D0966540

Accounting
for Managerial
Decision Making

Melville Series
on
Management, Accounting, and Information Systems

Consulting Editor   *John W. Buckley*

Accounting for Managerial Decision Making

Don T. DeCoster

Kavasseri V. Ramanathan

Gary L. Sundem

The University of Washington, Seattle

MELVILLE PUBLISHING COMPANY

Los Angeles, California

Copyright © 1974, by John Wiley & Sons, Inc.
Published by Melville Publishing Company,
a Division of John Wiley & Sons, Inc.

Library of Congress Cataloging in Publication Data
DeCoster, Don T.
    Accounting for managerial decision making.

    (Melville series on management, accounting, and
information systems)
        1.   Cost accounting—Addresses, essays, lectures.
2.   Decision-making—Addresses, essays, lectures.
I.   Ramanathan, Kavasseri V., joint author.
II.   Sundem, Gary L., joint author.   III.   Title.

HF5686.C8D29   6571.42   73-14884
ISBN 0 471 20502 8
ISBN 0 471 20501 X (pbk.)

Printed in the United States of America

10 9 8 7 6 5 4 3 2

Preface

Decision making and the role of information in making rational choices have been in the management and accounting literature for more than half a century. However, it was not until the early 1950s that the developments in establishing theories of decision making gained a noticeable foothold. This growth has occurred simultaneously in many disciplines including mathematics, statistics, economics, and psychology. Certainly this growth has created a pressure, coupled with an urgency, upon accountants to expand their function.

There are many signs of this pressure. In professional journals there has been a noted increase in the articles dealing with the planning and control aspects of accounting. This increased emphasis upon the managerial planning function points to the expanding scope of the use of accounting data for decision making. A principal concern has been the use of accounting data for the removal of uncertainty in projecting the future. At the heart of this interest in the future must lie the dynamics of making appropriate choices which optimize the behavior of the decision maker. Another example of the professional interest in accounting for decision making is the direct costing/absorption costing controversy. For almost 25 years the pros and cons of these two costing systems have permeated the literature. Proponents of direct costing argue that it is a superior costing system for managerial decision making. Proponents of absorption costing stress that the absorption of total production costs provides inventory and cost-of-goods-sold data consistent with stewardship reporting.

This increase in the role of accounting in decision making has also affected accounting education and professional entrance requirements. Over the past 20 years accounting education, both at the undergraduate and graduate level, has evolved to include more and more statistical decision making, microeconomics, mathematical models, and managerially oriented accounting data. This same trend has appeared on the Certified Public Accountant's examination. Over the years the exams have included more and more budgeting, direct versus absorption costing, capital budgeting, distribution, and short-run decision questions. To further highlight this trend, a new certificate entitled "Certified Management Accountant" was offered for the first time in 1972. Only one section of this exam was concerned with stewardship accounting. Other sections included

v

micro- and macroeconomics, organizational structures, capital financing, and managerial accounting. While it is too early to tell if this new program will be successful, it certainly indicates that many accountants are moving away from being concerned solely with the stewardship function.

These developments pose a major challenge to accounting educators in their attempts to introduce accounting students to the literature pertaining to managerial accounting. The difficulty arises from the fact that concepts and analytical tools from several different disciplines are relevant. These diverse tools need to be integrated with the accounting process of measurement and reporting if managerial decision making is to be brought to full bloom. Recent textbooks in managerial accounting have addressed themselves to this task with varying degrees of success. However, their basic emphasis has been on measurement and reporting techniques. Consequently, they fail to provide an adequate discussion of the interaction between the accounting process on the one hand and the concepts and techniques of the managerial process on the other.

One solution to helping meet the challenge facing accounting educators is a book of readings which concentrates on the interface between the accounting measurement process and the theories and methods found in disciplines relevant to the management process. Accordingly, the readings in this collection are designed to bring together notions from utility theory, decision theory, economic theory, and operations research techniques as they relate to managerial accounting. A basic criterion used in selecting individual articles is that they discuss the ideas in these areas in a manner which is simple, while simultaneously being capable of being related to the process of accounting. The readings do not require a mathematical or otherwise technical background on the part of the reader. Our emphasis is on making this collection an aid in teaching managerial accounting. Hence, we have not included articles devoted to research. The editors believe that the value of the readings to the student is enhanced considerably through periodic summarizations, evaluations, and directed reading. To provide continuity and flow the editors have included introductions to each section.

The present book is intended as a companion text for students in managerial accounting. Students who have had a preliminary exposure to microeconomics, statistics, operational research techniques, and organizational theory will gain the most from the readings. However, the editors believe that the great majority of the readings can be very meaningful to students with only a minimal background. The experience at the University of Washington indicates that both undergraduate and graduate students find the readings extremely helpful.

Based on their experience at the University of Washington in using these readings with regular texts in teaching managerial accounting, the editors offer the following suggested outlines.

The text chapters and the readings are shown for three popular cost accounting texts:

1. Horngren, Charles T., *Cost Accounting: A Managerial Emphasis*, 3rd edition (Prentice-Hall, Englewood Cliffs, New Jersey, 1972).
2. Matz, Adolph, and Othel J. Curry, *Cost Accounting: Planning and Control*, 5th edition (South-Western Publishing Co., Cincinnati, Ohio, 1972).
3. Shillinglaw, Gordon, *Cost Accounting: Analysis and Control*, 3rd edition (Richard D. Irwin, Inc., Homewood, Illinois, 1972).

The chapters in each text which relate to the readings in this book are as follows:

	Chapters in		
Reading No.	Horngren	Matz/Curry	Shillinglaw
1	1	1, 2	1
2	1, 23	2	1
3	1, 23, 27	2	1
4	1	2	1
5	1, 2	1, 2	1
6	2	3	2
7	10	3, 21	2, 9
8	—	—	—
9	8, 24	17	3, 17
10	3	23	3
11	7	17	3
12	9, 10	9, 10	8, 9
13	11	22	27
14	11	22	27
15	2	3, 17, 25	2
16	27	28	28
17	16, 24	17, 24	3, 11
18	10, 12	10, 21	20
19	13, 14	26	26
20	13, 14	26	26
21	5, 6	2, 15	14
22	5	15	14
23	5	16	14
24	5, 8	17	14
25	27	15, 16	14
26	5, 6	15, 16	14
27	5, 6	17	14
28	6, 25	10, 15	18

| | Chapters in | | |
Reading No.	Horngren	Matz/Curry	Shillinglaw
29	6	10	18
30	7, 9, 25	18, 19	20, 21
31	14, 21	26, 27	23, 27
32	21	27	22, 23, 26
33	22	27	23, 26

At the University of Washington the editors are using these readings as a supplement to the 3rd edition of *Cost Accounting: A Managerial Emphasis* by Charles T. Horngren in the required managerial accounting course for undergraduate accounting majors. A proposed course change would require undergraduate majors in accounting to complete two, instead of the current one, ten-week, three-credit courses in cost and managerial accounting. The general course outline for the two courses is:

I.   Costs and their Behavior—Weeks 1, 2, 3, 4

    Horngren: Ch. 1   "The Accountant's Role in the Organization"
              Ch. 2   "An Introduction to Cost Terms and Purposes"
              Ch. 3   "Cost-Volume-Profit Relationships"
              Ch. 8   "Flexible Budgets and Various Cost Behavior Patterns"
              Ch. 24 "Determination of Cost Behavior Patterns"
              Ch. 23 "Decision-Making, Uncertainty, and the Accountant"

    Readings: Section I   "Disciplining the Decision Process"
              Section II "The Accounting Discipline's Role in the Decision Process"
              Section III "Accounting for Short Run Decisions—General Concepts"

II.   The Traditional Cost Accounting Model

    A.   Job Order Accounting—Week 5

        Horngren: Ch. 4   "Cost Accumulation for Product Costing: Job Order Accounting"
                  Ch. 12 "Cost Allocation for Various Purposes"

    B.   Standard Costs—Weeks 6, 7, 8

        Horngren: Ch. 7   "Standard Costs: Direct Material and Direct Labor"

ACKNOWLEDGMENTS

The editors would like to thank the many people who assisted in the development of the manuscript. First, there were many faculty members of the University of Washington who made substantive suggestions. Eldon L. Schafer and William L. Felix, Jr. were particularly helpful. Second, there were the students who served as guinea pigs in the developmental phases. Finally, the editors would like to thank Mary Swain who fulfilled the taxing role of typist, coordinator, and decoder of three handwriting styles.

Don T. DeCoster
Kavasseri V. Ramanathan
Gary L. Sundem

x

Contents

Accounting
for Managerial
Decision Making

Some Reflections on Cost Accounting

J. Paul Sutter

Somewhere back in the dim ages, a man with a quill pen sat in front of a sheet of foolscap and reckoned the cost of the thing that he had made. Or was it a man with a stylus, before a tablet of wax? Or one with a reed in his hand and a papyrus leaf, picked on the banks of the Nile? Or perhaps a hairy, skin-clad man with a flint chisel, cutting pictures into a stone?

Whoever he was, or whenever he was, he has his memorial in every factory where things that are made are reckoned in figures. He started something. He was the first cost accountant. Peace to his ashes.

SOURCE: Reprinted by permission of *The Journal of Accountancy* (August, 1919). Copyright 1919 by the American Institute of Certified Public Accountants, Inc.

EDITORS' NOTE: This is extracted from the article with this title.

Disciplining the Decision Process

INTRODUCTION

Accounting is one segment of a complete decision system within an economic entity. The only reason for the existence of accounting is that it provides decision makers with information on which to base their decisions. A large number of decision makers are external to the economic entity; the study of financial accounting encompasses their needs for information and the systems which can supply this information. Other decision makers are within the firm; these are the managers making the firm's operating decisions. Managerial accountants supply them with the information they need for their decisions. The readings in this book describe the tools and concepts which are germane to managerial accounting.

One very basic difference between managerial and financial accounting is the extent of knowledge about the information needs of the decision makers. A financial accountant must produce data that are used by many different categories of decision makers, none of whom have explicitly defined information needs. This has caused the attempt to develop somewhat rigid rules regarding the form of financial accounting information systems. The result is the presentation of reports that are not precisely suited to any one decision maker's needs. Rather the reports reflect the average needs of all users of the information.

The managerial accountant, on the other hand, can identify the decision makers to whom he supplies information. Instead of designing an information system to meet externally imposed standards reflecting the needs of an "average" user of the information, he can tailor the system to fit the decision needs of the managers. The managerial accountant's objective is to design an information system to meet the needs of the decision makers at the lowest cost possible. Obviously, the benefit derived from using an information system for decision making must be greater than the cost of operating the system.

With this as his role, the managerial accountant must be an expert on decision making for two different reasons. First, he must know the effect of the information he generates on the decisions of the managers. Only by knowing how these managers make decisions can the accountant assess the impact of alternative types of information on the decisions. If certain elements of data are irrelevant for the decisions to be made, the accountant should not spend time and money collecting and presenting these data. If other elements are critical to certain decisions, these should be available before the decisions are made. A second reason for the managerial accountant to be familiar with decision making is that he is a decision maker himself. Just as other managers make decisions about production and marketing, the accountant makes decisions about the information system. He must be able to correctly establish his own objectives and select the alternative information system that best meets these objectives.

At first blush it appears that the managerial accountant must be an omniscient demigod, knowing not only how to make decisions about the information system but how all the managers in the firm make decisions. Of course, this cannot be the case. The separation of the decision-making function from the information-gathering and reporting functions is necessary if an entity is large since combining the functions would be completely unwieldy. The managerial accountant then is an expert in decision making about the information system, and he merely understands the decision systems and models used by the other managers in the firm.

Because any information produced by a managerial accountant must be judged in light of its ultimate effect on the decisions, a necessary precedent to a discussion of managerial accounting concepts is an understanding of decision making. The readings in this first section provide an insight into the general economic and psychological concepts that affect decision making as well as some of the specific models of rational decision making that have been developed.

The first reading, *The Accounting Discipline in 1999,* is a personal extrapolation by Professor Horngren. It must be obvious to the reader that the editors concur with Horngren since the goals of this book are closely allied with his discussion. There is an integration of many currently divergent research and teaching areas implied in Horngren's paper. Managerial accounting for decision making encompasses many subject areas and skills—microeconomics, decision theory, statistics, sociology, psychology, organizational theory, and, of course, the broad spectrum of the accounting discipline. The need for this multidiscipline blending places heavy demands on both the teacher and student. Yet there is a prevailing tone in this paper that this integration must take place if accounting is going to rise to its full potential. The mushrooming effect of the knowledge explosion has begun to shake the accounting world. A commitment to fulfill Horngren's vision will systematically transform the accounting profession. The days of quill pens, high stools, and green eye shades will soon be history.

The thrust of the second reading in this section, *Organization Decision Theory—A Synthesis* by Tersine, is the individual as a decision maker. Organizations are managed by individuals who make decisions; organizations themselves do not make decisions. Since all individuals are different, there is no one mode of decision making. However, there are some factors that are common to all decision situations. Based on these factors, models have been developed to prescribe how decisions should be made in varying circumstances and to describe how they are made by decision makers. Tersine blends a discussion of the role of decision makers in the organization with a presentation of several decision models. Knowledge of these models will help accountants both to understand how managers make decisions and to make their own appropriate decisions.

The theory of decision making is developed more completely by North in *A Tutorial Introduction to Decision Theory*. The general tools for a formal analysis of a decision situation are presented, and these tools are then used to solve a simple example. The emphasis is on clarity of exposition rather than on mathematical rigor.

The first tool that is presented is utility theory. Both an axiomatic and an intuitive development are presented. This is followed by a section on the use of probability theory to incorporate added information into the decision process. With these two tools the example is solved. Additional topics covered are decision making when a sequence of decisions is involved and determining the value of additional information. This latter topic is especially important for accountants because their job is to optimize the information system. This is only possible if the value of information can be determined. While a complete decision-theoretic approach as presented by North may not be possible in most real-world situations, the underlying principles must be applied, even if the application is entirely intuitive.

The final article in this section, *Accounting Information and Decision-Making: Some Behavioral Hypotheses* by Bruns, points out the role of the accountant as an information supplier to decision makers. While his ideas apply to both financial and managerial accounting, the emphasis on an assessment of the user's needs and reactions makes the conclusions more significant for managerial accounting than for financial accounting. The main point Bruns makes is that "relevance" is the primary criterion to use in deciding whether to present data. If the data are relevant to a decision maker, they have value; if they are not relevant they have no value. The main determinant of relevance is the possible effect the receipt of the information may have on the decision to be made. Several hypotheses about the information presented and the decision maker to whom it is presented indicate how one might judge the degree of relevance of accounting data. Relevance judged merely on the basis of a theoretical model is not sufficient; a decision maker's perception of the accounting data and the possibility of obtaining the same (or similar) information from non-accounting sources will affect the significance of the accounting information on the decisions that are made.

The Accounting Discipline in 1999

Charles T. Horngren

THE ESSENCE OF CHANGE

The change in the nature of doctoral training and faculty research of the 1960's finally affected the textbooks during the next two decades. A full discussion of these developments is beyond the scope of this discourse because my topic is accounting education, not research per se. But the enduring theme of much of the research is worth mentioning. The focus was on the relationship of accounting information to user needs. Because the user invariably utilizes the information for making a decision, the decision process became the starting point for analysis.

A body of statistical decision theory had developed during the 1960's, and interdisciplinary work in accounting pivoted increasingly around decision theory as a unifying element. In fact, the decision theory framework strongly influenced both the accounting curriculum and the entire business curriculum. Its major reasons for growth were its universality and its flexibility. Its focus on the decision maker applies to all management functions in nearly any context. Teachers found that its method can be implemented in a gamut of courses from freshman accounting to doctoral seminars; that is, decision models can be framed in the simplest of terms and relationships.

More specifically, decision theory and accounting fit together in the following way. A particular accounting system produces information to a decision maker, who may use the information in choosing an action. His action may

---

SOURCE: Reprinted with permission from *The Accounting Review,* Vol. 46, No. 1 (January, 1971), pp. 5-10.

EDITORS' NOTE: This reading is extracted from a larger discussion where the author takes the point of view of an accountant in 1999 assessing the developments in accounting during the past half century. These extracts, taken from the center section of his paper, deal with educational topics most relevant to the intent of this book.

influence, at least partially, subsequent events. The accountant must predict the relationships between the information system, the decision maker's prediction and action choice process, and the events that will occur.[13] The best accounting system is that which optimizes the objective function (the payoff) after all costs, including the costs of the information, are considered.

Note that this approach did not divide the world into quantitative and behavioral camps, as many accountants were prone to do in those days. Instead, it took the following view.

Decision making is choosing from among a set of alternative courses of action in light of some objective. The method for making the choice was termed a decision model. Decision models are often expressed formally in mathematical form. A mathematical decision model may indicate a choice which is nevertheless declined by management because of legal, political, behavioral, or other factors not incorporated in the specific model. In these cases, the output of the mathematical model is only one input into a more complicated, ill-defined decision model which includes considerations not explicitly quantified.

In many situations, mathematical models clearly provided better answers than would have been achieved with alternative techniques. However, the vastness and complexity of decision-making and implementation were also recognized. The management process has two important but interdependent parts: (1) decision model formulation and solution and (2) implementation. To formalize models, the model builder predominately used the tools and assumptions of economics to focus on the optimum allocation of the organization's scarce resources. Implementation relies on human and other means to assure that the chosen solution is achieved.

The major weakness of mathematical models was and still is their lack of completeness. Implementation is often a behavioral problem. As a supplier of information, the accountant has had to be concerned with both the economic decision models and their implementation as an entire package.

The trouble at that point was that our knowledge of behavioral effects was scanty indeed. Little systematic evidence was available concerning the complex effects of decision models and accounting information on user behavior. Instead, the relationship was either overlooked or it was described by over-simplified assertions that were valid only in one organization at one point in time.[14]

Some mathematical models had attempted to incorporate behavioral considerations explicitly (e.g., applying utility theory or adding behavioral constraints). These were admirable first steps on a long journey. In the year 1999, the frontier in this direction has been outlined but hardly penetrated.

There continues to be too much focus on the formal decision models and too little focus on the issues of implementation (which are largely behavioral issues). Accounting seems to attract individuals who are more prone toward the mathematical challenges of formal model building and less prone toward the difficulties of implementation. After all, such work is more tractable; the payoff is easier to see.

In contrast, the behavioral area is awesome and fuzzy. Laboratory and field experiments require a knowledge of both mathematical and statistical techniques and behavioral science methods. Moreover, the payoff is unclear because of doubts about our ability to generalize from findings.

In the 1960's there were many existing theories which were generated from business situations, but which were not generally transferable. That is, such theories may help explain behavior under a set of particular circumstances, but they do not help predict behavior under different circumstances. The latter is the goal. Findings about the following questions are slowly being gathered. Should accountants present one expected value (e.g., budgeted sales) or an entire probability distribution (e.g., probabilities associated with the entire range of sales)? Should reports present summaries (e.g., total costs) or details (e.g., unit costs) or both? Should reports present one income based on historical costs or one based on replacement costs or both?

To design an accounting system, ideally the accountant must predict how individuals will react to different sets of information.[15] Will a given configuration affect people differently? How? Why? What decisions about information can be made independently of personality differences? Since 1970, the quest has been toward building a theory that will predict behavior without being dependent on the differences in the individual personalities of the users.

The commitment of research in behavioral accounting is to discover stable patterns of behavior which are a function of general information processes rather than of unique situations and individuals.[16] The point is that ideally information systems should be tailored to the quirks and peculiar personalities of users. But that is an impossible goal for all except the tiniest organizations. Consequently, the search has concentrated on getting generalizations that may be used by systems designers without worrying about whether the organization has autocratic or democratic rule, or is populated by introverts or extroverts. This is in sharp distinction to attempts to arrive at a general theory of behavioral accounting by creating elaborate mosaics of individual needs, personality differences and particular modes of interaction.

COURSES IN INTERNAL ACCOUNTING

In 1970, management accounting was a diverse collection of techniques that had been useful in directing management's attention and in solving management's problems. It was more closely associated with manufacturing. The ensuing years saw more attention devoted to nonmanufacturing and international functions and enterprises. Moreover, as governmental bodies, medical institutions, and other non-business organizations grew in size and influence, they received increasing emphasis. The content of management accounting became more systematic, more geared to a fundamental body of decision theory that cemented the field.

New textbooks were written that were tied to the decision model and implementation framework. They examined various decisions and explored what information was needed to make choices and implement actions. For example, courses in internal accounting dealt with the problems of designing information systems that would serve management's needs for making capital budgeting decisions, product combination decisions, inventory control decisions, cost center or profit center decisions and their implementation. In addition to economics, quantitative training was routinely applied. Techniques like multiple regression, mathematical programming, and Bayesian analysis for dealing with uncertainty became commonplace. The courses now have a systems design perspective, including the use of the computer.

Behavioral aspects in management accounting courses have become especially prominent. In the 1960's, most accountants were utterly insensitive to these factors. Many accounting professors would continue to skip the "behavioral stuff" because it seemed strangely out of place. But now accountants and users are acutely aware of the behavioral aspects. At least accountants and managers are routinely asking the right questions in the area; such concern represents notable progress. The answers will continue to be elusive, but keeping the focus on the central issues of implementation is clearly a valuable contribution of formal education.

Courses are concerned with critical behavioral issues such as designing systems that motivate decisions which are congruent with top management goals. For example, planning and control systems that instructed managers to use discounted cash flow models for making investment decisions and then gauged performance with accrual accounting models often induced dysfunctional decision making. Now systems are more likely to be designed so that the models which evaluate performance are consistent with the models that guide planning decisions.

Empirical behavioral research in budgeting contexts has conclusively demonstrated that reports showing probabilistic information will generally lead to decisions having higher payoffs than reports that show only single values. Consequently, internal reports are routinely designed to communicate on a probabilistic rather than a deterministic basis.

Starting in the 1970's, empirical research in internal accounting also included the construction and reconstruction of information systems that better fit actual decision needs. Until 1970, for the most part, the models that examined information issues were postulated in the academic literature without any empirical evidence regarding their relevance to actual decision processes.[17]

COURSES IN EXTERNAL ACCOUNTING

The revolutionary changes in finance theory[18] and in teaching finance during the 1960's reinforced the fact that courses in so-called financial accounting were ripe for a movement in the direction of decision making. But the trend moved slowly, primarily because of institutional constraints and because of the widespread assumption that decision models of the unknown users were harder to specify. Annual financial reports attempt to satisfy simultaneously the information needs of many users, instead of generating several sets of statements that are aimed at specific users and decisions. Consequently, value judgments about the "correct" accounting method often assume some knowledge of user needs that are usually unproven hypotheses.

The changes in courses came in three phases, all of which overlapped somewhat. First, in the middle 1970's two new well-written texts that were exclusively devoted to "financial accounting" earnestly down-played procedures, bolstered the stress on theory and analysis, and forced the students to search for a logical framework for utilization by both the producer and consumer in judging the uses and limitations of financial statements. The approach was more normative. The student was not drenched with current practice as being the only acceptable way. The materials tended to concentrate on excerpts from annual reports and on current controversies, even in the early weeks of the first course.[19] These prodded student interest and helped to keep the spotlight on the users. By the late 1980's, such texts were dominating the market.

In the history of accounting education, these books marked the final turning point from the producer to the consumer. That is, the year-long, elementary courses in nearly all schools finally became fully focused on user needs. There were required courses in both financial and management accounting, and *both* courses emphasized the objectives of supplying information that will assist user decisions.

The second phase, which started with the thrust toward empirical research in the 1960's and boomed in the 1970's and 1980's, was a stress on the ability of external reports to facilitate the *prediction* of events of common interest to many external users, even though their specific decision models differ. For example, students examined the implications of alternative accounting methods for a growing list of predictive purposes, including the prediction of business failure,[20] the prediction of market prices,[21] and the prediction of security riskiness.[22]

The third phase in financial accounting, which has come during the late 1990's, has been a heavier incorporation of the relationship to information of formal decision models, mathematical techniques, and finance theory. Students are beginning to have more rigorous methods for deciding what accounting alternatives are best for external reports. This is largely attributable to the growth of knowledge produced by empirical research.

At first, the empirical research in the external area concentrated on improving the method of prediction, which is only one aspect of the decision process. But gradually the scope was enlarged. The main focus of research in external accounting was the relationship between accounting data and price behavior. Some preliminary work had already been accomplished by 1970. Tentative answers were being gathered to such questions as the following: What is the effect of annual earnings announcements on investor behavior?[23] How do security prices react to a change in accounting method?[24] Among alternative accounting methods, which method seems to be impounded in the market prices of securities (e.g., investments carried at cost or at equity)?

Such research provided us with more knowledge about how information is disseminated to external users and what role accounting data play in such a complex information and decision system. Such knowledge is now being increasingly incorporated in course material.

Incidentally, in 1970, nearly all existing curricula in accounting began with at least one term of external accounting and followed with internal accounting in a later course. There had been some attempts to reverse this sequence, but they had not been widely adopted. Now about eighty percent of the course sequences begin with internal accounting. This phenomenon is probably attributable to the decision theory framework as an approach to the whole field of accounting and management. In addition, empirical research has supported the idea that the decision models of managers (and the behavioral issues) are of wider interest and are easier to specify than the decision models of unknown users of external reports. Many of these elementary courses are no longer called financial or external accounting or management or internal accounting. Instead, they have a single name like "Accounting Information Systems for Decision Making."

FACILITATING THE CHANGES

Of course, the radical changes that transpired were facilitated by many factors besides the desire, talent, and energy of some determined college professors. The typical accountant and executive of the 1980's had a higher level of education than those in the 1960's. Moreover, their education markedly stressed the need for an analytical, questioning approach to accounting.

Accordingly, they were not satisfied with the 1950 and 1960 business and accounting methods. They were receptive to and, in fact, demanded more rigorous, fresh ideas. Therefore, the communications gap (that had peaked around 1970) narrowed throughout the remainder of the century. The result has been increasing financial support for accounting research from all sources. In addition to the public accounting profession, industry and not-for-profit sectors have helped finance research at a mounting rate.[25]

A key factor in accelerating the changes was the enlightened decision to broaden the content of the CPA examination. Earlier I mentioned the request of the MAS Committee in 1970 to admit non-CPA specialists to full membership in the AICPA. Its recommendation to have a special qualifying examination was seriously explored by another Institute Committee. But it was finally decided that the CPA examination itself should be broadened in keeping with the breadth of the CPA profession. There were many legal and institutional barriers to change, but now the examination has widened its scope, pruned the procedural, and accentuated the analytical. There is a plentiful use of optional questions so that the management service specialist can avoid answering a question that an income tax specialist would choose to answer, and vice versa.

The CPA examination is a potent influence on the content of accounting courses, even though its effects are frequently denied. Through the years, the CPA examination has affected the topics and homework material of nearly all leading textbooks in accounting. The CPA examination is regarded by many as a test of a minimum level of competence. If so, the preparers of the examination probably have the most awesome single responsibility in all of accounting education.

Until 1970 or later, there was a proverbial vicious circle between the CPA examination and the accounting curriculum. Some topics got in and never got out; others found entry difficult. The examiners recognized that progress could be made via breaking the vicious circle and assuming a leadership role. The inclusion of new topics and analytical material in the examination forced changes in the texts being used in a wide range of schools.

As before, strong accounting faculties, programs and texts were not directly influenced by the CPA exam. If anything, the CPA exam was more likely to be led by them. On the other hand, weak faculties, texts, and programs were and are directly influenced by the CPA exam. So the CPA exam has served a crucial function by upgrading weaker programs via its influence.

FOOTNOTES

13. Of course, decisions must be made by the accountant as well as the decision maker. These relationships are discussed more fully in Gerald A.

Feltham and Joel S. Demski, "The Use of Models in Information Evalua- tion," *The Accounting Review,* (October 1970).

14. Report of Committee on Managerial Decision Models, American Account- ing Association, *The Accounting Review,* Supplement to Vol. XLIV (1969), p. 41, 46.

15. Thomas R. Hofstedt and James C. Kinard, "A Strategy for Behavioral Accounting Research," *The Accounting Review* (January 1970), pp. 48–49.

16. Professor Alexander Bavelas, a psychologist who worked closely with several doctoral students in accounting, was a stimulating advocate of this approach.

17. Of course, the literature was not devoted exclusively to empirical research. In 1989, the 995th article on the merits of direct costing was published. This was quickly followed by the 995th article on the demerits of direct costing. In 1991, an *Encyclopedia of Direct Costing* containing 2,000 articles was printed.

18. For examples see Harry Markowitz, *Portfolio Selection* (John Wiley and Sons, Inc., 1959) and William F. Sharpe, "Capital Asset Prices: A Theory of Market Equilibrium Under Conditions of Risk," *Journal of Finance* (September 1964), pp. 425–42.

19. Of course, the work of the Accounting Principles Board (APB) continued to generate much scrutiny. Criticisms flowed from educators, students, industrialists, the Securities and Exchange Commission, and others. Most of the time, the APB felt like a lone tree in the midst of 1,000 dogs.

20. See articles by William Beaver in *The Accounting Review* (January 1968), *Journal of Accounting Research* (Autumn 1968), and *Journal of Account- ing Research Supplement* (1968).

21. R. Ball and P. Brown, "An Empirical Evaluation of Accounting Income Numbers," *Journal of Accounting Research* (Autumn 1968), pp. 159–78.

22. W. Beaver, P. Kettler, and M. Scholes, "The Association Between Market Determined Measures of Risk and Financial Statement Determined Measures of Risk," *The Accounting Review* (October 1970).

23. W. Beaver, "The Information Content of Annual Earnings Announce- ments," *Journal of Accounting Research Supplement* (1968).

24. T. Ross Archibald, "The Return to Straight-Line Depreciation: An Analysis of a Change in Accounting Method," unpublished doctoral dissertation, University of Chicago, 1968. A part of his dissertation is in *Journal of Accounting Research Supplement* (1970), pp. 161–86.

25. Of special note was the desirable proliferation of endowed chairs for accounting professors. For example, several Arthur Young Professorships were established throughout the country during the 1960's and 1970's. In passing, I note that my respected friend Sidney Davidson occupied the first such chair; by 1971 he had been in the chair so long that they renamed it the Arthur Old Professorship. A breakthrough in endowments occurred in 1995. Some benefactors financed the first endowed couch in accounting. Of course, the couch was occupied by a behavioral accountant.

Organization Decision Theory—A Synthesis

Richard J. Tersine

INTRODUCTION

While every rational being is an individual decision making mechanism, very little is known about what initiates this mechanism into action and how it operates. Decision making has been an integral part of the management literature for more than three decades. However, because of the emphasis on decision making as a hierarchical right, explorations of the behavioral aspects of the decision process were at a minimum for much of the time. It was not until the early 1950's that developments in decision theory gained a noticeable momentum. During this period, there emerged more powerful and sophisticated tools of mathematics and statistics as well as increased interest in the behavioral sciences. These influences have set the intellectual base for many of the current contributions on the subject.

The most significant aspect of the literature on decision making is what it does not contain. There are few, if any, systematic empirically based longitudinal studies on the decision process. There are relatively few articles classified as research although the literature abounds with limited and partial theories. Many of the theories have been developed by mathematicians and they are modifications of a completely rational man. Such theories in general ignore the psychological characteristics of men or the social environment in which they live.

Organizations per se do not make decisions, people and groups do. In many instances, the decisions made are compromise decisions. The decision

SOURCE: Reprinted with permission from *Managerial Planning* (July–August, 1972), pp. 18–26, 40.

15

maker as an individual, a member of the formal organization, and a member of an informal organization with his own philosophy and perception of the organization, selects solutions for optimizing value within organizational constraints. The organization has objectives, policies, and standards which must be balanced with technology, attitudes, and resources.

Professor Ansoff (2, pp. 5-6) cuts organizational decisions into three categories:

1. Strategic decisions—are primarily concerned with external rather than internal problems of the firm and specifically with the selection of the product mix which the firm will produce and the markets to which it will sell.
2. Administrative decisions—are concerned with structuring the firm's resources to create maximum performance potential. This can be sub-divided into:
   a. Organization structure—involves structuring of authority and responsibility relationships, work flows, information flow, distribution channels, and location of facilities.
   b. Resource acquisition and development—involves the development of raw-material sources, personnel training, personnel development, financing, acquisition of facilities, and equipment.
3. Operating decisions—are primarily concerned with the maximizing profitability of current operations. The key decisions involve pricing, establishing market strategy, setting production schedules and inventory levels, and deciding on the relative expenditures in support of R & D, marketing, and operations.

The process of management is fundamentally a process of decision making. The functions of management (planning, organizing, motivating, and controlling) all involve the process of evaluating, selecting, and initiating courses of action.

Decision making is at the center of the functions comprising the management process. The manager makes decisions in establishing objectives; he makes planning decisions, organizing decisions, motivating decisions, and control decisions. In this sense modern decision theory is a logical extension of the management process school. In addition, decision theory enters both the quantitative and behavioral domains.

Alexis and Wilson (1, p. 4) have specified three major approaches to organizational analysis which are:

1. Structural approaches—traced to early writings of Frederick Taylor, Henri Fayol, and Max Weber. (Line/staff, division of labor, coordination, scalar authority, span of control, unity of command, etc.)
2. Behavioral approaches—stress human variables. (Hawthorne studies and later behavioral research.)

3. Decision making approaches—stress human variables and technology. It views the organization from the locations of the actual decision makers.

One acting in the capacity of a manager or executive must make choices among various plans, policies, and strategies. These choices are made with varying degrees of information. Decision theory gives structure to the different conditions under which decisions are made. The decision making process used by management is becoming more organized and systematic than the intuitive process of the past.

Dahl and Lindblom[4] have suggested four broad influencing factors on the decision making processes in organizations:

1. Hierarchical—leaders are influenced by the structure of the hierarchy itself.
2. Democratic—leaders are influenced by nonleaders through such devices as nomination and election.
3. Bargaining—leaders are to some degree independent of each other and exercise reciprocal controls over each other. (labor vs. management)
4. Pricing system—leaders are influenced by the market place.

Basically, a decision must be made when the organization faces a problem, when it is dissatisfied with existing conditions, or when it is given a choice. A considerable amount of managerial activity precedes the actual decision. In large organizations these activities may be carried on by people other than the decision maker. Staff people and others in the line organization discover problems, define them, and prepare the alternatives for decision. The actual decision is only the conclusion of a process. The process in a broad sense includes (1) the activities of discovering and defining things to decide, (2) determining the objective of the organization, and (3) the enumeration and preparation of the alternative ways of making the decision (3, p. 269).

There is no unified agreed-upon structure for decision theory. This paper will add some structure to decision theory and also explore some of its dimensions.

FEATURES OF ORGANIZATIONAL DECISION MAKING

Setting of Objectives

The establishment and definition of the broad organizational goals of the firm is the basic requirement to all subsequent decisions to be made on a lesser level. From these broad objectives, strategies and departmental goals can be set to provide the framework for decision making at lower managerial levels. Even after organizational goals are set, other problems still exist such as:

1. Multiple objectives—decision making is complicated by the existence of many diversified objectives. A number of objectives may be difficult to characterize quantitatively. These goals reflect subjective values rather than objective values. Typical objectives involve growth, diversification, industry position, profit maximization, sales maximization, social responsibility, personnel development, employee attitudes, etc.
2. Conflicting objectives—any comprehensive list of organizational objectives will have areas of conflict. Social responsibility such as pollution control projects may adversely affect profit margins. Product diversification may initially stultify the return on investment during the introductory period.
3. Hierarchy of objectives—objectives of organizational units must be consistent with the objectives of higher organizational units. This means there are objectives within objectives, within objectives. If the cascade of organization objectives is not consistent, it results in suboptimization. Suboptimization occurs where a departmental level maximizes its own objectives, but in doing so it subverts the overall objectives of the firm. (Sales manager-large inventories; production manager-large production runs; warehouse manager-minimum inventory; purchasing agent-large lot purchases; etc.)

Planning Horizons

Decision making at various levels of management is concerned with varying degrees of futurity. Top management decisions involve longer time periods than lower level management decisions. Planning horizons precipitate the problem of temporal suboptimization.

Sequential/Interrelated Decision Making

Sequential decision making is the process of successively solving interrelated subproblems comprising a large complex problem. Because many managerial problems are extremely complex, organizations resort to specialization of labor or breaking the problem into many subproblems. Consider the problem of production where it is broken down into separate departments: procurement, scheduling, operations, quality control, shipping, etc.

Dynamic Decision Making

Dynamic decision making emphasizes that management's decisions are not usually a one-time event, but are successive over a time frame. Future management decisions are to some degree influenced by past decisions.

Programmed/Nonprogrammed Decision Making

Programmed decisions are those that are repetitive and routine. Organizations usually establish definite procedures for making them. In contrast, the nonprogrammed decisions are unstructured and novel; there is no set pattern for handling them. Higher levels of management are associated with the unstructured, nonprogrammed decisions.

Cost of Decision Making

Decision making has a cost, particularly the search process that precedes the decision. Management must determine if the cost of the search process is worth the reduced uncertainty. The cost of the search process should not exceed the benefits of improving the decision.

DECISION MODELS

One of the primary functions of management is to make decisions that determine the future course of action for the organization over the short and long term. There are two general types of broad decision models now in use; they can be classified as normative or descriptive. The normative framework describes the classical situation where a decision maker faces a known set of alternatives and selects a course of action by a rational selection process. The descriptive framework incorporates adaptive or learning features and the act of choice spans many dimensions of behavior, rational as well as nonrational.

There are at least six elements common to all decisions:

1. The decision maker—refers to the individual or group making a choice from the available strategies.
2. Goals or ends to be served—are objectives the decision maker seeks to obtain by his actions.
3. The preference or value system—refers to the criteria that the decision maker uses in making his choice. It could include maximization of income, utility, minimum cost, etc.
4. Strategies of the decision maker—are the different alternative courses of action from which the decision maker can choose. Strategies are based on resources under the control of the decision maker.
5. States of nature—are factors that are not under the control of the decision maker. They are aspects of the decision maker's environment affecting his choice of strategy.
6. The outcome—represents the resultant from a given strategy and a given state of nature. When the outcome is expressed in numerical terms, it is called a payoff. (The prediction of payoffs in a matrix is usually assumed to be perfect.)

Normative Decision Models

At the center of this framework is the concept of rationality. The normative models show how a consistent decision maker should act to be successful. Decision procedures are followed that will optimize something, usually output, income, revenue, costs, utility, etc. The ideal rational man makes a choice on the basis of (1, p. 150):

1. A known set of relevant alternatives with corresponding outcomes.
2. An established rule or set of relations that produces a preference ordering of the alternatives.
3. The maximization of something such as money, goods, or some form of utility.

The major features of a typical decision structure are the strategies of the decision maker, the states of nature, and the outcomes. A typical decision matrix is as follows:

Strategies	States of Nature				
	N_1	N_2	.	.	.	N_m
S_1	O_{11}	O_{12}	.	.	.	O_m
S_2	O_{21}	O_{22}	.	.	.	O_{2m}
.	.	.	.	.	.
.	.	.	.	.	.
.	.	.	.	.	.
S_n	O_{n1}	O_{n2}	.	.	.	O_{nm}

The matrix formulation of a decision problem permits recognition and identification of four distinct kinds of decision situations. The classification is based on what the decision maker knows about occurrence of the various states of nature. They are decision making under certainty, under conflict, under risk, and under uncertainty. Figure 1 illustrates a rational decision theory continuum.

Decision Making Under Certainty

Decision making under certainty is the simplest form of decision making. The outcome resulting from the selection of a particular strategy is known. There is just one state of nature for each strategy. Prediction is involved, but

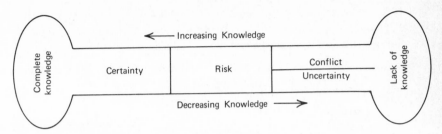

FIGURE 1. Rational decision theory continuum.

prediction is assumed to be perfect. There is complete and accurate knowledge of the consequence of each choice. The decision maker has perfect knowledge of the future and outcome. Certainty implies a state of awareness on the part of the decision maker that seldom exists. The probability that a certain state of nature exists is assumed to be one. The decision maker simply selects the strategy whose payoff is the best.

Examples of decision making under certainty are the simplex method of linear programming, the transportation method of linear programming, basic inventory models, breakeven analysis, etc.

Decision Making Under Conflict or Competition

The states of nature are subject to the control of an adverse intellect such as might be the case in competitive situations, bargaining, or war. The techniques for handling this type of a situation constitute the subject matter of game theory.[13] The states of nature of the decision maker are the strategies of the opponent. The decision maker is in conflict with intelligent rational opponents whose interests are opposed to his own.

Games are usually classified according to the degree of conflict of interest, the relationship between opponents, and the number of opponents. When one opponent gains at the loss of the other, it is called zero-sum games. A zero-sum game involves a complete conflict of interest. Games with less than complete conflict of interest are termed nonzero-sum games. In nonzero-sum games, the gains of one competitor are not completely at the expense of the other competitors. The majority of business competitive actions involve nonzero-sum games. The simplest type of game is the two-person zero-sum game.

The Two-Person Zero-Sum Game.   The players, X and Y, are equal in intelligence and ability. Each has a choice of two strategies. Each knows the outcome for every possible combination of strategies. The term "zero sum" is used because the sum of gains exactly equals the sum of losses. The four individual payoff possibilities are expressed as numbers; a positive number indicates a payoff to the player who plays the rows (X) and a negative number indicates a payoff to the player who plays the columns (Y). Each player desires to win or to minimize his losses, if he cannot win. An example matrix is as follows:

	Player Y	
	Strategy Q q_1	Strategy R q_2
Player X		
p_1 Strategy M	X wins 2	X wins 3
p_2 Strategy N	X wins 4	Y wins 2

$$\text{or } X \begin{pmatrix} & Y & \\ 2 & & 3 \\ 4 & & 2 \end{pmatrix}$$

A *pure strategy* exists if there is one strategy for player X and one strategy for player Y that will be played each time. The payoff which is obtained when each player plays his pure strategy is called a saddle point. The saddle point is the value of the game in which each player has a pure strategy. The saddle point represents an equilibrium condition that is optimum for both competitors. The Wald criterion, which is a variant of decision making under uncertainty, is a useful technique to determine if a pure strategy exists. A saddle point can be recognized because it is both the smallest numerical value in its row and largest numerical value in its column. Not all two-person zero-sum games have a saddle point. When a saddle point is present, complex calculations to determine optimum strategies and game value are unnecessary. The following two examples illustrate how to determine if a saddle point exists:

Example 1:

```
                      Row min.
        (2   3)          2          Strategies: X,1; Y,1
        (1  -2)         -2          Game value: +2
Column max.   2   3                 Saddle point
```

Example 2:

```
                      Row min.
       (-7 7 8)        -7           Strategies: X,2; Y,1
       (-4-3-2)        -4           Game value: -4
Column max.  -4 7 8                 Saddle point
```

When a pure strategy does not exist, a fundamental theorem of game theory states that the optimum can be found by using a mixed strategy. In a mixed strategy, each competitor randomly selects the strategy to employ according to previously determined probability of usage for each strategy. Using a mixed strategy involves making a selection each time period by tossing a coin, selecting a number from a table of random numbers, or by using some probabilistic process.

By referring to the originally stated matrix we will determine its mixed strategy. If p_1 and p_2 are the probabilities for player X strategies, and q_1 and q_2 are the probabilities for player Y strategies, we can find their values in the following manner:

$$\text{Expected value if } Q \text{ occurs} = 2_{p_1} + 4_{p_2}$$

$$\text{Expected value if } R \text{ occurs} = 3_{p_1} - 2_{p_2}$$

These two expected values must be equal. Therefore:

$$2_{p_1} + 4_{p_2} = 3_{p_1} - 2_{p_2}$$

$$p_1 + 6_{p_2}$$

$$\text{since } p_1 + p_2 = 1$$

$$6_{p_2} + p_2 = 1$$

$$p_2 = 1/7; \quad p_1 = 6/7$$

Under these conditions player X would play strategy M six-sevenths of the time and strategy N one-seventh of the time. In a similar manner, it can be shown that player Y will play strategy Q five-sevenths of the time and strategy R two-sevenths of the time. If player X uses a chance process with the derived probabilities, his expected benefit will be the same regardless of player Y's strategy.

If strategy Q: expected value = 6/7(2) + 1/7(4) = 16/7
If strategy R: expected value = 6/7(3) + 1/7(-2) = 16/7

If player Y uses a chance process with the desired probabilities, his expected benefit will also be the same regardless of player X's strategy. (Note signs of values in the matrix change when player Y's choices are considered.)

If strategy M: expected value = 5/7(-2) + 2/7(-3) = -16/7
If strategy N: expected value = 5/7(-4) + 2/7(2) = -16/7

As is always the case in the zero-sum game, player X's gain is player Y's loss and vice versa. The same procedure can be followed when a greater than two-by-two matrix exists, but it is usually easier to obtain the probabilities by using the simplex method of linear programming. When more than two competitors exist, various kinds of coalitions, treaties, and agreements can develop. The best example of zero-sum games are in problems of the military and various types of athletic competition (football, basketball, hockey, etc.).

The Nonzero-Sum Game.   The nonzero-sum games are closer to the actual problems that arise in everyday life and do not lend themselves to straightforward solutions. In most complex games there is no universally accepted solution for there is no single strategy that is clearly preferable to the others. Games with cooperative and competitive elements are usually more complex. Nonzero-sum games require that the payoffs be given for each player since the payoff of one player can no longer be deduced from the payoff of the other, as in zero-sum games. It is no longer true that a player can only benefit from the loss of his opponent. The outcome of the game is influenced by communication, the order of play, imperfect information, threats, agreements, side payments, personalities of the player, behavioral patterns, etc.

Although game models are not of particular value in their present form, they do provide a significant conceptional framework for analysis. They offer a meaningful guide for better decision making by focusing on pertinent problems that are prevalent in our everyday lives. They have found application in product development, product pricing, collective bargaining, athletic competition, war strategy, arbitration, foreign policy decisions, voting block coalitions, contract bidding, oligopolistic and monopolistic market conditions.

Decision Making Under Risk

Under this form the various states of nature can be enumerated and the long-run relative frequency of their occurrence is assumed to be known. The information about the states of nature is probabilistic. Knowing the probability distribution of the states of nature, the best decision is to select the strategy which has the highest expected value.

The following is an illustrative example of decision making under risk.

An organization is determining what size plant to build to produce a new product. Three different size plants are under consideration—small (S_1), large (S_2), and very large (S_3). The best plant size is dependent on the level of product demand—low (N_1), medium (N_2), and high (N_3). The possible payoffs and the probabilities of each state of nature obtained from market research are listed on the following matrix:

| | States of Nature | | |
Strategy	N_1 $\frac{1}{2}$	N_2 $\frac{1}{4}$	N_3 $\frac{1}{4}$
S_1	50	−8	0
S_2	−10	64	12
S_3	−20	12	80

S_1 expected value $= \frac{1}{2}(50) + \frac{1}{4}(-8) + \frac{1}{4}(0) = 23$
S_2 expected value $= \frac{1}{2}(-10) + \frac{1}{4}(64) + \frac{1}{4}(12) = 14$
S_3 expected value $= \frac{1}{2}(-20) + \frac{1}{4}(12) + \frac{1}{4}(80) = 13$

The best strategy with the highest expected value is S_1. Using this approach, a small plant would be built to manufacture the new product.

Examples of decision making under risk can be found in queuing theory, statistical quality control, acceptance sampling, program evaluation and review technique (PERT), etc.

Decision Making Under Uncertainty

In this case, you either don't know the probabilities associated with the states of nature or you don't know the states of nature. If you do not know the states of nature, additional research must be conducted before the problem can be approached. If you do not know the probabilities associated with the states of nature, you can use numerous techniques in arriving at a strategy. There is no one best criterion for selecting a strategy for a number of different criteria exist. The choice among the criteria depends upon the decision maker and the attitude or value system that he embraces (9, pp. 85-92). Examples of the applications of decision making under uncertainty are similar to those listed under decision making under conflict (see Figure 2).

Subjective Probabilities.   This approach assigns probabilities to the states of nature and reduces the problem to decision making under risk. Objective probability flows from the law of large numbers which asserts that the probability of any specified departure from the expected relative frequency of an event becomes smaller and smaller as the number of events considered becomes larger and larger. Objective or *a priori* probability of an event can be defined as the relative frequency with which an event would take place, given a large but finite number of observations. Unlike objective probability, subjective

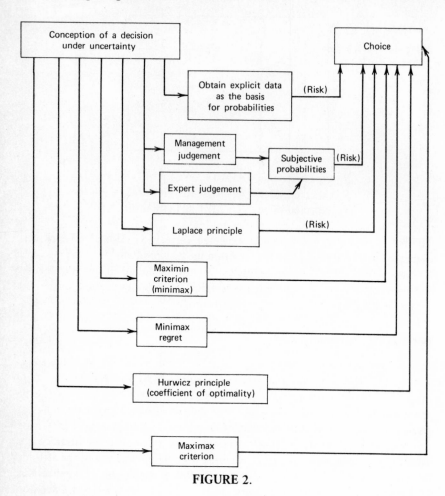

FIGURE 2.

probability is heavily behavioral in its approach and it interprets likelihoods in terms of personal perception. A decision maker's experience about a situation is, in reality, his probability distribution, and his objectives and values constitute his objective function about a given situation. Objective probability does become suspect on one of a kind or nonrecurring decisions. Bayes' theorem enables a decision maker to start with prior probabilities (which can be subjective) and by taking into account additional observational information to emerge with posterior probabilities, i.e., the revised probabilities as modified by the additional information.

Principle of Insufficient Reason (Laplace Criterion).   This approach assigns equal probabilities to each state of nature and treats it as decision making under risk. This method selects the strategy with the highest expected value.

Using this approach with the example given earlier of plant size, the probability of demand would be one-third for each state of nature. This method would select the very large plant size (S_3) since it has the highest expected value. The calculations are as follows:

Expected value of S_1 = 1/3(50) + 1/3(-8) + 1/3(0) = 12
Expected value of S_2 = 1/3(-10) + 1/3(64) + 1/3(12) = 22
Expected value of S_3 = 1/3(-20) + 1/3(12) + 1/3(80) = 24

Maximin Criterion (Wald Criterion).   This approach assumes the worst will happen and it selects the strategy that maximizes the minimum gain (or minimizes the maximum loss). Observing the smallest gain that could be achieved for each strategy, the strategy with the largest is selected. This criterion assures the decision maker of a payoff at least as large as the maximin payoff. The payoff will never be less than the maximin payoff.

Using this approach with the example given earlier of plant size, the small plant (S_1) would be selected. The strategy with the largest minimum value is S_1 as shown below:

$$S_1 = -8$$
$$S_2 = -10$$
$$S_3 = -20$$

Minimax Regret (Savage Criterion)[10].   An opportunity cost payoff matrix (regret matrix) is established. The decision maker attempts to minimize the regret he may experience. Regret is measured as the difference between the actual and possible payoff he could have received if he knew what state of nature was going to occur. The largest number in each column is subtracted from each other number in the same column. The strategy that minimizes the maximum regret is chosen.

Using this approach with the example given earlier of plant size, the large plant (S_2) would be selected as shown in the regret matrix below:

	N_1	N_2	N_3	Maximum Regret
S_1	0	72	80	80
S_2	60	0	68	68
S_3	70	52	0	70

Coefficient of Optimality (Hurwicz Criterion).   The coefficient of optimality is a means by which the decision maker can consider both the largest and smallest payoff, and weight their importance in the decision by his feeling of optimism. A probability is assigned to the largest payoff and also to the smallest payoff; the sum of these two probabilities equals one. The payoffs other than the maximum and minimum are neglected. The probabilities assigned tend to be subjective in nature and reflect how optimistic the decision maker is about the situation. The calculations are straight forward and the selection is determined by the strategy with the largest expected value. If the coefficient of optimality is one, the decision is the same as in the maximax criterion. If the coefficient is zero, the decision is the same as in maximin criterion.

Using this approach with the example given earlier of plant size with the coefficient of optimality equal to .6, the very large plant (S_3) would be selected as shown below:

$$S_1 \text{ expected value} = .6(50) + .4(-8) = 26.8$$
$$S_2 \text{ expected value} = .6(64) + .4(-10) = 34.4$$
$$S_3 \text{ expected value} = .6(80) + .4(-20) = 40$$

Maximax Criteria.   This approach is one of complete optimism. The decision maker assumes the very best outcome will occur, and he selects the strategy with the most optimum outcome, largest payoff.

Using this approach with the example given earlier of plant size, the very large plant (S_3) would be selected. The large plant had the largest payoff (80) of all the strategies.

Descriptive Decision Models

In the normative decision model, a few dimensions of the decision environment were admitted into the decision process and the decision maker was assumed to be a logical, methodical optimizer. The descriptive decision model is continually influenced by its total environment and it also influences the environment. It is concerned with how decisions are actually made. The decision maker is influenced by his personal values, the time available for decision, uncertainty, the importance of the decision, bounded rationality, satisfying behavior, etc.

The descriptive decision model is based on behavioral foundations and the decision maker is considered a complex mixture of many elements, including his culture, his personality, and his aspirations. The decision maker's behavior reflects his perceptions of people, roles, and organizations in addition to his own values and emotions. The whole collection of experiences and expectations, developed from recurring and nonrecurring situations, forms the premises for individual decisions.

An organization has the task of channeling person-centered behavior toward group-defined ends. Organizational structures provide status systems with defined roles. These become premises for individual decisions and hence behavior. The organization provides experiences and information through training and communication. These also are premises for decisions and can become powerful means of influencing individuals toward organizational goals (11, pp. 123-5). March and Simon offered a satisficing model in contrast to the classical economic rationality model. Their principle of bounded rationality stated that human beings seldom make any effort to find the optimum strategy in a decision problem. Instead, they select a number of possible outcomes of their available strategies which would be good enough.[7] Then they select a strategy that is likely to achieve one of the good-enough outcomes.

In the descriptive model, the decision maker can be characterized as passing through three time periods as shown in Figure 3 (1, p. 16) (6, pp. 333-78).

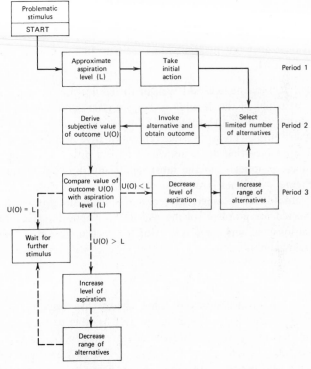

FIGURE 3.   Open decision model.

Period 1:   The individual starts out with an idealized goal structure. He defines one or more action goals as a first approximation to the "ideal goal" in the structure. The action goals may be considered as representative of the decision maker's "aspiration level."

Period 2:   The individual engages in search activity and defines a limited number of outcomes and alternatives. He does not attempt to establish the relations rigorously. His analysis proceeds from loosely defined rules of approximation. The alternatives discovered establish a starting point for further search toward a solution.

Period 3:   Search among the limited alternatives is undertaken to find a satisfactory solution, as contrasted with an optimal one. "Satisfactory" is defined in terms of the aspiration level or action goals.

Differences between normative and descriptive decision models are (1, p. 161):

1. Predetermined goals are replaced by some unidentified structure which is approximated by an aspiration level.
2. All alternatives and outcomes are not predetermined; neither are the relationships between specific alternatives and outcomes always defined.
3. The ordering of all alternatives is replaced by a search routine which considers fewer than all alternatives.
4. The individual does not maximize but seeks to find a solution to "satisfy" an aspiration level.

Descriptive decision models add realism to the decision-making framework. The human capacities of the decision maker are given some measure of recognition. They bring to bear the totality of forces—external and internal to the decision maker—influencing a decision. The normative decision models are the most valuable on recurring decisions which have a historical background; the descriptive decision models are the most significant on one-time, nonrecurring decisions. Figure 4 outlines basic approaches to decision making that can be used by organizational members in problem solving situations. The specific approach selected for problem solving will depend upon the given conditions, temporal relationships, and value system of the decision maker as modified by environmental restraints.

Conclusion

A framework for organizational decision theory has been outlined which includes normative and descriptive models as well as other pertinent dimensions. Decisions are made with varying degrees of information, and decision theory gives structure and rationale to the different possible environmental conditions.

The manager selects one strategy over others based on some criteria such as utility, maximum sales, minimum cost, or rate of return. The specific criterion or combination of goals is not entirely the manager's, for the value system is usually modified by groups with special interests such as stockholders, creditors,

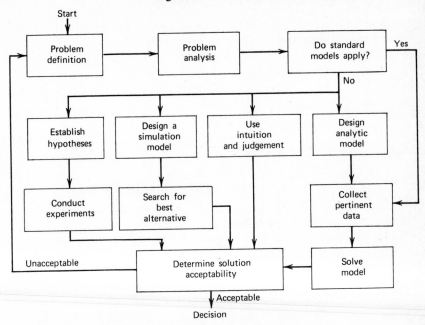

FIGURE 4.   Decision making approaches.

employers, unions, government, etc. In determining feasible strategies, many strategies can be omitted when they are dominated by a previously stated strategy. A decision is made by selecting one or reducing the number of strategies to one.

Frequently, the best strategy is that with the minimum disutility or the maximum expected utility. Utility tends to be consistent for a given individual, but for groups of individuals there tends to be inconsistence. The relationship between money and utility is complex and a doubling of profits usually does not double utility. Indifference curves are often used to forego the utility measurement in risk problems. The decision maker chooses a strategy that provides an acceptable combination of expected payoff and risk which is usually measured as the variance of return.[8] Indifference curves usually only consider two dimensions of the decision problem and they really have utility built into them. The development of indifference curves exhibits some of the same difficulties as utility indexes.

It is essential to an organization that its management develop rational decision-making procedures and strive to improve their decision-making capabilities. This can best be accomplished by analyzing their decisions and obtaining a better understanding of decision theory. An aim of decision theory is to better understand the decision process. Decisions are influenced by internal and external environmental factors; these factors have temporal variation which emphasize the dynamic nature of the decision process.

REFERENCES

1. Alexis, Marcus and Charles Z. Wilson, *Organization Decision Making*, Englewood Cliffs, New Jersey: Prentice-Hall, Inc., 1967.
2. Ansoff, H. Igor, *Corporate Strategy*, New York: McGraw-Hill Book Co. Inc., 1965.
3. Archer, Stephen H., "The Structure of Management Decision Theory." *Academy of Management Journal*, Vol. 7 (December, 1964) pp. 269–286.
4. Dahl, Robert A. and Charles E. Lindblom, *Politics, Economics, and Welfare*, New York: Harper & Row, 1953.
5. Hurwicz, Leonid, *Optimality, Criteria for Decision Making Under Ignorance*, Cowles Commission mimeographed discussion paper, Statistics No. 370, 1951.
6. Levin, Kurt *et. al.*, "Level of Aspiration," *Personality Disorders*, J. McV. Hunt, Ed., New York: The Ronald Press, 1944, pp. 333–78.
7. March, J. G. and Herbert A. Simon, *Organizations*, New York: John Wiley & Sons, Inc., 1958.
8. Markowitz, Harry M., *Portfolio Selection*, New York: John Wiley & Sons, Inc., 1959.
9. Miller, David W. and Martin K. Starr, *Executive Decisions and Operations Research*, Englewood Cliffs, New Jersey: Prentice-Hall, Inc., 1960.
10. Savage, Leonard J., *The Foundation of Statistics*, New York: John Wiley & Sons, Inc., 1954.
11. Simon, Herbert A., *Administrative Behavior*, New York: The MacMillian Co., 1957.
12. Simon, Herbert A., *The New Science of Management Decision*, New York: Harper and Bros., 1960.
13. Von Neumann, John and Oskar Morgenstern, *Theory of Games and Economic Behavior*, Princeton, New Jersey: Princeton University Press, 1953.

A Tutorial Introduction to Decision Theory*

D. Warner North

INTRODUCTION

The necessity of making decisions in the face of uncertainty is an integral part of our lives. We must act without knowing the consequences that will result from the action. This uncomfortable situation is particularly acute for the systems engineer or manager who must make far-reaching decisions on complex issues in a rapidly changing technological environment. Uncertainty appears as the dominant consideration in many systems problems as well as in decisions that we face in our personal lives. To deal with these problems on a rational basis, we must develop a theoretical structure for decision making that includes uncertainty.

Confronting uncertainty is not easy. We naturally try to avoid it; sometimes we even pretend it does not exist. Our primitive ancestors sought to avoid it by consulting soothsayers and oracles who would "reveal" the uncertain future. The methods have changed: astrology and the reading of sheep entrails are somewhat out of fashion today, but predictions of the future still abound.

SOURCE: Reprinted with the permission of the author and *IEEE Transactions on Systems Science and Cybernetics*, Vol. SSC-4, No. 3 (September, 1968), pp. 200–210..

EDITORS' NOTE: The mathematical techniques used in this article are more complex than in the rest of the book. However, many of the most important concepts can be understood without becoming involved in the mathematical complexity. Consequently, even students without a strong mathematical background can benefit from reading this article.

*Manuscript received May 8, 1968. An earlier version of this paper was presented at the IEEE Systems Science and Cybernetics Conference, Washington, D.C., October 17, 1966. This research was supported in part by the Graduate Cooperative Fellowship Program of the National Science Foundation at Stanford University, Stanford, Calif. The author is with the Decision Analysis Group, Stanford Research Institute, Menlo Park, Calif. 94025.

Much current scientific effort goes into forecasting future economic and technological developments. If these predictions are assumed to be completely accurate, the uncertainty in many systems decisions is eliminated. The outcome resulting from a possible course of action may then be presumed to be known. Decision making becomes an optimization problem, and techniques such as mathematical programming may be used to obtain a solution. Such problems may be quite difficult to solve, but this difficulty should not obscure the fact that they represent the limiting case of perfect predictions. It is often tempting to assume perfect predictions, but in so doing we may be eliminating the most important features of the problem.[1] We should like to include in the analysis not just the predictions themselves, but also a measure of the confidence we have in these predictions. A formal theory of decision making must take uncertainty as its departure point and regard precise knowledge of outcomes as a limiting special case.

Before we begin our exposition, we will clarify our point of view. We shall take the engineering rather than the purely scientific viewpoint. We are not observing the way people make decisions; rather we are participants in the decision-making process. Our concern is in actually making a decision, i.e., making a choice between alternative ways of allocating resources. We must assume that at least two distinct alternatives exist (or else there is no element of choice and, consequently, no problem). Alternatives are distinct only if they result in different (uncertain) rewards or penalties for the decision maker; once the decision has been made and the uncertainty resolved, the resource allocation can be changed only by incurring some penalty.

What can we expect of a general theory for decision making under uncertainty? It should provide a framework in which all available information is used to deduce which of the decision alternatives is "best" according to the decision maker's preferences. But choosing an alternative that is consistent with these preferences and present knowledge does not guarantee that we will choose the alternative that by hindsight turns out to be most profitable.

We might distinguish between a good decision and a good *outcome*. We are all familiar with situations in which careful management and extensive planning produced poor results, while a disorganized and badly managed competitor achieved spectacular success. As an extreme example, place yourself in the position of the company president who has discovered that a valuable and trusted subordinate whose past judgment had proved unfailingly accurate actually based his decisions upon the advice of a gypsy fortune teller. Would you promote this man or fire him? The answer, of course, is to fire him and hire the gypsy as a consultant. The availability of such a clairvoyant to provide perfect information would make decision theory unnecessary. But we should not confuse the two. Decision theory is not a substitute for the fortune teller.

It is rather a procedure that takes account of all available information to give us the best possible logical decision. It will minimize the consequences of getting an unfavorable outcome, but we cannot expect our theory to shield us from all "bad luck." The best protection we have against a bad outcome is a good decision.

Decision theory may be regarded as a formalization of common sense. Mathematics provides an unambiguous language in which a decision problem may be represented. There are two dimensions to this representation that will presently be described: value, by means of utility theory, and information, by means of probability theory. In this representation, the large and complex problems of systems analysis become conceptually equivalent to simple problems in our daily life that we solve by "common sense." We will use such a problem as an example.

You are driving home from work in the evening when you suddenly recall that your wedding anniversary comes about this time of year. In fact, it seems quite probable (but not certain) that it is today. You can still stop by the florist shop and buy a dozen roses for your wife, or you may go home empty-handed and hope the anniversary date lies somewhere in the future (Figure 1). If you buy the roses and it is your anniversary, your wife is pleased at what a thoughtful husband you are and your household is the very epitome of domestic bliss. But if it is not your anniversary, you are poorer by the price of the roses and your wife may wonder whether you are trying to make amends for some transgression she does not know about. If you do not buy the roses, you will be in the clear if it is not your anniversary; but if it is, you may expect a temper tantrum from your wife and a two-week sentence to the doghouse. What do you do?

We shall develop the general tools for solving decision problems and then return to this simple example. The reader might consider how he would solve this problem by "common sense" and then compare his reasoning with the formal solution which we shall develop later (Figure 2).

THE MACHINERY OF DECISION MAKING

Utility Theory

The first stage in setting up a structure for decision making is to assign numerical values to the possible outcomes. This task falls within the area covered by the modern theory of utility. There are a number of ways of developing the subject; the path we shall follow is that of Luce and Raiffa [16].[2]

The first and perhaps the biggest assumption to be made is that any two possible outcomes resulting from a decision can be compared. Given any two

Possible Outcomes

FIGURE 1.   Anniversary problem payoff matrix.

possible outcomes or prizes, you can say which you prefer. In some cases you might say that they were equally desirable or undesirable, and therefore you are indifferent. For example, you might prefer a week's vacation in Florida to a season ticket to the symphony. The point is not that the vacation costs more than the symphony tickets, but rather that you prefer the vacation. If you were offered the vacation or the symphony tickets on a nonnegotiable basis, you would choose the vacation.

A reasonable extension of the existence of your preference among outcomes is that the preference be transitive; if you prefer A to B and B to C, then it follows that you prefer A to C.[3]

The second assumption, originated by von Neumann and Morgenstern [22], forms the core of modern utility theory: you can assign preferences in the same manner to lotteries involving prizes as you can to the prizes themselves. Let us define what we mean by a lottery. Imagine a pointer that spins in the center of a circle divided into two regions, as shown in Figure 3. If you spin the

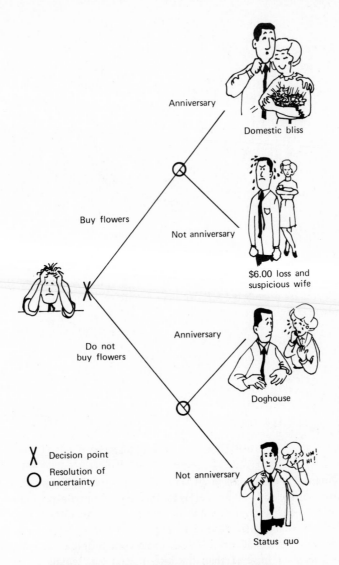

Anniversary

Domestic bliss

Buy flowers

Not anniversary

$6.00 loss and
suspicious wife

Do not
buy flowers

Anniversary

Doghouse

X   Decision point

O   Resolution of
    uncertainty

Not anniversary

Status quo

FIGURE 2.   Diagram of anniversary decision.

pointer and it lands in region I, you get prize A; if it lands in region II, you get prize B. We shall assume that the pointer is spun in such a way that when it stops, it is equally likely to be pointing in any given direction. The fraction of the circumference of the circle in region I will be denoted P, and that in

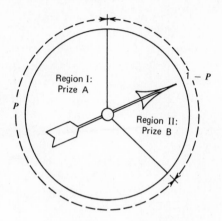

FIGURE 3.   A lottery.

region II as $1 - P$. Then from the assumption that all directions are equally likely, the probability that the lottery gives you prize A is P, and the probability that you get prize B is $1 - P$. We shall denote such a lottery as $(P,A;1-P,B)$ and represent it by Figure 4.

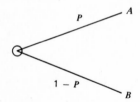

FIGURE 4.   Lottery diagram.

Now suppose you are asked to state your preferences for prize A, prize B, and a lottery of the above type. Let us assume that you prefer prize A to prize B. Then it would seem natural for you to prefer prize A to the lottery, $(P,A;1-P,B)$, between prize A and prize B, and to prefer this lottery between prize A and prize B to prize B for all probabilities P between 0 and 1. You would rather have the preferred prize A than the lottery, and you would rather have the lottery than the inferior prize B. Furthermore, it seems natural that, given a choice between two lotteries involving prizes A and B, you would choose the lottery with the higher probability of getting the preferred prize A, i.e., you prefer lottery $(P,A;1-P,B)$ to $(P',A;1-P',B)$ if and only if P is greater than P'.

The final assumptions for a theory of utility are not quite so natural and have been the subject of much discussion. Nonetheless, they seem to be the most reasonable basis for logical decision making. The third assumption is that there is no intrinsic reward in lotteries, that is, "no fun in gambling." Let us consider a compound lottery, a lottery in which at least one of the prizes is not an outcome but another lottery among outcomes. For example, consider the lottery $(P,A; 1 - P, (P',B; 1 - P', C))$. If the pointer of Figure 3 lands in region I, you get prize A; if it lands in region II, you receive another lottery that has different prizes and perhaps a different division of the circle (Figure 5). If you spin the second pointer you will receive prize B or prize C, depending on where this pointer lands. The assumption is that subdividing region II into two parts whose proportions correspond to the probabilities P' and $1 - P'$ of the second lottery creates an equivalent simple lottery in which all of the prizes are outcomes. According to this third assumption, you can decompose a compound lottery by multiplying the probability of the lottery prize in the first lottery by the probabilities of the individual prizes in the second lottery; you should be indifferent between $(P,A; 1 - P, (P',B; 1 - P', C))$ and $(P,A; P' - PP', B; 1 - P - P' + PP', C)$. In other words, your preferences are not affected by the way in which the uncertainty is resolved—bit by bit, or all at once. There is no value in the lottery itself; it does not matter whether you spin the pointer once or twice.

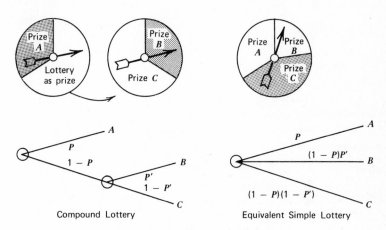

FIGURE 5.   "No fun in gambling."

Fourth, we make a continuity assumption. Consider three prizes, A, B, and C. You prefer A to C, and C to B (and, as we have pointed out, you will therefore prefer A to B). We shall assert that there must exist some probability P so that you are indifferent to receiving prize C or the lottery $(P,A; 1 - P, B)$ between A and B. C is called the certain equivalent of the lottery $(P,A; 1 - P, B)$, and on the strength of our "no fun in gambling" assumption, we assume that interchanging C and the lottery $(P,A;1 - P,B)$ as prizes in some compound lottery does not change your evaluation of the latter lottery. We have *not* assumed that, given a lottery $(P,A;1 - P,B)$, there exists a prize C intermediate in value between A and B so that you are indifferent between C and $(P,A;1 - P,B)$. Instead we have assumed the existence of the probability P. Given prize A preferred to prize C preferred to prize B, for some P between 0 and 1, there exists a lottery $(P,A;1 - P,B)$ such that you are indifferent between this lottery and prize C. Let us regard the circle in Figure 3 as a "pie" to be cut into two pieces, region I (obtain prize A) and region II (obtain prize B). The assumption is that the "pie" can be divided so that you are indifferent as to whether you receive the lottery or intermediate prize C.

Is this continuity assumption reasonable? Take the following extreme case:

$$A = \text{receive } \$1;$$
$$B = \text{death};$$
$$C = \text{receive nothing (status quo).}$$

It seems obvious that most of us would agree A is preferred to C, and C is preferred to B; but is there a probability P such that we would risk death for the possibility of gaining $1? Recall that the probability P can be arbitrarily close to 0 or 1. Obviously, we would not engage in such a lottery with, say, $P = 0.9$, i.e., a 1-in-10 chance of death. But suppose $P = 1 - 1 \times 10^{-50}$, i.e., the probability of death as opposed to $1 is not 0.1 but 10^{-50}. The latter is considerably less than the probability of being struck on the head by a meteor in the course of going out to pick up a $1 bill that someone has dropped on your doorstep. Most of us would not hesitate to pick up the bill. Even in this extreme case where death is a prize, we conclude the assumption is reasonable.

We can summarize the assumptions we have made into the following axioms.

A, B, C are prizes or outcomes resulting from a decision.

Notation:

$>$	means "is preferred to;"
$A > B$	means A is preferred to B;
$\sim$	means "is indifferent to;"
$A \sim B$	means the decision maker is indifferent between A and B.

Utility Axioms:

1. Preferences can be established between prizes and lotteries in an unambiguous fashion. These preferences are transitive, i.e.

$$A > B, B > C \text{ implies } A > C$$
$$A \sim B, B \sim C \text{ implies } A \sim C.$$

2. If $A > B$, then $(P,A;1 - P,B) > (P',A;1 - P',B)$ if and only if $P > P'$.
3. $(P,A;1 - P,(P',B;1 - P',C)) \sim (P,A;P' - PP',B;1 - P - P' + PP',C)$, i.e., there is "no fun in gambling."
4. If $A > C > B$, there exists a P with $0 < P < 1$ so that

$$C \sim (P,A;1 - P,B)$$

i.e., it makes no difference to the decision maker whether C or the lottery $(P,A;1 - P,B)$ is offered to him as a prize.

Under these assumptions, there is a concise mathematical representation possible for preferences: a utility function $u(\ )$ that assigns a number to each lottery or prize. This utility function has the following properties:

$$u(A) > u(B) \text{ if and only if } A > B \tag{1}$$

if $C \sim (P,A;1 - P,B)$,

$$\text{then } u(C) = P \cdot u(A) + (1 - P) \cdot u(B) \tag{2}$$

i.e., the utility of a lottery is the mathematical expectation of the utility of the prizes. It is this "expected value" property that makes a utility function useful because it allows complicated lotteries to be evaluated quite easily.

It is important to realize that all the utility function does is provide a means of consistently describing the decision maker's preferences through a scale of real numbers, providing these preferences are consistent with the previously mentioned assumptions 1. through 4. The utility function is no more than a means to logical deduction based on given preferences. The preferences come first and the utility function is only a convenient means of describing them. We can apply the utility concept to almost any sort of prizes or outcomes, from battlefield casualties or achievements in space to preferences for Wheaties or Post Toasties. All that is necessary is that the decision maker have unambiguous preferences and be willing to accept the basic assumptions.

In many practical situations, however, outcomes are in terms of dollars and cents. What does the utility concept mean here? For an example, let us suppose you were offered the following lottery: a coin will be flipped, and if you guess the outcome correctly, you gain $100. If you guess incorrectly, you get nothing. We shall assume you feel that the coin has an equal probability of coming up heads or tails; it corresponds to the "lottery" which we have defined in terms of a pointer with $P = 1/2$. How much would you pay for such a lottery? A common answer to this academic question is "up to $50," the average or expected value of the outcomes. When real money is involved, however, the same people tend to bid considerably lower; the average bid is about $20.[4] A group of Stanford University graduate students was actually confronted with a $100 pile of bills and a 1964 silver quarter to flip. The average of the sealed bids for this game was slightly under $20, and only 4 out of 46 ventured to bid as high as $40. (The high bidder, at $45.61, lost and the proceeds were used for a class party.) These results are quite typical; in fact, professional engineers and managers are, if anything, more conservative in their bids than the less affluent students.

The lesson to be learned here is that, by and large, most people seem to be averse to risk in gambles involving what is to them substantial loss. They are willing to equate the value of a lottery to a sure payoff or certain equivalent substantially less than the expected value of the outcomes. Similarly, most of us are willing to pay more than the expected loss to get out of an unfavorable lottery. This fact forms the basis of the insurance industry.

If you are very wealthy and you are confronted with a small lottery, you might well be indifferent to the risk. An unfavorable outcome would not deplete your resources, and you might reason that you will make up your losses in future lotteries; the "law of averages" will come to your rescue. You then evaluate the lottery at the expected value of the prizes. For example, the (1/2, $0; 1/2, $100) lottery would be worth $1/2($0) + 1/2($100) = 50 to you. Your utility function is then a straight line, and we say you are an "expected value" decision maker. For lotteries involving small prizes, most individuals and corporations are expected value decision makers. We might regard this as a consequence to the fact that any arbitrary utility curve for money looks like a straight line if we look at a small enough section of it. Only when the prizes are substantial in relation to our resources does the curvature become evident. Then an unfavorable outcome really hurts. For these lotteries most of us become quite risk averse, and expected value decision making does not accurately reflect our true preferences.

Let us now describe one way you might construct your own utility curve for money, say, in the amounts of $0 to $100, in addition to your present assets. The utility function is arbitrary as to choice of zero point and of scale factor; changing these factors does not lead to a change in the evaluation of lotteries using properties (1) and (2). Therefore, we can take the utility of $0 as 0 and the utility of $100 as 1. Now determine the minimum amount you would accept in place of the lottery of flipping a coin to determine whether you receive $0 or $100. Let us say your answer is $27. Now determine the certain equivalent of the lotteries (1/2, $0; 1/2, $27), and (1/2, $27; 1/2, $100), and so forth. We might arrive at a curve like that shown in Figure 6.

We have simply used the expected value property (2) to construct a utility curve. This same curve, however, allows us to use the same expected utility theorem to evaluate new lotteries; for example, (1/2, $30; 1/2, $80). From Figure 6, $u(\$30) = 0.54$, $u(\$80) = 0.91$, and therefore $1/2\ u(\$30) + 1/2\ u(\$80) = u(x) \rightarrow x = \$49$. If you are going to be consistent with the preferences you

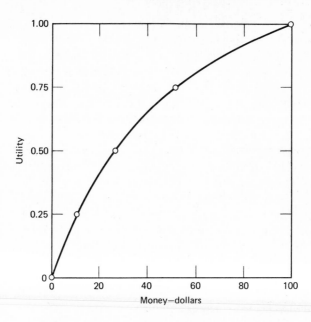

FIGURE 6.   Utility curve for money: $0 to $100.

expressed in developing the utility curve, you will be indifferent between $49 and this lottery. Moreover, this amount could have been determined from your utility curve by a subordinate or perhaps a computer program. You could send your agent to make decisions on lotteries by using your utility curve, and he would make them to reflect *your* preference for amounts in the range $0 to $100.

Even without such a monetary representation, we can always construct a utility function on a finite set of outcomes by using the expected value property (2). Let us choose two outcomes, one of which is preferred to the other. If we set the utilities arbitrarily at 1 for the preferred outcome and 0 for the other, we can use the expected value property (2) of the utility function to determine the utility of the other prizes. This procedure will always work so long as our preferences obey the axioms, but it may be unwieldy in practice because we are asking the decision maker to assess simultaneously his values in the absence of uncertainty and his preference among risks. The value of some outcome is accessible only by reference to a lottery involving the two "reference" outcomes. For example, the reference outcomes in the anniversary problem might be "domestic bliss" = 1 and "doghouse" = 0. We could then determine the utility of "status quo" as 0.91 since the husband is indifferent between the outcome "status quo" and a lottery in which the chances are 10 to 1 of "domestic bliss" as opposed to the "doghouse." Similarly, we might discover that a utility of 0.667 should be assigned to "suspicious wife and $6 wasted on roses," since our friend is indifferent between this eventuality and a lottery in which the probabilities are 0.333 of "doghouse" and 0.667 of "domestic bliss." Of course, to be consistent with the axioms, our friend must be indifferent between "suspicious wife, etc.," and a 0.73 probability of "status quo" and a 0.27 probability of "doghouse." If the example included additional outcomes as well, he might find it quite difficult to express his preferences among the lotteries in a manner consistent with the axioms. It may be advisable to proceed in two stages; first, a numerical determination of value in a risk-free situation, and then an adjustment to this scale to include preference toward risk.

Equivalent to our first assumption, the existence of transitive preferences, is the existence of some scale of value by which outcomes may be ranked; A is preferred to B if and only if A is higher in value than B. The numerical structure we give to this value is not important since a monotonic transformation to a new scale preserves the ranking of outcomes that corresponds to the original preferences. No matter what scale of value we use, we can construct a utility function on it by using the expected value property (2), so long as our four assumptions hold. We may as well use a standard of value that is reasonably intuitive, and in most situations money is a convenient standard of economic value. We can then find a monetary equivalent for each outcome by determining the point at which the decision maker is indifferent between receiving the outcome and receiving (or paying out) this amount of money. In addition to conceptual simplicity, this procedure makes it easy to evaluate new outcomes by providing an intuitive scale of values. Such a scale will become necessary later on if we are to consider the value of resolving uncertainty.

We will return to the anniversary decision and demonstrate how this two-step value determination procedure may be applied. But first let us describe how we shall quantify uncertainty.

The Inductive Use of Probability Theory

We now wish to leave the problem of the evaluation of outcomes resulting from a decision and turn our attention to a means of encoding the information we have as to which outcome is likely to occur. Let us look at the limiting case where a decision results in a certain outcome. We might represent an outcome, or an event, which is certain to occur by 1, and an event which cannot occur by 0. A certain event, together with another certain event, is certain to occur; but a certain event, together with an impossible event, is certain not to occur. Most engineers would recognize the aforementioned as simple Boolean equations: $1 \cdot 1 = 1$, $1 \cdot 0 = 0$. Boolean algebra allows us to make complex calculations with statements that may take on only the logical values "true" and "false." The whole field of digital computers is, of course, based on this branch of mathematics.

But how do we handle the logical "maybe?" Take the statement, "It will rain this afternoon." We cannot now assign this statement a logical value of true or false, but we certainly have some feelings on the matter, and we may even have to make a decision based on the truth of the statement, such as whether to go to the beach. Ideally, we would like to generalize the inductive logic of Boolean algebra to include uncertainty. We would like to be able to assign to a statement or an event a value that is a measure of its uncertainty. This value would lie in the range from 0 to 1. A value of 1 indicates that the statement is true or that the event is certain to occur; a value of 0 indicates that the statement is false or that the event cannot occur. We might add two obvious assumptions. We want the value assignments to be unambiguous, and we want the value assignments to be independent of any assumptions that have not been explicitly introduced. In particular, the value of the statement should depend on its content, not on the way it is presented. For example, "It will rain this morning or it will rain this afternoon," should have the same value as "It will rain today."

These assumptions are equivalent to the assertion that there is a function P that gives values between 0 and 1 to events ("the statement is true" is an event) and that obeys the following probability axioms.[5]

Let E and F be events or outcomes that could result from a decision:

1. $P(E) \geq 0$ for any event E;
2. $P(E) = 1$, if E is certain to occur;
3. $P(E \ or \ F) = P(E) + P(F)$ if E and F are mutually exclusive events (i.e., only one of them can occur).

$E \ or \ F$ means the event that either E or F occurs. We are in luck. Our axioms are identical to the axioms that form the modern basis of the theory of probability. Thus we may use the whole machinery of probability theory for inductive reasoning.

Where do we obtain the values $P(E)$ that we will assign to the uncertainty of the event E? We get them from our own minds. They reflect our best judgment on the basis of all the information that is presently available to us. The use of probability theory as a tool of inductive reasoning goes back to the beginnings of probability theory. In Napoleon's time, Laplace wrote the following as a part of his introduction to *A Philosophical Essay on Probabilities* (15, p. 1):

> Strictly speaking it may even be said that nearly all our knowledge is problematical; and in the small numbers of things which we are able to know with certainty, even in the mathematical sciences themselves, the principal means for ascertaining truth—induction and analogy—are themselves based on probabilities. . . .

Unfortunately, in the years following Laplace, his writings were misinterpreted and fell into disfavor. A definition of probability based on frequency came into vogue, and the pendulum is only now beginning to swing back. A great many modern probabilists look on the probability assigned to an event as the limiting fraction of the number of times an event occurred in a large number of independent repeated trials. We shall not enter into a discussion of the general merits of this viewpoint on probability theory. Suffice it to say that the situation is a rare one in which you can observe a great many independent identical trials in order to assign a probability. In fact, in decision theory we are often interested in events that will occur just once. For us, a probability assessment is made on the basis of a state of mind; it is not a property of physical objects to be measured like length, weight, or temperature. When we assign the probability of 0.5 to a coin coming up heads, or equal probabilities to all possible orientations of a pointer, we may be reasoning on the basis of the symmetry of the physical object. There is no reason to suppose that one side of the coin will be favored over the other. But the physical symmetry of the coin does not lead immediately to a probability assignment of 0.5 for heads. For example, consider a coin that is placed on a drum head. The drum head is struck, and the coin bounces into the air. Will it land heads up half of the time? We might expect that the probability of heads would depend on which side of the coin was up initially, how hard the drum was hit, and so forth. The probability of heads is not a physical parameter of the coin; we have to specify the flipping system as well. But if we knew exactly how the coin were to be flipped, we could calculate from the laws of mechanics whether it would land heads or tails. Probability enters as a means of describing our feelings about the likelihood of heads when our knowledge of the flipping system is not exact. We must conclude that the probability assignment depends on our present state of knowledge.

The most important consequence of this assertion is that probabilities are subject to change as our information improves. In fact, it even makes sense to talk about probabilities of probabilities. A few years ago we might have assigned the value 0.5 to the probability that the surface of the moon is covered by a thick layer of dust. At the time, we might have said, "We are 90 percent certain that our probability assignment after the first successful Surveyor probe will be less than 0.01 or greater than 0.99. We expect that our uncertainty about the composition of the moon's surface will be largely resolved."

Let us conclude our discussion of probability theory with an example that will introduce the means by which probability distributions are modified to include new information: Bayes' rule. We shall also introduce a useful notation. We have stressed that all of our probability assignments are going to reflect a state of information in the mind of the decision maker, and our notation shall indicate this state of information explicitly.

Let A be an event, and let x be a quantity about which we are uncertain; e.g., x is a random variable. The values that x may assume may be discrete (i.e., heads or tails) or continuous (i.e., the time an electronic component will run before it fails). We shall denote by $\{A|S\}$ the probability assigned to the event A on the basis of a state of information S, and by $\{x|S\}$ the probability that the random variable assumes the value x, i.e., the probability mass function for a discrete random variable or the probability density function for a continuous random variable, given a state of information S. If there is confusion between the random variable and its value, we shall write $\{x = x_0|S\}$, where x denotes the random variable and x_0 the value. We shall assume the random variable takes on some value, so the probabilities must sum to 1:

$$\int_x \{x|S\} = 1. \tag{3}$$

$\int$ is a generalized summation operator representing summation over all discrete values or integration over all continuous values of the random variable. The expected value, or the average of the random variable over its probability distribution, is

$$\langle x|S \rangle = \int_x x\{x|S\}. \tag{4}$$

One special state of information will be used over and over again, so we shall need a special name for it. This is the information that we now possess on the basis of our prior knowledge and experience, before we have done any special experimenting or sampling to reduce our uncertainty. The probability distribution that we assign to values of an uncertain quantity on the basis of this prior state of information (denoted $\&$) will be referred to as the "prior distribution" or simply the "prior."

Now let us consider a problem. Most of us take as axiomatic the assignment of 0.5 to the probability of heads on the flip of a coin. Suppose we flip thumbtacks. If the thumbtack lands with the head up and point down, we shall denote the outcome of the flip as "heads." If it lands with the head down and the point up, we shall denote the outcome as "tails." The question which we must answer is, "What is p, the probability of heads in flipping a thumbtack?" We will assume that both thumbtack and means of flipping are sufficiently standardized so that we may expect that all flips are independent and have the same probability for coming up heads. (Formally, the flips are Bernoulli trials.) Then the long-run fraction of heads may be expected to approach p, a well-defined number that at the moment we do not know.

Let us assign a probability distribution to this uncertain parameter p. We are all familiar with thumbtacks; we have no doubt dropped a few on the floor. Perhaps we have some experience with spilled carpet tacks, or coin flipping, or the physics of falling bodies that we believe is relevant. We want to encode all of this prior information into the form of a probability distribution on p.

This task is accomplished by using the cumulative distribution function, $\{p \leq p_0 | \&\}$, the probability that the parameter p will be less than or equal to some specific value of the parameter p_0. It may be convenient to use the complementary cumulative

$$\{p > p_0 | \&\} = 1 - \{p \leq p_0 | \&\}$$

and ask questions such as, "What is the probability that p is greater than $p_0 = 0.5$?"

To make the situation easier to visualize, let us introduce Sam, the neighborhood bookie. We shall suppose that we are forced to do business with Sam. For some value p_0 between 0 and 1, Sam offers us two packages:

Package 1: If measurement of the long run fraction of heads p shows that the quantity is less than or equal to p_0, then Sam pays us \$1. If $p > p_0$, then we pay Sam \$1.

Package 2: We divide a circle into two regions (as shown in Figure 3). Region I is defined by a fraction P of the circumference of the circle, and the remainder of the circle constitutes region II. Now a pointer is spun in such a way that when it stops, it is equally likely to be pointing in any given direction. If the pointer stops in region I, Sam pays us \$1; if it lands in region II, we pay Sam \$1.

Sam lets us choose the fraction P in Package 2, but then he chooses which package we are to receive. Depending on the value of p_0, these packages may be more or less attractive to us, but it is the relative rather than the absolute value of the two packages that is of interest. If we set P to be large, we might expect that Sam will choose Package 1, whereas if P is small enough, Sam will certainly choose Package 2. Sam wishes (just as we do) to have the package with the higher probability of winning \$1. (Recall this is our second utility axiom.) We shall assume Sam has the same information about thumbtacks that we do, so his probability assignments will be the same as ours. The assumption [utility axiom 4] is that given p_0, we can find a P such that Packages 1 and 2 represent equivalent lotteries, so $P = \{p \leq p_0 | \&\}$.[6] The approach is similar to the well-known method of dividing an extra dessert between two small boys: let one divide and the other choose. The first is motivated to make the division as even as possible so that he will be indifferent as to which half he receives.

Suppose Sam starts at a value $p_0 = 0.5$. We might reason that since nails always fall on the side (heads), and a thumbtack is intermediate between a coin and a nail heads is the more likely orientation; but we are not too sure; we have seen a lot of thumbtacks come up tails. After some thought, we decide that we are indifferent about which package we get if the fraction P is 0.3, so $\{p \leq 0.5 | \&\} = 0.30$.

Sam takes other values besides 0.5, skipping around in a random fashion, i.e., 0.3, 0.9, 0.1, 0.45, 0.8, 0.6, etc. The curve that results from the interrogation might look like that shown in Figure 7. By his method of randomly skipping around, Sam has eliminated any bias in our true feelings that resulted from an unconscious desire to give answers consistent with previous points. In this fashion, Sam has helped us to establish our prior distribution on the parameter p. We may derive a probability density function by taking the derivative of the cumulative distribution function (Figure 8): $\{p | \&\} = (d/dp_0) \{p \leq p_0 | \&\}$.

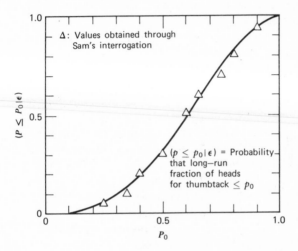

FIGURE 7.   Cumulative distribution function for thumbtack flipping.

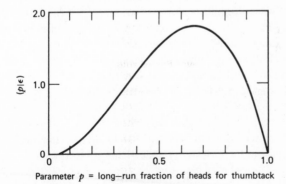

FIGURE 8.   Prior probability density function.

Now supposing we are allowed to flip the thumbtack 20 times and we obtain 5 heads and 15 tails. How do we take account of this new data in assigning a probability distribution based on the new state of information, which we denote as $\&, E$: our prior experience $\&$ plus E, the 20-flip experiment? We will use one of the oldest (1763) results of probability theory, Bayes' rule. Consider the prior probability that p will take on a specific value and the 20-flip experiment E will have a certain specific outcome (for example, $p = 0.43$; $E = 5$ heads, 15 tails). Now we can write this joint probability in two ways:

$$\{p, E \mid \&\} = \{p \mid E, \&\} \{E \mid \&\} \tag{5}$$

i.e., as the product of the probability we assign to the experimental outcome E times the probability we would assign to the value of p after we knew the experimental outcome E in addition to our prior information; or

$$\{p, E \mid \&\} = \{E \mid p, \&\} \{p \mid \&\} \tag{6}$$

i.e., the product of the probability of that experimental outcome if we knew that p were the probability of getting heads times our prior probability assessment that p actually takes on that value.

We assumed that probabilities were unambiguous, so we equate these two expressions. Providing $\{E \mid \&\} \neq 0$, i.e., the experimental outcome is not impossible, we obtain the posterior (after the experiment) probability distribution on p

$$\{p \mid E, \&\} = \frac{\{E \mid p, \&\} \{p \mid \&\}}{\{E \mid \&\}} \tag{7}$$

This expression is the well-known Bayes' rule.

$\{E \mid \&\}$ is the "pre-posterior" probability of the outcome E. It does not depend on p, so it becomes a normalizing factor for the posterior probability distribution. $\{E \mid p, \&\}$ is the probability of the outcome E if we knew the value p for the probability of heads. This probability is a function of p, usually referred to as the "likelihood function." We notice since p must take on some value, the expectation of the likelihood function over the values of p gives the preposterior probability of the experimental outcome:

$$\{E \mid \&\} = \int_p \{E \mid p, \&\} \{p \mid \&\}. \tag{8}$$

For the specific case we are treating, the likelihood function is the familiar result from elementary probability theory for r successes in n Bernoulli trials when the probability of a success is p:

$$\{E \mid p, \&\} = \frac{n!}{r!(n-r)!} p^r (1-p)^{n-r}. \tag{9}$$

This function is graphed for $r = 5$ heads in $n = 20$ trials in Figure 9. Multiplying it by the prior $\{p|\&\}$ (Figure 8) and normalizing by dividing by $\{E|\&\}$ gives us the posterior distribution $\{p|E,\&\}$ (Figure 10). In this way, Bayes' rule gives us a general means of revising our probability assessments to take account of new information.[7]

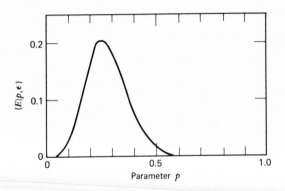

FIGURE 9.   Likelihood function for 5 heads in 20 trials.

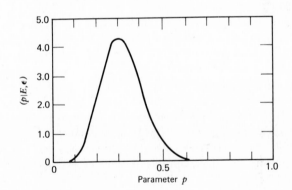

FIGURE 10.   Posterior probability density function.

SOLUTION OF DECISION PROBLEMS

Now that we have the proper tools, utility theory and probability theory, we return to the anniversary decision problem. We ask the husband, our decision maker, to assign monetary values to the four possible outcomes. He does so as follows:

Domestic bliss	(flowers + anniversary):	$100
Doghouse	(no flowers, anniversary):	$ 0
Status quo	(no flowers, no anniversary):	$ 80
Suspicious wife	(flowers, no anniversary):	$ 42

(For example, he is indifferent between "status quo" and "doghouse" provided in the latter case he receives $80.) His preference for risk is reflected by the utility function of Figure 6, and he decides that a probability assessment of 0.2 sums up his uncertainty about the possibility of today being his anniversary: the odds are 4 to 1 that it is not his anniversary. Now let us look at the two lotteries that represent his decision alternatives. If he buys the flowers, he has a 0.2 probability of "domestic bliss" and an 0.8 probability of "suspicious wife." The expected utility of the lottery is $0.2(1.0) + 0.8(0.667) = 0.734 = u(\$50)$. On the other hand, if he does not buy the flowers, he has an 0.8 chance of "status quo" and a 0.2 chance of "doghouse." The expected utility of this alternative is $0.8(0.91) + 0.2(0) = 0.728 = u(\$49)$. The first alternative has a slightly higher value to him so he should buy the flowers. On the basis of his values, his risk preference, and his judgment about the uncertainty, buying the flowers is his best alternative. If he were an expected value decision maker, the first lottery would be worth $0.2(\$100) + 0.8(\$42) = \$53.60$ and the second $0.2(0) + 0.8(\$80) = \$64$. In this case he should not buy the flowers.

The foregoing example is, of course, very trivial, but conceptually any decision problem is exactly the same. There is only one additional feature that we may typically expect: in general, decision problems may involve a sequence of decisions. First, a decision is made and then an uncertain outcome is observed; after which another decision is made, and an outcome observed, etc. For example, the decision to develop a new product might go as follows. A decision is made as to whether or not a product should be developed. If the decision is affirmative, an uncertain research and development cost will be incurred. At this point, a decision is made as to whether to go into production. The production cost is uncertain. After the production cost is known, a sale price is set. Finally, the uncertain sales volume determines the profit or loss on the product.

We can handle this problem in the same way as the anniversary problem: assign values to the final outcomes, and probabilities to the various uncertain outcomes that will result from the adoption of a decision alternative. We can represent the problem as a decision tree (Figure 11), and the solution is conceptually easy. Start at the final outcome, sales volume (the ends of the tree). Go in to the first decision, the sales price (the last to be made chronologically). Compute the utility of the decision alternatives, and choose the one with the highest value. This value becomes the utility of the chance outcome leading to that decision (e.g., production cost). The corresponding

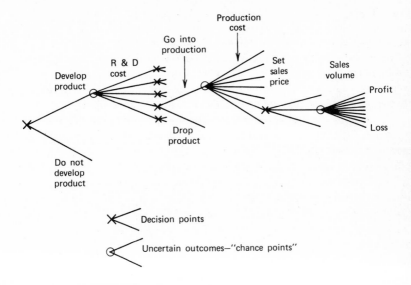

FIGURE 11.   Product development decision tree.

certain equivalent in dollars reflects the expected utility of reaching that point in the tree. In this fashion, we work backwards to the start of the tree, finding the best decision alternatives and their values at each step.

Many decision problems encountered in actual practice are extremely complex, and a decision tree approach may not always be appropriate. If all quantities concerned in the problem were considered uncertain (with prior distributions), the problem might be computationally intractable. It is often advisable to solve the model deterministically as a first approximation. We approximate all uncertain quantities with a single best estimate and then examine the decision; i.e., if research and development costs, production costs, and sales volume took the values we consider most likely, would it then be advisable to develop the product? This deterministic phase will usually give us some insight into the decision. Moreover, we can perform a sensitivity analysis by varying quantities that we believe are uncertain to determine how they affect the decision. The decision may be quite insensitive to some quantities, and these quantities may be treated as certain (uncertainty is neglected if it appears not to affect the decision). On the other hand, if a variation that lies within the range of uncertainty of a factor causes a major shift in the decision (i.e., from "develop the product" to "do not develop the product"), we shall certainly wish to encode our feelings about the uncertainty of that quantity by a prior distribution.[8]

THE VALUE OF RESOLVING UNCERTAINTIES

There is a class of alternatives usually available to the decision maker that we have not yet mentioned: activities that allow him to gather more information to diminish the uncertainties before he makes the decision. We have already seen how new information may be incorporated into probability assessments through Bayes' rule, and we noted that we can assign a probability distribution to the results of the information gathering by means of the pre-posterior probability distribution. Typical information-gathering activities might include market surveys, pilot studies, prototype construction, test marketing, or consulting with experts. These activities invariably cost the decision maker time and resources; he must pay a price for resolving uncertainty.

Let us return to the husband with the anniversary problem. Suppose he has the option of calling his secretary. If it is his anniversary, his secretary will certainly tell him. But if it is not, she may decide to play a trick and tell him that today is his anniversary. He assigns probability 0.5 to such practical joking. In any event, the secretary will spread the word around the office and our friend will get some good natured heckling, which he views as having a value of minus $10.

How will the secretary's information change his assessment of the probability that today is his anniversary? If she says, "No, it is not your anniversary," he may be sure that it is not; but if she says "Yes, it is," she could be joking. We can compute the new assessment of the probability from Bayes' rule. This new probability is equal to the probability 0.2 that she says yes and it really is his anniversary, divided by his prior estimate, $0.2 + 0.5 \times 0.8 = 0.6$, that she will say yes regardless of the date of his anniversary. Hence the probability assignment revised to include the secretary's yes answer is 0.333.

What is the value of this new alternative to our friend? If his secretary says no (probability 0.4), he may return home empty-handed and be assured of "status quo." On the other hand, if she says yes (probability 0.6), he will buy the flowers. In either case, he has incurred a cost of $10 which must be subtracted from the values of the outcomes. Calling the secretary then has a utility of

$$0.4 \, u(\$70) + 0.6 \, [0.333 \, u(\$90) + 0.667 \, u(\$32)]$$
$$= 0.344 + 0.416 = 0.760 = u(\$53.50).$$

Since this value of $53.50 exceeds the value of $50 for his previous best alternative (buy flowers), our friend should call his secretary. If the husband were an expected value decision maker, the alternative of calling the secretary would have a value of

$$0.4 \, (\$70) + 0.6 \, [0.333 \, (\$90) + 0.667 \, (\$32)] = \$58.80$$

which is less than the value of $64 for the "do not buy flowers" alternative; in this case our friend should not call his secretary. It is evident that in this example preference toward risk is very important in determining the decision maker's best course of action.

In the complex decision problems normally encountered in practice, there are usually several alternative options available for diminishing the uncertainty associated with the unknown factors. In theory, the expected gain for each type of sampling could be computed and compared with the cost of sampling as we have just done in the simple anniversary example. But these calculations can be quite involved as a rule, and there may be a great many alternative ways of gathering information. Often the relevant questions are, first, "Should we sample at all?" and then, "What kind of sampling is best for us?"

It is often useful to look at the limiting case of complete resolution of uncertainty, which we call perfect information. We can imagine that a gypsy fortune teller who always makes correct predictions is, in fact, available to us. The value of perfect information is the amount that we are willing to pay her to tell us exactly what the uncertain quantity will turn out to be. Note that her answer may be of little value to us—we may be planning to take the best decision alternative already. On the other hand, her perfect information may be quite valuable; it may allow us to avoid an unfavorable outcome. We are going to have to pay her before we hear her information; our payment will reflect what we expect the information to be on the basis of our prior probability assessment.

In the husband's anniversary problem, perfect information might correspond to a secretary who is certain to tell him if today is his anniversary. If he could act on this information, he would buy flowers if it were his anniversary and would not buy flowers otherwise. Since he feels that there is a 0.2 chance the secretary will tell him that it is his anniversary, the expected utility of the outcomes if he bases his decision on perfect information is $0.2 \, u(\$100 - b) + 0.8 \, u(\$80 - b)$ where b is the amount he must pay to get the information. By setting this expression equal to 0.734, the expected utility of his best alternative based on prior information, we can solve for $b = \$33.50$. The husband should consider for more detailed analysis only those opportunities for resolving his uncertainty that "cost" him $33.50 or less. If he were an expected value decision maker, perfect information would be of less value to him; he would be willing to pay a maximum of only $20 for it.[9]

SUMMARY

Decision theory is a way of formalizing common sense. The decision maker analyzes the possible outcomes resulting from his available alternatives in two dimensions: value (by means of utility theory) and probability of occurrence. He then chooses the alternative that he expects to have the highest value. He cannot guarantee that the outcome will be as good as he might hope for, but he has made the best decision he can, based on his preferences and available knowledge. Inference using Bayes' rule allows the decision maker to evaluate information gathering activities that will reduce his uncertainty.

Decision theory gives no magical formulas for correct decisions. In fact, it forces the decision maker to rely more strongly than ever on his own preferences and judgments. But it does give him a logical framework in which to work, a framework that is adaptable in principle to all decision problems, from the simplest to the most complex. As modern society continues to grow in size and complexity, such a framework for decision making will become more and more necessary.

ACKNOWLEDGMENT

The author is deeply indebted to Prof. R. A. Howard for valuable guidance and advice. Much of the viewpoint presented in this paper was acquired as a result of two years of assisting Prof. Howard in his course in Decision Analysis at Stanford University, Stanford, California.

FOOTNOTES

1. For further discussion of this point, see Howard [10] and Klein and Meekling [14].

2. The classical reference on modern utility theory is von Neumann and Morgenstern [22]. A recent survey of the literature on utility theory has been made by Fishburn [5].

3. Suppose not: you would be at least as happy with C as with A. Then if a little man in a shabby overcoat came up and offered you C instead of A, you would presumably accept. Now you have C, and since you prefer B to C, you would presumably pay a sum of money to get B instead. Once you had B, you prefer A: so you would pay the man in the shabby overcoat some more money to get A. But now you are back where you started, with A, and the little man in the shabby overcoat walks away counting your money. Given that you accepted a standard of value such as money, transitivity prevents you from becoming a "money pump."

4. Based on unpublished data obtained by Prof. R. A. Howard of Stanford University, Stanford, Calif.

5. Axioms 1. and 2. are obvious, and 3. results from the assumption of invariance to the form of data presentation (the last sentence in the

preceding paragraph). Formal developments may be found in Cox [3], Jaynes [12], or Jeffreys [13]. A joint axiomatization of both probability and utility theory has been developed by Savage [20].

6. We have equated the subjective probability that summarized our information about thumbtacks to the more intuitive notion of probability based on symmetry (in Package 2). Such a two-step approach to probability theory has been discussed theoretically by Anscombe and Aumann [1].

7. For certain sampling processes having special statistical properties, assumption of a prior probability distribution from a particular family of functions leads to a simple form for Bayes' rule. An extensive development of this idea of "conjugate distributions" has been accomplished by Raiffa and Schlaifer [19].

8. The decision analysis procedure has been described in detail by Howard [8].

9. Additional discussion regarding the value of information in decision theory is available from many sources, most notably Howard [8b], [9], [11] and Raiffa and Schlaifer [19].

REFERENCES

1. F. J. Anscombe and R. J. Aumann, "A definition of subjective probability," *Ann. Math. Statist.*, Vol. 34, pp. 199–205, 1963.

2. T. Bayes, "An essay toward solving a problem in the doctrine of chances," *Phil. Trans. Roy. Soc.* (London), Vol. 53, pp. 370–418, 1763.

3. R. T. Cox, *The Algebra of Probable Inference*. Baltimore, Md.: The Johns Hopkins Press, 1961.

4. P. C. Fishburn, *Decision and Value Theory*. New York: Wiley, 1964.

5. ——, "Utility theory," *Management Sci.*, Vol. 14, pp. 335–378, January 1968.

6. ——, "On the prospects of a useful unified theory of value for engineering," *IEEE Trans. Systems Science and Cybernetics*, Vol. SSC-2, pp. 27–35, August 1966.

7. R. A. Howard, "Bayesian decision models for system engineering," *IEEE Trans. Systems Science and Cybernetics*, Vol. SSC-1, pp. 36–40, November 1965.

8. a) ——, "Decision analysis: applied decision theory," *Proc. 4th Internat'l Conf. Operational Res.* (Boston, Mass., 1966).
   b) ——, "The foundations of decision analysis," this issue, pp. 211–219.

9. ——, "Information value theory," *IEEE Trans. Systems Science and Cybernetics*, Vol. SSC-2, pp. 22–26, August 1966.

10. ——, "The science of decision-making" (unpublished).

11. ——, "Value of information lotteries," *IEEE Trans. Systems Science and Cybernetics*, Vol. SSC-3, pp. 54–60, June 1967.

12. E. T. Jaynes, "Probability theory in science and engineering," Field Research Laboratory, Socony Mobile Oil Co., Inc., Dallas, Tex., 1959.

13. H. Jeffreys, *Theory of Probability*, 3rd ed. Oxford: Clarendon Press, 1961.

14. B. Klein and W. Meekling, "Applications of operations research to development decisions," *Operations Res.*, Vol. 6, pp. 352–363, May–June 1958.

15. P. S. Laplace, *Essai Philosophique sur les Probabilités* (Paris, 1814), translation. New York: Dover, 1951.

16. R. D. Luce and H. Raiffa, *Games and Decisions: Introduction and Critical Survey*. New York: Wiley, 1957.

17. J. W. Pratt, H. Raiffa, and R. Schlaifer, "The foundations of decision under uncertainty: an elementary exposition," *J. Am. Statist. Assoc.*, Vol. 59, pp. 353–375, June 1964.

18. ——, *Introduction to Statistical Decision Theory*. New York: McGraw-Hill, 1965.

19. H. Raiffa and R. Schlaifer, *Applied Statistical Decision Theory*. Boston, Mass.: Graduate School of Business, Harvard University, 1961.

20. L. J. Savage, *The Foundations of Statistics*. New York: Wiley, 1954.

21. R. Schlaifer, *Probability and Statistics for Business Decisions*. New York: McGraw-Hill, 1959.

22. J. von Neumann and O. Morgenstern, *Theory of Games and Economic Behavior*, 2nd ed. Princeton, N.J.: Princeton University Press, 1947.

Accounting Information and Decision-Making: Some Behavioral Hypotheses*

William J. Bruns, Jr.

Consider the following statements:

1. If accounting information is not considered relevant by a decision-maker to a decision under consideration, a change in the accounting information will not affect his decision.
2. The conception of accounting information held by a decision-maker—his opinion on how well the accountant and accounting system measures significant attributes and characteristics of factors affecting and affected by a decision—will affect the weight given to accounting information in the decision process when other information is available.
3. The availability of other information will be an important determinant of the weight assigned by a decision-maker to accounting information in the decision process.

Each of these statements has many characteristics of a truism. Many more like them, each concerned with the relationship between accounting systems,

SOURCE: Reprinted with permission from *The Accounting Review,* Vol. 43, No. 3 (July, 1968), pp. 469–478.

EDITORS' NOTE: The final two sections of this article dealing with research implications were omitted.

*Part of this work was completed while the author was a Faculty Fellow in the New York Office of Price Waterhouse & Co. However, the statements, opinions, and conclusions in this paper are solely those of the author.

accounting information, decision-makers, and decision-making could be easily constructed. Though behavioral relationships on which such statements rest are potentially important to the development of accounting theory and the design of information-decision systems, the study of those relationships is in the earliest stages.

Relatively little is known about the way in which information is used in decision-making, and without such knowledge it is difficult to predict the diverse effects which different accounting systems or information will have on decisions. A model developed below explicitly identifies and relates some factors which may determine when decisions are affected by accounting systems and information. The hypotheses on which this model is based are intended to stimulate and direct part of the study of accounting and decision-making. While the model is not tested here, some implications of the hypothesized relationships for both accounting theory and accounting systems are discussed.

RATIONALES FOR RESEARCH ON DECISION-MAKING AND BEHAVIOR BY ACCOUNTANTS

The problems that demand new research in behavioral aspects of accounting are familiar to almost all who have studied economics and accounting. The relationship between available information and decisions is basic to economic theories of decision-making. Knowledge about costs, prices, and competitors is assumed in almost all traditional theory, and much effort has been directed toward developing models of decision-making for use when information about one or more of these factors is unknown. As these models have been explored and modified, and as new procedures for analysis of alternative courses of action have been developed, new attention has been given to the role of data as determinants of decisions.

Accounting systems of firms are important sources of information for business decision-making. The information which systems provide for decision-making can be grouped in three classes: financial statements, quantitative reports on selected aspects of operations, and special analyses. Information from each class can be grouped with information from another, or with information from sources outside the accounting system in the set of information used by a decision-maker.

Almost all accounting information is affected by the body of rules and procedures called generally accepted accounting principles. Efforts to develop and improve generally accepted accounting principles have been underway since the 1930's, and since 1960 these efforts have found vigorous support from the accounting profession. Thus far, these efforts have not been notably successful, for there are few, if any, bases on which all accountants can agree to select among alternative general principles.

It is possible that much of the effort directed toward resolution of controversy about generally accepted accounting principles has been premature or misdirected. Accounting is a service activity carried out to provide information for decisions within and about business firms. Analyses of alternative sets of generally accepted accounting principles have often been based on the assumption that the relationship between an accounting report or information contained therein and each decision is direct. But this assumption has not been tested, and alternative hypotheses abound. When these have been tested and efforts to develop generally accepted accounting principles can be based upon knowledge of the manner in which accounting affects decisions about business activity, new and important criteria for selecting among alternative methods and alternative systems will be available.[1]

DEFINING ACCOUNTING SYSTEMS AND INFORMATION

One complication in the task of relating accounting information to decision-making is the fact that "accounting systems" are diverse and "accounting information" describes many different sets of data and information. For purposes of this paper, an "accounting system" will refer to the methods by which financial data about a firm or its activity are collected, processed, stored and/or distributed to members of the firm or other interested parties. It is possible to consider that any data or information which are obtained from or created in the accounting system of a firm are accounting information whether contained in a financial statement, a special report, or verbal statement. However, for our immediate purposes, that interpretation is too broad to be useful. Hereafter, "accounting information" will refer to written information of the type that might be contained in a complete or partial financial report— balance sheet, income statement, or funds flow statement—though in many cases this limitation is not critical to the discussion.

THE RELEVANCE OF ACCOUNTING INFORMATION FOR DECISION-MAKING

By definition, decisions affect future events, for future actions are determined as a decision is made. In the case of management decisions, decisions may affect only a single event or they may affect all events subsequent to the decision. But no event which has been completed can be altered by a decision.[2] Furthermore, accounting information, in the sense that we are using that term here, focuses on past events.[3] Accounting cannot change events or their effects unless it is through the decision process where future events and their effects are determined. Decision-making and accounting information focus on different time periods except to the extent that the decision process employs accounting information. An important question then is, when is accounting information relevant for decision-making?

In a recent paper, Ijiri, Jaedicke, and Knight have provided a framework which is extremely useful as a basis for discussing the relationship of accounting information and decision processes.[4] They represent a decision process as a function that relates a set of decision inputs to a unique set of decisions. Symbolically,

$$(z_1, z_2, \ldots, z_n) = h(x_1, x_2, \ldots, x_n).$$

Here $z_1, z_2, \ldots, z_n$ are a set of decisions based upon inputs, $x_1, x_2, \ldots, x_n$, according to a decision rule, h. Each set Z and X, must contain at least one element, but there is no requirement that the number of inputs be equal to the number of decisions.

Selection of a particular decision rule by a decision-maker is affected by many factors, among them his analytical capabilities and objectives. The rule associates inputs with decisions and selection of a decision rule establishes the degree to which objectives will be met by the expected effects of a particular set of decisions. The decision-maker explores the relationships between decisions and objectives prior to the selection of a rule by analysis and through evaluation of the effects of past events similar to those contemplated in the future.

If accounting information affects decisions, it does so through a decision rule which relates decisions to inputs, which include accounting information. The decision-maker uses or selects a decision rule which relates inputs to decisions in a manner consistent with his experience, perceptions, and his objectives. Suppose we let x_1 represent consistent accounting information, one element of a set of all decision inputs available at the time a set of decisions is to be made. The decision rule weights each decision input, which determines each decision in the set Z, and the weight assigned to x_1 will determine what effect, if any, accounting information has on decisions affecting future events. All other decision inputs, x_2 through x_n, are also weighted by the decision rule, and each affects the resulting set of decisions. These inputs may provide nonfinancial information essential to decisions, and in some cases their weights will overwhelm any possible effects of accounting information.

In selecting a decision rule, the decision-maker must consider all inputs available and their relevance to the set of decisions to be made. It is the decision-maker who decides whether any input is relevant or not. The perceived relevance of the decision inputs to the decisions at hand determine whether the decision rule selected will apply a weight different from zero to accounting information. If a weight different from zero is applied, accounting information may affect decisions; if not, decisions will not be affected by accounting information. Therefore, we hypothesize: *if accounting information is perceived as irrelevant for the set of decisions to be made, accounting information will not affect decisions; if accounting information is perceived as relevant to the set of decisions to be made, it may affect decisions.*

THE ROLE OF THE DECISION-MAKER'S CONCEPTION OF ACCOUNTING

Accounting is a systematic process of providing information about wealth and the effects of economic events. The methods, rules, and procedures that comprise accounting are here assumed to be familiar to the reader. However, there are reasons to believe that accounting is different things to different participants in economic events, and if so, the conceptions of accounting held by individuals or organizations may influence the impact of accounting information on behavior.

Away from reality, accounting can be regarded as a perfect measure. A perfect measure can be defined as a measure where there is a zero probability that the true measurement of an attribute differs from the reported measurement. We can assume that identifiable objects and legal rights have value and that these values are enhanced or destroyed as economic events occur, and we can assume that these values and effects are measureable. To many persons, accounting practice, carried out by trained observers applying consistent and objective methods of measurement and attested to by independent agents, holds the image of a perfect measure applied by professionals. There is an aura of authenticity that surrounds accounting data, and to the untrained user of information, accounting may appear to be a perfect source. We must recognize, however, that few, if any, of the persons who have processed or reviewed the data and the procedures that have converted it to information would consider it perfect.

More realistically, accounting can be considered as a process by which the value or effects of events is reported as accurately as possible but without pretense of being a perfect measure. Here, this conception of accounting will be referred to as an "imperfect measure." Such a measure is defined when the probability that the true value differs from the reported value is greater than zero. This conception is probably closest to that held by most practicing accountants. Errors and inaccuracy in the process of measuring, counting, and reporting are inevitable, and most persons who are familiar with accounting measures and procedures are familiar with these problems. This notion may cause accounting to have a different impact on behavior than the "perfect measure" notion. It allows for a "margin of disbelief" that may in some cases affect the kind of action taken as accounting information is used in decision processes.

A third conception of accounting is fundamentally different from the "perfect measure" or "imperfect measure" notions advanced above. Accounting information may be a goal for actors in economic events. When a businessman seeks profit, he does so for many reasons. For some purposes, the profit reported by accounting is far more important to the businessman or manager than the "true" or "perfectly measured" profit. Modern business organization has given this conception of accounting wide significance, and the implications of this notion for accounting warrant close examination.

Accounting becomes a goal when rewards or satisfactions accrue to a decision-maker as a result of accounting information, and the relationship of the true measure to the reported measure is unimportant. For example, if a manager hopes to advance and feels he will be promoted if he can effect cost reductions, and if accounting information will provide the basis for determining whether costs have been reduced, then it is the accounting information which shows reduced costs that becomes the goal. Likewise, where management is rewarded by stockholders with salary and perquisites on the basis of reported earnings or growth, the reports which result in these rewards may become more important—the goal of management decision-makers—than the long-run earnings or healthy growth which the stockholders really intend to reward.

While not exclusive, this brief recognition of diverse conceptions of accounting seems essential to understanding the effects of accounting information on behavior and decision-making. Below it will be assumed that any individual in a decision situation conceives accounting information either as a goal or at a point on a continuum on which accounting varies from a perfect measure to an imperfect one. This assumption is necessary to state a second set of hypotheses relating accounting information and decisions: *the conception of accounting held by a decision-maker will affect his selection of a decision rule to be used in reaching a set of decisions.* This hypothesis can be further specified by stating it in two parts:

1. If accounting information is both a decision input and an objective (goal) sought by a decision-maker, accounting information will affect decisions.
2. The more a decision-maker conceives accounting as being a perfect source of information, the more likely the decision-maker will select decision rules that weight accounting heavily, and the more likely accounting information will affect decisions.

CLASSIFYING DECISION-MAKERS

Because accounting information can be conceived as a goal, and because accounting information is determined in part by an accounting system, a classification of decision-makers provides insight into a final effect which accounting information may have on the set of decisions selected by the decision-makers. Three classes are suggested; first, decision-makers within the firm who make decisions both about operations and about the accounting system used to prepare reports; second, decision-makers within the firm who can make operating decisions but who cannot affect the methods used to prepare reports; and third, those outside of the firm who make decisions about the firm which may affect its environment and operations but who have no direct control over the operation of the firm or any activities in which it is engaged. The reasons for separating the first two classes of decision-makers, both of which are internal to the firm, will later become more obvious.

The first class of decision-makers is comprised of top management. Financial reports are the reports of this group and they are responsible for their preparation and presentation. If a choice must be made between accounting methods, this group is responsible for making that decision. This means that the set of possible decisions available to this class of decision-makers includes modification of the accounting system.[5]

The second class of decision-makers is distinguished from the first only in one important way. Their position in the organization precludes their determining the information included in accounting reports by modifying the accounting system. However, they make decisions about the activities of the firm and we can assume that accounting information enters into their decision processes. They can, of course, influence the content of accounting information by their decisions about activities, in which case accounting information may be affecting decisions.

The distinction between top management, who may affect accounting information, and internal decision-makers who cannot, is most critical where accounting information is conceived as a goal.[6] The decision function for such managers may contain important options between operating decisions and decisions to change the methods by which accounting information is prepared. In any event, decisions are affected, but predicting directions of the effects is much more complicated than it is for decision-makers who do not have authority to modify accounting methods or procedures. Requirements for independent audits and certification of consistency in methods between accounting periods reduces the significance of the two levels of management, though few would argue that this requirement is such that the effects of top management's discretion in accounting can be ignored.

The third class of decision-makers consists of several sets of interested outsiders. Investors, legally the owners of the firm but in fact usually somewhat removed from it, are ostensibly the group for which accounting information in published form is prepared. Creditors, in some cases merely another class of investors, usually seek the same information. A third major set of outsiders consists of government agencies who seek bases for taxation, regulation, and economic analysis. Each of these sets of outsiders makes decisions that may affect the firm and its operations, and to the extent that accounting information is utilized as part of their decision processes, it will affect these decisions. However, the goals of the decision-makers external to the firm presumably may differ from the objectives of the firm or objectives which concern decision-makers within the firm. This possibility (as well as the obvious diversity of goals in the sets of outsiders) makes analysis of effects of accounting information on decisions of this class of decision-makers very difficult.

Nevertheless, the classification of decision-makers yields an important hypothesis: *if a decision-maker can affect the accounting system as well as the activities of the firm, and if he conceives accounting information as a goal, accounting information will affect decisions about either or both the accounting system and operations.*

NON-ACCOUNTING INFORMATION

The final hypothesis to be introduced in this model concerns the role played by information which is not a product of the accounting system in determining the impact of accounting information on decisions. Above, accounting information was defined as information of the type that might be contained in a conventional financial report. In many respects, the effects of non-accounting information on decisions can be analyzed in the same framework as accounting information. However, the importance of non-accounting information here is that it may determine the effects of accounting information on decisions.

If non-accounting information becomes a goal or is perceived as having special relevance for decisions undergoing evaluation, the impact of accounting information will be reduced. If non-accounting information is not relevant to decisions, the effects of relevant accounting information will be enhanced. Therefore, we hypothesize: *the impact of accounting information on decisions is affected by the perceived relevance of other information also available to the decision-maker.*

A MODEL FOR ANALYZING THE EFFECTS OF ACCOUNTING INFORMATION ON DECISIONS

The hypotheses developed above are all summarized and their interrelationships are made clear in Figure 1. Rather than restate all hypotheses or describe the model in detail, a summary of hypotheses which lead to the principal outcomes predicted by the model will be used to reveal the interrelationships within it.

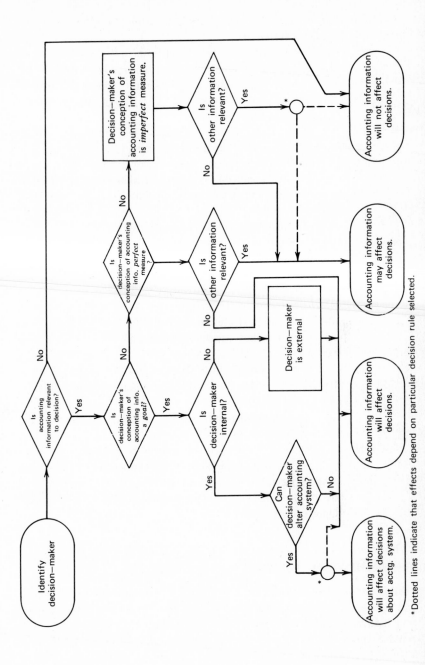

*Dotted lines indicate that effects depend on particular decision rule selected.

FIGURE 1. Accounting information and decisions. Dotted lines indicate that effects depend on particular decision rule selected.

1. *Accounting information will either affect decisions or affect decisions about the accounting system* if

    a.   accounting information is relevant to decisions,

        b.   the decision-maker conceives accounting as a goal, and

            c.   the decision-maker is a member of the firm who can control the selection and operation of the accounting system.

2. *Accounting information will affect decisions* if

    a.   accounting information is relevant to decisions,

        b_1.   the decision-maker conceives accounting as a goal, and

            c_1.   the decision-maker is a member of the firm who cannot control the selection and operation of the accounting system, *or*

            c_2.   the decision-maker is external to the firm,

  or b_2.   the decision-maker conceives accounting as a perfect measure, and

        c.   non-accounting information is not relevant to the decision.

3. *Accounting information may affect decisions* if

    a.   accounting information is relevant to decisions,

        b_1.   the decision-maker conceives accounting as a perfect measure, and

            c.   non-accounting information is relevant to the decision;

        b_2.   the decision-maker conceives accounting as an imperfect measure, but

            c.   non-accounting information is not relevant to the decision.

4. *Accounting information will not affect decisions* if

    a_1.   accounting information is not relevant to decisions; *or*

    a_2.   accounting information is relevant to the decision, but

        b.   the decision-maker conceives accounting information as an imperfect measure,[7] and

            c.   non-accounting information is relevant to the decision.

SOME FURTHER EXPLORATION OF THE MODEL

The flow chart format used in Figure 1 is extremely demanding and, possibly, too restrictive. This format demands that we state precisely what will happen at each branch of the model. Yet there appear to be some situations in which it would be more satisfactory to think in terms of effects along a continuum.

Examine, for example, the lower right-hand portion of Figure 1, where the model predicts the impact of other information when accounting has been perceived as relevant and when the decision-maker perceives accounting information as being either perfect or imperfect. The model predicts that accounting information perceived as perfect may have some effect on decisions. However, when the decision-maker perceives accounting information as being something less than perfect (for example, recognizes that errors or biases may have been introduced into the measurements reported), the impact of other information becomes less certain. The degree of conceived imperfection and the amount and quality of other information are important variables in such cases. Likewise, even in cases where accounting information is perfect, and other information is relevant, the decision might be affected but not altered by accounting information. Similar questions can be raised at other points and simply reinforce conclusions about the need for testing the hypotheses on which this model is based.

While these uncertain conclusions beg for clarification and discriminating research, they are perhaps the least interesting. In cases where decisions may be little affected by accounting information, the choice of a particular accounting system, or particular accounting methods used in that system, may be of little importance. It is at the other extreme, where the model predicts that accounting information will affect decisions that the choice of accounting systems and methods becomes critical.

INTERACTION WITHIN THE MODEL

Further complications in interpreting or using the model stem from possible interaction between the method of accounting used and/or the accounting system developed and the perceived relevance of accounting for decision-making purposes. If the decision-maker feels that a particular method or system of accounting is inappropriate as a basis for measurements relating to a particular problem, he will be led to a position where the effective accounting information will be reduced. Unless we know something about the particular class of decision-makers and their perceptions of accounting methods, it is difficult to predict whether any examination of the conception of accounting held by the decision-maker will be of importance. Likewise, if the method chosen, or the process of selecting a method, affects the conception of accounting held by the decision-maker, then this will affect the relationship between a particular method and decisions.

A DIGRESSION: THE MEANING OF RELEVANCE

The proposal made here to recognize relevance as a primary determinant of the effect of accounting on decision-making is not new. The degree of relevance has frequently been suggested as a basis for choosing between alternative accounting methods and forms of accounting information. This has been particularly true in the literature relating to accounting within the firm, where it is frequently asserted that those methods that result in revelation of cost-volume-profit relationships are most appropriate. Likewise, in the recent *Statement of Basic Accounting Theory,* formulated by a committee of the American Accounting Association, relevance is proposed as a primary standard for selecting among alternative forms of accounting information.[8]

However, the meaning of relevance appropriate for its use as a criterion in the development of accounting methodology and theory is not clear. While users are frequently the point of reference in analyses employing "relevance," the determination of "relevant information" is left to the accountant, who uses some standard, generally accepted model for decision-making as the criterion in determining what should be reported. In the formulation which has been presented above, relevance is determined by the user of the information, and the effect of this choice creates several problems which require careful consideration before this criterion is employed.

If the user determines relevance, we should expect that, in some cases, what the user feels is relevant would not be relevant in those standard, accepted models with which we are familiar, such as those drawn from economics, Suppose the accountant knows the objectives of the firm and those objectives correspond to those in an accepted model of decision-making, but the decision-maker feels the relevant information is different from that called for by the model. The accountant may be placed in a position of second guessing the user, in order to provide the data that will allow him to make a correct decision, because the user's idea of what information is relevant is wrong from the standpoint of the decision models. This is a position in which I believe most accountants would feel somewhat uncomfortable.

We must also be concerned with the possibility that the conception of accounting held by the decision-maker affects the perception of relevance to a significant degree. The more a decision-maker conceives of accounting as being perfect, the more relevant accounting information is likely to be for decision-making purposes, and the more importance can be attached to the part that accounting systems and methods will play in the decision-making process. In so far as this writer is aware, this relationship has seldom been considered, and never carefully explored.

If the hypotheses developed in this paper are valid, then it is clear that relevance alone cannot serve as a primary standard for the development of accounting theory and methods. If accounting is to serve users of accounting information then something besides whether or not the data is relevant must be known. These hypotheses would lead us to believe that critical variables are the conception of accounting held by a decision-maker and the perceived relevance of other kinds of information to the problems under examination at the time the user chooses to employ or not to employ accounting information.

FOOTNOTES

1. This call for attention to the relationships between accounting, decision-makers, and decisions is not new. See for example Carl T. Devine, "Research Methodology and Accounting Theory Formation," *The Accounting Review* (July, 1960), pp. 387–399; Myron J. Gordon. "Scope and Method of Theory and Research in the Measurement of Income and Wealth," *The Accounting Review* (October 1960), pp. 603–618; and the more recent *Statement of Basic Accounting Theory* (American Accounting Association, 1966), especially Chapter 5.

2. Here we approach an interesting point about which more will be said later. Decisions about the accounting methods to be used can alter the *reports* of events which have occurred in the past. It is the effect of these *reports* which is the principal topic of interest here.

3. In many cases assumptions about future events affect reports of past events. Depreciation accounting is a good example of this; an asset may be assumed to have value in future events, and therefore, its cost is not charged only against events which occur in the period of acquisition.

4. Yuji Ijiri, Robert K. Jaedicke, and Kenneth E. Knight, "The Effects of Accounting Alternatives on Management Decisions," *Research in Accounting Measurement* (American Accounting Association, 1966), pp. 186–199.

5. There are, of course, limits to the modifications of the accounting system which can be effected. For example, requirements for consistency prevent selection of different inventory valuation or depreciation methods each year. However, methods used for new acquisitions can be selected, and questions about expense vs. capitalization arise frequently and can be answered uniquely as they arise.

6. An example of this would arise where management wished to report a particular amount for earnings per share.

7. The degree of conceived imperfection is important for this conclusion. If accounting information is conceived as being so imperfect it is of no use it will not affect decisions in this case. If, however, the degree of imperfection conceived is not great enough to preclude the use of accounting information in the decision process, accounting information may or may not affect decisions.

8. *A Statement of Basic Accounting Theory* (American Accounting Association, 1966), especially Chapter 2.

The Accounting Discipline's Role in the Decision Process

INTRODUCTION

Accounting literature implies that accountants feel themselves torn between two opposing professional stances. On the one hand many accountants see the necessity of remaining personally objective so that they can obtain objective, verifiable data to fulfill their "stewardship" role. The stewardship function has been the foundation upon which traditional accounting has rested. The bookkeeper, who is responsible for recording historical transactions, and the independent auditor (CPA), who is responsible for the verification of the historical reports, are natural offsprings of the stewardship function. In a nutshell, the stewardship role of the accountant is to insure that the resources of the firm are adequately protected, classified, cataloged, and ultimately reported to interested parties.

There is a passivity in stewardship reporting which is not present in the other stance the managerial accountant often takes. The articles in the first section were pointed towards the necessity of choosing between alternative courses of action when the consequences resulting from this choice were imperfectly known. Decision making has a dynamic quality; historical record keeping has a stagnant flavor. The stewardship activities report what has happened as a result of the firm's choices, while the decision-assisting activities are directed towards "optimizing" the firm's choices. The accountant's role in decision making is at times unclear. Many accountants, particularly in older articles, have stressed the line/staff dichotomy. By insisting that the accountants fulfill a staff role, they feel they can continue the aloof, objective posture necessary for stewardship reports while simultaneously providing data for decision making.

The traditional accounting model has been predicated upon a transactional approach where historical, arm's-length transactions involving the firm's financial resources are recorded. This model provides definite limitations upon those transactions which are recorded. Examples of transactions which are excluded from the model are numerous; human resources, customer goodwill, unusual product marketability, superior employee or plant productivity, costs of foregone opportunities, and the economic concepts of marginal and incremental costs. If accountants expand their role to transcend the stewardship model, these concepts often fall within the bounds of useful data. Perhaps the crucial question is, "Can accountants properly serve the two functions of stewardship reporting and assisting decision making without becoming dysfunctional in either or both?"

The editors believe that current accounting students must extend their horizons beyond the bookkeeping, stewardship, and audit functions. Historical data, particularly as represented in the traditional balance sheet and income statement, will increasingly become a smaller proportion of accounting services if accounting continues to be a viable, active discipline.

The first section of readings dealt with a relatively puristic approach to decision making. The concern of these authors was oriented towards how to discipline the decision process. Obvious to even the casual reader was the fact that all four authors considered not only the more rational, mechanistic tools used by decision makers but also the more subjective, emotional side of the decision maker. This section begins to elaborate upon the accountant's role in the process of making choices. Certainly accountants are a prime source of data potentially useful for decision makers.

The first article in this section, *Extending the Dimensions of Accounting Measurement* by Churchill and Stedry, suggests some of the new fields of information and data open to accounting. They explore both monetary and nonmonetary measures that accounting must consider if it is to move away from the stewardship function. These authors offer a number of provocative ideas although their discussions do not lead to prescriptive statements. Perhaps the most cogent of their ideas is the differentiation of data needs between planning models and stewardship reporting. Where do the data concerning the myriad of planning variables come from when the accounting system is oriented primarily towards stewardship? Is an historically based transaction model adequate to provide these data? One of the hopes the authors give to these questions is a total on-line, real-time information system where information is stored in retrievable, combinable, and recombinable "bits."

The second article, *An Interpretive Framework for Cost* by Haseman, begins with a traditional definition of cost. Since a principal component of any planning and control model is cost, the ability of the accountant to adequately forecast and measure cost is paramount in making optimizing choices. An analogy might clarify the objective of this article. There is an old story about the group of blind men examining an elephant. One touches the tail and states, "An elephant is much like a cobra." Another touches the leg and says, "You are wrong, the elephant is like a tree." A third man touches the elephant's trunk and exclaims: "You are both wrong! The elephant is similar to a heavy rope." This little story of differential perception fits well into the goals of Professor Haseman. Taking the concept of cost, he views it from many different perspectives. Most of these ideas are probably not novel to the reader, but the classification system offered should facilitate the reader's ability to deal with the multidimensional concepts.

Picture a simple transaction that might occur in a normal business day, i.e., the purchase of a fire insurance policy. Now picture the problems of a coding system that would examine this simple transaction from the many vantage points suggested by Professor Haseman. Even the viewing of this after-the-fact, historical transaction from the many different objects being costed is difficult. Now, let your imagination wander a little and then begin looking at this cost as a single variable in some future decision which includes many variables and you can see the problems of "different costs for different purposes."

The third article in this section deals with an issue that has been relatively active for many years—the direct costing/absorption costing controversy. In many ways this issue is a confrontation of the question, "Should accountants be more concerned with their stewardship function or with their function of assisting managers make optimizing decisions?" The advocates of absorption costing are those accountants primarily concerned with external financial reporting—CPA's, auditors, tax accountants, and SEC accountants. They argue quite simply that inventory and cost of goods sold should include all allocated cost of production if net income and the residual assets are to be meaningful. A diagramatic representation of the absorption costing is:

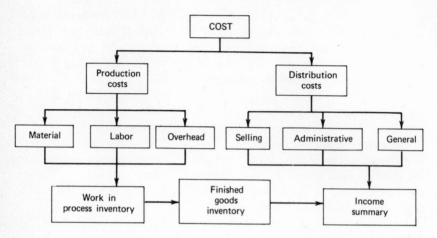

The inflows into work–in–process includes *all* costs of production. The outflow from work in process is represented by "total average cost" to produce a unit of product. Since this average cost to produce a unit includes many allocated costs, particularly in the overhead, the advocates of direct costing feel that it is not useful in managerial decision making. Direct costers believe that a more useful cost flow can be established to assist the managers in making short-run production and distribution decisions. Their suggested cost flow pattern is:

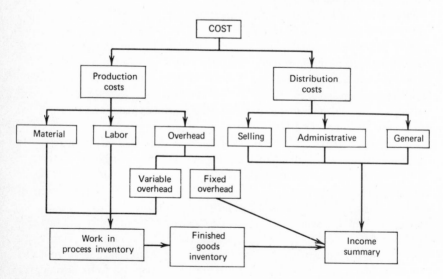

The variable costs of production flow into work–in–process, which provides a "variable cost" to produce a unit of product. In many short-run decisions this unit cost provides a reasonable approximation of the marginal cost.

Mr. Dudick, in *Alternative Costing Methods for Reporting And Pricing Purposes,* contrasts these two costing systems. There are two points in his article which differ from most other articles. First, he states that managers insist upon full costing. This has not been proven empirically! It is rather the impression of the editors that managers use all data at their disposal when making decisions and that if they are introduced adequately to a direct costing system, they prefer it over absorption costing for decisions. It is difficult to reconcile this statement by Mr. Dudick with the fact that the great majority of proponents of direct costing are accountants who are involved in the management accounting function. Second, Mr. Dudick implies that absorption costing methodology allocates fixed costs to the products upon the basis of the *optimum* utilization of the equipment. This would be desirable, but it is not true in the majority of firms that use absorption costs. Rather they allocate costs upon the *actual* utilization of equipment. While at first blush this may appear a moot point, it is not. A cost allocation based on the optimum utilization provides an estimate of the minimum cost incurrence pattern, while the allocation upon actual utilization may not.

In the final article in this section, *Uniform Cost Accounting Standards: Past, Present and Future,* Professor Wright traces the development of the Cost Accounting Standards Board. The author feels that the board may engage in two efforts. The first stems from the fact that the law requires that the board report to Congress within 24 months concerning its progress in promulgating cost standards. The second effort will be that of preparing a statement of basic concepts and cost accounting principles.

It is apparent that regulatory agencies such as the Securities and Exchange Commission, Interstate Commerce Commission, and the Internal Revenue Service would find their tasks considerably easier if there were a standardization of accounting theories, procedures, and techniques. Further, it is logical to assume that groups such as these apply pressure upon industry to become more homogeneous in their accounting process. In the area of cost accounting there is a trend for standardization similar to that found in external financial reporting. A principal motivation for this standardization has been cost accounting problems in governmental contracts.

At the present time the board is in the process of obtaining empirical evidence upon the actual operating situations faced by the firms. It is far too early to tell what the ultimate impact of the Cost Accounting Standards Board might be. However, it is possible to make a few reasoned guesses. First, the board will achieve a degree of standardization in cost accounting in firms that deal with the federal government in cost-plus contracts. This homogeneity may come at the cost of a loss of accounting freedom within the firm. Second, the orientation of the Cost Accounting Standards Board will be to remove uncertainty for the governmental agencies in their procurement decisions.

The orientation will *not* be to remove management's uncertainty about the choices they face. In this sense the cost standards are more likely to be stewardship-oriented than they are to be decision-oriented. Third, if we generalize from the impact that the Internal Revenue Service has had on the accounting profession, it can be hypothesized that the cost standards will affect accounting processes not directly regulated by the Cost Accounting Standards Board. Accounting is not a cost-free activity. To minimize the cost of cost accounting there will be pressure, and subsequently a movement, for firms to adopt the cost standards because it is parsimonious to do so. It is easy to say in a blasé fashion that firms will keep two accounting systems— one for regulatory purposes and one for internal decision-making purposes. However, in practice this can be accomplished only with additional cost. Fourth, it can be postulated that the government will move to total average cost concepts rather than marginal cost concepts. Two cogent questions arising from these thoughts are: "Is accounting an art or a science?" and, "Does the adoption of uniform cost standards create a response set on the part of the user that accounting is a science?"

Extending the Dimensions of Accounting Measurement*

*Neil C. Churchill &
Andrew C. Stedry*

New techniques for management planning and control make possible the use of more and different kinds of data. The requirements for implementing these techniques have characteristics quite different from those associated with traditional methods of business management. Thus it is important to examine some aspects of the impact that management science and the technology of total information have had and may have on accounting and accounting measurement.

Traditionally, accounting measurement has been made in terms of money. When a significant event occurs, the decision as to whether it should be recorded in the accounting records depends primarily on whether it can be expressed in terms of money. Consequently, some matters of a trivial nature are recorded, while significant events that are measurable in terms of some quantity other than dollars (say, the number of skilled workers employed or the number of lost sales) and non-quantifiable events (the development of a new process or the choice of the corporation's next president) are effectively ignored.

SOURCE: Reprinted by permission of *Management Services* (March/April, 1967), pp. 15–22. Copyright 1967 by the American Institute of CPAs.

*This article was developed from a paper presented at a Seminar in Basic Research in Accounting Measurement at Stanford University and published in the collected papers, R. K. Jaedicke, Y. Ijiri, and O. Nielsen (Ed.), *Research in Accounting Measurement,* American Accounting Association, Evanston, Illinois, 1966.

The necessity for expression in a single common denominator has diminished as we have become more sophisticated in dealing with vector and matrix representations in many dimensions. The reduction of all events to a single dimension, with a consequent loss of certain significant information, is a necessary accompaniment of our historic proclivity to deal only with quantities that could be measured on a simple scale. However, this now outdated requirement should not be perpetuated as a desirable characteristic of contemporary accounting measurement. To emphasize the value of eliminating this constraint on accounting measurement, we will examine some common situations which illustrate that accounting expertise could be applied to a greater proportion of significant events were the constraint of collecting data solely in monetary units to be eliminated.

CRITERIA OF RELIABILITY

The traditional concept of accounting measurement is closely associated with the practice of recording historical costs. An event is recorded, where possible, at the amount and price of an actual exchange. Such an exchange usually produces documentary evidence of its occurrence. To the extent possible the price used in recording the transaction is based on "arm's length" bargaining, emanating from the notion of the free market as an objective and impersonal judge of value.

The historical role of accounting is that of stewardship: The owners' assets are to be protected against the unscrupulous or incapable employee or manager. Therefore, the amounts recorded should be subjected to as little manipulation by the manager as possible. The attractiveness of objectivity (in the accounting sense) and verifiability of market-based historical costs is clear.

The stewardship reports provide, although imperfectly, both forecasts and controls. It is generally assumed that if a report reveals poor management or defalcation, it is an indication (i.e., a forecast) that such behavior will be repeated unless preventive action is taken. Also, it is assumed that the disclosure, or threat of disclosure, of such behavior will tend to reduce its incidence of occurrence.

Contemporary financial statements are used to provide indications of future earnings and solvency for outsiders, while internal reports, generally considered a function of managerial accounting, provide data on which to base plans and by which to evaluate and reward managers, thus affecting or controlling the behavior that takes place within the enterprise. The usefulness of the qualities of verifiability and objectivity in certain of these non-stewardship roles will not be overlooked in the process of suggesting possible departures from current accounting theory and practice. On the contrary, we wish to emphasize the benefits of retaining much of the basic framework and methodology of accounting and accountants' activities. We shall attempt to do this through justifying our suggestion that the role of the accountant be extended into newer areas of measurement and, at the same time, that accounting methodology be altered and expanded.

For example, in the absence of truly sophisticated forecasting procedures, simple extrapolation of reliable historical data may yield far better results than more elaborate techniques using subjective estimates of future events. However, the development of more sophisticated forecasting techniques utilizing other than historical data has made the relevant problem, in part, that of obtaining reliability of measurement of non-historical data comparable to that of conventional accounting data.

RELIABILITY NOT ALWAYS VITAL

The point to be made here is not that a high degree of reliability is necessary for all measures or even that complete reliability is beneficial in all circumstances. For example, the value of a conservative forecast produced by a sales department is questionable, even though it proves to be accurate, if a more optimistic forecast would have resulted in higher sales. Rather, the suggestion is that we do not "throw the baby out with the bath water." In most business firms accounting data are frequently the only data available whose collection proceeds regularly without missing observations and, generally, with recurrences of similar events recorded consistently in the same category. We suggest that this expertise be adapted to the information requirements presented by new management techniques—through expansion of the scope of the definition of accounting and its methodology. The alternative would seem to be the development of an entirely new measurement theory and practice divorced from the data collection and verification traditions of accounting and the discipline of the accounting profession.

PLANNING MODELS

Conventional financial statements have been used to estimate future income, sales, cash requirements, etc. To this extent they have played a role in affecting management decision making.[1] These extrapolations have generally been made in accordance with assumptions that no assumed structural changes will take place other than those already indicated by trends in the data. The forecasting model, of itself, is naive, and adjustments to the forecasts are usually made on the basis of information fed in after the computations of the model have been performed. Thus, information beyond that which can be readily extrapolated is injected outside the forecasting model. Such techniques have been found to be useful where the required adjustment is small and, in general, the planning model for which the forecasted data serve as input is similarly naive.

Developments in management science (a field of research not even recognized as such before 1940) have provided increasingly sophisticated planning and coordination techniques. Their input data requirements are not readily satisfied by data currently collected within accounting systems. However, for these techniques to reach their full potential, the periodic updating of their data inputs, similar to the periodic posting of inventory accounts, must be undertaken. The close relationships between posting and updating suggest extending the boundaries of accounting measurement and broadening the application of the expertise developed in the collection and verification of financial data to include the provision of data inputs for planning models. Therefore, we shall examine some of the characteristics of data required by these new techniques.

Although these techniques frequently use a profit cirterion, much of the data required involve quantities that cannot be expressed in dollar terms. Planning models are currently capable of handling thousands of variables and constraints. Consider techniques incorporating linear programing models.[2] Usually the most numerous required inputs are the coefficients of the variable elements in the inequalities that represent capacity limitations, product interdependencies, and the like. In general, they are measured in physical rather than monetary terms. Furthermore, the solutions obtained are most sensitive to inaccuracies in such data. The extension of accounting measurement to the direct determination of these parameters appears critical if accounting is to play a role in the determination of data for planning models. Interestingly, costs are frequently the data whose accuracy is least critical. Furthermore, even these cost measurements are only infrequently required in the form in which costs are normally collected by the accounting system.

Another distinction between current accounting measurement and the production of data required for planning models is the size and type of the units measured. Planning models require parameters such as rates of output (e.g., tons per hour) as opposed to the number of hours a particular individual worked on a particular day. The development of standard cost systems represents progress in recording accounting data in a more global context. However, the recording of the movement of small quantities of material over small distances remains a part of accounting measurement quite distinct from the data required by planning models. Furthermore, the practice of attaching dollar figures to physical changes or movements of a detailed nature frequently militates against the development of data, in the required physical terms, for larger quantities.

'DIAGNOSIS' VS. 'CURE'

Finally, and perhaps most critically, the question of the scope or range of the data required for planning models must be considered. Prior to the development of techniques for analyzing a wide variety of possible modes of behavior, there was little justification for estimating the impact of decisions on other parts of the organization far removed or far into the future. The use of accounting data within the organization was confined largely to control rather than to planning. The results recorded after the fact were compared with previous results, goals, or other evaluation yardsticks. If unfavorable trends were observed, search was made for specific remedies to apply to apparently malfunctioning subsystems. This process, generally referred to as "management by exception," serves to indicate areas where some action is desirable. However, the actual remedies are not found within the accounting system itself, or even as direct consequences of the data collected. The action required must be determined separately, while the system only indicates that "something" should be done. By contrast, the planning models we have been discussing develop the decisions and actions to be taken directly from their data inputs.

Therefore, these data inputs must encompass the entire range of possibilities for decisions available to the model. These models require knowledge not only of how a machine has performed but how it would perform, say, if it were run 50 hours a week rather than 40. The data required must be more sophisticated than simple extrapolations; they must be estimates of behavior (forecasts) under conditions that may be quite different from those previously experienced. These forecasts cannot always be based on objective and verifiable data in the conventional accounting sense—but are another step removed.[3] For some models it is even necessary to go beyond the prediction of these quantities (generally, the determination of expected values in the statistical sense) and estimate a frequency distribution of other possible occurrences about the expected occurrence.

DATA REQUIREMENTS FOR CONTROL

Although the development of planning models has been dominant in management science applications, another area with particular data requirements is the application of mathematical techniques to the problems of organizational control.

We have alluded to the notion of control both in the context of the stewardship function and as it relates to management by exception. More generally, the control problem may be defined as the problem of implementing decisions made in the planning process, including motivation of the people involved in the implementation process. The control aspect of stewardship accounting is the possible prevention, through threat of disclosure, of fraud, waste, etc. This might be viewed as raising the expected penalty for these undesirable activities, thereby lowering the motivation to engage in them. Similarly, the comparisons used in management by exception, by calling to the attention of supervisors discrepancies between goals and performance, may well serve to motivate people to seek to avoid these discrepancies, which necessarily carry implicit, if not explicit, penalties.[4]

In management science investigations attention has been focused on the determination of goal-setting policy so as to maximize performance. It has been shown empirically that goals set at the planned levels of performance more often produce performance that falls short of the planned levels than goals set at more ambitious levels.[5] Work with models of the process of allocating managerial effort among various performance activities indicates that the optimal goal-setting policy is not equivalent to translating plans directly into goals.[6] The precise levels at which goals should be set for optimal performance depend upon the motivation of the individual manager—how he thinks about attaining the goals, the probabilities of rewards for attaining them, and the technological and behavioral factors determining the performance of the unit he supervises.

In a field study of foremen's response to supervisors' goals it was found that the extent to which the foremen found a challenge in the goals seemed to have a marked effect on overall performance.[7]

Such research findings indicate a need for some types of data nor normally collected in organizations. The studies suggest a need for the regular and systematic collection of behavioral data (e.g., on goal perceptions, conflicts between subgoals and overall goals, audit criteria, and behavioral response to audits and budgetary controls) if problems of organization control are to be treated rationally. Relying on our earlier assumption that the regular and systematic collection of data is an area of accounting expertise, the suggestion that accounting measurement concepts be extended to behavioral data follows immediately.[8] The problems involved in this extension are certainly not trivial. But the disturbing thing is that as yet they are not even under investigation in the field where data collection expertise is most apparent—accounting.

On the other hand, the problems of performance measurement for control purposes do not seem as formidable in terms of current accounting measurement conventions.[9] Unlike parameters for planning models, performance evaluators need not be particularly accurate, and the form in which they are expressed— monetary or otherwise—is not generally critical. They need only be effective. For example, suppose a goal is to be set to increase the effort allocated to improving quality. The important consideration would then seem to be the individual's response to a discrepancy between the goal and his previous performance. Such behavioral responses are probably more closely related to the consistency, verifiability, and objectivity of the measure that is to be used to evaluate performance (properties we have attributed previously to current accounting data) than to any economic concept of value or replacement cost. Extensions of this idea that might be suggested (such as the evaluation of morale in a manager's unit through measurement of employee absenteeism and turnover rates), as part of a widening of the definition of the control function, are of a different order from the estimation of parameters for planning models. Such extensions can be viewed in the context of historical data. They do not require the estimation of behavior in situations never experienced. The changes required would be in the extension of the scope of the data, for example, to include behavioral data of a nonmonetary character, rather than in the methodology (i.e., from measurement to estimation).

INFORMATION SYSTEMS

The separation of information systems technology from management science is in part artificial. The application of computer science to management problems might well be classified under management science. On the other hand, the total information systems[10] on the drawing boards and in various stages of implementation include management science planning models as an integral part of the information generation process.

The concept of "total information" is an awesome one. It embodies the notion that all of the relevant data for decision making and control can be stored in an electronic computer and disseminated as needed and in the appropriate form to all those requiring such data. Clearly, even the formulation of such a concept has awaited the availability of computer hardware capable of storing and obtaining reasonably rapid access to amounts of data large enough to represent a significant subset of "total." The process of recording in computers all *accounting* data under current definitions of accounting measurement is both manageable and even, by contrast, a trivial problem. It has been feasible for some years and has been realized on much less sophisticated hardware than is currently available.

RECORDING ONLY ONE STEP

However, the recording of data is only one part of a total information system. The data inputs are merely the raw materials for the information outputs that can be used by members of the organization. A parameter in a thousand-variable planning model—say, the units per hour of product 243 that can be produced on machine A17B—is, of itself, useless. The decisions produced by obtaining the optimal solution to the planning model—produce 1000 units of product 243 on machine A17B on March 10—constitute usable information.

The parameter itself, however, will generally be a figure derived from the compilation and analysis of still less aggregated data.

The process of information generation in such total systems as are currently predicted is intimately related to their existence as "on line-real time" systems. The data collection facilities of such on line-real time systems are designed to be instantly responsive to changes. An order filled from stock results in the immediate reduction of an inventory quantity; a change in the temperature of steel in a blast furnace is instantaneously recorded. The notion of waiting until the end of a day or week to post transactions is not relevant to such systems.

In these systems, and even in others less sophisticated, the data are collected in minute units. Some are retained to be aggregated in various ways. Others are translated immediately (in combination with others) into required action or other forms of information and then discarded. The measurement of actions or events that form the basic entering information will take place at a level of aggregation far below what is envisioned in current accounting measurements. Practically speaking, the transaction as we know it today will no longer be the basic unit of recorded information.

MULTIPURPOSE DATA

Implicit in these remarks is another data characteristic whose impact must be assessed. The basic data entries in an on line-real time or a totally integrated system are multipurpose. A particular input will be subjected to various manipulations and aggregations before it is used for specific purposes. A process flow figure may simultaneously become an input for a product availability computation (marketing), a product improvement analysis (engineering), a production schedule (planning), and the control of a process (production). The information processing system will be able to produce common information for use in all management functions. The existence of separate organizational units for generating different types of information seems unlikely. Rather, the current trend is toward the development of a centrally located unit in which programs convert data of joint value into the requisite special-purpose information—accounting reports, for example.

Thus the major impact of information systems technology on accounting measurement may be the imposition of a requirement for criteria of measurement at the level of minute data "bits." This would include the development of techniques for verification of data at these "micro" levels as well as the redefinition of objectivity criteria in these new terms. Obviously, if accounting is to be involved in the process of aggregating these "micro" units into transactions, the basic elements of accounting data, accountants must develop concepts for these aggregation functions and must acquire the required knowledge and skills associated with information systems.

Another effect will be that the techniques for combining the data into the levels of aggregation which we now consider as the province of accounting measurement will be internal to the machine program. This will require the development of new concepts of audit such as the audit of the machine aggregation programs as well as verification of the disaggregated inputs. The problems involved here are obviously difficult ones. However, if accountants do not consider these problems, it is unlikely that accounting measurement will be relevant to the management information systems, or even to the accounting reports, of the future.

FUTURE TRENDS

In examining the impact that developments in management science and in total information systems are having on accounting measurements, two simultaneous and, at first glance, conflicting trends are observed.

The first is a trend toward planning and control at a more microscopic level. As developments in managerial accounting have shifted the focus of accounting from the firm as a whole to sub-units within the firm, the focus of the information system is now shifting from profit and cost centers to individual machines, production lines, inventory files, etc. The basic data collection point is moving downward in the organizational hierarchy as well as across present functional areas. This trend seems destined to become more pronounced as more and more firms obtain high-capacity, multiple-input equipment. This will not alter the correctness of present accounting cost collection systems—but will simply render them largely irrelevant.

Large-scale planning models will require increased amounts of more refined data. Computers will become more and more capable of handling larger and more detailed models, thus allowing the extension of central planning to smaller, more homogeneous, and less aggregated units and sub-units within the enterprise. The accountant's focus can and should become finer and sharper. He can concern himself more with the classification of the basic primitive transaction and leave the routine processing of data to the computer program, once the program is developed. In addition, relieved from routine processing activities, he can turn his attention to the more important problems of quantification of events now accorded only qualitative description. Thus the accounting department could consist of a small group concerned with the preparation of programs to produce routine reports from the disaggregated data and a much larger group concerned with measurement, systems requirements, and special studies, reports, or projects.

The second trend is toward increased attention to the interrelationships among the enterprise's various units and functions. The development of mathematical models that can take greater numbers of factors into account permits planning in detail; it also facilitates the analysis of interdependencies among large organizational units whose import heretofore could only be surmised. The "total systems approach" has focused attention on the existence of interconnections; computer technology has made the solving of large problems feasible; and, finally, increased knowledge of the firm and its processes has resulted in detailed studies and reports that have a global focus. That is, it is becoming increasingly feasible to determine the effect of a decision made by (or for) a sub-unit on all interrelated activities throughout the enterprise. This means that planning and control studies and techniques will expand to embrace *macroscopic* considerations—considerations of operational strategies for the attainment of the overall objectives of the firm that previously were simply not feasible to implement. Accounting, too, must focus on these broader considerations if it is to remain relevant to the operations of the organization.

CONCLUSION

Changes prompted by these systems do not, of course, diminish the role of management or the need for managers to obtain information. The breaking down of conventional functional units and the increased capability for dealing with interrelationships place a greater demand on the accounting and information systems. These systems must provide managers with the information they need to make correct decisions in a more complex organizational environment. More data are available; more combinations of information are possible; and the time allowance for their acquisition is compressed. Taken in total, the magnitude of these changes is such as to make the problem of information organization and presentation appear almost totally new.

The factors involved in managerial response to the selection, timing, and presentation of a vastly expanded information flow need increased attention. The effect on accounting-based institutions such as audits, budgets, and financial reports needs further study.

We have attempted to point out the relevance of the expertise and traditions of accounting to the reliability of collected information. The areas of application being opened for accountants by the management and behavioral sciences and by information systems technology are far more numerous than those being closed by automation. These new areas offer a challenge and an opportunity. Someone must rise to it. By tradition and by proven record it ought to be the accountants.

FOOTNOTES

1. It should be noted that we distinguish between planning and control. E.g., the principle of "management by exception" involves a management decision to allocate effort (attention) to a particular area. However, this decision is more closely related to the process of control, that is, the implementation of plans.

2. For a thorough treatment, see A. Charnes and W. W. Cooper, *Management Models and Industrial Application of Linear Programing*, vols. I and II, John Wiley & Sons, Inc., New York, 1961. Actually, although this discussion focuses on programing model requirements in order to avoid a proliferation of model descriptions, most of the characteristics of data required by other models are similar to those outlined here.

3. A more elaborate examination of the requirements for such data and a detailed illustration can be found in N. C. Churchill and A. C. Stedry, "Some Developments in Management Science and Information Systems With Respect to Measurement in Accounting," in Jaedicke, Ijiri, and Nielsen, *loc. cit.*, pp. 28–48.

4. The motivational effect of accounting-related activities has been demonstrated in the organization related effects produced in differing degrees by both the anticipation of an audit and by its actual occurrence. See N. C. Churchill and W. W. Cooper, "Effects of Auditing Records: Individual Task Accomplishment and Organizational Objectives," in W. W. Cooper, H. J. Leavitt, and M. W. Shelly (Ed.), *New Perspectives in Organization Research*, John Wiley & Sons, Inc., New York, 1961, pp. 250–275.

5. A. C. Stedry, *Budget Control and Cost Behavior*, Prentice-Hall, Inc., Englewood Cliffs, N.J., 1960.

6. A. Charnes and A. C. Stedry, "Exploratory Models in the Theory of Budget Control," in W. W. Cooper, H. J. Leavitt, and M. W. Shelly (Ed.), *loc. cit.*, pp. 212–249.

7. A. C. Stedry and E. Kay, "The Effect of Goals on Performance: A Field Experiment," *Behavioral Science*, April, 1966.

8. Indeed, one of the peripheral findings of the field study discussed above was that no performance measure, however trivial, could be traced for an individual for any length of time without coming upon missing observations, obvious inconsistencies, etc., *unless the measure was collected through the regular accounting mechanism* in the plant. The researchers found that measures of foremen's performance, considered by their supervisors to be more meaningful indicators than the accounting measures,

could not be used because neither the supervisors who purported to use them for evaluation, nor anyone else, collected them with sufficient regularity for a satisfactory analysis.

9.   The qualification stated previously—that planning activities are considered and possibly provided for separately rather than classified under the control function—is assumed here.

10.   We are indebted to R. A. Gilbert of the Mead Corporation and F. Carr and F. Heath of the Westinghouse Electric Corporation for helping us to gain insights into the current capacities and the potential capabilities of information systems in industry.

An Interpretive Framework for Cost

Wilber C. Haseman

Cost is a complex and illusive term. The word is used in a variety of contexts to convey different shades of meaning. The precise meaning intended usually is left for the reader to deduce, and this commonly leads to faulty communication, and, in some instances to outright confusion. The purpose here is to examine the meaning or meanings of the term, COST, in a comprehensive way, with the objective of providing an interpretive framework to assist in communicating cost information with greater precision and, thus, to assist in utilizing cost information more effectively. Such an interpretive framework should be useful to accountants charged with the responsibility of compiling and communicating cost information, and to the users of cost information whose conclusions and/or decisions depend at least partly upon an interpretation of this information.

THE PROCESS OF COST INCURRENCE AND RECOVERY

Paton and Littleton explained the basic principles of cost incurrence and recovery more than a quarter-century ago, and they are still relevant.[1] Alternative courses of action are evaluated by managers in the light of enterprise objectives, and the problems and opportunities posed by internal and external economic factors. Formulated plans tend to commit the enterprise to cost-generating activities, yet costs are considered to be initially incurred only when goods and services are purchased or otherwise acquired from outside parties. As these purchased goods and services are converted into different types of goods and services through enterprise operations, the originally

---

SOURCE: Reprinted with permission from *The Accounting Review,* Vol. 43, No. 4 (October, 1968), pp. 738–752.

recorded costs are regrouped in various ways to represent the newly generated goods and services, and to measure other important characteristics of the conversions such as operational efficiencies (use of variances), cost responsibilities (segregation into controllable and non-controllable categories for specific management levels), and cost behavior patterns (segregation according to variability with volume, experience—the learning curve, pace of operations—PERT cost, or other causal factors). As newly generated goods and services are consumed (not just converted) through sale, or in providing support for sales or other revenue-earning operations, or by loss (having no future benefit potential)— the costs representing what was consumed are matched (as expenses or losses) in some appropriate mode with the revenue earned to determine whether costs are recovered, and what amount of profit or loss resulted. Costs not consumed are held in suspense, treated as assets having a future benefit potential.

In this process of cost incurrence and recovery, so many different specific applications and adaptations are made of cost information that it is not surprising when people become confused as to the meaning of COST.

SOME POINTS OF CONFUSION

Accounting measurements of cost are used in manifold ways to express different aspects of enterprise operations. These uses for cost measurements frequently require different interpretations of cost, and it is in this regard that confusion may arise. Consider, for a moment, some of the cost concepts now in use and varied related uses for cost information.

Cost Flow

In the process of recording events as they occur within an enterprise, costs are used as the valuation base for goods and services purchased by an enterprise. As purchased goods and services gradually are used to create other goods and services, costs originally belonging to what was purchased are transferred, following the concept of cost flow, so that they now become the valuation base for the newly created goods and services. Eventually these same costs are expensed, matched with revenue in the process of income determination. Thus, for example, costs originally identified as purchased labor, supplies, and plant and equipment may now be identified as parts of the cost of a newly created service, "maintenance," and, also (through overhead applications in one or more steps), as parts of the cost of a newly created product for sale. Eventually, when goods are sold, these same cost elements are identified as expense (cost of goods sold). These cost flows are diagrammed in Figure 1.

Although the concept of cost flow, illustrated here, is familiar to accountants, it is likely to be confusing to others. That a cost originally identified as labor,

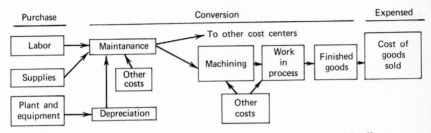

FIGURE 1. The cost flow paradox. The paradox costs originally identified as labor, supplies, plant and equipment, etc., later become identified under different titles.

or supplies, or plant and equipment could later also be a cost identified as "maintenance," "machining," "work in process," "finished goods" and "cost of goods sold" *is* confusing unless one clearly understands the cost flow concept and the resulting differences in cost contexts implied by the various account titles involved.

Cost Classification

The point of confusion growing out of the cost flow concept becomes even more complex when one considers still other ways in which a given group of enterprise costs may be classified and reported. Thus, an enterprise which incurred $100,000 of costs during a period of time for purchased goods and services might regroup these costs in such a way as to identify (1) "What we purchased" (natural classes), (2) "What activities we generated with what we purchased" (functional classes), (3) "What assets, whether still on hand or not, resulted from the activities performed" (product classes), (4) "What part of the period's costs should be treated as expenses and losses and what part as assets" (expense-loss-asset classification), (5) "What costs are the result of different ventures or projects" (project classes), (6) "Which costs are responsive to changes in volume and which are not" (variability classes), and (7) "Which costs are responsive to the decisions and actions of specific managers" (responsibility classes).

The fact that a given group of costs may be subdivided and reported in so many different ways tends to be confusing. The point is, that a particular cost measurement has meaning only when viewed in the context for which it is prepared. If we want to know the costs of the goods and services we purchased, then we organize costs using a natural classification of some type. If we want to know the costs of the activities generated with what we purchased and used, then we organize costs using a functional classification of some type. In a similar way, the other bases for cost classification tend to provide a rationale for organizing costs to fit specific needs.

What Costs To Include?

As cost flow concepts are used in determining the cost of purchased or self-created goods and services, there is always the question, "What costs to include?" When material is purchased, for example, should the inventory be charged for costs of processing the purchase order, transportation-in, receiving, inspection, and material handling to the storeroom? In a very real sense, these costs are part of the investment made in the units by the time they have reached the storeroom. We would have to agree that the material "costs" more because of these operations performed on it before it reaches the storeroom, and that the inventory probably has a higher future earning capacity because of these operations.

In a similar way, when labor costs are incurred should the associated costs of payroll taxes, vacation pay, annual bonuses, insurance and other employee benefits, training programs, employment and personnel offices, and employee facilities be included as part of the cost of labor? Rather obviously, these items do increase the cost of labor; at least, they increase the eventual cost to make labor available to the enterprise.

In regard to overhead costs and their allocation among cost centers and manufactured products, there are numerous questions regarding what should be included. Should top management and general administrative costs be allocated so that a portion of it is included in manufacturing overhead? What about research and product development costs? At what point does the manufacturing process end? Are the costs of delivering the finished product to company-owned warehouses inventoriable product costs? What about the cost of warehousing the finished product? Several alternative reasonable cost flow assumptions could be made, resulting in different amounts of cost for goods and services created by the enterprise.

These and other related questions have been debated by cost accountants for years with no conclusive answers.[2] So, when we ask the question, "What did it cost?" there is room for confusion.

Yet, the question, "What costs to include?" is even more complicated than this. For what stage in the full cycle of events relating to the created product or service is the cost to be computed? Also, do we mean full cost, or incremental cost? Should losses associated with waste and inefficiency be included, or should these be handled separately? All of these points are likely to lead to further confusion when one asks,—"What did it cost?"

Assets, Expenses, and Losses

Costs are used as the valuation for most assets, expenses, and losses. Thus, in referring to a cost, one may be speaking of any of these three categories. Many people find this point confusing, yet it is simply a matter of relating costs to the events which have occurred up to a specified point in time. Because of these events, some costs are treated as expenses or losses, and others are treated as assets. The tendency to think erroneously of all costs as expenses, or of cost connoting something bad or undesirable prevents a clear understanding of the meaning of cost.

In many instances, however, this three-way analysis of costs is not the important thing. In speaking of the cost of a product manufactured for sale, for example, it may not be important to know whether the product actually has been sold (in which case the cost is an expense) or whether the product is still in inventory (in which case the cost is an asset). The important thing may be just to know what the cost of the product *is*: for purposes of judging whether costs are reasonable, whether the cost-sales price-margin on the product line would yield an adequate profit or return on investment, or whether the cost of manufacturing it in one way is better than manufacturing it in another. These uses for cost information do not require identification of the cost with expense, loss, or asset categories. Such identification would be irrelevant and, therefore, unimportant.

Cost Responsibilities

Effective control of costs requires identification of the managers responsible for costs. Thus, the costs traced through cost flow concepts to cost centers, divisions, or other segments commonly are separated into those which are considered to be "controllable" by the manager of that segment and those which are considered to be controllable by others. Some people find it confusing that only a part of the costs traced to a segment are considered to be "controllable."

The point is that almost all costs are controllable to some extent by some manager if given sufficient time to work out new decisions and actions, but only certain costs are controllable by a specific manager within a relatively short time horizon. The authority of each manager only extends over certain enterprise events so that there is only a limited number of ways his decisions and actions can influence enterprise costs. Also, a time interval is needed to work out new decisions and actions so that the shorter the time period, the smaller the degree of controllability. It is important to identify those costs which are responsive in the relatively short run to each manager's decisions and actions, because this becomes one important way of judging managerial performance.

Cost Measurements for Future Events

For the purpose of planning and as a basis for identifying waste and inefficiency, anticipated costs are needed. In most regards the concepts underlying anticipated costs are the same as those previously discussed in relation to historical and current costs. The question simply is: "If done in this way, what will it cost?," rather than "Since it was done in that way, what did it cost?" Yet some uses for anticipated costs involve cost concepts which are different from those for which historical and current costs are used. Among these are the opportunity cost concept, and recognition of the role time plays in the process by which costs are influenced. The concept of opportunity costs furnishes still another point of view regarding the nature of the sacrifice to be embodied in a cost measurement. Opportunity costs are sacrifices evolving from opportunities lost.[3] We might ask, "What is the cost of that unit of equipment, *if it is to be used in company operations*?" If the equipment is to be used in company operations, the opportunity of selling it as used equipment is lost. Therefore, one view of the cost sacrifice involved is the opportunity cost foregone by using it rather than selling it. Its book value (undepreciated part of original cost) might be $10,000 and its market value as used equipment might be $12,000. From a very real point of view, the cost of the equipment is $12,000, if the company decides to continue using it rather than selling it. This is the amount of opportunity foregone.

The concept of opportunity costs can be seen in the prevailing practice of valuing marketable securities and inventory at the lower of cost or market. The market valuations, in these cases, can be viewed as opportunity costs. Beyond that, proponents of direct costing and relevant costing have set forth the "cost avoidance" argument in support of marginal cost inventory valuation methods for external reporting. Their arguments also have tinges of the opportunity cost concept.[4]

Many persons find the opportunity cost concept confusing because it violates their traditional way of thinking that the term, cost, should be confined, somehow, to *historical* costs traced to, and embodied in, the object being costed.

Costs are caused by, and the result of, events occurring within and to the firm. Time is required to set these events in motion. Furthermore, once certain cost-generating events are set in motion it becomes difficult or expensive to change them. Finally, we have already seen that some costs are long-lived, so that their full effect upon enterprise operations may endure for some time. When all of this is coupled with the ideas of risk and uncertainty, it becomes evident that an understanding of the meaning of COST involves an understanding of the relationship between cost, uncertainty, and the passage of time.

The events which generate enterprise costs are, to an important extent the result of enterprise managers' decision-making and control. While managers certainly cannot control all events which might happen to the firm (because many are set in motion by competitors, customers, suppliers, government agencies, etc.), they can and do anticipate these other happenings and react to them. In this sense, therefore, even the impact upon the enterprise of happenings set in motion by others can be, and is, influenced by enterprise managers. Thus, the cost impact upon a steel consumer of a rise in steel prices or of a shortage of steel supply because of a labor dispute in another industry, can be blunted if the managers of the consuming enterprise recognize the developing problem early enough to react to it.

A FUNDAMENTAL DEFINITION FOR COST

The discussion up to this point has probably raised more questions than it has answered. If this is so, its purpose has been achieved. COST *is* a complicated word, it *does* have a confusing way of changing its meaning when applied to different situations. In spite of these complexities, COST should have some fundamental meaning.

In its most fundamental meaning, *the term COST would seem to refer to some type of measured sacrifice evolving from an operational sequence of events and centering upon a particular activity or product.* The ideas contained in this cost definition emerge from the earlier discussion, but are not entirely unique. Evidence supporting them could be cited by referring to the etymological derivation of COST, accepted usages in economics, law, business, and accounting. and authoritative pronouncements of accounting and other professional associations. Rather than attempting at this point to prove the logic of this definition let us tentatively accept it and examine in more detail what it implies regarding the meaning of COST in specific situations.

The definition is worded in very general language, so general, in fact that some might object to it on the basis that it permits manifold interpretations. On the other hand, this is precisely what is needed in the way of a fundamental definition because COST *is*, and *should be*, used, even by a single professional group such as accountants, to mean different things in different situations. The important point is that we have reached a stage in accounting where usage of the term, COST, must be accompanied by an explanation (implied or specified) in order to make the meaning of the term precise. COST has become a generic term, referring to a whole family of specific meanings; in fact, there is strong evidence that it always has been a generic term, but, in technical accounting usage, one meaning (embodied historical cost) has dominated.

How, then, can the meaning of COST be made specific in individual situations? The answer advocated here is by providing an interpretive framework which will guide accountants into specific formulations of cost information to fit each situation, and will guide users of accounting data into the specific meaning intended.

AN INTERPRETIVE FRAMEWORK

An understanding of the meaning of COST in specific situations seems to require an understanding of five inter-related things: (1) the purpose of the cost measurement, (2) the object to which the cost attaches, (3) the operational sequence of events reflected in the cost, (4) the type of sacrifice being measured by the cost and (5) the terms in which the cost sacrifice is measured. Specifications for these five things must be set forth or clearly implied before an accountant can determine how to formulate and communicate cost information; they must also be set forth or clearly implied before the user of cost information can make an accurate interpretation.

The Purpose of the Cost Measurement

Identification of the purpose for which a specific cost measurement is made probably is the key to an understanding of the meaning of COST. The object to which the cost attaches, the operational sequence of events reflected in the cost, and the type of sacrifice involved, all depend upon the purpose for the cost measurement. A Committee of the American Accounting Association has expressed the view that the term, COST, may mean any number of things depending upon the purpose in measuring that cost as well as the ability to measure costs in terms suited to that purpose.[5] The Committee categorized the many specific purposes for cost measurements under three main groups:

1. *Planning*—deciding upon best future courses of action to follow.
2. *Control*—regulating action so that it conforms to plans by effectively communicating to and motivating managers, and by effectively appraising the products, activities, and projects with which they are concerned.
3. *Periodic external reporting*—income determination and asset valuation for the business entity as a whole.[6]

For purposes of planning, costs are *anticipations* of what the future sacrifices will be, evolving from a *proposed* operational sequence of events and centering upon *planned* activities, projects, or products. In most planning situations historical and current cost information also is available for background. Such information, however, is not relevant for deciding future courses of action because it does not reflect the future sequence of events which will determine costs. The basic problem of developing cost anticipations for planning purposes, however, is much the same as that for developing historical and current cost information. Costs are the result of the operational sequence of events which creates the product or activity being costed; it is just a question of which sequence of events—those which have already taken place or those which will take place in the future. Of course there is less certainty regarding anticipated events than for those which have already taken place, but once a cost generating sequence of events has been formulated, the process of translating it into cost information is the same for cost anticipations as for historical costs.

For purposes of control, both anticipated and current cost information are needed to serve different aspects of the overall control process—to regulate action so that it conforms to plans. Managers must know, first of all, what the plan is and what level of performance is expected of them. Thus *anticipated* costs together with other performance data for the plan of action decided upon need to be communicated to individual managers in such a form as to motivate and guide each of them to conform to his part of the plan. Secondly, *current* cost information together with other data are needed to measure performance in regard to products, activities, and projects assigned to individual managers. When current costs are compared to previously anticipated or planned costs, and analyzed in relation to the operational sequence of events which caused the costs, performance may be appraised to determine its quality (to what degree was control achieved?) and the causes and responsibilities for failure to control (what needs to be done to reestablish control?).

For the purpose of periodic external reporting, there is more reason for narrowing the range of meanings of the term, COST. Stockholders, investors, and others for whom such reports are prepared need to make inter-period and inter-company comparisons, for which purpose a high degree of uniformity in cost meaning is desirable. In the context of summarized income determination and asset valuation for a given period of time, costs tend to be a *specific type* of measured sacrifice (historical cost),[7] evolving from a *single, rather formalized view* of the operational sequence of events which create them (full costs including a pro-rata share of joint costs), and centering mainly upon *broad groupings* of activities and products, and, all this, *viewed as important because of the time period involved* (separation of expensed costs and capitalized costs).

This discussion of the relationship between the purpose of the cost measurement and the meaning of cost has been only exploratory. A full appreciation of the relationship can be gained only by establishing the relationships between the purposes of cost measurements and the other four criteria in the interpretive framework for costs. There are a multitude of specific purposes under each of the three main categories discussed above; many of these call for different cost formulations and meanings. Furthermore, there are alternative views which might be taken regarding the best way of categorizing the purposes of cost measurements; for example, the purposes might be stated in a manner cutting across the three purposes previously outlined:

1. To determine the costs of the various activities carried on by an enterprise, composing together the totality of its operations.

2. To determine the costs of goods (including materials, supplies and equipment) purchased, or manufactured and sold, at different stages of the complete process by which they are acquired, processed, sold, billed and collected.
3. To determine the managerial responsibilities for costs.
4. To determine the causes for costs.

Regardless of the view one takes regarding the purposes of cost measurement, the different purposes require different cost formulations and lead to different meanings for the term, COST.

The Object to Which the Cost Attaches

COST always is the cost of *something*. This *something* must be clearly identified before the term, COST, has meaning, in specific situations. The object to which the cost attaches depends upon the purpose of the cost measurement, and, in various situations may be a product, facility, service, activity, or project. It may be acquired from a second party (such as purchased material or equipment; purchased labor, insurance, electricity or other services; purchased maintenance, advertising, research, or other activities); or it may be produced internally (such as manufactured products, self-constructed equipment, self-generated electricity, company-operated maintenance, selling, administrative, or research activities). Furthermore, at any given point in time, the object in question may be an asset (having some future earning potential), or it may be an expense or loss (having no future earning potential).

The relationship between the purpose of the cost measurement and the object to which the cost attaches is difficult to describe in general terms. Yet, the ideas: (1) that there *is* an important relationship between these two, and (2) that an understanding of this relationship is important, for giving meaning to the term, COST,—are rather obvious. Some purposes for cost information require that costs be organized along *product* lines, with specified product categories as the objects to which costs attach. Other purposes require that costs be organized along *functional* lines, or *project* lines with quite different specifications for the objects to which the costs attach.

For example, if the purpose of the cost measurement is planning sales prices, determining the cost of goods sold during a period, or determining a valuation for goods in inventory at the end of a period, then, costs should be organized along product lines and the object to which the costs attach is the specific unit or units of product in question. On the other hand, if the purpose of the cost measurement is planning operating methods, determining the cost of a particular activity carried on during a period, or fixing responsibility for cost inefficiencies, then, costs should be organized along functional lines and the object to which costs attach is the particular activity in question. In some situations, the purpose for the cost measurement is planning or review of a project cutting across functional or product lines; some examples include: the consequences of a promotional campaign, a proposal to replace or expand facilities, or the introduction of a new product line. In these situations, the specific project in question becomes the object to which the costs attach and an attempt is made to isolate the influences that the project has upon enterprise costs and profits.

Thus the object to which costs attach becomes an important basis for *cost classification*, and the *matching* of costs with the objects to which they may properly be attached becomes an important cost accounting procedure. This is not to say that these are the only bases for cost classification and cost matching, because there are several others; but only to place this concept of identifying the object to which costs attach in proper perspective with regard to the more familiar cost ideas of classification and matching.

Operational Sequence of Events Reflected

Costs are the result of what happens in, and to, an enterprise. These happenings or events produce costs. Most cost figures are condensations of the collective result of a rather long sequence of events. In the process of condensation, the details of the sequence of events tend to become merged and hidden from view. Yet, to understand fully the meaning of a cost measurement one must understand what particular sequence of events is reflected in that measurement. To understand the meaning of cost in this manner, is to understand the causes for that cost.

There are two aspects to this idea that an understanding of COST requires an understanding of the operational sequence of events reflected in specific cost measurements. The first point has to do with the stage of completion or state of the object being costed. The other has to do with the operating conditions and methods for reaching this state. To illustrate the first point: the cost of a unit of product partly completed may be $10: by the time that unit is completely manufactured its cost may be $20; after it is warehoused, sold, delivered, and the customer billed its cost may be $30. To say that the product costs $10, or $20, or $30 means nothing unless one understands what product state is reflected in the cost—how far the product cost reaches along the sequence of operating events which, for a salable product, eventually culminates in cost recovery. And then, there are still questions regarding whether joint costs such as those for top management, and research and product development are reflected in the measurement.

Now to illustrate the second point. In the previous example, the $20 figure measured the cost of the product when it had reached the finished goods warehouse. Knowing the stage of completion reflected in the cost measurement gives some meaning to the term, COST. Yet there are still some nagging questions regarding the meaning of that cost figure: "Why was the cost that amount? What particular events took place and how did each event influence costs?" To answer these questions specifically requires reconstruction of the details of the sequence of events reflected in the cost, exploring them so as to reveal the manner by which they influenced cost. Such a specific answer is not needed in most instances. Usually it is sufficient simply to understand what particular methods of purchasing, conversion, selling, etc., the events reflect. In our example, the cost was $20 because of the unique operating conditions and methods which were involved in a particular sequence of events. Presumably a change in these conditions and methods would have resulted in a cost figure higher or lower than $20 for the stage reached by the product.

Types of Sacrifice

Knowing the object being costed and the operational sequence of events to be reflected in a cost is not sufficient to give meaning to COST in specific situations because there are alternative ways in which a cost sacrifice can be viewed and expressed. For example, the cost sacrifice may be expressed in terms of *full cost* for the stage of completion or state of the object, or it may be expressed in terms of *incremental cost.* Furthermore, the sacrifice may be expressed in terms of *embodied costs* which focus upon what was done to the object being costed or it may be measured in terms of *displaced costs*[8] which focus upon what this did to the rest of the enterprise (the opportunity cost concept).

To understand the different ways for expressing a cost sacrifice requires examination of different *concepts of sacrifice,* as well as different *terms of measurement.* At this point, let us concentrate on concepts, and take up the measurement problem later. Admittedly the two aspects are closely related, and in some regards are difficult to separate.

A basic meaning of sacrifice is the giving up of something desirable or valuable. But do all desirable or valuable things given up qualify as a sacrifice in the business and economic cost context? Who must do the giving-up? What sorts of things given up by that person or group qualify? To whom must the thing given up be valuable? The replies to these questions, and others, suggests a number of different concepts of sacrifice which might have relevance to business and economic cost problems. These are outlined below in such a manner as to identify the aspect of sacrifice being interpreted and to show at least two contrasting concepts of interpretation.

1. *Person or group making the sacrifice.*
   a. Social cost concept—sacrifices by society at large.
      Illustration: A piece of equipment manufactured by us has involved society's sacrifice of the natural resources, human talent, and space

and time resources contained in, or displaced by, it. This sacrifice is difficult to measure; among other things, it contains no profit element for processing by our suppliers.

b. Entity cost concept—sacrifices by a specific economic entity within society at large (a corporation, firm or other definable economic entity, including consolidations or sub-divisions thereof).

Illustration: The manufacture of the piece of equipment, referred to in (a) above has involved a sacrifice by our corporation (the economic entity assumed) for the material, labor, and services contained in, or displaced by, it. These sacrifices are measurable in various contexts referred to in (2), (3), (4), (5), and (6) below.

c. Personal cost concept—individual sacrifices by the persons composing the economic unit, including owners, managers, and workers.

Illustration: The manufacture of the piece of equipment has involved personal sacrifices by owners (for capital consumption and use) by managers and workers (for human effort and time including the sacrifices associated with development of skills and experience, and with risks of injury and loss).

Most business and economic applications involve the entity cost concept.

2. *Discernibility of the things sacrificed.*

a. Physical cost concept—sacrifices of or pertaining to natural or material things, largely discernible and subject to measurement.

Illustration: In the manufacture of the equipment, material, labor, and services (physically discernible things) were sacrificed.

b. Psychic cost concept—sacrifices of a mental, emotional, or spiritual character, lying outside the realm of known physical processes, hardly discernible except by the person making the sacrifice and not subject to measurement.

Illustration: In the manufacture of the equipment, the persons involved in the operational sequence of events underwent pain, inconvenience, emotional stress, body fatigue and anxiety. On the other side, they may also have experienced satisfaction, elation, emotional uplift, and pleasure reducing the net psychic cost.

Most business and economic applications involve the physical cost concept.

3. *Embodiment in the object being costed.*

a. Embodied cost—sacrifices measured in terms of their origins, reflecting what was originally given up to acquire and convert the object being costed.

Illustration: In the manufacture of the equipment, the cost sacrifice is measured by the original cost embodied in the material, labor, and services consumed to produce the object in question.

b. Displaced cost—sacrifices measured in terms of their ultimate effects upon the group making the sacrifice, reflecting the opportunity lost by, or the adverse consequence resulting from, the sacrifice in question.

Illustration: In the manufacture of the equipment, the cost sacrifice is measured by values displaced when the material, labor, and services were consumed in this particular way:

(i) the loss of revenue from failure to sell the material, labor, or services singly or as they might have been embodied in an alternative saleable product, or

(ii) the future cost necessary as a going concern to replace the items in question.

Some business and economic applications involve the displaced cost concept while many others involve the embodied cost concept.

4. *The joint sacrifice problem.* Is a lump sacrifice for a group of objects also a sacrifice for each object viewed individually?

a. Full cost—the aggregate sacrifice, including a fair share of fixed and otherwise joint sacrifices as well as the incremental sacrifice identifiable with the object being costed.

Illustration: In the manufacture of the equipment, certain facilities made available for the processing of various other cost objects were used (e.g., fixed assets, facilities for purchasing, storage, labor relations, machining, assembly). These facilities, in turn, probably share benefits provided, at some cost sacrifice, by still higher order facilities (e.g., top management costs). Full costs result when material, labor, and services are charged to the equipment in such a manner as to include an allocated share of these "joint costs."

b. Incremental cost—the increase in total sacrifice identifiable with the specific object, or group of objects, being costed, recognizing that fixed and otherwise joint sacrifices may be increased little, if at all, because of what was done to or for the specific object being costed.

Illustration: In the manufacture of the equipment, what was done to or for the equipment has caused an increased level of activity and, perhaps, also, an increased character of activity in the various facilities which compose the economic entity. These changes increased entity costs. Incremental costs result when material, labor, and services are charged to the equipment in such a manner as to reflect only this increase in aggregate entity costs.

In some business and economic applications the full cost concept is used while in others, the incremental cost concept is used.

5. *Controllability by entity managers,* reflecting the combined effect of two aspects of a sacrifice: (1) the extent to which a sacrifice is subject to influence by the decisions and actions of entity managers, and (2) the time allowed for these influences to have their effect.
    a. Manageable uncommitted costs—sacrifices influenced to an important degree by managers' decisions and actions with plenty of time for these influences to have their effect.
    b. Manageable committed costs—sacrifices influenced to an important degree by managers' decisions and actions but these influences have already had most of their effect, setting in motion the chain of events which largely determines the sacrifice in question.
    c. Unmanageable uncommitted costs—sacrifices largely influenced by factors or forces outside managers' control with plenty of time for these influences to have their effect.
    d. Unmanageable committed costs—sacrifices largely influenced by factors or forces outside managers' control and already set in motion to such an extent that influences have had most of their effect.
    Illustration: The controllability aspect of a cost sacrifice becomes important when attention is being directed to cost responsibilities. *As a manager looks ahead,* only the manageable uncommitted costs are responsive to his new decisions and actions and, thus, are costs he can reasonably be held responsible for. The manageable committed costs are already influenced and set in motion for a predestined outcome by his previous decisions and actions. The unmanageable costs, committed and uncommitted, are not subject to his influence. *As a manager looks back* over his accomplishments somewhat the same interpretation of manageable and unmanageable sacrifices is relevant. However, the length of the time period will influence what should be considered as manageable uncommitted costs.

6. *The present value problem*—extent to which the sacrifice reflects a present value, recognizing at least two influences; (1) price level changes and (2) the time value of any desirable thing.
    a. Historical, previous value cost—sacrifices expressed in terms reflecting an older, outdated valuation scale.
    b. Historical, present value cost—sacrifices originating from an older valuation scale but adjusted (if necessary) to reflect present values.
    c. Futuristic, contemporary cost—anticipated sacrifices expressed in the contemporary valuation scale without adjustments for anticipated price level changes or the time value of any desirable thing.
    d. Futuristic, present value cost—anticipated sacrifices adjusted (if necessary) to reflect present value.

Illustration: A $10,000 figure for the cost of the item of equipment has very little meaning until it is related to a time scale. Is the $10,000 a valuation for a sacrifice made some time ago? If so, the things sacrificed are probably now worth more than $10,000 partly because of inflationary price-level changes, and partly because of the time value of money (the things sacrificed would have been earning a return had they not been sacrificed).

The preceding outline of different concepts of sacrifice probably needs to be refined, because it does contain some conflicting interpretations. For example, how can a displaced cost also lend itself to an incremental cost interpretation? Despite such inconsistencies as this, the outline may prove of value in diagnosing the type of cost sacrifice needed for specific situations. The outline suggests that the type of sacrifice reflected in a cost measurement may be any one of a very large combination of possible variations. The outline considers six aspects of a sacrifice and there are two or more variations regarding each aspect. This creates 384 possible combinations (3 X 2 X 2 X 2 X 4 X 4). While it is probably true that a very small number of the 384 possible combinations account for the vast majority of specific cost measurements, there are at least some isolated cases of cost measurements where most of the other types of sacrifice would be appropriate. Furthermore, when the 384 possible combinations of different sacrifice concepts are considered together with the number of alternatives for objects to which a cost may attach, operational sequences of events which may be reflected, and different terms of measurement, then the number of combinations of meanings which may be attributed to a cost measurement becomes truly astronomical.

Terms of Measurement

Having identified the cost object, its operational sequence of events, and the type of sacrifice which are appropriate to a specific purpose or need for cost information, there is still the problem of how to quantify that cost. In essence, this problem is solved by translating the three conceptual things already identified for that cost into an appropriate measure. Since COST is a *measured* sacrifice, it must be quantified and cannot, in specific cases, be left just as a set of concepts or ideas.

Cost measurement involves decisions regarding the measuring unit, the recognition procedure, and the necessary degrees of objectivity, verifiability, relevance, and precision of the resulting measure. These decisions regarding the terms of measurement logically should be based upon what has already been identified regarding the object to which the cost attaches, the operational sequence of events to be reflected in the cost, and the type of sacrifice to be expressed.

The scope of this article does not allow for a full exposition on this final stage in the interpretive framework for cost; nor was that the purpose of the article. However, a few points relating to terms of measurement will be made. We should note that the measuring unit for cost is not necessarily restricted to money. If the purpose of the cost measurement is the operating foremen's control of labor costs, for example, it may be more appropriate to express the variation between actual labor costs and budgeted or standard labor costs in terms of labor hours. The foremen probably can be held responsible for the labor hours used to produce what was produced, but they probably cannot be held responsible for the hourly labor rates. In a similar way other non-monetary, physical measuring units for cost such as pounds of material, number of salesmen's calls, or number of invoices processed may be more appropriate reflections of the cost sacrifice intended, than money terms. Selected ratios computed from monetary or non-monetary units also may appropriately reflect certain cost sacrifices. Nevertheless, money would be the appropriate measuring unit for many cost sacrifices largely because it is a common denominator versatile enough to allow merging of practically all types of cost flows.

The recognition procedure establishes a technique or method to quantify the appropriate operational sequence of events and modes of cost sacrifice for specific cost measurements. Whether monetary or non-monetary units of measure are to be used, there is still the problem of establishing a measurement procedure to convert the concepts or ideas regarding the appropriate cost sacrifice into *numbers* which recognize what we are trying to measure. The recognition procedure may be some part of the traditional double entry bookkeeping procedure for recording historical costs; in other instances it may be the procedures of job or process costing, cost departmentalization, responsibility accounting, or direct costing; but in many other instances mathematical or statistical procedures outside those of double entry, historical cost keeping will be needed to provide an appropriate measure.

Decisions regarding the necessary degrees of objectivity, verifiability, relevance, and precision in a cost measurement are based upon the purpose of that measurement and the type of sacrifice this involves. These decisions are stated here as a part of the terms-of-measurement problem (rather than earlier in the framework) simply because this is the point where the accountant must come to grips with them. In choosing a recognition procedure to quantify what we are trying to measure, consideration must be given to certain technical characteristics of the measure (objectivity and verifiability), as well as to its ability to express the object being costed, the appropriate operational sequence of events, and the proper type of cost sacrifice (relevance and precision). We should note that objectivity and verifiability may compete with relevance and precision in such a way that a high degree of the former may require a

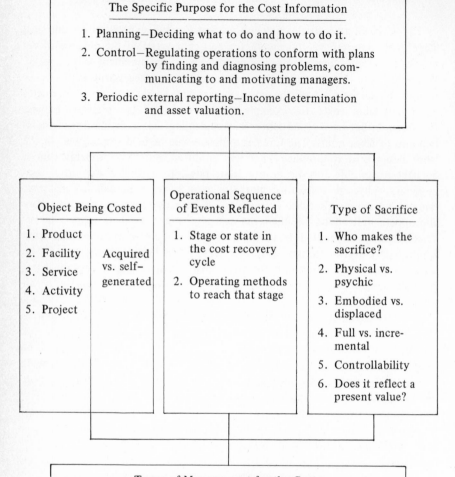

The Specific Purpose for the Cost Information

1. Planning—Deciding what to do and how to do it.
2. Control—Regulating operations to conform with plans by finding and diagnosing problems, communicating to and motivating managers.
3. Periodic external reporting—Income determination and asset valuation.

Object Being Costed

1. Product
2. Facility
3. Service
4. Activity
5. Project

Acquired vs. self-generated

Operational Sequence of Events Reflected

1. Stage or state in the cost recovery cycle
2. Operating methods to reach that stage

Type of Sacrifice

1. Who makes the sacrifice?
2. Physical vs. psychic
3. Embodied vs. displaced
4. Full vs. incremental
5. Controllability
6. Does it reflect a present value?

Terms of Measurement for the Cost

1. Measuring unit—monetary vs. nonmonetary
2. Recognition procedure—what costing technique?
3. What degrees of objectivity, verifiability, relevance, and precision?

Figure 2.   A framework for interpreting the meaning of cost in specific situations.

lower degree of the latter. Thus the recognition procedure may have to be a compromise insofar as the desired objectivity, verifiability, relevance and precision of a cost measurement is concerned.

CONCLUSIONS

COST *is* a complex and illusive word. It has a confusing way of changing meaning from one business situation to another. Because of this, the meaning of COST in specific situations may frequently be misunderstood. What is needed is an interpretive framework to guide both accountants (who make the cost measurements), and statement readers (who attempt to understand the cost measurement and apply it to business problems). Such an interpretive framework has been described and is summarized in Figure 2.

Determination of the meaning of cost in specific situations requires, first of all, a clear understanding of the purpose of the cost measurement. From this can be deduced three things: (1) the appropriate object to which the cost attaches, (2) the appropriate operational sequence of events to be reflected in the cost, and (3) the appropriate type of sacrifice involved. Finally, from these three, an appropriate set of terms for measuring the cost can be determined.

FOOTNOTES

1.   W. A. Paton and A. C. Littleton, *An Introduction to Corporate Accounting Standards* (American Accounting Association, 1940).

2.   Company practices have been reported in various NAA *Research Reports.* See "Costs Included in Inventory," (August 1947); "Accounting for Labor and Labor Related Costs," (November 1957).

3.   For an excellent discussion of the accountant's view of opportunity costs see Charles T. Horngren, *Cost Accounting, A Managerial Emphasis,* 2nd edition (Prentice-Hall, Inc., 1967), p. 424.

4.   Charles T. Horngren and George H. Sorter, "Direct Costing for External Reporting," *The Accounting Review* (January 1961), pp. 84–93, and "Asset Recognition and Economic Attributes—The Relevant Costing Approach," *The Accounting Review* (July 1962), pp. 391–399.

5.   Committee of Cost Concepts and Standards, American Accounting Association, "Tentative Statement of Cost Concepts Underlying Reports for Management Purposes," *The Accounting Review* (April 1956), p. 183.

6.   *Ibid.,* pp. 184–193.

7.   In the framework developed in a later section of this article, the specific type of sacrifice would be called entity-physical-embodied-full-manageable and unmanageable committed-historical previous value cost.

8.   The cost terms, *embodied* and *displaced,* were introduced, with somewhat different meanings by Ralph C. Jones, "Some Aspects of Cost," *1941 Proceedings of the 54th Annual Meeting, American Institute of CPA's.*

Alternative Costing Methods for Reporting and Pricing Purposes

Thomas S. Dudick

A great deal has been written in the past two decades on the virtues of direct costing versus absorption costing versus distribution. Like our two-party system of government, members of the accounting profession have developed their "pro" and "con" points of view. Either they enthusiastically endorse the one costing concept or they condemn it. This article will explore a number of considerations and will try to evaluate the arguments advanced. Since direct absorption costing proponents raise the loudest arguments we shall start there.

HISTORY OF DIRECT COSTING AND ABSORPTION COSTING

The deluge of literature on direct costing in recent years fosters the general belief that direct costing is a new concept. Actually, it is not new—it predates absorption costing.

This is logical because high fixed costs, as we know them today, did not exist in the early years of this century. In fact, in the early 1900's profits were calculated before any provision was made for amortizing equipment costs. As soon as the amount of profit became known, a decision was made as to how much depreciation would be deducted from the current year's profits.

SOURCE: Reprinted by permission of *The Journal of Accountancy* (October, 1967), pp. 49–54. Copyright 1969 by the American Institute of Certified Public Accountants, Inc.

As mechanization increased, the investment in equipment grew larger and larger. The use of judgment in determining the amount of depreciation to be taken into expense was considered to be too haphazard—the need for a more scientific approach became obvious. The method adopted was to ascertain the useful life of the asset; determine the annual depreciation provision; and then include the annual cost in an overhead (burden) rate based on an indicator of activity such as direct labor. When the level of activity for the period became known, the overhead rate would be extended by the direct labor volume and this became the cost transfer into inventory. This is how absorption costing was born.

The controversy between advocates of direct costing and absorption costing involves two areas: management reporting and product pricing.

MANAGEMENT REPORTING

In this area, the supporters of direct costing are principally interested in the simplicity of reporting afforded by the direct costing concept.

In a direct costing format, the direct or variable costs are segregated from the fixed or period costs. A profit contribution calculation is made after direct costs are deducted from sales. This profit or marginal contribution can be conveniently compared with the period costs to show the impact of volume of sales. The amount of profit must be great enough to cover all fixed or period costs to achieve a breakeven situation.

Early writers and speakers on the subject of direct costing challenged the absorption costing practice of allocating period-type costs to the various product lines. They argued that since committed costs were there anyway, nothing was to be gained by spreading these costs to products when determining profitability. Their recommendation for an operating statement format by product line is shown in Exhibit 1.

Total sales and direct (variable) costs are broken down by products. The total variable cost as a percentage of sales indicates that Product B is the most profitable because a greater percentage of the sales dollar is left to cover fixed costs than is left for Products A and C. Product C is the least profitable because the percentage left to cover fixed costs is the smallest of the three.

Critics of direct costing were quick to contest the validity of this method for determining product profitability. They asserted that the investment required to produce various products differed; therefore profitability could not be determined without recognizing these differences. A car rental agency could be used to illustrate this point. Assume that various makes in the low-priced compact, the medium and the luxury sizes are rented. Gauging profitability on an overall basis without considering the differences in depreciation in the

EXHIBIT 1.   Product-Line Operating Statement

	Total	Product A	Product B	Product C
Sales	$1,000,000	$100,000	$410,000	$490,000
Variable costs				
Material	170,000	20,000	60,000	90,000
Direct labor	118,000	8,000	40,000	70,000
Overhead	142,000	12,000	55,000	75,000
Commissions	60,000	6,000	24,000	30,000
Total Variable Cost	490,000	46,000	179,000	265,000
Variable cost % of sales	49%	46%	44%	54%
Fixed costs				
Overhead	300,000			
Administration	25,000			
Selling	112,000			
Total Fixed Cost	437,000			
Profit Before Taxes	73,000			

Cadillac, Ford and Volkswagen would be quite misleading. The more recent writers and speakers on direct costing have been recognizing the need to consider fixed costs in determining product profitability.

The argument raised by the direct costers against absorption costing is that when volume is higher than normal a greater amount of fixed cost is absorbed into production and therefore transferred to inventory. The difference between the amount absorbed and the amount which, under direct costing would be considered a period cost, is reflected as a favorable volume variance. Conversely, if the volume of production is lower than normal, a lesser amount of fixed cost would be absorbed into inventory. The difference between this amount and that which would have been reflected as a period expense becomes an unfavorable volume variance. Direct costers argue that many nonaccounting managers are confused by accounting statements that reflect volume variances.

Also, because of the difference in method of treating fixed costs, profits under absorption costing procedures fluctuate with changes in production—profits are greater when production increases and vice versa. Under direct costing; profits fluctuate with sales, rather than with production.

Whether one sides with the direct or absorption costers depends on one's point of view as to what costs should be charged into inventory. Consider the case of a company that automates a hand assembly operation which requires ten man-hours per unit. At $2 per hour, this results in a direct labor cost of $20 per unit. If the machine costs $100,000, has a life of ten years, and will produce 1,000 units per year, the cost per unit is $10. In this example, depreciation expense has been substituted for direct labor cost. It is rather difficult to build a logical case for inventorying the entire cost of the hand assembly operation, but not inventorying the depreciation which amounts to 50 per cent of the original direct labor cost. This would be the case under pure direct costing theory.

Direct costing advocates recognize the pressure from two major sources to provide full costs. These are:

1. The Internal Revenue Service and the Securities and Exchange Commission, both of whom require that inventories be valued at full manufacturing cost.
2. Company managers who, pressured by the forces of competition and the relentless demand for higher wages try to reduce overall costs through the introduction of labor-saving equipment. The operating manager will insist on being given information that will disclose full product costs so he can ascertain whether the investment in automation is paying off.

Proponents of direct costing, recognizing that these requests must be fulfilled, have proposed that such costs as depreciation and the related support services be assigned to the products to which these costs are related without going through the absorption costing process.

This recommended procedure, while suitable for a simple operation where only a few items are involved, is inadequate for the more complex situations. The reason is that such period costs as depreciation and the related services must be identified by the cost center or manufacturing process before they can be identified by product. Since the products of most manufacturers are a mixture of parts and subassemblies that flow through a number of processes, each represented by different cost centers, overhead can be assigned on an equitable basis only through the absorption process. Then, as the various parts and subassemblies, many of which are common to a number of products, are put together to form a finished product, each product will be assigned its full share of overhead cost—both fixed and variable.

Take for example the following hypothetical illustration of two radios. Radio A has manual tuning but Radio B utilizes push buttons. As a result, Radio B requires a greater amount of metal stamping and plastic molding of the parts making up the push button assemblies. This means more plating, painting and hot stamping at overhead rates that are relatively high because of the greater use of higher cost equipment in these operations. The computation of overhead costs by process for the two products is demonstrated in Exhibit 2.

Note that the overhead cost per hour for Radio A is $4.91 while the same cost for Radio B is $5.21. This cost difference must be recognized in the

EXHIBIT 2

| | Overhead cost per hour | Overhead cost per 100 radios | | | |
| | | Radio A | | Radio B | |
		Hours	Overhead cost	Hours	Overhead cost
Metal stamping	$10.00	15	$150.00	20	$200.00
Plating	7.50	5	37.50	7	52.50
Painting	6.75	2	13.50	3	20.25
Plastic molding	8.50	10	85.00	12	102.00
Hot stamping	3.50	2	7.00	3	10.50
Assembly	3.00	66	198.00	68	204.00
		100	$491.00	113	$589.25
Overhead cost per hour			$ 4.91		$ 5.21

selling prices of the two radios. The most accurate method for determining this difference is the recognition of cost center overhead rates. This is the essence of absorption costing.

Absorption costers would seem to have the weight of government authorities and company managers on their side.

However, absorption costing supporters who blindly reject a report format merely because they disagree with direct costing theory are depriving their managements of a useful analytical tool that is not readily available in the conventional absorption costing format.

PRODUCT PRICING

The supporters of direct costing with respect to product pricing stress the importance of marginal pricing—where direct costs are compared with selling prices of various products to determine the amount of the selling price left (after direct costs) to cover fixed costs and profits. This information is frequently used to "shave" prices by willingness to accept less than full recovery of fixed costs.

The basic assumption is that by reducing prices, volume will increase. Although the profit per unit will be smaller, the increased volume will result in a greater total profit. In a check of 14 companies it was found that almost half stated they used the marginal contribution concept for pricing.

Marginal pricing advocates meet strong resistance from absorption costing proponents who remind them that price reductions are only temporary because competitors will react quickly to meet the reduced price—with the result that prices have been reduced but the anticipated increase in volume will not materialize. Another disadvantage frequently cited is that the marginal approach to pricing, if not carefully controlled, could result in a "houseful" of unprofitable business.

As companies automate certain products and reduce the direct costs, it is conceivable that marginal contribution approaches to pricing could, in addition to these reductions, result in selling prices that further reduce the recovery of fixed costs that permitted the reduction of direct costs in the first place.

The supporters of absorption costing suggest that a more logical method of competitive pricing is to:

1. Spread fixed costs on the basis of optimum utilization of equipment. If purchase of a machine was justified on the basis of operating two full shifts, then spread the fixed costs over the volume generated by a full two-shift operation. The selling price will then provide for a recovery of investment on a competitive but equitable basis, thereby eliminating guesswork.
2. Base direct labor and material costs included in the selling price on an efficient operation exclusive of excessive rework, scrap and downtime.

Use of this approach in developing cost-selling price comparisons results in consistency among the various products in the line and these same costs can be used as standards to measure performance.

SELLING-MARKETING-DISTRIBUTION EXPENSES AND PRODUCT PROFITABILITY

Differences of opinion between direct costing and absorption costing proponents are usually confined to the area of manufacturing cost. Both sides generally agree on classification of these expenses—that such items as commissions, freight and cooperative advertising are variable but salesman costs, warehousing and institutional advertising are properly treated as period costs. Both groups normally calculate product-line profitability by allocating these expenses, both variable and fixed, on the basis of the sales of the various products.

"Absolutely wrong!" say the distribution cost accountants, who in many companies hold positions as controllers. They support their contention with examples similar to the following:

Company A sells its products to several sister divisions as well as to distributors and to other companies. The sales department effort required to sell to sister divisions and to distributors is minimal as compared with the direct contact required in selling to other companies. The major effort in selling to a company's own divisions is in the order entry and billing activity. The same is true when selling to distributors because orders are larger and more routine in nature. But in the sales effort required in selling other companies, the average sale is much smaller; personal contact and extensive travel on the part of the salesman is required.

Under these circumstances, the distribution cost accountant correctly asks, "How can you allocate the cost of sales on a pure dollar volume basis?"

One will find, in analyzing direct sales, that many companies have a small number of large house accounts. Such accounts are based on the personal contact of one of the executives of the company—rather than a member of the sales staff. Orders from such accounts are often automatic and do not require salesman servicing. Here again, the sales department cost cannot arbitrarily be assigned on the dollar volume basis, otherwise management would be misled on the profitability of various classes of sales.

Warehousing expenses, likewise, influence product profitability, depending upon the method of assignment of this cost to class of sale. The shelf item type of product generally requires substantial warehousing throughout the country or territory. The customized version of the same product, which is made to order, requires no warehousing. To assign this cost on the basis of sales volume could misstate profitability.

The same principal applies to institutional advertising—the company does not need to advertise in order to sell to one of its divisions. Bad debt expense, likewise, is neither incurred by a sister division nor by the large, triple A credit rated house account.

The operating statement shown in Exhibit 3 demonstrates how the profitability by class of sales can vary. Note that the total profit amounts to 4.9 per cent of sales of $15,377,000. But when these sales are broken down by sales to other divisions, sales to distributors and sales made by the company's own sales force through direct selling, the profit varies from 14 per cent for interdivision sales to breakeven for direct selling. Interdivision sales are more profitable than the other classes because no advertising expenses are required for this type of selling. At the same time, sales department expenses are minimal. Direct selling, on the other hand, requires a high degree of sales effort as well as advertising.

Even the direct sales can be broken down by classes with varying degrees of profitability. Exhibit 4 demonstrates how the total direct selling is broken down by three categories: one large customer (house account), special custom line, and all others.

Although the total direct sales category shows breakeven results, the large house account shows a 4.9 per cent profit on sales. This class of sale requires less sales effort because of a standing relationship with one of the nonsales executives. Orders are forwarded regularly on a release basis with no need for salesmen to call on a regular basis. Of the remaining two classes, the special

EXHIBIT 3. Operating Statement by Major Class of Sale

	Total	Inter-division	Distrib-utors	Direct Selling
Gross sales	$15,377,000	$5,126,000	$5,126,000	$5,125,000
Less: Discounts and allowances	676,000	163,000	513,000	–
Royalties	176,000	59,000	59,000	58,000
Net sales	$14,525,000	$4,904,000	$4,554,000	$5,067,000
Cost of sales	11,610,000	3,870,000	3,870,000	3,870,000
Gross operating profit	2,915,000	1,034,000	684,000	1,197,000
Selling expenses	676,000	101,400	101,400	473,200
Product service expenses	220,000	110,000	–	110,000
Warehouse expenses	144,000	24,000	24,000	96,000
Advertising	801,000	–	400,500	400,500
Bad debts	74,000	–	37,000	37,000
Eng'g and product design	242,000	81,000	81,000	80,000
Total expense	$ 2,157,000	$ 316,400	$ 643,900	$1,196,700
Pretax profit	758,000	717,600	40,100	300
% Profit on sales	4.9%	14.0%	.8%	

EXHIBIT 4. Breakdown of Direct Selling

	Total direct selling	One large customer (house account)	Special custom line	All others
Gross sales	$5,125,000	$1,708,300	$1,708,300	$1,708,400
Less: Discounts and allowances	–	–	–	–
Royalties	58,000	19,300	19,300	19,400
Net sales	5,067,000	1,689,000	1,689,000	1,689,000
Cost of sales	3,870,000	1,290,000	1,290,000	1,290,000
Gross operating profit	1,197,000	399,000	399,000	399,000
Selling expenses	473,200	71,000	201,100	201,100
Product service expenses	110,000	36,700	36,700	36,600
Warehouse expenses	96,000	48,000	–	48,000
Advertising	400,500	133,500	133,500	133,500
Bad debts	37,000	–	18,500	18,500
Eng'g and product design	80,000	26,700	26,700	26,600
Total expense	$1,196,700	$ 315,900	$ 416,500	$ 464,300
Pretax profit	300	83,100	(17,500)	(65,300)
% Profit on sales	–	4.9%	(1.0%)	(3.8%)

custom line is less unprofitable because warehousing costs are generally unnecessary for custom products.

(Although the per cent of profit on sales has been compared for the various classes of sales for illustrative purposes, it would be well to bear in mind that the per cent of return on investment would be a more appropriate measure of profitability.)

It is unfortunate that professionals in the cost accounting field are so fragmented in their areas of interest that it is necessary to clear away the clouds of controversy among three different groups to find meaningful answers to a relatively simple problem.

SUMMING UP

Direct costing provides information to management that is invaluable for profit planning and control. It includes such techniques as breakeven analysis, profit planning, profit-volume relationships and determination of relative profitability of products in the line.

While some direct costing advocates would consider marginal pricing an important tool for management, the absorption costing proponents make a good point when they emphasize that a more logical method for costing products would be to base costs on optimum utilization of equipment, direct labor and material. The same cost used for product costing and competitive pricing would provide management with a measuring stick to evaluate performance against these standards.

The proponents of both direct costing and absorption costing are guilty of concentrating their attention on manufacturing product costs without recognizing other major cost areas that can have a marked effect on profitability of various classes of sales, for example, if not properly assigned.

Although direct costing is based on the concept that fixed costs will be charged off as period costs, IRS and SEC requirements for full costing of inventories necessitates a change in approach in this respect. The modification proposed by the direct costers, although probably acceptable to the government agencies, would not equitably assign fixed costs to the various products (where there are significant disparities in amount of investment) without pursuing the absorption costing process through use of cost center overhead rates.

The executives responsible for operating their businesses on a profitable basis in a highly competitive environment are confused by the diversity of opinion among the professionals upon whom they rely for advice. They care not a whit whether the cost system is called direct costing, absorption costing or any other name. Nor are they interested in becoming arbiters in an academic debate. But if management were asked to arbitrate, the decision would undoubtedly be: "Utilize the best features of all systems."

Uniform Cost Accounting Standards: Past, Present, and Future

Howard W. Wright

Cost problems in government contracting are not new. In his book, *History of American Sailing Ships,* Howard Chapelle reports that a warship built in 1791 encountered some difficulties of this nature: "The *Massachusetts* was built in Newburyport, Mass., and was to cost $1,440. However, her captain had the builder alter the vessel during construction without authorization. The government finally accepted her and paid the builder for the changes."

Some version of defense cost principles have been around for a long time: T D 5000, T M 14-1000, the Navy's Green Book, the first Armed Services Procurement Regulations (ASPR) in effect from 1949 to 1959, and the current ASPR in effect since 1959. Each set of regulations has been more detailed than its predecessors. I like to think that the present set established a broad conceptual framework for the first time, thereby providing a more flexible document.

WHY UCAS?

The present Part 2, Section XV of the ASPR was only three years old when the first proposals for uniform cost accounting standards (UCAS) were head. Admiral H. G. Rickover, one of the most vigorous advocates of UCAS, said in a speech before the Federal Government Accountants' Association last June: "I first raised the issue of cost accounting standards for defense contracts before

SOURCE: Reprinted with the permission of the *Financial Executive* (May, 1971), pp. 16–23.

119

Congress in 1963. Each year thereafter I testified before Congressional committees about the serious need for such standards. Finally, in 1968 the House of Representatives passed a bill requiring the development of uniform cost accounting standards for defense contracts. Even at that late date the accounting profession gave little heed to the problem."

His voice wasn't very effective for five years. But, by the spring of 1968, the mood of the country had changed. We had war, not peace; inflation, not price stability; large deficits, not balanced budgets. The "military-industrial complex" fell into disfavor in many parts of the land and with some members of Congress.

I believe that the legislative actions of the spring and early summer of 1968 were politically inspired. The legislation did not arise from any major problems identified by the Department of Defense, NASA, GAO, or the contractors. At the Senate Hearings on June 18, 1968, Frank Weitzell, then the Assistant Comptroller General, did about everything he could to sabotage the proposed legislation. No spokesman from the executive branch even bothered to testify. The representatives of accounting organizations and trade associations uniformly opposed it. In my opinion, no need for legislation of this magnitude had ever been demonstrated.

The Comptroller General's feasibility study was required by the 1968 legislation. The 18 months following the passing of the legislation were devoted to research and writing. The Comptroller General's "Report on the Feasibility of Applying Uniform Cost Accounting Standards to Negotiated Defense Contracts" was published in January 1970. To no informed observer's surprise, it determined that such standards were, and are, feasible. S 3301, a bill calling for such standards, had already been introduced in the Senate a month before.

Senate hearings were held in early spring of 1970. In the prior two years, many things had happened to ease the path of UCAS legislation. The Vietnamese War became even more unpopular. The anti-defense group in Congress had become larger and more influential. Inflation was worse. Lockheed's C-5A and other problems were common knowledge, as were over-runs on other systems. A crisis of confidence was developing in the nation. The Accounting Principles Board was having its problems with earnings per share, poolings and purchases, and intangibles. One prominent partner of a national CPA firm said: "UCAS is an idea whose time has come."

The 1970 Senate hearings were very different from those of 1968. The Comptroller General strongly supported the legislation. Somewhat milder support came from the AICPA, the NAA, the AAA, several prominent individuals, and one association. FEI, myself, and the other associations opposed. We lost 99–1 in the Senate. The House action was preordained. The legislation was signed in August 1970.

Why UCAS? Maybe it is an idea whose time has come. Perhaps, as the Comptroller General said once, the Pentagon mechanism for making changes in the ASPR cost principles is too much influenced by the contractors and their trade associations. Maybe it is a device to get free TV coverage in election years for Congressmen up for re-election. Regardless of the reasons, the Cost Account- ing Standards Board is now a fact. Like the Russians, you may not like them, but you had better learn to live with them.

COST ACCOUNTING STANDARDS BOARD

Public Law 91–379 enacted in the fall of 1970 established a Cost Accounting Standards Board as an agent of the Congress. The Board consists of the Comptroller General of the United States and four members to be appointed by him. Two are to be appointed from the accounting profession, one from industry, and one from the federal government.

In mid-January, the Comptroller General announced his appointments. In my opinion, all are excellent, and they should do much to allay the concern headlined in the Wall Street Journal of last November 10: "Defense Contractors Fear New Standards for Calculating Costs May Be Catastrophic." I'll mention each briefly:

1. Herman Bevis is the retired managing partner of Price Waterhouse and Co. He has served as a member of the AICPA government contracts committee and, for some years, as a member of the Comptroller General's advisory council. He has always been fair, unhurried, and objective.
2. Charles Dana is manager of government contract accounting for Raytheon Corp. He has been a highly vocal critic of the increasing intrusion of govern- ment in the contractor's business for many years.
3. Robert Mautz is professor of accounting at the University of Illinois. He has been president of the American Accounting Association and is a member of the AICPA Executive Committee. He is well known for his research on problems of reporting of diversified companies which he did for FEI. Professor Mautz also supervised the GAO questionnaire analysis which was a part of the Comptroller General's feasibility study.
4. Robert Moot is Assistant Secretary of Defense (Comptroller). Formerly he was administrator of the Small Business Administration. He is known to be a very thorough, fair-minded person.
5. Elmer Staats is Comptroller General and chairman of the Cost Accounting Standards Board. He served under four Presidents in the Bureau of the Budget, and he has been Comptroller General for about five years. Those

who experienced the jaundiced views of the GAO in the pre-Staats decade know how much better balanced they have become since he took over.

I have high hopes for the fairness and objectivity of the Board. If we have to have one, and the legislation says that we do, I say that the composition of this one is outstanding.

FEASIBILITY OF STANDARDS

About a year ago the word "uniform" was dropped from "uniform cost accounting standards" because of its redundancy—a standard must be for uniform application.

I am sure that I can find a set of cost accounting standards; I can, in fact, find many! The problem is that all sets will differ in some degree. No generally accepted definition of cost accounting standards has yet emerged. This should not be frightening. We don't have any generally accepted definition of "generally accepted accounting principles" either.

What is involved here is not so much a matter of definition. Rather, it is a matter of preparing an operational document to be used in a contract. We now have such a document: Part 2, Section XV, ASPR. It has been judged by the Congress of the United States to be inadequate. So either this existing document will be amended or a new one will be prepared.

Neither a new document nor a modification of the present Section XV will be able to offer a set of standards consisting exclusively of self-evident truths and axioms which have a degree of universality and permanence and which underlie, or are fundamental to, cost accounting practices. The present Section XV is not exclusively a statement of cost accounting principles. For example, it disallows costs for reasons of public policy (e.g., fines and penalties, entertainment), costs for administrative convenience (e.g., bidding expense), and, for no apparent reason, it disallows the cost of stock options. Because it is a regulation, it is quite detailed in order to close loopholes and to guard against abuses. Any new version will have the same objectives and characteristics.

Some clues as to the nature of cost accounting standards can be found in the Comptroller General's feasibility study, which concluded the following:

- Emphasis should be directed to disclosure, consistency, and establishment of criteria for the use of alternative accounting methods.
- To the extent that contractors or divisions of contractors could be grouped on the basis of similarities in their operations or in contracting situations, the standards for such groups could be stated in more specific terms.
- Advance written agreements concerning accounting methods will insure consistency between bid and proposal, contract performance, and final settlement.

- More explanatory material and better criteria for identifying, measuring, and allocating indirect costs are needed.

These recommendations fall into two categories: those of an accounting nature and those of an administrative nature. The latter category includes recommendations for greater disclosure, consistency, and advance written agreements. The recommendations concerning accounting deal with the establishment of criteria for the use of alternative accounting methods, including methods for indirect cost allocation.

I expect that the Board will curtail alternatives currently available under generally accepted accounting principles or specify criteria for their use. For example, it would not be surprising if the Board placed a ceiling on the cost of minor asset acquisitions or improvements charged to expense. And it may curtail alternative treatments for research and development expenditures.

The Board's efforts to eliminate alternatives or to set forth criteria for determining which alternatives may be used will set it up in competition with the Accounting Principles Board. Certainly there is nothing new in this. The present Part 2 Section XV is already more rigid than generally accepted accounting principles. The impact of the Cost Accounting Standards Board's pronouncements is on defense contracts only, so it is doubtful that such pronouncements will be accepted as more authoritative than those of the Accounting Principles Board.

Although the Cost Accounting Standards Board's current jurisdiction extends only to defense contracts, Lyman Bryan reports in his Washington Background column in the February *Journal of Accountancy* that "UCAS-like provisions have begun to appear in bills outside the defense areas, including health care, regulatory bills and grants in aid." The appearance of UCAS outside defense areas is entirely consistent with the recommendations of the Comptroller General's feasibility study. Also, the Comptroller General believes that similar cost accounting standards for the $7-billion depot maintenance program of the Department of Defense are both needed and desirable. The FEI Government Procurement Policies Committee made similar recommendations to the Comptroller General in October 1969.

The other half of the Board's accounting efforts will deal with cost accounting: the identification and allocation of costs. The Comptroller General's feasibility study is quite specific on this point. Most of the 120 "horror cases" reported in that study involved problems of cost allocation. Virtually all of the cases I deal with in my private practice are in this area. So we can expect a major thrust here.

The present Part 2, Section XV includes only a few paragraphs dealing with indirect cost allocation. While these paragraphs provide cost accounting standards, the Comptroller General's report has labeled them as inadequate because they do not provide specific guidance. I expect that what is now a few paragraphs will be expanded into many pages. Criteria for the composition of overhead pools will be set forth in substantial detail. Equal space will be devoted to acceptable bases for distribution and the composition thereof.

While not directly relevant here, it is interesting to note that the Department of Defense currently is considering eliminating cost of sales as a distribution base for the allocation of general and administrative expenses. This action can be traced directly to the Commissioner's decision in the Court of Claims in the Litton Industries case. While not final, the decision would reverse that of the Armed Services Board of Contract Appeals.

Very briefly, the facts of the case are that Litton had consistently used the cost of sales base for general and administrative (G&A) allocations. Its inventories were rising consistently over a period of years. The DCAA auditor wanted Litton to shift to a cost input base, which would lower the G&A rate during a period of rising inventories. Litton refused because of its long-lead backlog plus the retroactivity of the change. The ASBCA upheld DCAA; the Court of Claims Commissioner upheld Litton, reversing the Board. The Court of Claims decision has not been handed down.

The expected changes mentioned in the few preceding paragraphs can be viewed as mere patches on the existing Part 2, Section XV. Most of them are suggested by the Comptroller General's feasibility study. But other, somewhat more cohesive (and more extensive) approaches have been proposed.

The outline for one such approach has been proposed by Dr. Robert Anthony, Professor at the Harvard Graduate School of Business and a former Assistant Secretary of Defense (Comptroller). Anthony identifies 20 definitions, characteristics, and problems which could be included in the new cost standards. Most of them are included in the present cost principles implicitly rather than explicitly and, in some instances, he differs with the existing concepts or prefers a more extensive treatment than is offered by present cost principles. Some of the more obvious items he mentions include definitions of direct costs, indirect costs, overhead pools, bases for distribution, period and product cost. He suggests inclusion of two definitions not currently included in ASPR—"materiality" and "consistency." He would like to see the cost of capital dealt with in the new cost standards.

A more complete view of Anthony's ideas about cost can be found in his article "What Should Cost Mean?" in the May–June 1970 *Harvard Business Review*.

It is not beyond the realm of possibility the Board will engage in two efforts that may go on simultaneously, or perhaps sequentially. The first has to do with the fact that the law which created the Board requires that it "shall report to the Congress not later than 24 months after the enactment of this section, concerning its progress in promulgating cost accounting standards. . . ." As eight months have passed since the law was enacted, the next 16 may see a flurry of tire-patching activity.

But the second effort the Board may undertake is a more difficult and time-consuming task: that of preparing a statement of basic concepts and cost accounting principles. Such a statement could be much like Statement No. 4 of the Accounting Principles Board, published in October 1970 and entitled "Basic Concepts and Accounting Principles Underlying Financial Statements of Business Enterprises." This statement covered more than 1,000 pages of definitions, concepts, and principles.

Of more than passing coincidence is the fact that both Statement No. 4 and the Comptroller General's original definition of cost accounting standards includes three levels, with increasing degrees of specificity as one nears practical application. Thus, Statement No. 4 presents Pervasive Principles, Broad Operating Principles, and Detailed Accounting Principles. The Comptroller General's definition included the three levels Cost Principles, Cost Accounting Standards, and General Rules of Procedure. The similarity in structure is striking.

I would like to make three suggestions for concepts to be included in the highest tier—the pervasive principles perhaps—to illustrate what such a level might contain if the Board were to draw up such a statement.

The first suggestion for items to be considered in the top level is the fact that all cost accounting systems are based on assumptions of normality and continuity. Thus, the costs accumulated within a given system are valid only so long as this assumption is valid. Changing circumstances require a continuing re-examination of the system. Where terminations occur, new product lines are introduced, or present subsidiaries are disposed of, results of the system may be different from those contemplated at the negotiation of the contract.

I believe this suggestion is particularly important in view of the emphasis in the Comptroller General's feasibility study on consistency of accounting method throughout the proposal, performance, and settlement stages of defense contracting. If his recommendations are followed literally, no major contractor ever could change his system because of the overlapping of contracts.

The second suggestion for items to be considered is labelled the law of large numbers. It also might be called the compensation of errors. (Anthony partly gets at the same thing when he discusses tradeoffs.) The problem I am concerned with here can best be illustrated by depreciation. When discussing depreciation, many people draw conclusions as though they were discussing a single asset, while in fact a major business will have tens of thousands of assets acquired at different times. Depreciation on a single asset is irrelevant for all practical purposes; it is measured for the group of assets. Similarly, one should not look at one cost element of an overhead pool as having little traceable relationship to a cost objective without looking to all elements in the pool to see if possible errors aren't being compensated for.

The third suggestion is equity. This is a concept which is easy to talk about, harder to write about except in generalities, and very difficult to apply because equity is in the mind of each individual. Yet equity is what this game is all about. Negotiations of contract price are intended to substitute for the automatic equity arising from the arm's length bargaining of the market place. The use of accounting in negotiations and settlements should ease the path to an equitable price or settlement. Accounting (or bookkeeping) form should never be permitted to get in the way of an equitable amount.

The concept of equity already exists in the present cost principles. For example, Par. 15-201.4, in defining allocability states: "A cost is allocable if it is assignable. . .in accordance with the relative benefits received *or other equitable relationship.*" Thus, even now equity transcends benefit. Equity is mentioned several times in detailed paragraphs in 15-205, but each of these is a somewhat incidental reference. What is needed is a full presentation of equity as one of the pervasive principles.

The intermediate level of principles could consist of the definitions of direct costs, indirect costs, composition of pools, and basis for distribution. Other definitions might well be included. The intermediate would be the level consisting of broad operating standards equally applicable to all contractors. The lowest level would consist of the detailed guidelines, perhaps somewhat in the nature of the present 15-205 without the administrative instructions. Alternatively, this level might include some paragraphs to be applied only to certain industries or groups, and not to others. The Comptroller General's report includes the recommendation: "To the extent that contractors or divisions of contractors could be grouped on the basis of similarities in the nature of their operations or in contracting situations, the standards for such groups could be stated in more specific terms."

It is very clear to me that cost accounting standards can be developed. In fact, they have existed for many years in the present Section XV. If they are inadequate in this form, they will be expressed in different words. Such is the charge of the Cost Accounting Standards Board.

CONCERN FOR THE FUTURE

I know that those who are going to be affected by the new cost standards have a nagging fear that whatever the government does it will only worsen things; they never get better. For this reason, I opposed the UCAS proposals before two Senate committees. But I'm not as fearful now as I once was.

On the negative side, there will be some confusion arising at the time of changeover. I don't know how the changeover will be made. If changes are made from time to time by the Board on a piece-meal basis, they will have to be reflected in each contract as it is made. While this is no different from what contractors have been experiencing with changes in ASPR XV, up to now the changes have been minor and infrequent. The next 18 months may bring about quite a few changes.

Also on the negative side is the probability that the Board will require advance written agreements for disclosure, consistency, and criteria for the use of alternative accounting methods. This was emphasized so much in the Comptroller General's report that I believe he will not back away from it without good reasons. It is imbedded too extensively in the legislative history to be forgotten.

I oppose advance written agreements as being costly to prepare, wasteful of administrative effort, and difficult to change when changing circumstances require. Requiring advance written agreements is one of the biggest red herrings in the entire UCAS history. It is based on an assumption that contractors are free to change their accounting methods at will, without regard to the doctrine of consistency, the DCAA, or their own CPA. I am hopeful that, in the interest of economy and efficiency, the cost standards will be written in such a way as to avoid an annual hassle over the accounting system.

Somewhat by way of the silver lining in what one may otherwise see as a dark cloud is the fact that government auditors also will be bound by the cost accounting standards. No longer will they be able to select a method which is most advantageous to them while denying reimbursement. There may be a significant advantage in having an independent board promulgate the standards. No longer will DCAA act as both the writer of the rules and the referee. If your flexibility is going to be limited, so is theirs.

I don't believe that we need have any fear that the entire nature of defense contract accounting will change. No one has attacked the soundness of the conceptual framework of the present Section XV. At worst, it has been attacked for its lack of specificity: for being implicit, rather than explicit. Therefore, we can expect the changes I've detailed earlier.

I may be naive, but I believe that few defense contractors will have to make any changes in their accounting. They have been living with Section XV for 11 years. If their systems are sound, few if any changes will be needed. If my experience is at all reliable, few contractors abused the flexibility of Section XV; DCAA was guilty about as much. If few were taking advantage of its flexibility, only those few will be adversely affected by its removal.

Another fact which provides substantial hope is the composition of the Cost Accounting Standards Board. As I mentioned earlier, it is composed of people in whom we can have confidence. The membership is far from pro-government. If anything, the balance tips in favor of industry. The government official who called me to tell me of the appointment said: "Elmer (the Comptroller General) has opened the doors to the treasury and has thrown away the key." His judgment is more extreme than mine. I don't expect any hasty, rash, or unfair actions by this board, but I *do* expect sound judgments based on careful research and extensive consideration.

Obviously, however, one should not be unaware of what happens to such boards in Washington. Usually, if in the Executive Branch, they become havens for non-expert political appointees. Thus, our confidence in the present appointees does not extend to their successors until they are known, although I believe that the Comptroller General, whoever he may be, will have different motivations from those of the President when making appointments.

WHAT CAN BE DONE?

It is too early to know precisely how the Board will proceed or what its output will be. It is clear to me, however, that any major pronouncements of the Board will be based on empirical research. The Comptroller General's feasibility study included the following comment in its recommendations: "Considerable research in actual operating situations will be necessary and should be done in close cooperation with contractors, procuring agencies and professional accounting organizations."

In the last analysis, much of what is produced by the Cost Accounting Standards Board depends on defense contractors. I believe that the Board is made up of intelligent, fair-minded men. If we want accounting flexibility, if we wish to preserve our right to choose among alternatives, if we believe that differing circumstances justify differing accounting treatments, we must respond to calls for research data. The Board's staff cannot do the research sitting in Washington. Corporate executives have the data in their organizations. If they want freedom and flexibility, they must earn them by demonstrating their need.

Accounting Analysis for Short-Run Decisions— General Concepts

INTRODUCTION

At the heart of the use of costs in planning decisions lies the ability to estimate costs with an acceptable degree of validity and reliability. The cost concepts most relevant in this area come from microeconomic theory, which assumes that the goal of decisions is to maximize the value of the firm. Of particular interest are two cost concepts. The first concept is that of marginal cost. Marginal cost is defined as the additional cost required to produce one additional unit. The optimum economic decision is to move to the point where the marginal costs equal the marginal revenue. The second cost concept widely used is that of opportunity cost. An opportunity cost is the amount of foregone revenue. Stated another way, the opportunity cost is what would have been earned had the decision maker taken the next best available alternative.

129

When accounting focuses upon an historical, transactional model, it does not readily provide a useful estimate of either the marginal cost or of the opportunity cost. Advocates of the direct costing flow system (discussed in the previous section) imply that the variable production costs are reasonable approximations of the marginal costs, except where the plant is operating at full capacity. In this respect the managerial accountant, when he advocates direct costing, believes that he is providing data for the managers' decisions congruent with basic economic theory. In a practical day-to-day setting the measure of variable cost is used as an estimate of the marginal cost, even though it does not completely match the economist's definition of marginal cost.

While the separation of costs into their fixed and variable components offers a practical way of operationally defining marginal costs, there is *no* practical way to operationally define opportunity costs on a continual basis. There is no accounting system that systematically measures opportunity costs. Opportunity costs are situation specific. That is, the opportunity costs present in one decision are not the same opportunity costs present in another decision. They are not generalizable! It should be obvious that if the accounting model is concerned with measuring the results of past transactions, and that opportunity costs are the revenues *not* earned because a transaction was not culminated, then accounting systems and opportunity costs are incompatible by definition. As a result, all estimates of opportunity costs lie outside the domain of traditional accounting and must be derived from special studies.

Fortunately accountants can provide useful data for making choices via the fixed and variable cost perspective. While the flexible budget[1] is not a cure-all, particularly for measuring opportunity costs, it is a significant advancement over historical, total average cost. A flexible budget provides many benefits. First, and probably most important, the variable costs provide reasonable estimates of marginal costs, and fixed costs provide an estimate of committed costs. This opens many vistas for marginal production and distribution decisions. Second, and perhaps a variation of the first benefit, the flexible budget opens the door to the whole area of cost-volume-profit analysis. This analysis is often diagrammatically expressed in the form of break-even graphs or marginal graphs. Third, the flexible budget provides a parsimonious and efficient way of forecasting and predicting future cost incurrences, given a choice that is within the relevant range of output. Finally, the flexible budget is valuable for cost control. By allowing management to compare actual costs with a budget estimate of what costs should be for the output volume, management can adjust its control mechanisms.

There is a danger in the consideration of fixed and variable costs which should be recognized. When the managerial accountant states that "the fixed costs are $100,000 and the variable costs are $10 per unit produced," too many people accept this as an irrefutable fact. The concepts of fixed and variable costs are only perceptual views of a cost. In that sense they are hypothetical constructs. There are many examples of hypothetical constructs from other disciplines. In Freudian psychology the use of the terms id, ego, and super ego are hypothetical constructs. The geological ages such as the Pleistocene and Miocene are hypothetical constructs. So also are the concepts of extrovert, introvert, and ambivert. All of these have in common the fact that they are not irrefutable. What they represent are devices for classifying data that are useful in explaining and describing a particular phenomenon. The division of costs into fixed and variable portions is situation specific; this is especially true because the time horizon for the decision at hand affects this division.

This section introduces the reader to the concepts of fixed and variable costs. The articles in this section make no attempt to use these concepts in a dynamic decision-making context. Rather they are concerned with problems of delineating and understanding the concepts.

The first article in this section, *Difficulties in Flexible Budgeting* by Koehler and Neyhart, discusses the accountant's problems in determining fixed and variable cost estimates. Their discussion centers upon two important topics—the selection of a volume base and the methods of separating fixed and variable costs. The previous discussion of fixed and variable costs as hypothetical constructs is implied in this article. For each methodology of separating fixed and variable costs, regardless of its sophistication, the process of fitting the regression line to the historical data results in deviations from the line. The presence of these deviations points to the fact that fixed and variable costs are not facts but conceptual classification schemes. Some students with a mathematical background suggest that the deviations can be eliminated by fitting a curvilinear line with one bend in the curve for each observation. While this method would make the line fit the data perfectly, and hence avoid deviations, the resultant expression would be of no value in predicting future cost behavior.

The second article, *Break-Even Charts Versus Marginal Graphs* by Bell, is important to the understanding of the problems of the relationships of accounting data and economic decision making. Traditional economic theory makes some different assumptions regarding costs and revenues. For example, the economist assumes that as production increases and approaches plant capacity, the point of diminishing returns will be reached. The marginal cost will then increase. Also economists assume that as production and sales increase, the selling price per unit will decline. Professor Bell discusses some of these crucial differences between accounting and economics.

Professors Summers and Welsch in their article, *How Learning Curve Models Can Be Applied to Profit Planning,* introduce the widely observed phenomenon of the learning curve. Dating back in business application to the early 1930s, this method of budgeting labor cost variations has been widely accepted in many industries, most prominently the air frame industry. Certainly the fact that people improve their performance with repetition and practice, particularly when this improvement can be quantified, is a significant tool in forecasting labor time and labor cost. This technique is most applicable in firms that have high proportion of direct labor costs. Firms that would not find the learning curve as useful would be those with a continuous, automated production line. The learning curve, like many planning and control tools, rests upon a body of theoretical literature, but its measurement, and therefore its usefulness, can only be discovered empirically.

The final article in this section, *How Should Costs Be Determined*, is an application of the cost variability principles to the problems of determining the costs which would be applicable to alternative courses of action. The problem posed by the dialogue between the accountant and the restaurant owner, while posed in a seemingly unimportant and oversimplified setting, is crucial to managerial decision making. Lying behind this simple illustration are the complex issues of cost allocations, absorption versus direct cost systems, marginal versus average cost meanings, relevant versus nonrelevant costs, decision cost systems versus historical stewardship cost systems, and fixed and variable cost notions. It has been said that the allocation of fixed or indirect costs to departments and products causes more interpersonal fights in business, and greater confusion about the meaning of costs, than any other one technique. Could this be true?

FOOTNOTE

1.   The editors define a flexible budget as a statement of how costs behave (change) with changes in output. Thus if a firm says the fixed production costs are $100,000 per year and the variable costs are $10 for each unit produced, it has a flexible budget.

Difficulties in Flexible Budgeting

Robert W. Koehler & Charles A. Neyhart, Jr.

INTRODUCTION

The planning and control advantages of flexible budgeting are widely known. Evidence suggests that most large firms use flexible budgeting procedures. In our recent survey of 40 such firms, 22 of the 28 respondents[1] indicated that they employed flexible budgeting at least partially. Another questionnaire revealed that very few (about 15 percent) small industrial firms prepare flexible budgets. We believe that there is a scarcity of literature on this topic in relation to its importance. This paper presents our findings on some of the problems of this technique.

The first problem in preparing a flexible budget centers around the selection of the most appropriate volume base or measure of output. Unit volume, physical measures of volume, direct labor hours, machine hours, and dollar volume of output are the most common of the possibilities. It is possible for the wrong volume base to be used inadvertently particularly in departmental flexible budgets. Correlation analysis coupled with a test for significance provides assurance in selecting the best base.

A commonly discussed problem involves semi-variable expenses. It is a relatively simple clerical task to determine the fixed and variable expenses for each level of activity under consideration. However, some expenses, maintenance for example, contain both fixed and variable elements. It can be very difficult to budget these.

SOURCE: Reprinted with permission from *Managerial Planning* (May–June, 1972), pp. 21–28.

The following variety of methods have been used to separate the fixed and variable components of a mixed or semi-variable cost:

1. Treat the expense as either all variable or all fixed depending upon which category it most closely approximates.
2. High-low method.
3. Least squares regression analysis (including the "eye ball" method).
4. Work measurement techniques.

We have developed a hypothetical example to test the effectiveness of the first three of these methods. We will relate our results to work measurement techniques.

In addition to developing a model for the selection of the volume base and testing the various methods of separating the fixed and variable elements of a mixed cost we have suggested a basis for estimating a *range* within which the costs should fall when control is being maintained.

SELECTION OF VOLUME BASE

As we pointed out in the introduction, correlation analysis can be used to select that base which is most strongly related to the expense item being budgeted. It is regrettable that more emphasis has not been given to this application of correlation. We have found only an article[2] and a case study[3] that devoted significant attention to this important application.[4]

Mr. Gynther comments that:

> The absence from the literature of advice on the selection of a suitable unit (volume) to which to relate the variable expenses may have turned some people away from the separation of fixed and variable portions of semi-variable expenses or may have been the cause of use of incorrect bases. If incorrect volume bases are used, inaccurate results will follow whether the method of least squares, scatter-charts or any other lesser-used separation method is employed.[5]

The following hypothetical example is similar to the Touche Ross case; however, in order to assure that a correct volume base has been selected we have extended our example to include a test for significance. The importance of this refinement will be emphasized shortly.

Assume that Red Niblick produces liquid chemical detergent for industrial use in units ranging from 50 gallons to 200 gallons. The liquid detergent is the only product produced by Red Niblick. In November 1970 "Big Red," the controller, decided to adopt flexible budgeting in order to achieve a more efficient overall cost control system.

Because employee wages in the packaging department represented a rather significant mixed cost, Red decided to initiate these procedures here. Packaging department employees receive bulk liquid from the inspection station, package it in aluminum drum containers of appropriate size, and place the drums on a conveyer belt to the shipping department. Their wages should be classified as a mixed overhead cost rather than as direct labor because a minimum crew must be on hand at all times regardless of the level of activity. Also, the amount of their wages seems to depend on both units packaged and gallons packaged.

Intuitively Red believed that units packaged represented the best volume base. He had used this measure in the past in preparing fixed budgets. At this time he asked Carl Davis, his young assistant, to help him determine if his intuition was correct. Fortunately, Carl had taken several quantitative courses in college. Before their morning meeting he had accumulated the information shown in Table 1. He had also found in his statistics textbook the formula for calculating the coefficient of correlation, r.[6] With this the men quickly obtained the r value of 0.48 for units packaged. Both thought the correlation would be higher and rechecked their calculations.

Red asked, "How do we interpret this coefficient?" Carl answered, "Actually the coefficient of determination, r^2, is used to interpret the results. It expresses the proportion of the total variance in the dependent variable (wages) that is explained or accounted for by its linear relation to the independent variable (units packaged). In this case the r^2 or 0.23 indicates that 23 percent of the variations in employee wages are explained by variations in units packaged. The other 77 percent of the variations in employee wages are explained by gallons packaged and possibly other factors not considered in our calculations such as inefficiencies and errors in accumulating the data."

Red responded, "I still think units packaged is our best single measure of output." Carl replied, "You may be right. Let's test this coefficient for significance then make the same calculations for gallons packaged just to see what we come up with."

Red asked, "What do you mean by the test for significance?"

"Well," said Carl, "we want to answer the question: Does our coefficient of correlation, r, which in this case is 0.48, indicate a real relationship between wages and units? We must answer no if we could reasonably expect to obtain a coefficient this high from unrelated variables taken at random. *So we want to calculate the probability of obtaining an* r *value at least as high as 0.48 due to chance when there is no relationship between the variables.* We can do this because we know that the distribution of sample r's is t distributed when the sample size, n, is under 30."

At this point Red interrupted, "Our sample size is 12 isn't it?" Carl nodded his head in agreement. Red continued, "Now what do you mean by 't distributed'?"

Carl responded, "A t distribution is symmetrical and approaches normality when the sample size reaches 30. In other words it is somewhat flatter than the normal curve. Like the normal curve it is completely defined by its mean and standard deviation, that is, once we find the number of standard deviation units between the mean, which is zero since we are assuming no relationship (see italicized sentence above), and 0.48, we can convert this into the appropriate area under the distribution by using a t table. This area can then be interpreted in terms of the probability we are after.

"Let's do the arithmetic. It should clarify the explanation. The standard error of correlation is given by the formula:

$$s_{r_O} = \sqrt{\frac{1 - r^2}{n - 2}}$$

After plugging in the numbers we get $s_{r_O} = 0.277$.

Next we will find the number of standard deviation units between 0.48 and the hypothesized population coefficient, p, which we are assuming to be 0. In other words we will convert r into a t value according to the following formula:

$$t = \frac{r - p}{s_{r_O}}$$

Substitution gives us:

$$t = \frac{.48 - 0}{.277} = 1.733$$

A table of the distribution of t indicates a probability that somewhere between 5 and 10 percent of the sample values will fall outside 1.733[7] when there is no relationship. That is, the probability of obtaining a coefficient of 0.48 when $p = 0$ is greater than 5 percent but less than 10 percent."

Red commented, "This shows us that we are 'likely' to get an r value at least as great as 0.48 when there is no real relationship." Carl agreed, "That's right."

Both men were relieved when they obtained the correlation coefficient of 0.921 between wages and gallons packaged. In testing for significance they obtained a t value of 7.49. Almost never would they obtain a t this high if there was no relationship between these variables. Only one time in a thousand would a t value exceed 3 if there is no correlation. Hence, we have shown almost conclusively that there is a relationship between wages and gallons packaged.

Red asked why they couldn't have determined the best volume base by selecting the one with the highest correlation coefficient. Carl admitted that "the highest coefficient would identify the best volume base but this could still involve an insignificant relationship in at least the following circumstances:

1. Improper method of accumulating or presenting the data.
2. Lack of cost control resulting in unstable relationship between best volume base and cost.
3. Coefficient based upon two few observations.[8]
4. Change in the operation (such as purchase of more efficient machinery) causing the historical relationship to change."

Red added that "we would want to identify any of these situations. If the highest coefficient was insignificant, we would know to look for these occurrences and to refrain from using the historical data for budgeting purposes. This would call for work measurement procedures."

Carl cited the following comment from Welsch:

> Cost variability is frequently meaningless because an incorrect factor (volume base) is being used, showing low correlation between cost and activity. Another problem is the tendency of a factor gradually to become inadequate. For example, the installation of additional or new machinery in a department may necessitate a change from direct labor hours to direct machine hours as the measure of output. A factor should not be assumed to be valid for all time.[9]

Carl concluded that "correlation can frequently be helpful in determining the best volume base. Once correlation analysis is completed the test for significance is merely a procedural detail although some effort is required to understand the interpretation. I have been unable to find any tests for significance in correlation applications to flexible budgeting in the literature. Even the Gynther article and the Touche Ross case failed to extend their procedures to include this important test.[10] No doubt the test has been used in practice but it is more frequently overlooked."

Both men agreed to base the budget for wages in the packaging department on gallons packaged. They now had to decide which method to use in separating the fixed and variable elements of this expense.

A TEST OF THE METHODS OF SEPARATING THE FIXED AND VARIABLE ELEMENTS OF MIXED COSTS

They decided to use the data for the past year (shown in Table 1) to determine budget formulas assuming complete variability, the high-low method, and the least squares regression technique. They will then determine what the monthly

TABLE 1.   Actual Results, Red Niblick Packaging Department

November of 1969 to October 1970

Month	Employee wages	Units packaged	Gallons packaged
November	$ 2,100	413	10,000
December	2,130	430	10,500
January	2,240	435	11,500
February	2,350	440	13,000
March	2,270	430	12,000
April	2,180	430	11,000
May	2,250	400	9,000
June	1,860	410	7,500
July	1,770	400	5,500
August	1,700	430	7,000
September	1,890	390	8,000
October	1,960	390	9,000
	$24,700	4,998	114,000

budgets would have been based upon each of these formulas. Computation of the standard deviations about these budgeted values will provide evidence for electing the best method.

The formula assuming complete variability is easily found by dividing the total number of gallons packaged during the last 12 months into the total wages.

$$\text{Variable cost per gallon} = \frac{\$ \ 24,700}{114,000} = \$0.217$$

The budgeted figures in Table 2 were calculated by multiplying the number of gallons packaged for each respective month by $0.217. For example, the figure for November is 10,000 gallons packaged X $0.217 = $2,170.

TABLE 2.   Variance Report Based on Complete Variability

Month	Actual wages	Budget	Variance[11]
November	$ 2,100	$2,170	(70)
December	2,130	2,278	(148)
January	2,240	2,496	(256)
February	2,350	2,821	(471)
March	2,270	2,604	(334)
April	2,180	2,387	(207)
May	2,250	1,953	297
June	1,860	1,627	233
July	1,770	1,194	576
August	1,700	1,519	181
September	1,890	1,736	154
October	1,960	1,953	7
	$24,700		

The calculation of the budget formula under the high-low method is shown below. Table 3 presents the variance report based on this formula.

	Wages	Gallons
High activity (February)	$2,350	13,000
Low activity (July)	1,770	5,500
Difference	$ 580	7,500

VC = $580/7,500 = $0.077
FC = $TC - VC$
    = $2,350 - (13,000) (0.077)
    = $1,349

Budget Formula = $1,349 + $0.077 (per gallon packaged)

TABLE 3. **Variance Report Based on High-Low (Activity)**

Month	Actual wages	Budget	Variance
November	$ 2,100	$2,119	(19)
December	2,130	2,158	(28)
January	2,240	2,235	5
February	2,350	2,350	0
March	2,270	2,273	(3)
April	2,180	2,196	(16)
May	2,250	2,042	208
June	1,860	1,927	(67)
July	1,770	1,773	(3)
August	1,700	1,888	(188)
September	1,890	1,965	(75)
October	1,960	2,042	(82)
	$24,700		

Red noted that "in a month to month comparison of the variances reported in Table 2 and 3 the variances in Table 3 (based on the high-low method) are lower for each month except for August where the variance based on the high-low method is only $7 more than that based on complete variability. This is certainly strong support for favoring a budget formula based on high-low over one based on complete variability. Now how do we determine the budget formula based on the least squares method?"

Carl explained that the formula pertains to the line of average relationship between the variables which are plotted in Figure 1. The method derives its name from the fact that the line is determined in such a way that the sum of the squares of the differences between each point and the line is less than it

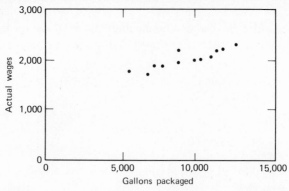

FIGURE 1.   Graphic relationship between wages and gallons.

would be for any other line that could be drawn. Like any straight line the general formula for this line of average relationship is $y = a + bx$. Of course, a represents the fixed cost and b represents the variable cost per gallon packaged. In graphic terms, a is the height of the line at the y intercept and b is the slope of the line. We simply use our data to find the values of the constants a and b.

The slope is computed by the following formula:

$$b = \frac{\Sigma XY - \dfrac{(\Sigma X)(\Sigma Y)}{n}}{\Sigma X^2 - \dfrac{(\Sigma X)^2}{n}}$$

where Y represents employee wages and X represents gallons packaged. Substitution yields a value of $0.088 per gallon packaged.

The fixed portion of employee wages is determined by the formula $a = \overline{Y} - b\overline{X}$ where:

$$\overline{Y} \text{ (mean of } Y) = \$2,058$$
$$\overline{X} \text{ (mean of } X) = \ 9,500$$
$$a = \$2,058 - (0.088)\ 9,500$$
$$a = \$1,222$$

Hence, the formula for budgeting employee wages in the packaging department for various possible levels of activity is:

$$\$1,222 + 0.088X$$

This line can be viewed graphically in Figure 2.

The resulting variance report is shown in Table 4. Red could not refrain from making a month to month comparison of the variances in Table 4 resulting from the least squares method with those in Table 3 resulting from the high-low method. These comparisons which are summarized in Table 5 indicate that the least squares method produced lower variances.

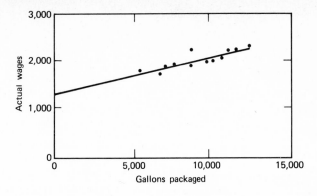

FIGURE 2.   Least squares line.

TABLE 4.   Variance Report Based on Least Squares Method

Month	Actual wages	Budget	Variance
November	$ 2,100	$2,102	(2)
December	2,130	2,146	(16)
January	2,240	2,234	6
February	2,350	2,366	(16)
March	2,270	2,278	(8)
April	2,180	2,190	(10)
May	2,250	2,014	236
June	1,860	1,882	(22)
July	1,770	1,706	64
August	1,700	1,838	(138)
September	1,890	1,926	(36)
October	1,960	2,014	(54)
	$24,700		

TABLE 5.   Monthly Comparisons of Variances Resulting from
High-Low and Least Squares Methods

Month	High-low has higher variances	Least squares has higher variances
November	$ 17	
December	12	
January		$ 1
February		16
March		5
April	6	
May		28
June	45	
July		61
August	50	
September	39	
October	28	
	$197	$111

Carl, however, suggested that "a comparison of the standard deviations of the variances about the budgeted values under each of the three methods is a more scientific analysis. These figures are easily obtained by taking the square root of the mean of the sum of the squared monthly variances.[12] The calculation could be depicted by the following formula:

$$\sqrt{\frac{\Sigma(\text{Monthly variance})^2}{12}}$$

While they took a coffee break Carl gave each of the variance reports to one of his co-workers who shortly returned with these standard deviations for each of the methods.

Method	Standard deviation of actual wages about the budgeted values
Complete variability	288.6
High-low	89.86
Least squares	83.79

It was apparent that the least squares method was most favorable although in this case the high-low method didn't look too bad. Carl reasoned that "the least squares method should always produce better results because it accounts for the information for each month. More important, by definition the values are determined in such a way that the standard deviation about these least squares values is less than for any other set of values."

Red added, "With these formulas available the least squares calculations are not significantly more time consuming than the calculations of the other methods. There is still something that bothers me though. The variance for the month of May is quite high—over 10 percent of the budget."

DATA ADJUSTMENTS AND WORK MEASUREMENT TECHNIQUES

Carl also recognized this difficulty. He explained that "our analysis is based on past information. Our results were affected by any inefficiencies or errors that were reflected in past results. Sometimes statisticians exclude data that result from extraordinary circumstances. We could try to determine if the "high" wages in May resulted from irregularities. If so, it would be appropriate to drop the results for May and to recalculate the budget formula."

At this point both men performed these calculations in order to study the effect of the change. By dropping May from the analysis, they found that the least squares budget formula changed to $1,182 + 0.09X$. With this the standard deviation about the budgeted values is 46.08 which is a much more favorable measure than the 83.79 obtained by least squares with May's data included in the analysis. Carl reasoned that "since the correlation analysis for this volume base is so highly significant ($r = 0.975$ after eliminating May) and since the least squares method is really part of a correlation analysis we can probably be satisfied with this adjustment to our data.

"For other operations we may want to conduct work measurement methods. These methods would include time and motion studies. We might also want answers to such questions as: What should the fixed costs be? (As opposed to, What do we estimate them to have been?) Are these costs step costs rather than semi-variable costs? Are these costs so dependent upon two volume bases that both should be used to determine the budget formula?"[13]

To test his understanding, Red reviewed the concepts he learned from their study. "Statistics will not solve all of our problems but it can help us in preparing our flexible budgets for operations which are substantially in control. It also signals trouble and the need for work measurement techniques when, for example, we are unable to obtain a significant correlation coefficient. A year after work measurement has been applied correlation will indicate whether control has been maintained. If so, least squares can be used in determining future budget formulas."

Carl was pleased that Red had understood the points that he was trying to convey, but he still felt that their analysis should be extended further. The variances—even those constructed after the elimination of the May data (shown in Table 6)—make it clear that it is impossible to budget the wages perfectly. He remarked, "Even when the correlation coefficient is 0.975 the variances

TABLE 6. Variance Report Based on Least Squares Method with May Eliminated

Month	Actual wages	Budget	Variance
November	$ 2,100	$2,082	$18
December	2,130	2,127	3
January	2,240	2,217	23
February	2,350	2,352	2
March	2,270	2,262	8
April	2,180	2,172	8
June	1,860	1,857	3
July	1,770	1,677	93
August	1,700	1,812	(112)
September	1,890	1,902	(12)
October	1,960	1,992	(32)
	$22,450		

for July and August are over 5 percent of the budget. Perhaps in our budget we should consider the range within which the wages can be expected to fall. This will be helpful in planning, control, and sometimes in decision-making."

BUDGET RELIABILITY AND CONTROL

Red reacted favorably. "Knowledge of such a range would be useful but how do we determine the limits?"

Carl stated, "Fortunately one of the assumptions of least squares analysis is that the points are t distributed about the regression line.[14] In our example this means that the actual wages should be t distributed about the budgeted values. An important characteristic of this distribution is that about 95 percent of the values lie within 2.228 standard deviations on either side of the mean when there are 12 observations and 10 degrees of freedom. Actually, once we know the mean and the standard deviation we can set up a range for various probability levels.

"Let's see how this works in our example. Based on your latest formula with the May data eliminated Table 6 shows that we budgeted wages for July at $1,677 [$1,182 + .09 (5,500 gallons)]. This figure is the height of the line of average relationship, where $x = 5,500$. In other words, $1,677 represents the mean wages when 5,500 gallons are packaged. We would then expect the wages to fall within the following interval 95 percent of the time:

$$\$1,677 \pm 2.228 \ (46.08) = \$1,677 \pm 102.67 = \$1,574.33 \text{ to } \$1,779.67.$$

(You recall that we previously found the standard deviation about the budgeted values to be $46.08.)

"Our flexible budget could portray a range of possible costs for each possible level of activity. Table 7 illustrates a possible format which we could extend to include other activity levels and other cost classifications. This notion of limits is also appropriate for variable and managed costs as well as for mixed costs.[15] We might also find that ranges other than the 95 percent confidence interval are more useful."

Red thought they were embarking on an area that would be extremely helpful. He remarked "This way we will have a whole series of budgets. We can lay plans for the best and worst events as well as for what we consider to be most likely. However, I am still somewhat concerned about budgeting a range of costs for a given activity level. Shouldn't we budget the costs at what they should be and take investigative action if they differ?"

Carl replied, "When do we ever have a variance report with zero variances? We always accept some variance because people simply can't perform completely uniformly and they can't explain why. Since we can't find a cause we should

TABLE 7.   Flexible Budget Format, Packaging Department
Month of_____

Cost	Gallons packaged					
	5,500			7,000		
	Lower limit	Mean	Upper limit	Lower limit	Mean	Upper limit
Employee Wages	$1,574	$1,677	$1,780			

not investigate. The budget format in Table 7 simply gives recognition to these chance variances."

Red understood. "Then this budget format should be useful for control purposes too. We should investigate if the wages fall outside the budgeted limits."

Carl said, "Exactly. Eventually we should try to find the most economical limits.[16] We must also keep in mind that the most effective and timely control must emanate at the performance level. However, the monthly report can review control effectiveness."[17]

Red noticed that it was 5 o'clock and concluded, "This has been a very productive day. Thank you, Carl, for directing my thinking along these useful lines."

FOOTNOTES

1. Twenty-six of the 28 respondents were in Fortune's 500.

2. R. S. Gynther, "Improving Separation of Fixed and Variable Expenses," *NAA Bulletin,* (June 1963), pp. 30–36.

3. Touche, Ross, Bailey, and Smart, *Ralston Electric Company* (Mimeographed).

4. The following article did, however, employ multiple correlation which simultaneously considers more than one volume base: George J. Benston, "Multiple Regression Analysis of Cost Behavior," *The Accounting Review,* XLI, No. 4, (October 1966), pp. 657–672.

5. Gynther, *op. cit.,* p. 30.

6. $r = \dfrac{n\Sigma XY - (\Sigma X)(\Sigma Y)}{\sqrt{[n\Sigma X^2 - (\Sigma X)^2]\ [n\Sigma Y^2 - (\Sigma Y)^2}}$

7. This value can be found in most statistics textbook tables under Distribution of t. This value is based on 10 degrees of freedom $(n - 2)$ when p is assumed to be 0. The tables are not normally refined enough to give the

exact percentage. The value corresponding to $t_{.10}$ is 1.372 and the value corresponding to $t_{.05}$ is 1.812.

8. The fewer the observations the higher the coefficient must be to be significant. In the case of two observations a coefficient of 1 is not significant because the coefficient will always be 1 whether or not the variables are related. This can be seen by plotting the data. Since two points determine a straight line, both observations must lie on the line. Thus, we have perfect correlation.

9. Glenn A. Welsch, *Budgeting: Profit Planning and Control,* (Englewood Cliffs, New Jersey: Prentice-Hall Inc., 1957), p. 169.

10. In a slightly different context the following article did include a significance test: John S. Chiu and Don T. DeCoster, "Multiple Product Costing by Multiple Regression Analysis," *The Accounting Review,* XLI, No. 4, (October 1966), pp. 673–680.

11. The parentheses ( ) in the variance column indicates that actual wages were less than the budget resulting in a favorable variance.

12. Those with a knowledge of statistical terminology will recognize that the accountant's use of the word "variance" as presented on the variance reports is different from the statistician's use of the word (the standard deviation squared). Since our discussion is directed primarily to accountants we thought this approach without symbolic notation would be more understandable.

13. This would involve using multiple regression. See the George J. Benston article referred to in footnote 4.

14. The terms regression line, least squares line, and line of average relationship are used synonymously. The distribution becomes normal when the number of values reaches 30.

15. Professors William Ferrara and Jack Hayya presented an excellent paper on this subject at the Notre Dame Convention of the American Accounting Association held in August of 1969. Their paper entitled "Toward Probabilistic Profit Budgets" estimated the probabilities of various activity levels and combined these with the probabilities for the related expenses to arrive at a probability distribution for profits. The first part of this paper was awarded a Certificate of Merit from the National Association of Accountants for 1969–1970 and has been published under the same title in the October 1970 issue of *Management Accounting.*
    Robert K. Jaedicke and Alexander A. Robichek published an article involving the use of normal curve probabilities in decision making. See *The Accounting Review,* XXXIX (October 1964), pp. 917–26.

16. For a discussion of the factors involved see Robert W. Koehler, "The Relevance of Probability Statistics to Accounting Variance Control," *Management Accounting* (October 1968), pp. 35–41.

17. Robert W. Koehler, "Statistical Variance Control: Through Performance Reports and On-the-Spot Observation," *Management Accounting* (December 1969), pp. 42–46.

Break-Even Charts Versus Marginal Graphs

Albert L. Bell

The break-even chart is a very useful device for analyzing the cost-volume-profit relationships and for predicting the probable profit effect of changes in output, revenue and costs. However, there is need for further synthesis of the break-even technique and price theory. The inter-action of the new ideas and techniques of cost accounting with the research which is being done in statistics, operations research and economic theory will help to bridge the gap between the empirical data of the accountant and the price theory of the economist. Thus break-even analysis can provide a major link between business behavior and the theory of the firm.

The purpose of this article then is twofold. It is an attempt to clear up some of the misunderstanding which still exists because of the apparent disparity between what is taught in accounting and what is taught in economics. It is also the aim of this paper to continue the work of providing a better fusion of these two bodies of knowledge in order to provide a better basis for management decisions.

COMMON DIFFERENCES

The vital factor in profit planning is the relationship between revenue, cost and volume. There are two different methods of showing this: the marginal graph and the break-even chart.

The marginal graph was designed to provide the theoretical framework for economic analysis concerning the general relationships between selling price

SOURCE: Reprinted from *Management Accounting* (February, 1969), pp. 32-35, 48. by permission of National Association of Accountants, New York, N.Y. Copyright 1969.

and costs of production at different volumes. Specifically, it shows the relation-ship between marginal revenue and marginal cost in an effort to determine the point of most profitable output.

The break-even chart is a diagram of the relationship between the total revenue and the total cost as volume changes. It assumes linearity of this relationship and shows a definite break-even point with the implications that the profit area will continue to widen as the volume increases and that the point of most profitable output is at full capacity.

These two methods vary because of differences in point of view and in assumptions. Break-even analysis is primarily concerned with the effect of changes in quantity on costs and profits. On the other hand, economics is primarily concerned with resource allocation and, hence, interested in the effect of price on the quantity sold. This divergence of interest leads to a basic difference in the calculation of revenue.

Economic theory assumes that under conditions of imperfect competition additional units can be sold only by lowering the price. This means that the total revenue line (TR) is concave to the base (Exhibit 1).

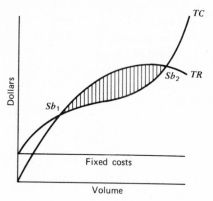

EXHIBIT 1.   The economist's graph

The accountant, however, assumes that the selling price is constant over the relevant range of output for the firm and therefore the total revenue line is a straight line (Exhibit 2). This means that the average revenue is the same as the price and is a horizontal straight-line.

In calculating the total cost and in diagramming the corresponding curve a divergence is encountered similar to that in the treatment of total revenue. Because of the behavior of variable cost as volume changes (this will be explained later) the economist shows the total cost line as curvilinear (Exhibit 1). The accountant, on the other hand, finds the average variable cost to be the

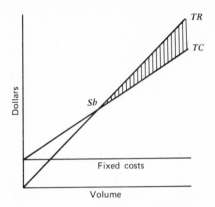

EXHIBIT 2.   The accountant's graph

same over the relevant range in volume and therefore shows the total cost line as linear (Exhibit 2).

When the total cost curve and the total revenue curve of the economist are placed on a diagram, they appear as in Exhibit 1. The points Sb_1 and Sb_2 are break-even points and the area between Sb_1 and Sb_2 represents the profit area.

When the accountant's linear total revenue line and total cost line are plotted (Exhibit 2), there is only one break-even point, namely Sb, and the profit is shown by the shaded area. The limit to this profit area is the capacity of the firm. These differences are fundamental and will be explained in subsequent sections of this paper.

Another difference that normally exists is that the economist's curves are usually drawn in terms of unit price instead of totals, as in the case of break-even charts. In order to make the economist's data comparable to the accountant's total figures, the economist's unit costs are translated into the totals as shown in Exhibit 1.

REVENUE

The economist knows that under any form of imperfect competition the entrepreneur cannot determine accurately the demand schedule for his product or products and thus cannot calculate precisely the total revenue, the average revenue, or the marginal revenue. However, the economic theorist knows that the producer has some control over price, and he is also aware of the law of demand. Thus it is concluded that the firm must lower its price if it desires to sell additional units. Therefore, the hypothetical problems which are drawn up show that as the price is lowered the quantity demanded is increased.

As long as the percentage increase in the quantity sold is greater than the percentage decrease in the price, the total revenue will increase and the *TR* line will move upward. As soon as the percentage increase in quantity is less than the percentage decrease in price, the total revenue will decrease and the *TR* line will bend downward.

Break-even analysis assumes that the firm can sell all that it can produce at the current market price and therefore the total revenue line is linear. This is a realistic assumption for most firms which are in industries where the short-run prices are inflexible over the relevant range of output.[1] This relevant range is within the outputs which they have been producing and with which they have had recent experience. However, after the accountant has plotted the *TR* line for those relevant outputs then the line is extended to the origin. It would probably be better and cause less confusion if the *TR* line was not extended to the origin.

Perhaps the curvilinear *TR* line of the economist could be explained as being made up of a series of the short-linear sections drawn by the accountant. This explanation would be more nearly correct than the traditional diagram because outside of this relevant range these same relationships are unlikely to exist.

There are probably several explanations or justifications for this assumption of administered (fixed) prices. In the first place, if the selling price is set by competition, as is assumed under pure competition, then the sales line (*TR*) is a straight-line. Conversely, if the firm is a leader in the industry and is in a position to set and control the price then the *TR* line is linear for the output which it sells.

The assumption of a fixed price for the other types of market structure is more difficult to explain. Probably the simplest explanation is that most firms use average cost pricing (profit target pricing) in arriving at the selling price.[2] The managers believe that prices are determined by costs and that prices are built up out of costs by calculating the average total cost and then adding a mark-up designed to achieve the attainable profit target.[3] In order to provide price stability the producers typically do not raise prices when the demand increases, because they do not regard this as an increase in demand but as a movement along the revenue curve. On the other hand, price theory regards any increase in the *quantity* demanded *without* a change in price—as an increase in demand which means that the demand line has shifted to the right and the entire revenue line has moved up.

Turning to the supply side, as it affects selling price, we find that an increase in costs under average cost pricing will increase prices by more than the full amount of the cost increase. This is likely to be the case when the managers know that their competitors are subject to the same increases such as occur in a new round of wage increases arrived at under industry-wide bargaining. Of course if the price is changed the total revenue line will be changed, and if the wages increase the total cost line will be changed, thus requiring a new break-even chart.

Another factor reinforcing the assumption of a fixed price for the seller's output is that for most manufacturing firms, competition takes the form of non-price rather than price competition. This gives the producer some assurance that the firms within the industry will try to increase the volume by such means as advertising rather than by changing the price.

In arriving at the conclusion that total revenue can be realistically represented as a straight-line, it is necessary to assume a constant sales mix, because if the sales mix changes the total revenue will most probably change and the break-even point is altered. In most firms the various products have different price-volume ratios, i.e., different contribution ratios; consequently, if there is a change in the product mix then there is a change in the profit pattern and a shift in the break-even point.

It may be concluded then that the inability of the economist or the business manager to construct a demand schedule is not a conceptual flaw but an empirical problem. To overcome this problem the manager assumes that in the short-run the price will remain unchanged for the volume relevant to this firm and that the total revenue line is linear. Neither the economist nor the manager is deceived into believing that the sales line is a demand curve. It simply shows the total revenue if the price remains unchanged.

COSTS

The next important difference between the figures in break-even analysis and the data in economic theory is the costing area. The term cost has different meanings to different groups of users. The broadest concept is the one which the economist uses which regards cost as the level of compensation paid to the owners of the factors of production to provide the incentive for these owners to continue to supply the firm. Economic analysis measures this compensation in terms of the other opportunities which are available or in terms of the foregone opportunities. This is another way of saying that the cost of a factor is equal to what the factor could command in its most profitable use. Therefore, costs in economics mean opportunity costs.

The compensation to the factors of production supplied by outsiders involves payment and are called explicit cost. The compensations for the factors supplied by the owners are referred to as implicit costs and do not necessarily involve payment at all. Under the principle of opportunity costs it is necessary to include as a cost an amount for wages of management which under a single proprietorship is a sum equal to what the proprietor could receive managing another business. Likewise it is necessary to include as cost a figure for implicit interest which represents a normal return on the funds supplied by the owner or owners. The inclusion of these two items is required in order to state the total cost as conceived by the economist.

Even in dealing with the explicit costs the economist is not satisfied with the figures as supplied by the accountant. These are past costs and in order to conform to the principle of opportunity costs these must be converted into current costs. This is particularly true in accounting for plant and equipment because the depreciation is calculated on original cost and must be converted to a replacement cost basis.

The same is true in the pricing of inventories and in the calculation of cost of goods sold. The use of the traditional "cost or market, whichever is lower" will not reflect current costs; therefore, the economist adjusts these to a current-dollar basis. It must be added, however, that to the extent that "Lifo" is used, the cost of goods sold will more nearly approximate current costs and thus more nearly satisfy the demands of economic analysis.

In contrast to the economic concept of cost developed above, the accounting concept views costs as an outward flow of assets that usually arise out of business transactions, represent expenditures and are expressed in terms of dollars based on original cost. The accountant does not include implicit costs and therefore does not regard dividends paid to the stockholders of a corporation as a cost of producing income, but instead regards it as a distribution of income to the stockholders. He does not attempt to convert costs to a current basis but is interested in matching the costs of the period with the revenue of the period in order to arrive at the net income.

In order to overcome the conceptual difference involving dividend payments, some break-even charts show not only the break-even point using traditional accounting costs but also the volume necessary to cover the regular stipulated dividend on the preferred stock and a "normal" dividend on the common stock. It is obvious that this does not satisfy all the criticism from the field of economics but it does help to bridge the gap between the accountant's concept of cost and the economist's concept of cost.

VARIABLE COSTS

Not only do the two bodies of knowledge differ conceptually, but they differ empirically. As was stated earlier, price theory shows the total cost line as curvilinear, while the break-even analysis shows that the total cost line is linear. The difference in the assumptions about the behavior of the two total cost curves is explained by the difference in the behavior of the variable costs.

The break-even analysis assumes that the average variable cost per unit (*AVC*) is the same throughout the entire range of output; therefore, the total variable cost line and total cost line are linear and the average variable cost is the same at all volumes. Studies have been made which indicate that this is so for several enterprises.[4] However, in these studies data were not available for the extremes and therefore the behavior of costs for very low or very high volumes was not included. For example, it is quite possible that at very high volumes the average variable cost and the average total cost will increase. Therefore, it is much safer to draw the cost curves only for the *relevant* range for which verifiable objective evidence is available. So then the curvilinear cost curves of the economist can be thought of as a combination of a series of short linear cost sections provided by the accountant.[5]

On the other hand, economic theory considers that average variable cost is not the same throughout, but will decline initially (as long as there are increasing returns), will remain constant (as long as the average physical product per unit of input is constant) and eventually will increase (after the point of decreasing average return has been reached). This causes the total cost line to behave as in Exhibit 1. It also causes the average variable cost (*AVC*) line and the average total cost (*ATC*) to be somewhat U shaped and the marginal cost (*MC*) to move upward (Exhibit 3). According to the definitions used, assumptions made, and problems constructed, these cost curves are correct.

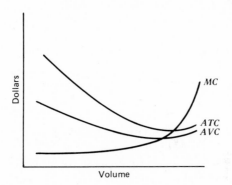

EXHIBIT 3.   Average costs and marginal costs

This concept of increasing average variable cost and increasing marginal cost rests on the famous economic law of diminishing returns (law of variable proportions). This is certainly true of agriculture where in the short-run you hold one factor fixed, namely land, and increase the other factors.

The modern manager questions the relevance of this principle to the operation of a manufacturing plant. In manufacturing he sees no fixed factors because, unlike land, more machinery can be secured so small doses of a variable factor are not added to a fixed factor. Instead, the different factors of production are added in packages and the manager contends that diminishing returns is not applicable.[6]

This reasoning does not invalidate the law of diminishing returns nor the idea of increasing marginal cost. Both are short-run concepts and by definition the short-run is a period so short that the plant capacity cannot be changed. Therefore, by definition, more machinery cannot be added and there is a fixed factor, namely plant.

The above illustrates the need for a synthesis of the two ideas and shows the relevance of both in management decisions. In industry it can be shown that as soon as increased output begins to press on capacity management takes steps to increase the capacity in order to prevent the operation of diminishing returns and increasing marginal costs. The manager must realize, however, that the fixed costs have changed and it is necessary to draw a new break-even chart.

DIRECT VS. MARGINAL COSTS

Another source of confusion and disagreement concerning marginal cost stems from the fact that some accountants confuse average direct cost with marginal cost. Since direct costs include principally direct materials and direct labor, the average direct cost seems to be constant. Therefore he concludes that marginal cost is constant.

The economist contends that, besides direct materials and direct labor, the figure for marginal cost must include items such as the extra wear and tear on machinery, the extra risk of break-downs and the costs of bottle-necks as the production process is speeded up to turn out the extra units.[7] Therefore, economic theory says that the marginal cost curve will turn up gradually, not simply as some of the diagrams show, because none of the above items would cause an increase of this magnitude.

When using the concept of marginal cost for planning, the economist is willing to concede that the marginal cost curve will not be a fine line, but because of the unpredictable nature of the above items it will be a broad line. Further he contends that this will not render it useless because decisions based upon a thick marginal cost line that has the proper shape are better than those based upon marginal cost as a straight line.

The conclusion of the theorist on this point is succinctly summarized by P. J. D. Wiles when he states that, "It is of course a grave error to hold that imprecise concepts cannot be precisely reasoned with, and made to produce imprecise but very useful answers."[8]

Other economists feel that the idea of constant average variable cost is erroneous because it is derived from the use of standard costs in cost accounting. Under a standard cost system the costs for direct material, direct labor and overhead are pre-determined costs, and the differences between these standard costs and the actual costs are shown as favorable or unfavorable variances. Since direct materials and direct labor are charged into production at a standard cost which is the same for each unit of a product, the average variable cost will be the same at each output and any divergence from standard will be shown in the variances. Cost accounting has been concerned primarily with the setting of standards and norms by which management could judge performance. Its goal has been to keep efficiency up to some predetermined mark, rather than to determine incremental costs at different volumes.

SEMI-VARIABLE COSTS

Another source of trouble is that break-even equations and charts typically assume that all costs be either fixed or variable over the entire range of output. This causes great difficulties since accountants have recognized for many years an intermediate category referred to as semi-variable costs. These vary with volume, but they vary in steps, as for example the wages and salaries of supervisory personnel. The cost accountant shows this by means of preparing flexible budgets for the various volumes, but still within the relevant range.

The economist quite largely avoids this problem by not having a category of costs called semi-variable. Nevertheless, the break-even analysis must take cognizance of the different levels at which the important "stepped semi-variable expenses" increase because all costs must be separated into fixed and variable[9] in order to calculate the contribution margin and to arrive at the break-even point.

POINT OF MOST PROFITABLE OUTPUT

The most important difference between the findings of break-even analysis and the conclusions reached by economic theory has to do with the calculation of the point of most profitable output. Since on the break-even chart the difference between the average total cost and the selling price of a unit is the same at all volumes, then it follows that profits are maximized at full capacity. In fact it is impossible to use a marginal diagram inasmuch as the marginal revenue line is a straight horizontal line and the marginal cost line is another horizontal straight line running parallel, so these two lines cannot cross and there cannot be a point of equilibrium.

However, on the marginal graph under any form of imperfect competition the marginal revenue is falling and the marginal cost is rising, so the point of most profitable output is where the two lines cross and *MR* is equal to *MC* (Exhibit 4). This shows that the firm will sell quantity *Q* at a price *P* and that the profit rectangle is represented by *RPST*.

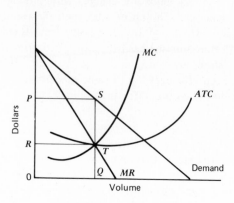

EXHIBIT 4.   *MR = MC*

If the empirical data conform to the economic theory then the theory is able to go one step further than the break-even chart and indicate not only the break-even point, but also any equilibrium condition. This is the point of maximum profit and shows the volume at which the firm should endeavor to operate. Even if the data are not available for this calculation, the economic principle provides an important analytical framework within which the manager may make better decisions.

CONCLUSIONS

The break-even chart based upon the assumption of a constant selling price and constant average variable cost has been a useful classroom device for showing cost-volume-profit relations. It has also made a major contribution to profit planning by showing in a simple way the effect of changes in volume on costs and profit. However, today's management is more aware that the break-even point is valid only under the conditions which are assumed to exist and that profits are the result of many more factors than can be shown on a two-dimensional graph.

In the meantime business has continued to become more complex so that the accountant has developed a more complete break-even system. This system takes into account changes in selling price, volume, product-mix, efficiency and technology. The statisticians use regression analysis to study items that are not constant, and construct probability tables to cover these items.

These refinements and explorations provide management with a tremendous amount of valuable information. The new break-even system with its sophisticated techniques and additional data has certainly overcome some of the criticisms of economic theory. It is hoped that the above explanations will help to continue this fusion of empirical data, statistical techniques and economic theory and also it is hoped that the above will help to clear up the confusion between what is taught in economics and what is taught in accounting.

FOOTNOTES

1.   Joel Dean, *Managerial Economics*, Prentice-Hall, Inc., Englewood Cliffs, N.J., 1951, p. 334

2.   *Ibid.*, pp. 444–50.

3.   John F. Due, *Intermediate Economic Analysis*, Richard D. Irwin. Inc., Homewood, Ill., 3rd edition 1956, pp. 268–80.

4.   Joel Dean, "Cost Structures of Enterprises and Break-Even Techniques." *American Economic Review*, May 1949, pp. 150–60.

5.   D. Vickers, "On the Economics of Break-even," *The Accounting Review*, July 1960, p. 411.

6.   J. R. Burchard, "A Critical Look at the Marginal Graph Technique," *N. A. A. Bulletin*, May 1961, p. 31.

7.   P. J. D. Wiles, *Price, Cost and Output*, Frederick A. Praeger, New York, 1963, pp. 51–2.

8.   *Ibid.*, p. 55.

9.   Spencer A. Tucker, *The Break-Even System: A Tool for Profit Planning*, Prentice-Hall, Inc., Englewood Cliffs, N. J., 1963, p. 27.

How Learning Curve Models Can Be Applied to Profit Planning

Edward L. Summers &
Glenn A. Welsch

Since World War II a substantial amount of literature has been devoted to a behavioral phenomenon known as the "learning effect." The learning effect refers to the potential efficiency to be gained from repetition of a manufacturing procedure, process, or operation.

Learning-curve theory has particular relevance for accountants and others concerned with historical costs, projected costs, and budgets. It is an important factor to be considered in developing realistic cost estimates and profit projections where repetitive manufacturing or operational activities are involved.

A high degree of realism and accuracy in cost and profit forecasts enables management to develop competitive and economically sound pricing policies, particularly where price depends in large measure on costs. Other significant consequences include effective planning and control of cash flows, costs, and personnel requirements. This article reviews learning-effect theory and suggests some relevant applications in profit planning and control.

SOURCE: Reprinted by permission of *Management Services* (March/April, 1970), pp. 45–50. Copyright 1970 by the American Institute of CPAs.

The learning effect is the relevant factor underlying what have come to be known as learning-curve manufacturing progress models. Development of the ballistic missile provided the basis for a widely cited illustration of the learning effect. During the early and middle 1950's, when the research and development of ballistic missiles reached a payoff stage, cost projections for the first production models emerged. The cost of one ballistic missile from the first production line was in excess of the cost of a single strategic bomber. It could have been argued (aside from the fact that the bomber was manned and the missile was not) that, since bombers were less costly to produce, they should be produced in preference to the apparently quite expensive missiles.

However, the decision was to produce missiles. The decision rested in part upon the knowledge of learning-curve models and significance of the learning effect gained from the experience of the aerospace industry. That experience had enabled planning and budget executives in the Department of Defense to forecast realistically that the production cost of a ballistic missile could be reduced to approximately one million dollars, far less than the "matured" cost of a strategic bomber. The expectation of substantial and dramatic reduction in cost was based on the explicit assumption that there would be significant learning efficiencies as more and more missiles were produced. With cumulative experience, less material waste, less labor, and less overhead should be incurred for each missile produced.

THE LEARNING CURVE

Practically all manufacturing experiences are subject to the learning effect in varying degrees. In particular, a production run of finite size and possessing some degree of complexity is susceptible to the learning effect. The learning effect may be described quantitatively by an exponential function which relates the resources required to produce one unit to the total number of units produced. One commonly observed learning-effect function has the resources required per unit produced decreasing by 20 per cent each time the production quantity is doubled. Thus, if the first unit produced required $10 million in resources, the second unit would require $8 million, the fourth unit $6,400,000, and so on. These costs, plotted on a vertical axis against total units produced on the horizontal axis, represent a *learning curve*.

The learning effect concept of cost measurement may be compared with the standard cost concept in managerial accounting. A standard cost normally is held constant in the short run, subject to the effects of discretionary management decisions and externally imposed price changes of specific resources. The learning model holds that the cost of resources included in a product in addition is affected by other variables that are controllable by the firm. The standard cost concept implicitly assumes that the learning effect (if it exists) has been realized; i.e., that the firm is operating on that segment of the learning curve that is asymptotic to the horizontal axis. To restate it another way, a standard cost is a "mature" cost; the assumption is that sufficient experience has been gained so that any further learning effect is negligible. In contrast, the learning-effect model explicitly states that many of the operations and resource commitments involved in a producing situation (particularly where the product involves complex operations and the production run is limited) are continuously subject to the learning effect as more and more units are produced. The learning-curve model does not assume a mature cost as the on-going situation. If the conventional concept of standard cost is utilized in developing the cost budget for manufacturing in a situation where the learning effect is significant, the budget standards are apt to be excessively liberal and the resultant variances in performance reports misleading. The inclusion of learning-effect models in the development of manufacturing cost budgets in "immature" situations clearly should serve to improve managerial planning and control of operational costs.

CLASSIFYING ACTIVITIES

At any one point in time, not all activities of a firm are subject to the learning effect. Those activities which are subject to the learning effect should be identified and evaluated so that relevant cost concepts can be applied to them in the profit planning and control process. Activities that are subject to learning curve analyses are:

1. Those that have not been performed or have not been performed in their present operational mode. In contrast, any activity which has long been performed by the firm in a particular way is not subject to the learning effect.
2. Those which are being performed by new workmen, new employees, or others not familiar with the particular activity. In contrast, activities being performed by experienced workmen thoroughly familiar with those activities will not be subject to a learning effect.
3. Those involving utilization of raw materials which have never been used by the firm before, or never have been used in this particular fashion by the firm. In contrast, familiar and regularly used materials generally do not reflect the learning effect.
4. Those production runs which are of short duration, especially if there is a possibility of follow-on production runs (by short duration we mean perhaps less than 10,000 units although "short" is a relative concept).

CURVES VARY WIDELY

From the control point of view the learning effects should be identified with responsibility and decision centers primarily associated with service or overhead operations. In general, one should not expect that normal service or overhead operations will be subject to a learning effect in a significant degree since they tend to be routine and to be continuously performed in essentially the same manner for long periods of time. However, exceptions should be anticipated such as the maintenance of new types of equipment; in such cases maintenance in the early periods is likely to be significantly less efficient than maintenance after a record of experience is attained. The supervisory function initially is apt to be subject to a learning curve effect; for example, when a new plant is acquired supervision initially may be less efficient than after the plant has been in operation for a period of time.

In applying learning curve models it is important to recognize that not all learning effects can be described by the same quantitative formulas although some formulas do have wide application. For example, the "80 per cent learning effect" has been found to be widely applicable to a variety of simple manufacturing operations. It may be applicable in the aggregate to the assembly of a product that involves a large number of independent operations, each individually subject to a different learning effect. Yet there are a number of situations where the 80 per cent curve would be inappropriate.

Although there are many instances of complex mathematical analysis in the literature with respect to the learning effect, one of its pragmatic attractions is that it can be described simply and applied with a minimum of mathematical sophistication. The essential technique employed is to plot certain selected values on log-log paper (graph paper on which the scales are expressed in terms of logarithms rather than absolute values). The learning effect may be expressed as a straight line on log-log paper; therefore, only two points (or one point and a slope) are necessary for plotting. Each point plotted will represent values for a pair of variables: first, the dependent variable—the measure, in dollars or other units, of the resource used; second, the independent variable—the measure of output, usually the number of units produced. The terms "resource used" and "number of units produced" are generalizations and are used to suggest definitional requirements appropriate to each particular application. (As another example see Figure 1.) Two-cycle log-type paper generally is adequate for these purposes. Once the required initial data are obtained and plotted, the resource input for each individual unit in a production run can be read directly from the graph. Since direct reading is tedious it is generally preferable to employ a formula for estimating the total resource input for any given number of units produced.

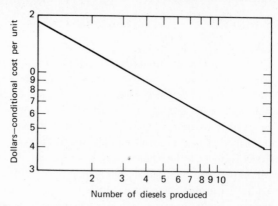

FIGURE 1. Conditional costs per unit versus total number of diesels produced.

FORMULA FOR RESOURCE INPUT

The formula for the resource input (Y) of the xth unit in a production run is:

$$Y_x = Y_1 x^n$$

where Y_1 = resource input for the *first* unit in the production run, and n, the learning constant, is

$$n = \frac{\ln(1-K)}{\ln 2}$$

where K = fractional reduction in resource required per unit for each 100 per cent increase in total units produced.[1]

The cumulative resource input is:

$$\Sigma Y = Y_1 + Y_2 + \ldots \text{etc.}$$

If N units are to be produced, this expression may be integrated from $x = 0.5$ to $x = N + 0.5$ to give

$$\underset{N}{\Sigma Y} \equiv T_N \approx \frac{Y_1}{1+n}\left[(N+0.5)^{1+n} - (0.5)^{1+n}\right]$$

which is the desired formula.

This formula can be modified to give the average cost per unit in a production run which is subject to the learning effect:

$$Y_{(N)} \approx \frac{\underset{N}{\Sigma Y}}{N} = \frac{Y_1}{N(1+n)}\left[(N+0.5)^{1+n} - (0.5)^{1+n}\right]$$

Consider the following brief example which illustrates utilization of these formulas:

Let Y_1 = 962 direct labor hours (DLH)
      K = 0.18
      x = 12th unit
      N = 24 units of output

Then

$$N = \frac{\ln(1 - 0.18)}{\ln 2} = -\frac{.198}{.694} = -.286$$

$$Y_{12} = 962 \, (12^{-.286})$$

$$= 962 \, (.49)$$

$$Y_{12} = 471 \text{ DLH}$$

The total DLH requirement for 24 units is approximately

$$T_{24} \approx \frac{962}{1.0 - .286} \, [(24 + 0.5)^{1.0 - .286} - 0.5^{1.0 - .286}]$$

$$\approx 1350 \, (9.2)$$

$$\approx \underline{\underline{12400 \text{ DLH}}}$$

The average number of DLH in each of these first 24 units would be

$$Y_{24} = \frac{12400}{24} = \underline{\underline{517}}$$

(compare this with the 962 DLH in the first unit)

The primary difficulty in measuring the learning effect is development of the initial data (values for Y_1 and K) that are required to formulate the relevant models. Cost projections frequently must be developed prior to the production of a single unit. In such circumstances, the resource input for the first unit, or the average cost in a production run, may be unreliable. There is little help that we can provide to resolve this rather sticky problem, except to note that through experience many firms have developed their own heuristics for estimating its significance.

For example, the quantity n in the preceding formulas is termed the "learning constant." The learning constant tends to be stable within certain classes of activity; a repetitive activity such as "fitting" might justify a constant of .9; and for another activity such as "painting" the constant might be .75. As a consequence, when a new product is produced, these two learning constants should be appropriate for "fitting" and "painting" if these two activities are required to produce the new product. When a totally new operation is to be performed for the first time it may be possible to conduct pilot runs of the new operation–and from these runs useful estimates of the learning constant may be made.

ABSOLUTE PRECISION IMPOSSIBLE

With respect to the value of K in a given production run we must observe that it is practically impossible to develop absolutely precise estimates. However, the accountants, budget executives, and engineers who work cooperatively to prepare cost projections usually can specify K with sufficient precision to provide, on the average, a usable learning effect description.

Incorporation of the learning effect in the budgetary process introduces a complexity somewhat greater than when standard costs are utilized. The non-linear relationships explicit in learning curve theory require some added sophistication; effective use of the non-linear cost function is a skill that the budget executive should acquire. The budget executive should be competent to select and apply relevant learning models to those costs which should reflect a significant learning effect and to incorporate them in a budget along with costs that do *not* involve a learning effect. To do this, another classification of costs based upon learning-effect theory should be added to the system.

HOW TO BUDGET

For example, consider the problem of budgeting by quarters. Let us assume that in each quarter 100 units of a particular new product will be produced. In the first quarter costs of production subject to the learning effect will be higher than they will be, say, in the fourth quarter. Assuming stable quarterly production, it would be unrealistic to allocate the total estimated manufacturing costs for the year in equal amounts to each quarter should some of those costs involve a learning effect. Rather, the learning-curve costs should be separately evaluated and projected by quarter and then combined with those costs not subject to the learning effect. Consequently, the resultant budget variances are apt to be more useful as instruments of effective managerial control. The same procedure should be applied by weeks if budget variances are reported in that time dimension. Budgeting learning-effect costs in this way serves to explain to management many mysteriously occurring variances whose causes are not suggested by the conventional variance analysis. It is also possible to compute a "learning-effect variance" to measure whether incurred costs subject to the learning effect reflect an acceptable level of improvement in the performance of the activity.

To appreciate the potential influence of the learning effect on managerial decisions, consider the implications in a situation where standard or budget costs have not incorporated the learning effect. Significant variations are apt to be reported, creating concern and misunderstanding by the management. The management might be provoked to unwise decisions (such as overpricing a new product) that application of learning-curve theory could have prevented. High costs during the early production period also may be accepted as representative and used as a basis for budget projections, thereby tending to deprive the firm of potential cost reductions due to the learning-curve effect.

When budgeting for the learning effect it is important to identify other factors that affect learning-curve costs. Some of these factors tend to offset, and thereby submerge the learning-curve effect. Inflation and price changes affecting specific resource inputs may escalate the cost of material or labor as much as 15 per cent in a single year. In some situations it might be desirable to develop an index of prices to compensate for inflation and price changes in the cost estimation models.

Several uses of cost data that have been adjusted for the learning effect were suggested in the preceding paragraphs. The use of cost data adjusted for the learning effect potentially can also enhance the accuracy of cost-volume-profit analyses and provide more realism in the establishment of the pricing policies of the firm.

To illustrate in moderate detail one application of cost data (adjusted for the learning effect) in the development of pricing policy assume a fact situation in which a firm was preparing a bid on a contract to produce diesel engines. There was a strong possibility of a follow-on production run. The learning effect was substantial, but the firm was not aware of the learning effect and other firms with which it was competing for the contract presumably *were* aware of this effect.[2]

The Sampson Machine and Tool Company was a custom machine and tool manufacturer. The company was preparing a bid for a production contract for eight large diesel engines incorporating newly designed features. There was a strong possibility of a follow-on order for eight more. John Brown, manufacturing cost analyst, developed manufacturing cost estimates for the engine contract based on standard costs. His estimate was:

First engine direct costs	$ 200,000
Each subsequent engine, direct costs	180,000
Total direct costs	1,460,000
Conversion costs and profit at 100 per cent of direct costs	1,460,000
Total bid, first contract	$2,920,000
Total bid, second contract	$2,900,000

Glen Campbell, director of marketing services, was concerned when he heard (reliably) that a competing firm was planning to submit a bid of $2,500,000 for the first contract and $2,000,000 for the second contract. These bids were far below the prices that Mr. Brown felt Sampson would have to obtain in order to realize an acceptable profit.

Mr. Campbell felt that "something" had been overlooked in preparing the Sampson bid. "Surely," he said, "it doesn't cost as much to make the eighth unit as it costs to make the first or second unit, and our figures don't take that into account."

"You may be right," said Brown. "We have never been too successful in bidding on high-cost, low-volume production contracts, either. However, we have quoted average costs." The two men agreed to call in Tom Sawyer, a quantitative analysis specialist from the engineering department. After reviewing the situation, they asked him to "analyze the facts and let us have your suggestions."

Within two days Mr. Sawyer was back. "Look," he told them, "here are some cost figures from the Robbins contract, which was similar to this diesel affair. Our direct costs on the first unit were $34,000, and for the second unit, $26,800, and so on. Now, as I see it, approximately $24,000 of the costs on the first unit were subject to the learning effect, which means that they decreased as experience was gained. Let's call these our "conditional" costs, that is, costs subject to the learning effect. I estimate there were $16,700 conditional costs on the second Robbins unit, and so on down to $6,750 on the twelfth and last unit. Note here that all these points fall in essentially a straight line on this log-log paper."

"What about the costs not subject to this learning effect?" asked Brown. "What happens to them?"

"They just stay about the same; they aren't particularly affected by experience. Now the interesting thing is that I plotted this straight line on the log-log paper with conditional costs against total units produced for several other recent contracts, and each time I got a line with a slope of about –0.7."

"Are you implying that the slope of the line for conditional costs versus total production on our diesel contract would be the same?" asked Campbell.

"Yes, and I have assumed a slope of –0.7 in preparing this other graph (Figure 1) for the diesel contract," Sawyer answered. "I assumed that the first-unit cost would be $200,000 in direct costs; that $20,000 of direct costs would not be subject to the learning effect; and that none of the conversion costs and profit would be subject to the learning effect."

Sawyer continued: "Note that the vertical axis is in dollars of cost per engine produced. The horizontal axis is scaled in engines produced. The line intercepts the vertical axis at $180,000, which is the avoidable direct cost on the first engine. The line was plotted by computing the conditional direct cost of the first, second, fourth, eighth, and sixteenth units. Each of these was computed as 0.7 of the cost immediately preceding it. The figures on the other sheet (Figure 2) summarize the computation of bids from the graphs."

Conditional direct costs on unit	1	$ 180,000
	2	126,000
	3	102,000
	4	88,200
	5	78,000
(Read from graph)	6	71,000
	7	65,000
	8	61,740
		771,940
Unconditional direct costs on 8 units		160,000
Subtotal		931,940
Conversion costs and profit		931,940
Total Bid First Contract		$1,863,880

Conditional direct costs on unit	9	$ 57,500
	10	54,500
	11	52,000
	12	49,500
	13	47,300
(Read from graph)	14	46,000
	15	44,000
	16	43,200
Subtotal		394,000
Unconditional direct costs on 8 units		160,000
Subtotal		554,000
Conversion costs and profit		554,000
Total Bid Second Contract		$1,108,000

FIGURE 2.

After glancing at the sheet (Figure 2), Campbell said: "Does this mean that you are prepared to suggest what our bid prices should be?"

"Obviously," Sawyer responded, "these are suggested bids that I have developed, and the bids of $1,863,880 and $1,108,000 will beat the competition's bids of $2,500,000 and $2,000,000, and we would still do okay on the profits. In fact, if the information about the competitive bids is reliable, and if those would be the low bids without Sampson, sound bidding strategy would indicate that the bids I have computed could be inflated somewhat to provide additional profit and less money left on the table. You should bear in mind that the costs will not behave this way because a learning model indicates they should, but that the model describes objectively an observed phenomenon. It would be up to us to meet the learning-curve targets."

FOOTNOTES

1. "ln x" is the logarithm to the base e of x, i.e., the natural logarithm of x.
2. This illustration is based on a case prepared by one of the authors and appearing in *Short Cases in Managerial Accounting*, Prentice-Hall, Inc., 1970.

How Should Costs Be Determined?

The method for computing costs for purposes of determining the comparative costs of alternative courses of action or for comparing costs with benefits can have an important effect on the results. Should costs be determined on the basis of fully allocating all applicable costs or should they be determined on the basis of including only the incremental costs incident to a change? The method used normally assumes the greatest importance in costing an additional activity or in measuring the savings which would result from discontinuance of an existing activity.

The following sketch provides a useful as well as entertaining insight into some of the considerations involved in this issue.

WHAT PRICE PROGRESS

In discussing the costs incident to various types of operations, the analogy was drawn of the Restaurant which adds a rack of peanuts to the counter, intending to pick up a little additional profit in the usual course of business. This analogy was attacked as an over-simplification. However, the accuracy of the analogy is evident when one considers the actual problem faced by the Restauranteur (Joe) as revealed by his Accountant-Efficiency-Expert.

Eff Ex: Joe; you said you put in these peanuts because some people ask for them, but do you realize what this rack of peanuts is *costing* you?

Joe: It ain't gonna cost. 'Sgonna be a profit. Sure, I hadda pay $25 for a fancy rack to holda bags, but the peanuts cost 6¢ a bag and I sell 'em for 10¢. Figger I sell 50 bags a week to start. It'll take 12½ weeks to cover the cost of the rack. After that I gotta clear profit of 4¢ a bag. The more I sell, the more I make.

EDITORS' NOTE: The author of this article is unknown. It has been previously published in several sources including *GAO Review* (Fall, 1969), pp. 47–49.

Eff Ex: That is an antiquated and completely unrealistic approach, Joe. Fortunately, modern accounting procedures permit a more accurate picture
which reveals the complexities involved.

Joe: Huh?

Eff Ex: To be precise, those peanuts must be integrated into your entire
operation and be allocated their appropriate share of business overhead. They must share a proportionate part of your expenditures for
rent, heat, light, equipment depreciation, decorating, salaries for your
waitresses, cook,——

Joe: The *cook*? What'sa he gotta do wit' a peanuts? He don't even know I
got 'em!

Eff Ex: Look, Joe, the cook is in the kitchen, the kitchen prepares the food,
the food is what brings people in here, and the people ask to buy
peanuts. *That's* why you must charge a portion of the cook's wages,
as well as a part of your own salary to peanut sales. This sheet contains
a carefully calculated cost analysis which indicates the peanut operation should pay exactly $1,278 per year toward these general overhead
costs.

Joe: The peanuts? $1,278 a year for overhead? The Nuts?

Eff Ex: It's really a little more than that. You also spend money each week to
have the windows washed, to have the place swept out in the mornings,
keep soap in the washroom and provide free cokes to the police. That
raises the total to $1,313 per year.

Joe: (Thoughtfully) But the peanut salesman said I'd make money—put
'em on the end of the counter, he said—and get 4¢ a bag profit——.

Eff Ex: (With a sniff) He's not an accountant. Do you actually know what the
portion of the counter occupied by the peanut rack is worth to you?

Joe: Ain't worth nothing—no stool there—just a dead spot at the end.

Eff Ex: The modern cost picture permits no dead spots. Your counter contains
60 square feet and your counter business grosses $15,000 a year.
Consequently, the square foot of space occupied by the peanut rack
is worth $250 per year. Since you have taken that area away from
general counter use, you must charge the value of the space to the
occupant.

Joe: You mean I gotta add *$250 a year more* to the *peanuts*?

Eff Ex: Right. That raises their share of the general operating costs to a grand
total of $1,563 per year. Now then, if you sell 50 bags of peanuts per
week, these allocated costs will amount to 60¢ per bag.

Joe: WHAT?

Eff Ex: Obviously, to that must be added your purchase price of 6¢ per bag, which brings the total to 66¢. So you see, by selling peanuts at 10¢ per bag, you are losing 56¢ on every sale.

Joe: Somethin's crazy!

Eff Ex: Not at all! Here are the *figures*. They *prove* your peanut operation cannot stand on its own feet.

Joe: (Brightening) Suppose I sell *lotsa* peanuts—thousand bags a week 'stead of fifty?

Eff Ex: (Tolerantly) Joe, you don't understand the problem. If the volume of peanut sales increases, our operating costs will go up—you'll have to handle more bags, with more time, more depreciation, more everything. The basic principle of accounting is firm on that subject; "The Bigger the Operation the More General Overhead Costs that Must be Allocated." No. Increasing the volume of sales won't help.

Joe: Okay. You so smart, *you* tell *me* what I gotta do.

Eff Ex: (Condescendingly) Well—you could first reduce operating expenses.

Joe: How?

Eff Ex: Move to a building with cheaper rent. Cut salaries. Wash the windows bi-weekly. Have the floor swept only on Thursday. Remove the soap from the washrooms. Decrease the square foot value of your counter. For example, if you can cut your expenses 50 percent, that will reduce the amount allocated to peanuts from $1,563 to $781.50 per year, reducing the cost to 36¢ per bag.

Joe: (Slowly). That's better?

Eff Ex: Much, much better. However, even then you would lose 26¢ per bag if you charge only 10¢. Therefore, you must also raise your selling price. If you want a net profit of 4¢ per bag you would have to charge 40¢.

Joe: (Flabbergasted) You mean even after I cut operating costs 50 percent I still gotta charge 40¢ for a 10¢ bag of peanuts? Nobody's that nuts about nuts! Who'd buy 'em?

Eff Ex: That's a secondary consideration. The point is, at 40¢ you'd be selling at a price based upon a true and proper evaluation of your then reduced costs.

Joe: (Eagerly) Look! I gotta better idea. Why don't I just throw the nuts out—put 'em in a ash can?

Eff Ex: Can you afford it?

Joe: Sure. All I got is about 50 bags of peanuts—cost about three bucks—so I lose $25 on the rack, but I'm outa this nutsy business and no more grief.

Eff Ex: (Shaking head) Joe it isn't that simple..You are *in* the peanut business! The minute you throw those peanuts out you are adding $1,563 of annual overhead to the *rest* of your operation. Joe—be realistic—*can you afford to do that?*

Joe: (Completely crushed) It'sa unbelievable! Last week I was a make money. Now I'm in a trouble—justa because I think peanuts on a counter is gonna bring me some extra profit—justa because I believe 50 bags of peanuts a week is a easy.

Eff Ex: (With raised eyebrow) That is the object of modern cost studies, Joe—to dispel those false illusions.

Accounting Analysis for Short-Run Decisions— Pricing Policies

INTRODUCTION

Marketing decisions are the most crucial and most difficult decisions made by firms. There are great differences among firms regarding how accounting data are used in making these decisions. In some firms, pricing and promotion decisions are derived directly from accounting cost figures using some heuristic (that is, a rule-of-thumb). In other firms costs are ignored completely. In these firms a subjective assessment of the market is the only information used for marketing decisions. The readings in this section point out that an effective approach to marketing decisions would require a simultaneous consideration of accounting data and projections of market demand functions under different external and internal situations.

The pricing decision is the principal marketing decision. The subject of price theory in economics has developed an elegant basis for pricing to achieve maximum profits assuming different levels of competition in the market. A brief review of some of this theory is presented next, and it is followed by a discussion of its implications (and its weaknesses) in practical decision situations.

First, consider a firm selling a product in a perfectly competitive market. In this case no pricing decision need be made. All units produced can be sold at the prevailing market price. The accounting cost data, however, become important for setting the quantity to be produced. With fixed capacity a point is reached where the cost of producing one extra unit (i.e., the marginal cost) is greater than the selling price. Production should be set at a level such that the marginal cost of the last unit is not greater than the selling price, P_1, or at Q_1, in the following graph:

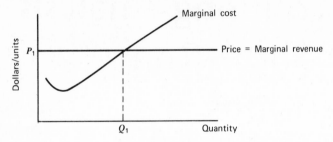

If the firm sells a product that is perceived as having some unique qualities it has a potential for monopoly profits. The marginal revenue curve is no longer a horizontal line; the quantity produced and sold will be a function of the price charged. In this case both the price charged and the quantity produced are dependent on the cost and revenue functions. The quantity produced (Q_1) is that where marginal cost equals marginal revenue, and the price charged (P_1) is the average revenue at that production quantity:

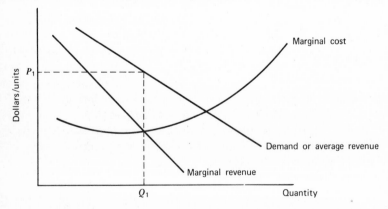

Despite the well-developed theory, applying price theory in practice is extremely difficult. The three main reasons for the difficulties are uncertainty, exogenous (nonprice) influences on the quantity sold, and actions of competition.

Price theory has been developed under the assumption of perfect knowledge of future costs and revenues. Obviously this assumption is not true in real situations. Prediction of demand and marginal costs is an extremely difficult and possibly expensive task. Demand functions are especially hard to determine, but even the cost functions create some difficulties. For instance, accountants often accept variable cost as an approximation of marginal cost. The same variable cost is applied to a whole range of production levels, usually to all relevant production levels. This may be a useful assumption for many decision-making situations, but it is inconsistent with the use of marginal costs in price theory. The difficulties in determining marginal cost and demand functions are partly responsible for the use of heuristics rather than economic theory in setting prices.

Another weakness of price theory in a practical setting is that it separates the pricing decision from other marketing decisions. There is a necessary interaction between pricing, promotion, sales force deployment, and other related policies. When price theory assumes that demand (and thus the quantity produced and sold) is a function of price alone, it ignores all of these other influences. Optimizing the marketing strategy requires a simultaneous consideration of all these aspects. Because the conceptual and modeling ability of people is limited, a complete consideration of all these aspects is quite expensive at best, and it is probably next to impossible in the real world. Hence, simple heuristics are generally used for all these marketing decisions.

The final complication to price theory is competitive action. Any demand function is based on assumptions about the prices and strategies of competitors. However, their actions will depend on the actions of all other firms (including the firm making the pricing decision), and consequently a decision cannot be made without assessing the impact of that decision on the demand function. Again, optimization becomes so complex that heuristics become welcome alternatives.

Despite these shortcomings, price theory provides a good basis on which to judge alternative heuristic pricing models, but price theory alone is not sufficient. It is basically a model of short-run optimization. A realistic pricing policy sets prices applicable in each short-run period after taking into consideration all the long-run implications for the firm. Therefore, pricing models must be looked at as part of both the long- and short-run planning models as well as basic decision models.

In *An Evaluation of Product Pricing Models* Brenner describes the basic alternative pricing models that are used. He brings out the considerations that enter into the selection of a pricing model and briefly mentions the role of costs in pricing decisions. After describing the alternatives, he presents a brief evaluation of each.

One aspect of the role of costs in pricing decisions that is ignored by Brenner is the prediction of competitors' prices. This is especially important when prices are in the form of bids for a given job. If a firm knows its own cost behavior and knows the significant differences between its production process and that of a competitor, it can more easily predict the bids of competitors and therefore tailor its bid accordingly.

An important question that appears to be in the back of Brenner's mind throughout the article is the role of the accountant in the pricing process. This question is not resolved in the article or in practice. Accountants obviously are involved with cost determination and estimation. Should they also participate in demand forecasts? Does the accountant even need to know the pricing model that is used? In thinking about these questions, consider the role of the accountant as one who optimizes the inputs into decision models. In that role it is mandatory for the accountant to at least understand both the prediction model used for forecasting market demand and the decision model used for price determination.

Oxenfeldt and Baxter, in *Approaches to Pricing: Economist Versus Accountant,* discuss more specifically how costs can be useful in making pricing decisions. After first presenting objections to cost-plus pricing and showing why marginal costs are more appropriate for pricing from a theoretical point of view, the authors put forward their preferred pricing model. This model does not ignore costs, but the role of the accountant is different from the one traditionally taken. Instead of being a producer of historical cost, the accountant is charged with predicting opportunity cost. If cost-plus pricing is a surrogate for an opportunity cost pricing model, it may provide acceptable decisions. If cost-plus has no relationship to opportunity costs, its use in pricing is highly questionable.

An Evaluation of Product Pricing Models

Vincent C. Brenner

INTRODUCTION

Probably no one single marketing tool is so critical from both an economic and social standpoint as price. Yet, as important as it is, less is probably known about how an industry establishes prices than is known about any other single marketing tool.[1]

The purpose of this paper is to analyze various aspects of pricing. No attempt is made to discover how an industry actually does reach its pricing decision, but rather, an investigation is made of several models, presently set forth in the literature. This investigation is made in order to determine which single method is most theoretically sound, yet applicable in practical situations. To be theoretically sound the method must take into consideration all factors which affect a pricing decision. To be applicable in practical situations it is necessary that these factors be quantified so that their effects on the pricing decision can reasonably be determined.

The first section of this paper is concerned with setting forth those factors which have a strong influence on pricing decisions. These factors will be described and analyzed in order to determine how they may affect a pricing decision. The next section sets forth several pricing models describing them and finally evaluating them in terms of their comprehensiveness in considering those factors which affect the pricing decision.

SOURCE: Reprinted with permission from *Managerial Planning* (July-August, 1971), pp. 17-26.

177

FACTORS AFFECTING PRICING DECISIONS

There are many factors which come into play when pricing decisions are to be made. The list of factors presented are those which, in general, will exert the greatest influence upon pricing decisions. The factors to be considered are: overall company goals, costs, consumer demand, competition, legal influences, and social responsibilities. The order of their presentation is not intended to reflect their degree of influence. For any decision their arrangement, according to importance for that decision, may change. Thus, no specific ordering can be made applicable to all pricing decisions.

OVERALL COMPANY GOALS

> Since pricing is not an end in itself, but a means to an end, an explicit formulation of the company's pricing objective is essential. The fundamental guides to pricing are the company's overall goals.[2]

In cases where overall company goals are specifically stated and well defined they may become synonymous with pricing objectives. For purposes of this paper no distinction between the two will be attempted, rather, the impact of company objectives on pricing is of major concern.

Pricing objectives can be broken down into three major areas:

- *Target return objective*—This may include desiring a specific return or investment, sales or costs.
- *Profit maximization objective*—This is usually desiring large return on investment, profitable growth, or all the traffic will bear.
- *Nonprofit oriented objectives*—These may be expansion or growth, maintaining or increasing market share, preserving a status quo position, etc.

Thus, it can be seen that a company may choose among a wide range of pricing objectives. In a study conducted of twenty large corporations it was found that 50% of the firms had pricing objectives of a target rate of return.[3] Maintaining or increasing market share was the objective of 30% of the firms.

In most cases a firm will have both primary and secondary pricing objectives. A target rate of return might be of primary concern while increasing market share is secondary. Thus the firm will try to reach its target return, upon doing so, it may alter its price or some other variable to increase its market share.

Pricing objectives play a very important role in pricing decisions. If the company's objectives are to be met, pricing decisions must be made in light of those objectives. For example, a company wishing to increase its market share would not do so if it were to price above other sellers in the market; other things being equal.

Primary pricing objectives are generally long run in nature while pricing decisions themselves are short run. Since the conditions surrounding a pricing decision are in a constant state of flux, it is an exceptional situation to have a pricing decision remain in tack for a long length of time. Perhaps the best example of an exception is the five cent candy bar. In this case the price is customary or expected by the buyers. The manufacturer considers price as a fixed factor and adjustments are made through other factors in the marketing mix, such as product.

Since pricing decisions are generally short run in nature their effects on long run objectives command the consideration of those objectives. A firm with a long run objective of a target rate of return will find that in the short run, if it tried to attain its return, it may be forced from the market by competition. Thus, the firm may find it necessary to price below its target rate to retain its share of the market, which will better ensure achievement of its long run objectives.

Any decision process requires the implementation of some sort of guide(s) to action. Overall company goals fulfill this need in pricing decisions. To attempt reaching a price decision without them would be analogous to selecting a price at random.

COSTS

The importance of costs in pricing decisions seem to be self evident. If a firm does not price so as to meet costs, it will go into bankruptcy. This approach is highly oversimplified. What costs must be covered by price? Do prices have to cover costs at all times? To answer these questions it is necessary to become more specific as to what role costs play in pricing.

Types of Costs

In general pricing decisions deal with two types of costs; full costs and incremental or marginal costs. Full costs may be defined as the total costs expended in order to get the product to the point of sale. This includes total production, marketing and administrative costs. Incremental cost, on the other hand, is the expenditure required to get one additional unit of product to the point of sale. In accounting terminology full cost includes both direct and indirect costs while incremental costs includes only direct costs. Direct costs are those which can be traced to each unit of product, whereas, indrect costs lack this quality.

Role of Costs in Pricing

Costs may play various roles for pricing decisions. "The basic use of costs in pricing is . . . to forecast the profit consequences of various alternative prices."[4]

Thus, once a price has been set, cost should be used to determine if that price, with its expected volume, will bear sufficient profits in light of the firm's objectives.

Joel Dean also points out that there are cases when costs play a more direct role in pricing.[5] Among these are (1) product tailoring; (2) refusal pricing; (3) monopsony pricing; and (4) public utility pricing.

Product tailoring is closely akin to purely competitive markets where the individual seller cannot affect the market price; he must take the price as given. In this case the seller knows for what he can sell his product and must adjust his costs accordingly if he is to make a profit. For example, if a seller's original cost estimates are above selling price he will have to shave costs rather than raise his price if entry into that market is desired.

Refusal pricing refers to specially designed products manufactured for a single buyer. In this instance the product may be priced on the basis of incremental costs plus a gross margin which is equivalent to what the producer could get if he chose the next best alternative. This price would at least set a floor price. This method assumes that the producer has other avenues available in order to make use of his facilities. What if the producer had no alternatives available, or in other words, he had idle capacity? Here again, incremental costs play an important role. Any price, in this case, which is above incremental costs would contribute to overhead and/or profits. Thus, a producer with idle capacity would be better off, in the short run, if he could get a price greater than incremental costs.

Monopsony pricing is concerned with the situation where a producer has only one buyer. Here, the producer's price must be less than what it would cost the buyer to produce the product himself. "Thus the seller's cost in this kind of pricing is only an indicator of the relevant basis for setting the price that will keep competition out."[6]

Public utility pricing is determined by costs. In this case it is the full or average costs that are most relevant. Since utilities are regulated and held to reasonable returns it becomes necessary to use full costs as a basis for pricing decisions. If utilities were to use incremental costs, plus their profit percentage there is a strong possibility that they would not cover average costs and eventually would leave the industry or have to be subsidized by the government.

Another area which relates closely to public utility pricing is the use of costs for price justification. In this situation costs may not play a direct role in setting price, but it would play the major role in justifying a price, once set. This area has become increasingly important since the enactment of the Robinson-Patman Act.

Costs play an important role in any pricing decision, whether they be considered directly or indirectly. At a very minimum costs should be used to evaluate different prices and their effect on profitability. In other cases costs may be the starting point of the pricing process.

There are cases where prices are set below or equal to cost as long run policy. This may be so where a firm produces complementary products. For example, razor blade companies may sell razors at, or below cost in order to sell razor blades, their primary products. Even in these cases cost is important in determining the profitability of the firm as a whole.

CONSUMER DEMAND

General Characteristics

In any pricing decision it is imperative that the demand for the product be considered. Demand sets forth the relationship between price and consumer behavior.

> Two economic principles state this relationship in a manner helpful to marketing executives. The first is the "law of demand," which states that more units will be purchased at low prices than at high prices. The second . . . is known as "price elasticity of demand." Price elasticity of demand describes in a precise quantitative manner the sensitivity of buyers to changes in price.[7]

The law of demand principle assumes a rational and knowledgeable buyer. This is not always the case in a real world situation. Where price is the only comparable feature between products the opposite may hold true. D. S. Tull and others conducted a study on the relationship between price and imputed quality which supports this.

> The findings . . . strongly suggest that consumers rely heavily upon price as a predictor of quality when there is a substantial degree of uncertainty involved in the purchase decision.[8]

Thus, the law of demand does not hold true in all cases, but generally we can assume that it does. A firm with a given price can sell more if it reduces its price and vice versa.

The second concept, price elasticity, enables a seller to determine what the effect of a change in price will be on demand. If a small cut in prices brings about a large increase in sales, we say the demand is elastic. Demand is inelastic when a substantial cut in prices is required to increase sales. Although the concept is referred to as "price" elasticity other factors affect the elasticity of demand.

> There is strong reason to believe that the sensitivity of sales to a given percentage change in price will vary from brand to brand and from one local market to another.[9]

The degree of product differentiation may be a strong factor in elasticity. If products are homogeneous, a price reduction may bring about a greater increase in sales than if the products are highly differentiated. The effect of price changes on demand will also differ among different market segments. A price reduction in a high income segment will generally not have as great an effect on relative demand as would the reduction in a low income market segment.

DETERMINATION OF DEMAND

In making a pricing decision, a firm must be able to determine the demand for its product in order to substantiate the price set. Several methods of determining demand have been set forth in the literature. Joel Dean set forth the steps to be taken when pricing a new product. These are:

1. . . . Find out whether or not the product will sell at all, assuming that the price is set within the competitive range.
2. . . . determine the competitive price range
3. . . . try to guess the probable sales volume at two or three possible prices within the range
4. . . . consider the possibility of relation by manufacturers of displaced substitutes.[10]

This method could apply equally well to existing product pricing by leaving out the first step.

Other methods of determining demand are set forth by Alfred Oxenfeldt.[11] Among these are statistical techniques of multiple correlation. This technique ties together past demand with some closely associated factor. It yields a formula for forecasting future demand based on that factor.

Another method assumes that demand is relating to national income. Here changes in national income are used to estimate changes in demand for a firm's product. More recent methods include personal interviews and test marketing. In these cases the demand is extrapolated from the test market to the firm's total demand for its products.

Thus, there are many ways through which a firm can estimate the demand for its product. The techniques range from very sophisticated studies to "seat of the pants" guesses. No matter what method is used some sort of demand schedule must be employed in setting product prices.

ROLE OF DEMAND

No matter what the company's pricing objectives may be, demand is one factor to be considered. For any specific price the demand must be known in order to evaluate that price in terms of the company's objectives. For example, if the firm's objective is a specific rate of return on assets, the demand must be known for various prices to determine which price will enable the firm to reach its target rate. Thus, demand is used to narrow down a price range to a specific price which will best enable the firm to reach its goals.

COMPETITION

> Competition by its very nature tends to set an upper limit on pricing. Whenever a company desires to make any price move it must anticipate the action of its competitors.[12]

This statement is true except in cases where the structure of the market is purely competitive. In this case no one seller can affect the market price and therefore must take the price given. In other market structures the consideration of competition must play a prominent role. These other market structures are the oligopoly and the monopoly.

OLIGOPOLY

There are two types of oligopolistic structures which are characterized by homogeneous and heterogeneous products. In the homogeneous oligopoly there are few sellers each selling a product which the consumer views as being equal in quality or value. This being the case, the buyer would have no reason to pay more than the lowest priced product of the homogeneous group. A price reduction by one seller may greatly increase his sales at the expense of the other sellers, assuming they took no retaliatory action. Usually this would not be the case. A price cut by one seller which increased his sales, would generally induce retaliation from competitors.

> As a result, they would reduce price only if they thought they would gain from such behavior even though their competitors matched the price reduction.[13]

In the heterogeneous oligopoly the products of the different sellers are viewed as different in quality or value. A seller may have a range of prices within which he may operate without retaliation by competitors. Above this price range customers may be lost to competition, while below the range customers might be drawn from competitors.

> The amount of variation in price depends on the degree of difference that customers believe exists between individual products, and on the importance of such differences to the customer.[14]

Thus, competition in a heterogeneous oligopoly must be considered in pricing decisions. The firm may price within the range allowed by its product differentiation without fear of retaliation by competitors. In setting a price outside this range, the reaction of competitors must be considered in determining the profitability of that price.

MONOPOLY

In the case of the monopoly and pricing decisions one might say there is no need to consider competitors because there are none. This is true to some extent. In the short run a company, which is a monopoly, can charge the highest price the market will bear for its product without the fear of losing sales to competitors. The importance of competition under this structure is not actual competitors but potential competitors. Pricing decisions in this case must take into consideration the inducement it may give others to enter the field. Thus, in the short run, a monopoly may charge high prices generating large profits, but in the long run this practice would induce others to enter the market, thereby, reducing the monopoly's long run profit potential.

Since the majority of market structures in the United States are oligopolies, it is easy to see the importance of competition in pricing decisions.

LEGAL INFLUENCES

There are many ways in which the government can influence prices. Direct price setting, public utility regulation, anti-trust laws, limitations on competition and laws restricting supply are the major ways in which government has influenced pricing decisions. It is beyond the scope of this paper to consider all these different methods. "The law that most directly affects the prices businessmen can charge is the Robinson-Patman Act...."[15] Thus, the provisions of this act are our major concern.

The most important change that the Robinson-Patman Act made over the Clayton Act was the prohibition of discrimination that would "... injure, destroy, or prevent competition with any person who either grants or knowingly receives the benefit of such discrimination or with customers of either of them." The specific types of transactions made unlawful by this act are:

1. Transactions in which goods of similar quality are sold to two firms at different prices.
2. Transactions in which, as a result of these price differences, the buyer paying the higher price has been injured or in which it seems reasonably possible that he will be injured. Injury need not take the form of bankruptcy or severe financial embarassment; the loss of sales is enough to constitute injury.

3. Transactions in which the price difference is not attributable to corresponding cost differences arising from special economics in delivery or to economics resulting from differences in the size of the order.
4. Transactions in which conditions have not altered during the interval between the two sales in a manner that would account for a change in price.
5. Transactions in which the lower price did not result from necessity to meet competitor's price.[16]

Thus, pricing decisions must also take into account any government legislation to determine if the price set is within legal bounds. If this is not done the seller may receive the brunt of repercussions by the government.

SOCIAL RESPONSIBILITY

In setting prices a firm must take into consideration the impact of that price on society as a whole. Generally, this factor will come into play only when the seller sells large quantities of goods on a nationwide scale. In these cases the seller should not set a price which may be considered detrimental to society as a whole. The social factor has gained increasing importance, especially in recent years. This is a result of the desire to maintain price stability in the economy. A price increase by a seller whose product is widely used in the economy may find repercussions from society, especially if this increase is made in the face of inflation. Recent occurrences in the steel and aluminum industries have exemplified this fact. A steel price rise during the Kennedy administration met such strong opposition that it was cancelled. The aluminum industry was also pressed into cancelling a price hike. The Johnson administration felt that the price increase was inflationary and therefore detrimental to society as a whole.

It, therefore, has become increasingly important for firms to consider the effects their price will have on the economy as a whole. Recent history has pointed this out very emphatically.

APPROACHES TO PRICING

Now that the critical factors that must be considered in a pricing decision have been set forth, consideration will be given to the price decision itself. In this section an examination of different techniques of pricing is set forth. These techniques are restricted to a sample of those from the economic, accounting and statistical areas. The first part of this section is descriptive in nature in order to give an understanding of the working of the different techniques. The second part presents an evaluation of the techniques using the factors set forth in the first section of this paper as a guide.

DESCRIPTION OF THE TECHNIQUES

Economic

The basic economic techniques for pricing under different market structures revolve around the same principle. The basic economic analysis assumes the firm's objective is to maximize profits. Given this objective, and that the firm knows its demand curve, the economic approach determines a price by finding that price at which marginal revenue equals marginal costs. The price where this condition holds true is the point of maximum profit for the firm.

Geometrically it would look as follows:

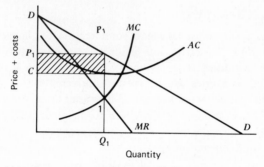

On the x axis is shown price and cost in dollars, while the y axis shows the quantity of output. The line DD is the demand curve for the seller and, as stated before, is assumed to be known. MR is the marginal revenue line, it represents the additional revenue obtained from each additional unit of output. The curve MC is the marginal cost curve representing the additional cost of producing each additional unit of output. The AC curve represents the average cost per unit of the product over the range of quantities. If we look at the point where $MR = MC$ (point 1), their point of intersection, and draw a line, perpendicular to the y axis, through this point and upwards to meet the demand curve we can determine the proper price. The appropriate price is P_1. How do we know this is the price that will yield maximum profits? The profits at this point can be determined by comparing our average cost with the price. The shaded area P_1ABC represents the profit. If we were to set the price above or below P_1, we would find that the profit area would be less than at P_1. Thus P_1 must be the optimum price for maximizing the firm's profits.

The basic notion of marginal costs equaling marginal revenue to determine price is common under all industry structures. In pure competition, where price is given, the analysis is used to determine what level of output is most profitable for the firm. Under pure competition the mechanics of the approach may differ but the underlying theory is the same. Applying the basic theory to monopolies and oligopolies closely approximates the geometrics previously presented. The only difference between the two will be their demand curve. In the oliogopoly solution the demand curve is generally said to be kinked because of competition. The economic approaches do take into account competition, such as in the case of an oligopoly. In this case actions by existing or new competitors may be represented by a shift in the demand curve.

The economic approach may be applied to any market structure. To be able to employ this approach, it is necessary that the firm know its demand at various prices and maintain a pricing objective of maximizing profits.

Accounting (Cost-Plus)

The basic premise around which accounting techniques justify their type of pricing is that cost must be covered.

> One complete pricing method is used more commonly than all others combined. This method, variously called "cost-plus pricing" and "average cost pricing," calls for the addition to some base cost of a margin to cover profit.[17]

The firm, in this approach, computes its total average cost per unit of product then to this adds the desired profit margin. In its most simple algebraic form it looks as follows:

$$Price = \frac{Total\ Cost + Profit}{Quantity}$$

From this basic form have evolved numerous attempts to come up with a more meaningful pricing formula. What amount of profit should be plugged into the formula? If the firm's pricing objective is a specific rate of return (15%) on assets we can modify the formula as follows:

$$Price = \frac{Total\ Costs + (15\% \times Assets)}{Quantity}$$

The problem with this sort of formula is that it does not take into consideration those costs and elements of capital employment which vary with volume. Thus, there have been those who have tried to overcome this by refining the formula. These points can be overcome by the following formula.

$$Net\ Unit\ Price = \frac{(C' + UV + RF)/V}{1 - RW}$$

The symbols indicate the following:

C'—fixed costs
U—variable cost per unit

R—percentage return desired on capital employed
F—fixed portion of capital employed, e.g., property, plant and equipment
W—variable capital employed expressed as a percentage of sales volume
V—annual sales volume in units[18]

Thus, this formula fulfills the objections concerning variable costs and variations in capital employed. Even at this there still remains the basic flaw of the majority of the cost plus pricing techniques, that being the ignoring of demand. To overcome this flaw other cost oriented approaches have been developed.

As was stated in the first section of this paper the major role of costs in a pricing decision is that of determining the effects on profitability of the different prices. With the problems of demand and costs in mind, Robert Beyer has developed a different method of the cost approach to pricing.[19] Instead of using costs and desired profit to determine price, he starts with a price and then evaluates its profitability. Essentially his approach can be seen from the following hypothetical example:

Possible prices:	$ 5.00	$ 5.25	$ 4.90
What is volume?	1,100	1,000	800
Sales revenue	$5,500	$5,250	$3,920
Variable costs			
($2/unit)	$2,200	$2,000	$1,600
Gross profit	$3,300	$3,250	$2,320
Fixed costs	$1,500	$1,500	$1,500
Net profit	$1,800	$1,750	$ 820

Thus, we can see that certain specific prices are chosen and that these are used to determine what the volume of sales will be. Demand for the product is considered in this approach and it uses costs properly in the pricing decisions. In a strict sense the last technique cannot be considered a cost-plus pricing approach. Traditionally, cost-plus pricing has referred to the previous approaches presented. It was presented here because it is an approach set forth by an accountant.

The presentation of the cost-plus pricing approaches has in no way been an exhaustive one. Rather, the main purpose here was to set forth the basic characteristic of that approach. "Formulas for cost-plus pricing differ widely among industries and even among firms within an industry."[20]

Statistical (Bayesian)[21]

The difficulties involved in price decisions are many, as one author writes:

> ... pricing decisions necessarily involve considerable guessing—at least about general business conditions, political events, international relationships, climatic conditions, etc., and about the probable response of competitors and customers.[22]

Notice that the need for guessing and probabilities is set forth. The Bayesian approach fulfills this need.

> In highly oversimplified terms, the Bayesian approach to decision-making under uncertainty provides a framework for explicitly working with the economic costs of alternative courses of action, the prior knowledge or judgment of the decision maker, and formal modification of these judgments as additional data are introduced into the problem.[23]

The most distinctive feature of Bayesian statistical analysis is that it employs the use of personalistic interpretation of probabilities. That is, it uses the subjective probabilities placed by management, on the outcomes of different states of nature. These probabilities may later be revised by actual sample evidence.

A detailed description of this approach is beyond the scope of this paper. Rather a very general description will be presented. The following is a description given by Harry V. Roberts.

> Assessments are made of probabilities of events that determine the profitability of alternative actions open to a decision maker. Assessments are also made of profit (more generally, utility) for each possible combination of action and event. For each possible action, expected profit can then be computed, that is, a weighted mean of the possible profits, the weights being the probabilities mentioned above. The action is chosen for which expected profit is highest. The dominating principle of decision, then, is maximization of expected profit (or utility).[24]

The complexity of problems that can be solved by this approach is exemplified by Paul Green's article which presents an application of

> ... the use of Bayesian decision theory in the selection of a "best" pricing policy for a firm in an oligopolistic industry where such factors as demand elasticity, competitive retaliation, threat of future price weakness, and potential entry of new competitors influence the effectiveness of the firm's courses of action.[25]

As a pricing decision tool this approach offers definite advantages over the previous approaches mentioned. The Bayesian method provides for consideration of alternative states of nature and the assigning of prior to subjective probabilities to their occurrence. The method also provides for "testing the sensitivity of the study's outcomes to departures in the basic assumptions."[26]

EVALUATION OF APPROACHES TO PRICING

The point has now been reached where an evaluation of the different approaches to pricing can be made. Presentation has been made of those factors which affect a pricing decision. The general theories of several approaches to pricing have also been presented. Since we know what factors must be considered in a pricing decision, it is necessary that any techniques used in reaching a price decision contain their consideration. It is only in this way a technique can be completely applicable in practical situations. Let us, therefore, turn our attention to an evaluation of the different techniques in terms of their comprehensiveness in dealing with those factors mentioned, which affect pricing decisions.

Economic Approach

There are two basic weaknesses in the economic approach. They are (1) the assumption that the firm's goal is that of profit maximization, and (2) the assumption that the firm's demand curve is known. As was pointed out earlier, it appears that the majority of the firms in this country do not subscribe to the objective of profit maximization, but rather, a specific rate of return. Thus, it can be conjectured that the first assumption will not hold true in the majority of cases. This approach, therefore, does not take into consideration our first factor affecting pricing, overall company goals, except in a few cases.

The economic approach does make full consideration of costs by using both average (full) and marginal costs in its decisions.

Regarding its treatment of demand it assumes that the firm's demand curve is known.

> The traditional demand and supply curves of the economists hardly exist in real life. Thus, the marginal theory tends to build theoretical models on figures that are either incomplete or subject to substantial errors of estimation.[27]

We can, therefore, say that the approach does consider demand although maybe not in an exacting way.

The economic approach also considers competition but can only consider one reaction of competitors. The approach does not consider all possible actions of competitors. Thus, this approach includes the competitive factor, but in a somewhat limited manner.

The last two factors, legal and social influences, are not considered in any explicit manner. It is possible that these could be considered implicitly in the determination of the demand curve, but no evidence of this has been found in current literature on pricing. Even if this were the case, it would appear that explicit consideration should be given, especially when profit maximization is assumed. Under this assumption, more than under other assumed goals, is there the danger of these factors having great influence on the price decision.

Accounting (Cost-Plus)

The imperfections of cost-plus pricing are cited throughout literature.[28] This approach is essentially one which considers the firm's pricing objective to be a specific rate of return. In this sense we can say that it will in the majority of cases take into consideration overall company goals.

The traditional cost-plus approach ignores demand. It does not consider the buyer's needs or willingness to pay, which affect the volume at different prices. The approach involves circular reasoning. It uses volume to determine price and price, in turn, is used to determine sales.

The approach also ignores competition. The formulas do not take into consideration rivals, reactions nor the possibility of the potential competitors entering the market.

Traditionally, cost-plus pricing deals only with average or full costs. As was pointed out in the section under costs, there are times when marginal, rather than full costs, are relevant for pricing decisions. In these cases cost-plus pricing is inadequate, and cannot be said to consider the cost factors to an adequate extent. In times of changing volume it can lead to wrong decisions. If sales are falling, and it is felt that a new price is needed, the cost-plus approach would result in a higher price. With decreasing volume, fixed cost would be spread over fewer units, making the average cost higher. This would result in a higher price, since price is based on average cost. In times of increasing volume the cost-plus formula would indicate a reduction in price.

Legal influences could be considered only in specific cases. Generally, legality with reference to public utilities could be worked into the formula. In this situation the government limits the company to a specific rate of return which is easily worked into the formula. The formula could also be used in cost-plus contracts with governmental agencies. In overall consideration of legal influences, the approach is very weak.

The cost-plus approach also fails to take into consideration the aspects of the firm's social responsibility. The approach provides no means of working this into the formula.

Statistical (Bayesian)

In the past there have been difficulties in applying statistics to marketing problems. As one writer states it "no theoretical bridge existed between 'statistics' and 'business judgment'."[29] Bayesian statistics fulfills this need by explicit use of subjective probabilities in its approach. The problem now is that of application of the approach. Since the approach can make analysis of all the different states of nature surrounding the pricing decision, there develops a large amount of arithmetic detail. In many cases this commands the use of a computer. Many firms lack computer facilities and, therefore, find it difficult to make use of this approach.

Another factor required for its application is a statistician. Again, many firms do not employ statisticians, thus making its application impossible without incurring the cost of hiring someone outside the firm.

A third factor is the general lack of an understanding of the approach by those in the business world. Businessmen are reluctant to employ a technique about which they have little or no knowledge.

Given the general circumstances surrounding the application of the approach, let us turn our attention to its consideration of the factors set forth which affect a pricing decision. As was pointed out earlier, the decision rule for this approach is to choose that alternative which provides the greatest expected profits. This would lead us to believe that the only company goal which this approach considers is that of profit maximization. However, this does not necessarily have to be the goal. Once the expected profits of the different prices are known, other decision criteria may be applied. If the firm's objectives were a specific rate of return on sales or assets, the expected profits of the different prices could be examined to determine which results in the desired rate of return. The approach could also be applied where the objective is to maximize sales. In this case the different prices could be evaluated in terms of which provides the greatest volume of sales. Thus, the approach can be applied under any company goals by the use of different decision criteria.

In consideration of costs the approach is not bound by the use of a specific cost concept, such as full cost. The approach is capable of taking into account any costs which are relevant to the price decision. The approach even goes so far as to use costs of sampling in determining whether or not market surveys, etc. should be conducted in light of expected profits to be derived from a decision. Thus, the Bayesian approach can provide for extensive consideration of costs.

This approach also takes into consideration consumer demand and reaction of competitors at different price levels. Since the approach considers all possible states of nature, it can make estimates of consumer and competitive reaction, to be used in the process of determining an optimal price. Management's probabilities of the occurrence of different events are combined with the probabilities acquired through some type of sampling technique in order to determine expected occurrences of events.

This process can also be used to encompass the influences of governmental and social pressures on the company. Given certain prices, management can be asked to place probabilities on each, concerning what effect these prices will have regarding government and society.

SUMMARY AND CONCLUSIONS

Six important factors that must be considered when making a pricing decision were set forth. These factors were overall company goals, costs, demand, competition, legal influences and social responsibility. The general characteristics of each was described and their role in pricing decisions set forth. Next, several approaches to pricing were analyzed. These approaches were from the general areas of economics, accounting and statistics. The basic theory of each was set forth. Following this an evaluation was made of the various approaches by examining their comprehensiveness in accounting for the factors set forth that influence price decisions. . . .

As was set forth previously, for a pricing technique to be theoretically sound it must take into consideration all the factors affecting a pricing decision. To be applicable, the pricing technique must be able to quantify the effects of the different factors. . . .these is only one approach fulfilling these requirements. This is the statistical or Bayesian approach to pricing. Through the use of management probabilities and data collected from sampling the approach quantifies all those factors which must be considered. Thus, the approach is theoretically sound and applicable in the real world.

The other two approaches cannot be considered theoretically sound because they fail to consider all the relevant factors. The economic approach is applicable to the real world only if the demand curve of the firm is known, which is not often the case. The accounting approach is also, restrictively, applicable to the real world. Even though these last two approaches can be applied, they can be done so only to the extent that management is not concerned with the factors which these techniques do not consider. Thus, it appears that their application is meaningful only in a few cases.

Since we have found that the statistical approach is theoretically sound and also applicable to the real world situations it seems reasonable that this approach should have widespread use. At present this is not the case. The application of this approach is relatively new, thus, there exists a lack of its understanding by those in the business world. Since the approach is the best of those set forth, it seems imperative that businessmen acquire an understanding of it. It is the writer's opinion that as soon as businessmen become more knowledgeable concerning the approach, they will apply it in their business. The resulting effect of this should be better pricing decisions.

FOOTNOTES

1. Richard H. Buskirk, *Principles of Marketing* (New York: Holt, Rinehart and Winston, 1961), p. 385.

2. Joel Dean, *Managerial Economics* (New York: Prentice-Hall, Inc., 1951), p. 399.

3. Robert F. Lanzilloti, "Pricing Objectives in Large Companies," *American Economic Review*, Vol. XLVIII No. 5 (December, 1958), pp. 921–40.

4. Dean, *op. cit.*, p. 454.

5. *Ibid.*, p. 454.

6. *Ibid.*, p. 456.

7. Alfred R. Oxenfeldt, *Pricing for Marketing Executives* (San Francisco: Wadsworth Publishing Company, Inc., 1961), p. 26.

8. D. S. Tull, *et. al.*, "Relationship of Price and Imputed Quality," *Journal of Business*, Vol. 37 (April, 1964), p. 191.

9. Oxenfeldt, *op. cit.*, p. 26.

10. Joel Dean, "Pricing a New Product," *The Controller* (April, 1955), p. 164.

11. Alfred Oxenfeldt, *Industrial Pricing and Market Practices* (New York: Prentice-Hall Inc., 1951), pp. 124–126.

12. Martin Zober, *Marketing Management* (New York: John Wiley & Sons, Inc., 1964), p. 76.

13. Oxenfeldt, *Pricing for Marketing Executives*, p. 38.

14. *Ibid.*, p. 37.

15. *Ibid.*, p. 35.

16. Oxenfeldt, *Industrial Pricing and Market Practices, op. cit.*, pp. 420–21.

17. Oxenfeldt, *Pricing for Marketing Executives*, p. 70.

18. Wayne Keller and William Ferrara, *Management Accounting for Profit Control*, Second Edition (New York: McGraw-Hill Book Company, 1966), p. 570.

19. Robert Beyer, *Profitability Accounting for Planning and Control* (New York: The Ronald Press Company, 1963), pp. 322–23.

20. Dean, *Managerial Economics, op. cit.*, p. 445.

21. For an excellent book on this topic see Robert Schlaifer, *Probability and Statistics for Business Decisions* (New York: McGraw-Hill Book Company, Inc., 1959).

22. Oxenfeldt, *op. cit.*, p. 20.

23. Paul E. Green, "Bayesian Decision Theory in Pricing Strategy," *Journal of Marketing*, Vol. 27 (January 1963), p. 5.

24. Harry V. Roberts, "Bayesian Statistics in Marketing," *Journal of Marketing*, Vol. 27 (January 1963), p. 1.

25. Green, *op. cit.*, p. 5.

26. *Ibid.*, p. 14.

27. N. K. Khalla, "The Art of Product Pricing," *Management Review*, Vol. 53 (June 1964), p. 65.

28. See: *Ibid.*, p. 64; Dean, *op. cit.*, pp. 450–451; Oxenfeldt, *op. cit.*, p. 72; and Charles M. Hewitt, "Pricing–An Area of Increasing Importance," *Business Horizons* (February 1961), p. 109.

29. Roberts, *op. cit.*, p. 4.

Approaches to Pricing: Economist Versus Accountant

Alfred R. Oxenfeldt &
William T. Baxter

This article examines the part played by the cost accountant in fixing a firm's prices, and especially his assumption that cost plus or full cost is a useful and logical basis for price. It also undertakes the difficult task of reconciling the almost flatly contradictory views of the cost accountant and the economic theorist on pricing.

Generalizations about the two professions must, of course, be unsatisfactory. Since the terms "cost accountant" and "economist" cover many persons with a wide-range of views, a short article must omit many desirable qualifications and do injustice to many individuals. However, few who are familiar with both costing and economics would fail to recognize the gulf that often separates the respective approaches to price. It is generally true that the cost accountant fails to state his assumptions about the firm's aims and pays scant attention to demand; he collects cost data and arrives at price by manipulating these. The economist, on the other hand, starts by assuming that the firm is trying to maximize something, for example, profit; he then shows how the firm should study demand as well as cost in an attempt to find this maximum output level.

SOURCE: Reprinted with permission of *Business Horizons* (Winter, 1961), pp. 77–79.

COST-PLUS

The cost-plus procedure is too familiar to need extended description.[1] In the multiproduct firm, the formula for finding the price of a job runs somewhat as follows: (1) find the job's direct costs—mainly material and labor; (2) add a charge for indirect costs (by allocating these overheads as a rate on a unit such as the wages or hours of direct labor, or machine-hours); and (3) add a further sum for profit—often calculated as a percentage of the total under (1) and (2).

Objections to Cost-Plus

It is not hard to ridicule the logic of the cost-plus doctrine. Its "cost" is objectionable on at least three grounds—time, jointness, and opportunity.

Time.   The avoidable cost of any job depends on the firm's degree of commitment at the time in question. Since this may change with each decision and act, a job has not one cost but a range of costs varying with its stage of completion and at best a cost figure can be right at only one stage. The cost accountant's sums, however, are based on historical records that do not change with changing commitments.

Jointness.   A job is normally a joint product in the sense that other jobs use the same resources. The cost of such resources is thus common to many jobs and there is seldom an unimpeachable basis for dividing it among the jobs (since the resulting figures rarely show what will actually be saved if a given job is not done). Yet full cost includes an allocated slice of common cost.

Opportunity.   Costing tends to concentrate on expenditures of a given work program. It seems to ignore the alternatives open to the enterprise, or to assume that the alternative is idleness. Yet displaced opportunities are vital in making a business decision, which might indeed be defined as the process of selecting among alternatives.

The objections to the "cost" in the cost-plus formula are only part of the problem; economists criticize the "plus," too. The use of a somewhat rigid margin suggests that the firm does not want to find the price levels at which its total profits will be highest—or at least that it is oddly indifferent to the power of demand and of competition. Yet competition in some cases may be strong enough to take price decisions right out of the firm's hands. In other cases, surely the starting point in pricing should be the study of demand (whether, for example, it is elastic or inelastic) and the realization that each possible price may entail a different output and profit.

Superficially, it appears that if a firm adds a margin to costs to cover overheads and profit, it thereby ensures itself some profit. But, of course, this is true only in favorable markets. If cost-plus produces a price so high relative to customer valuations that few sales are made, losses will be sustained. No mechanical pricing formula can guarantee a profit, although, unfortunately, cost plus gives the impression of doing so.

Cost and Displaced Alternatives

Costing thus seems to violate a central cost principle of the economist, that cost can be measured realistically only by taking into account the alternative opportunities open to the firm. To find the sacrifices that will result from the decision to do a job (the economist argues), we must logically look only to the period that still lies in the future at decision date, and must estimate the changes in future expenses and revenues that result from the decision, a procedure that obliges us also to estimate what these expenses and revenues would look like if the job is not done.

It will therefore be helpful to classify costs under two heads. The first agrees with what is commonly understood by "cost" (except that it insists on a cause-and-effect relation between decision and sacrifice), while the second differs from the everyday definition of the word in that it is concerned with potential gains displaced by the given job.

First, compare expenses if the firm does Job A, with its expenses if it does nothing. In this way, we find the expenses that should appear in an ordinary budget—the sacrifices that the firm can avoid by not doing A or anything in its place. We shall call these potential savings *avoidable costs.*

Second, compare the firm's balance sheet after doing Job A with its balance sheet if it instead puts its assets to their next best uses (for example, employs plant on other work, or lends cash at interest). The net revenue that the firm would gain by applying its resources to their next best use is part of the sacrifice of doing A. We shall henceforth use *opportunity cost* in this narrow meaning of net revenue foregone. The total sacrifice involved in doing Job A may thus include both avoidable cost and opportunity cost.[2]

Business Acceptance of Cost-Plus

The objections to cost plus sound formidable in the classroom, but cut remarkably little ice outside. The cost accountant often concedes that they have some validity in private discussion; yet he ignores them in his published writings, and his accounts continue in the main to be filled with historical costs and allocations. These seem to impress executives and to serve as satisfying guides to policy. Cost-plus is probably the primary method of fixing price in American industry (and is perhaps even more usual abroad).

The main attraction of cost-plus is, of course, that it offers a means by which plausible prices can be found with ease and speed, no matter how many products the firm handles. Moreover, its imposing computations look factual and precise, and its prices may well seem more defensible on moral grounds than prices established by other means. Thus a monopolist, threatened by public inquiry, might reasonably feel that he is safeguarding his case by using cost-plus; also when the "just price" of part of a firm's output is at issue (as in contracts for military supplies), cost-plus may be the best short-run method of fixing price. For these and other reasons, the appeal of cost-plus to harassed executives is plain, even though some of them may look on it privately as no more than an expedient ritual. We must indeed ask whether those of us who are its spoken critics would in fact wholly reject it if we were ourselves responsible for pricing.

The gulf between practice and doctrine is thus extremely wide.[3] In an effort to appraise the issues, we shall now look more closely at the cost accountant's figures under various circumstances. We shall, for instance, compare different market structures and contrast single-product with multi-product firms.

SINGLE-PRODUCT FIRMS

Where a firm makes only one product, the cost accountant generally summarizes his results as averages. Average cost seems at first sight to serve many useful ends. In particular, it can readily be compared with price and for this reason it is a handy test of whether the firm is earning profits—provided the implied guesses at total cost and volume prove correct. However, average cost becomes less attractive when we distinguish various markets in which the one-product firm may find itself, and consider the pricing problems that these markets sometimes pose.

Where Markets Are Purely Competitive

Although examples of pure competition are probably not to be found anywhere, rough approximations to the economic theorist's model do exist. Agriculture, organized commodity markets, and some branches of the textile industry come fairly close. In such purely competitive markets, the businessman needs no cost data for pricing purposes. He has no power over price, being compelled to accept the prevailing one, or wait to sell his wares at another time, since price is determined by the interaction of all buyers and sellers, and is not subject to perceptible influence by any one of them. Therefore, cost cannot be the basis for price.

Accounts, however, may still be guides to business policy. Every firm should consider whether it can better itself by altering its scale of operation; the cost accountant would be doing useful work if he drafted budgets of total cost and revenue at various levels of activity. These would show which level is the most profitable, or even that none of the levels is profitable, in which case the firm would do better to switch to other products, or go right out of business. With change in scale comes change in cost; thus, under pure competition, it is price that fixes cost rather than vice versa.

Where the Product Differs from Competing Products

A firm making a single product that differs from the offerings of rivals generally has some discretion over price.[4] Its price decisions will influence, perhaps strongly, its physical volume of sales. It should presumably try to find the price and volume that bring the highest profit; it may decide to charge a price far below what its rivals ask for competing wares, or to sell at a premium. Only rarely will its best price be the same as its rivals' prices. More important, only rarely and by accident will its most profitable price (in the short run or the long run) be average cost plus a constant conventional margin. Sometimes the firm with the lowest unit costs can command the highest price because of attractive features in its product. To reap the rewards of its skill, such a firm must depart from routine cost-plus. As a minimum, it should raise its "plus" when it produces an outstanding product; conversely, when its model is a failure, it may be forced, in order to get rid of the batch, to shift from cost-plus to cost-minus.

Where Different Prices Are Charged

Under the two kinds of markets outlined above, we have assumed that the firm sells all units of its one product at the same price. In practice, however, a firm often sells at different prices. The price may be changed rhythmically over time (with seasonal shifts in demand, for instance), or different prices may be charged at the same time in different markets—customers being ostensibly distinguished by location, size of order, or promptness of payment, but in fact by intensity of demand. Many firms believe that they raise their profit by varying price in this way; indeed, there seems to be a trend in retailing away from the one-price system and back to old-fashioned higgling.

On occasion, the prices of some units may with advantage be put *below* average cost; as long as sales in the low-priced market exceed the avoidable costs of the extra goods, the firm's net profit is raised. For instance, hotels and airlines sometimes gain by cutting off-peak rates to less than average cost. Comparison of the cut rates with average costs serves little purpose, except perhaps as a clumsy reminder of the deficit to be made good at the peaks.

When one-product firms vary price in such ways, they have presumably rejected cost-plus. Here then are cases where our opening statement about the widespread use of cost-plus does not apply, and where firms apparently agree with the view that cost-plus can impair profit.

For the reasons just given, one might almost say that any reference to average cost will be downright harmful at the pricing stage. Average cost becomes useful after the firm has chosen the best price for the given output program, because comparisons of price and average cost then form a handy miniature budget for predicting period results, and may well suggest a need to change the program. But a miniature budget of this kind cannot give a more accurate financial picture of total revenue and cost than a full budget; in fact, it is likely to be less accurate.

MULTIPRODUCT FIRMS

The firm with many products is, in its extreme form, the individual job shop that makes unique goods to order—for instance, the engineering shop that bids for special projects. Most common is the firm producing substantial numbers of several standardized products. In such firms, both cost accountant and price fixer are confronted by far harder tasks and, consequently, are all the more apt to take refuge in cost-plus.

Demand Difficulties

As we have said, the economist insists that demand should be consciously weighed when price is being fixed. But the labor and skilled guesswork needed for making detailed demand studies for a wide range of items would generally be prohibitive. Systematic comparison of the firm's prices with those of rivals is perhaps the simplest part of the task, and yet this is often burdensome and confusing. Even the firm that is a price leader might well throw up its hands at the costs of fully estimating demand for each product. Clearly, no firm selling hundreds of products could afford to make careful demand estimates for each; in any case, many of the estimates would be out of date by the time they could be used.

Thus, the accountant has a strong argument in that his system is simple, quick, and cheap. Moreover, and this is a most important point, it lets a manager delegate pricing. Such advantages, coupled with the inevitable vagueness of demand estimates, no doubt go far to explain its wide acceptance.

On the other hand, inability to estimate demand accurately and in time scarcely excuses the substitution of cost information for demand information. Crude estimates of demand might substitute for careful estimates of demand, but a cost gives remarkably little insight into demand.

Allocation of Indirect Cost

If asked to explain his charges for indirect costs, the accountant will perhaps explain that a job makes a drain on the firm's manufacturing resources—its plant and space, supervisors, design talent, and the like—and this drain is a cost of the job. Since a big job makes a big drain, cost varies with size.

Here the views of accountant and economist are poles apart. The accountant in effect believes that the total historical cost of providing the plant can be divided up into separate sacrifices for each job. The economist contests the worth of such figures and offers instead his opportunity cost argument: If the firm has excess capacity (plant, supervisors, cash, and so on), *no* sacrifice is involved in using these idle resources on the particular job,[5] if the firm has other uses for the resources, then the cost of assigning them to this job is the sum they would earn (less avoidable costs) in their best alternative uses. Opportunity cost in a range from zero to a large sum is very different from the account's layers of overhead.[6]

Overhead allocation is arbitrary in that the choice of any particular basis (for example, direct wages or machine-hours) is hard to justify; in addition, each of the possible bases gives figures that may differ greatly from those found on another basis. Moreover, allocation invests the "fixed costs of the job" with an air of reality that at times deceives some managers, who may, for instance, let plant stand idle rather than use it on jobs that yield less than its full slice of overhead. However onerous—even disastrous—fixed commitments like rent and interest are to the firm, they are not sacrifices for which the individual job is responsible, and are irrelevant in pricing it.

Costs bind the firm, not its customers. In the case of a product, if the avoidable costs exceed its price, the firm can at least stop making it, but where allocations of fixed costs are concerned, this remedy may not help. A firm that cannot turn to more rumunerative jobs should carry on with those that fail to cover their share of overhead; such a firm can only hope that the gross margin (revenue minus avoidable cost) on all jobs will meet fixed cost and leave a profit.

Relevance of the Master Budget

In a firm of any sophistication, job costing (whether in forward-looking budgets or backward-looking accounts) is intimately linked with the firm's plans as stated in its master budget, the budget of total revenue and total cost for the next period. Sometimes such budgets merely give combined figures for the firm's total operations, but generally—if subdivision is feasible—they allow individually for each of the main products. The master budget's projection of revenue implies a specific level of price (hopefully resting on the most competent analysis of market conditions that management can make). Both revenue and cost figures similarly imply forecasts of volume and mix.

From the master budget, with its implicit price and cost per unit, one can derive an average margin per unit. In other words, it is the master budget that gives the rates of allocated overhead and profit for each job. This holds whether the budget is full and formal, or merely a tentative forecast.

If costing and pricing are integrated with a master budget, then several extremely important corollaries seem to follow.

Pricing Objectives. The master budget presumably states the firm's realistic plans and expectations, and reflects what it is trying to maximize. The economist summarizes the relevant forces in his diagrams of total or marginal cost and revenue, and suggests that the firm will trim its output until it arrives at the point of maximum profit. The master budget seems to be the firm's forecast of its cost and revenue at that point. The maximand may in fact be profit— probably for the long run rather than the budget period alone; more likely, it is some compromise among such advantageous factors as profit, a safe cash position, growth, and prestige.

Considering the importance of the master budget, costing writers are curiously silent about its construction, and add little to our scant understanding of the mental steps behind the big decisions. Their reticence compels the critic to put his own interpretation on this fundamental part of costing theory, but it is doubtful that these writers seriously challenge the economist's view of the firm's aims and methods *at the budget stage.*[7] They must surely regard maximum long-run profit as an important part of the goal—at least in the sense that the less costly method is better than the more costly, and a very low profit is a danger sign.

Measures of Activity and Size of Job with Diversified Output. Some multi-product firms have no obvious unit with which to measure the size of jobs. Such firms cannot readily link budget figures with units produced, or speak of unit cost and unit price, nor can they in any direct way compare the profits and costs of different jobs.

We suggest that the one object of job costing is to overcome this difficulty, and to find units where these are not provided by the nature of the job. In a few cases, an artificial unit of output can be devised, such as the "bus mile" or "passenger mile" of a motor bus. Where no common unit of output can be found, the accountant for want of something better may take a unit of input, like wages or hours of direct labor, or machine-hours. The master budget can thus be regarded as a plan for a certain volume of activity measured in man-hours, or some other selected unit. The cost estimate for each job likewise makes use of the same unit for allocating indirect costs and finding price; in this way, cost and price are linked with the job's size.

Average Cost per Unit with Diversified Output.   If this interpretation is right, then the accountant's measure of indirect costs for a job is often akin to an average that is weighted to allow for the job's size, measured in the chosen input units. It has therefore much the same demerits and merits as average cost in the one-product firm. It fails to show the real sacrifice involved in doing the job, but it serves under some circumstances as a miniature forecast of the firm's annual results, and so gives advance warning of a need for revising, say, the scale of operations.

The Costing Margin as a Processing Charge.   Again, just as the one-product budget shows both the number of units to be produced and total revenue, so a multiproduct budget shows planned production in input units and total revenue. But the one-product budget may sensibly deal with unit price whereas to speak of average price per unit in the multiproduct firm usually does not mean much.

If the margin added to direct cost to arrive at price is explained as so much indirect cost and profit per input unit, it has little to recommend it. But if it is regarded as a price per unit—for example, the firm's estimate of the best average price to charge per man-hour for the service of converting direct materials into finished goods—it may be both useful and intellectually defensible. The price quoted for a job could then be regarded as avoidable cost plus a processing charge—with no mention of overhead cost. This idea comes close to the method called "contribution costing," which is used by certain cost accountants when they express the margin on a job as a rate per machine-hour, that is, as the earnings per hour of some key machine that the job utilizes.

A firm in its master budget should presumably try to forecast the number of input units and the average price for each that will give best results. Then, in its day-to-day decisions, it should implement the budget strategy. Suppose, for instance, that the planned costing margin is m per man-hour. A job needing x man-hours is priced at mx (plus direct costs), not because mx measures meaningful slices of overhead, but because this is the price that the firm must charge if it is to carry out its budget decisions. Cost-plus, then, represents an administrative trick for putting a price policy into action.

The Costing Margin and Opportunity Cost.   Our interpretation thus implies that a costing margin should be regarded as a tacit allowance for opportunity cost, among other things. The firm first decides that it can maximize profit by selling so many input units of service at a certain price; given this assumption, to do Job X at a lesser rate is to lose greater potential revenue. The loss may arise because X's buyer would in fact be willing to pay more, or because X displaces a better job, or because the firm would need to cut prices all round when X's price became known.

This view, if correct, would go far to explain why costing seems to serve business needs despite its shaky logic. It does not do what it professes to do, but it may do something better; the traditional costing margin—overhead plus profit—may serve as a rough guide to opportunity cost. On the other hand, if costing derives its virtue in this way, then recognition of its true nature would prevent errors based on misinterpretation and would enable accountants to improve their figures.

There are obvious objections to our interpretation of the costing margin, to which we shall return shortly. It does, however, stress one important point; in real life, the alternative to Job X is usually not a known Job Y that neatly duplicates X in everything save profit. The alternative, which may still be unknown when a price is put on X, may consist of several small jobs or part of a large one; it may demand more or less time, space, and money than X. Job-by-job comparisons of profit may, in fact, be impossible or meaningless. Conceivably, operational research will someday help to simplify this issue; in the meantime, probably the best the firm can do is to allow roughly for X's displacement power by means of a load that depends—like the costing margin— on how much of the firm's resources are engaged in the production of X.

Job Costs and Marginal Analysis

A further conclusion may perhaps follow if the foregoing argument is correct. The conflict between accounting and economics seems, in this area, somewhat unreal; both may simply be dealing with different stages of the production program.

When the economist considers the problem of profit maximization, he is generally thinking of the stage at which the firm is still trying to find its best scale of operation for the next period. He considers, for instance, the results on expected cost and revenue of expanding the next period's output from n units to $n + x$ units. (x is here the marginal quantity, and its avoidable cost is the relevant marginal cost.)

Costing is more often concerned with what happens after these plans have been made. As we have seen, estimates for single jobs or small batches assume that the master budget for the period has already been drafted and that the figures of the budget (including planned physical activity of n units, however these are measured) have been used to find rates for burden and profit at the start of the period. Later, at some point during the period, a given job is considered. Costing tries to estimate inputs of this job, its size (x units), and, thus, its weighted average cost. But the master budget is not changed by the job; output is still expected to total only n (not $n + x$) by the close of the year, for x is merely a part in the planned flow of output. Consequently, the job, its cost, and its revenue do not appear to be marginal in the economist's usual sense; a textbook diagram whose horizontal axis shows total output is helpful for explaining the composite program, but is irrelevant to any job within that program. We suspect that, when economists question businessmen on how the fundamental decisions are made, there may be sad muddling of budget strategy with costing tactics.

Objections to the Costing Margin

In our attempt to interpret the costing margin as a measure for pricing, we have deliberately passed over the flaws in the argument.

1. One weakness is that the interpretation has never to our knowledge been put forward by a cost accountant.
2. Another lies in the notion of omniscient budgets and clear-cut budget periods; plainly, a costing margin found by a master budget cannot measure opportunity costs at all closely, for the budget assumes such costs to be the same for every date during its period and for all the products. The day-by-day state of the market ought to change a manager's views on the period's possibilities; if he gets a big order, he must, at least mentally, revise his budget totals somewhat. Consequently, a cost margin found at the budget stage may soon be out of date.
3. Again, the argument makes sense only where the firm can in fact switch from one product to another. This is often difficult or impossible, because, for instance, the products emerge in fixed proportions, or plant is built to do only one job. If there is no alternative, there is no opportunity cost.
4. Further, the argument assumes that the chosen input unit correlates with costs and demand in much the same way as the output units of the single-product firm. This is a tall assumption. In some firms, any given input unit seems likely to vary too much with each job's peculiarities to be a good general index of size for all jobs, and there may be no common denominator for size if each job is a distinctive bundle of materials, skills, and services.
5. A customer, to take the demand point of view, will not base his valuations on any internal unit used by his supplier. His test of a job's size is how much he wants it, and his price ceiling is the lower of this subjective value and the price he must pay for a similar article elsewhere, or for substitutes. This composite force on the demand side, and not the supplier's cost and effort, is what enables the supplier to charge more for the big job—and indeed to earn any revenue at all. Accordingly, a prime criterion in choosing a unit should be that it serves as a guide to the bids of rivals; the more their productive methods differ from those of the given firm, the less sound will the latter's input units be as guides.

6. Finally, just as one-product firms may find that it pays to charge different prices in different markets, so the multiproduct firm may benefit by varying its margin per unit on its different products. A firm of jobbing engineers, for example, may make each of its tenders in somewhat different demand conditions; here the case for flexible pricing is very strong.

Although these objections to the use of the costing margin as an indicator of opportunity cost and price are formidable, the pricer in the multiproduct firm must have some measure of the size of each job in order to determine how much of the firm's productive resources (man power, machinery, space, and executive direction) the job will consume. Even when these resources involve no added expense or outlay, they do represent the firm's opportunity to create net income, and some price must be placed on their use if the firm has alternatives. The costing margin may be a crude and imperfect tool, and yet be the least objectionable one that is available.

Perhaps the correct attitude toward the costing margin is to regard it in practice as the best starting point for pricing. When the appropriate price for the size of the job has been found by this omnibus formula, management can consider whether the master budget's assumption about the general state of trade still applies or whether demand for the particular article warrants a change in the margin. Considering such factors, they may, perhaps without realizing the extent of their intervention, modify the costing price substantially.[8]

The Firm with a "Line of Products"

A good example of the need to modify prices found by means of a costing margin occurs when a firm sells many different products to the same customer. Such firms may be said to sell a "line of products." A new customer means sales of many products; a lost customer means lost sales of many products.

Cost-plus, strictly applied, would often rob the firm of the benefits that come from pricing its wares as a "team" in which some items clear the ground for others. The price line, with the low-price, low-margin items whose function is to "build traffic" and arouse customer interest, and the high-price, high-margin, and high-quality item that brings prestige to the entire line and aids the medium-priced items, is commonplace in many industries. Other firms use the variation of periodically cutting prices of some items for a short time.

Could costing at least show which items to promote and which to drop? There are several difficulties in using accounts to this end. First, the cost side would include some arbitrary allocations; many of the overheads charged to the item under scrutiny would not be reduced to nil by dropping it. Second, the revenues are likely to understate the item's contributions; inclusion of an item in the line may well explain how important customers have been won and held. Finally, the decision maker must look to the item's future rather than its past.

Accordingly, this kind of firm is likely to be led astray–both in fixing prices and in deciding whether to promote, drop, or maintain items–if it relies on traditional accounts. It is far better for an expert price fixer to guess clumsily at the right factors than to measure precisely those that are irrelevant. He should estimate the demand for those products that are unique in some degree and arrange prices on the team principle; when he is considering whether to drop an item, he should guess at what it adds to revenue by boosting the sale of other products. The mechanical application of a generalized budget formula is here most unlikely to measure opportunity costs. A cost estimate of the savings from dropping the item may be useful, but it should be an *ad hoc* estimate, confined to costs that will in fact be changed by the omission.

SUGGESTED PROCEDURE

Early in this article, we posed two problems. Why is cost-plus so popular, despite its crude logic? And, would we, if we were in positions of business responsibility, reject this approach? We shall now try to answer both questions by outlining the way in which we think the cost accountant should help with pricing.

Formula Versus Individual Analysis

The central problem is whether any general formula, such as cost-plus, suitably reinterpreted, can with advantage be put in the place of individual decisions about each price.

The two main factors to be weighed by a pricer are demand and cost. Demand should ideally be studied with the utmost care by persons of outstanding discernment. We believe that no formula can accurately assess all the pulls and shifts of the living market, and that management must in the end bear full responsibility for estimating demand. A formula can be defended only on the grounds that careful judgments on each separate price are either not feasible (because of the need for quick decisions on many articles) or not worth-while (because of the high risk of error). The retail shop provides an apt analogy: its owner might well maximize profit by bargaining afresh with each customer on each visit over each unit of stock, but in practice he is usually forced by the difficulties of doing otherwise to put the same price ticket on all like units.

Cost may at first sight seem easier to reduce to a formula. If, however, it is looked on as a choice between alternatives, it too becomes subjective and hard to weigh. Ideally, a job's cost should be estimated by senior managers after full consideration of the likely alternatives and all their impacts on future possibilities. We accept that no formula will do justice to a host of dimly foreseen and hypothetical events, and that management must shoulder the task of choosing between alternatives. But a formula may still be defensible, if only on the grounds that it winnows out the obviously unattractive plans, and leaves managers free to work on plans that offer a good prospect of success.

In short, the formula can be defended only as a last resort. Our task is to consider the circumstances in which it is most likely to be a useful supplement to special studies, and the means by which its defects can be minimized.

Building the Master Budget

As we have seen, the formula implies the existence of some sort of forecast—at its best, a full budget of the firm's revenue and costs. Such a budget seems desirable in any case. Before it is drafted, certain basic questions might well be explicitly posed. Is it the firm's aim to win maximum profit, at least in the long run and with various provisos? Is there a point on the firm's scale of activity at which profit is maximized, and on either side of which profit declines through the combined action of cost and demand forces? Practical men will know that such questions cannot be answered without qualifications, and that no one can pinpoint the quantities at stake. The important thing is to be clear on the objective and plan of attack.

Demand and price should play a big part in the plan. Our discussion has stressed the major influence of demand, and how this varies in different markets. In some markets, the firm has no discretionary power over price; the only major decision concerns scale of output. In others, the firm must simultaneously envisage price, demand, volume, and cost as interrelated parts of the budget problem.

In firms facing several types of demand, or making several products with very different cost patterns, the budget should be split up between home and foreign markets, or time of year, or type of product, and so forth. The firm must study demand in each market, and try to map out the best price policy in each; it must also draft separate budgets for each department that has a fairly uniform cost pattern.

The Task of the Formula

The budget establishes the general plan—scale, level of prices, and so on. The formula tries to put this plan into effect when the minor decisions are later made on each job.

One must in each case ask whether the firm can foresee the future clearly enough to establish such an all-embracing plan. If conditions change so fast that even supplementary budgets soon lag behind events, then a predetermined formula seems likely to do mischief. The same holds if the various jobs differ greatly, whether on the side of demand or costs. The formula presumably assumes stability and sameness in day-to-day operations; it relies on "what things usually cost" or "what we can usually charge," and thus breaks down if there is no "usual."

For reasons set out earlier, we cannot accept the normal wording of the formula in terms of allocated overhead, and so on. We prefer to interpret it as a measure of contribution, that is, what the firm believes to be its best price, per unit of activity, for converting direct inputs into finished goods.

If the formula is to work well, it must allow for three quantities that would otherwise need to be found by special estimate:

1. Concealed and remote avoidable costs.
2. Opportunity costs, that is, the contribution to overhead and the profit that could be obtained by doing other jobs instead.
3. Any further contribution from this particular job.

The formula's claims may be tested by following the build-up of a price, step by step; we shall, if we do not state the contrary, deal with single jobs rather than large flows.

Building a Price.   The first step is to find the avoidable costs. Though the direct costs of the accountant may often be very similar to the obvious avoidable costs, the accountant's figures are based on clerical convenience rather than a cause-and-effect relationship between decision and sacrifice.[9] They will thus on occasion need amending in two ways: The money values attached to some ingredients must be changed, for example, by substituting current for historical cost; and the list of direct costs must be extended to include those avoidable costs that accounting classes as indirect. By their very nature, items on this extended list may be hard to detect and evaluate; even a special study for the job might end with a very vague guess at the sums in question. Therefore, it does not seem unreasonable to allow for them roughly with a rate per unit of size, unless the job has individual peculiarities that call for a special estimate. Size in this context seems more likely to be a function of time (man-hours or machine-hours) than of direct expenses.

If we ignore odd cases like the loss-leader, avoidable cost will be the lowest price at which the firm will ever take on work. This minimum will, however, need to be raised if the given job displaces other profitable opportunities. Accordingly, the next step is to estimate opportunity cost.

Opportunity Cost.   The alternatives to the given job may be known and clearly measurable. If they are, straightforward comparison between the job and the best alternative should be easy, and will show which work yields the biggest margin. If they are not, then a margin based on normal yields per unit of activity seems likely to be helpful, at least as a starting point. However, since such a margin cannot be more correct than the master budget from which it springs, the pricer should consider whether the budget still holds good. There may be a temporary change in activity, or new trends may be emerging, in the light of which the load for the given job should be trimmed. Unless the margin rate keeps pace with the order book, it is a poor guide to opportunity cost.

Which unit of activity from contenders such as direct labor cost or machine-hours should the formula employ to measure opportunity cost? Presumably the firm must find out by experience which unit best satisfies a double test: (1) prices based on this unit must attract the desired volume of activity; and yet (2) the items bought at these prices must not displace more remunerative items. The right unit is thus part of the price mechanism that equates demand with supply; customer reactions to the unit are important as well as the firm's internal workings. When one starts to find out whether a given job will displace other work, one's first inclination is perhaps to look for any scarce factor that acts as a bottleneck in production. Such a factor may exist; if, for example, labor is short, man-hours may be a good index of displaced jobs. Under imperfect competition, however, a firm may have plenty of "slack" in a physical sense, and yet continue to charge a margin. Here the bottleneck is not physical; it is the firm's own policy of restricting sales volume by keeping up prices: In this case, therefore, one should not search for bottlenecks in the plant, but should use the unit that rations sales most profitably (particularly in markets that are subject to destructive price cutting). Once again, a unit based on time seems most likely to work well; but, conceivably, the best unit for measuring opportunity cost is not the best for measuring concealed avoidable cost.

Profit Margin.   When the pricer has estimated the job's avoidable and opportunity costs, his next and final step is to ask how much more can be added as pure profit.

In many cases, the ceiling is obvious—the price charged by rivals (adjusted to allow for any special features in the firm's own product). If this is less than total cost, the firm will withdraw from the race. If it is more, the pricer must judge how near it to pitch his figure, a calculation for which direct comparison would seem a better guide than the formula.

But, where the product is new or a tender has to be made for a special job, the firm may not yet know the competing prices. Here one of the chief aims of the cost department might be to guess the prices charged by rivals. If the latter rely on a formula, then a formula may be a useful tool for predicting their prices; indeed, the normal full-cost estimate may be defensible on the grounds that it suggests not the firm's own costs, but the prices of competitors (actual or potential). Presumably the formula should not be used blindly, but should be adapted in the light of what is known of the rival's ways. For instance, a special estimate might be needed if the rival has a different method of production.

There may be a wide space between the cost floor and the demand ceiling. In that case, bargaining skill rather than economic factors may fix the position of price, or the firm may gain by charging a low price, perhaps because this will mean many future sales. An omnibus formula can scarcely respond to situations of this type. Nor can it weigh the eagerness of particular customers or the merits of a particular product. Such factors strengthen the case for using individual decisions to modify the formula's figure for profit.

Cost and Price for Large Batches.   Our approach must obviously be modified when we pass from the individual job to many sales of like units. Here the pricer faces nearly all the complexities of the complete budget in a single-product firm: cost may vary with volume, which may vary with the price that he is trying to find. No mechanical approach that relies on the use of a formula can do justice to such a problem.

The accountant can help by providing cost estimates at several points of the scale of output; the pricer must try to guess demand at corresponding points, and so find the optimum scale of operations. As the drafting of many precise estimates would involve much work, there may be good reason for using a formula in the preliminary stages. When the choice has been narrowed, special studies of avoidable and opportunity cost may become worth-while, particularly if the given batch of new articles is big enough to suggest that it amounts to a change in the master budget.

Importance of Demand.   Our review of the forces at stake has emphasized the supreme importance of demand. Though this force is hard to gauge, the pricer's success must in the long run depend on his flair for assessing it.

Part of his problem stems from the effect that frequent price changes may have in the long run on customer relations. He should be equipped with a clear statement of the firm's policy on this point. Does the firm feel that isolated price concessions will involve a serious handicap in the future? The top executive might even be called upon to set a figure that measures the size of the handicap; for instance, he might estimate that price stability would in the long run justify a drop in current profits of up to $25,000.

The pricer may sometimes get helpful impressions from other members of the firm. If, for example, he is trying to set prices for a line and to employ the team-pricing concept, men in the sales department are likely to be the best source of information about which items to treat as promotional numbers, how much to charge for a prestige model, and the probable gain in general sales from having a particular item in the line.

The pricer should gather data and impressions from others within the firm, including data from specific studies specially undertaken for him by the market research department. In the end, however, he must size up all the relevant forces for himself. He cannot move directly from cost to price; he cannot even assign clear values to many of the forces. He can probably do his job best by drawing up a schedule covering the main factors at stake, and by making his own estimate, however crude, of their values. Such schedules would call for different information according to the type of product and market. Once prepared, however, they would be helpful starting points the next time a price decision for the same product was needed.

In the procedures described above, costs are still important, and it is to be hoped that the cost accountant will help to make the estimates. Since he is the man most at home with the firm's cost structure, he can give much useful information.

However, if the cost accountant is to play his full part, he must adopt an approach that is still alien to his tradition; any attempt to kill two birds with one stone (that is, to use his ledger balances for pricing as well as for their more fitting task of control) will fail. He must abandon a classification that depends on clerical traceability; he must look forward rather than back, and must cease to imagine he can perform the miracle of splitting common cost. Further, he must recognize the need for a wider range of information, much of it subjective; opportunity costs depends on factors about which the accountant in many firms is at present not kept informed, such as the nature of the market and the state of the order book. Thus, he must keep in close touch with other departments, notably the sales department.

Such a task would be an exacting challenge to the cost accountant. But it would make for much closer ties between him and the managers, since he would have to be privy to their intentions and alternative plans, and, in consequence, it would greatly enhance his status.

Our approach can in part be summarized as a plea for cost statements with more precise words and less precise figures. The words ought to serve as clear explanations of the different kinds of sacrifice—obvious avoidable costs, hidden avoidable costs, and opportunity costs. Many cost figures must inevitably be guesswork, and this should be made plain; on occasion, they will be none the worse for being expressed as a range of probabilities, or for being sprinkled with question marks. Such vagueness accords with the facts of business life better than a facade of precision.

Clear words would also show the nature of each computation, whether it is the passive product of a formula, or a special estimate. A pricer must choose between the two. The special estimate is plainly superior in the sense of being more logical and flexible; but, as none of us has boundless wisdom, time, and energy, there may often be a sound case for the critical use of a formula.

FOOTNOTES

1. Costing practices are described in countless textbooks. For a description of U.S. pricing practices, see Theodore Karger and C. Clark Thompson, "Pricing Policies and Practices," *Conference Board Business Record,* XIV (September, 1957), 434–42; Joel Dean, *Managerial Economics* (New York: Prentice-Hall, 1951), pp. 444–57; Alfred R. Oxenfeldt, *Industrial Pricing and Market Practices* (New York: Prentice-Hall, 1951), pp. 156–65; and A. D. H. Kaplan, Joel B. Dirlam, and Robert F. Lanzillotti, *Pricing in Big Business* (Washington: The Brookings Institution, 1958).

2. This approach to cost assumes that the cost figures are to be used only for decision on pricing or the like. Some accountants now say that the merits of costing lie more in *control* (of waste, and so on) than in pricing. For control, the right cost may well be historical cost, possibly compared with standard or budget figures.

3. Considering the size of the gulf, it has excited surprisingly little comment. Costing authors are usually too swamped in massive computations to say what their end-figures mean. Economists tended to ignore costing until the late thirties, when articles by R. H. Coase and R. S. Edwards—republished in David Solomons, Ed., *Studies in Costing* (London: Sweet & Maxwell, 1952)—criticized costing theory; and when, for example, R. L. Hall and C. J. Hitch, "Price Theory and Business Behaviour," *Oxford Economic Papers,* No. 2 (May, 1939), pp. 12–45, pointed out that businessmen's descriptions of their own behavior fail to tally with those in economic writings. P. W. S. Andrews in *Manufacturing Business* (London, 1949) went on to suggest that the economist's description is therefore wrong. Such backsliding evoked many retorts, including: Austin Robinson, "Pricing of Manufactured Products," *Economic Journal,* LX (December, 1950), 771–80; and Fritz Machlup, "Marginal Analysis and Empirical Research," *American Economic Review,* XXXVI (September, 1946), 519–54. The virtues and limitations of the economist's approach are ably set out by R. A. Gordon, "Short-Period Price Determination in Theory and Practice," *Studies in Costing,* pp. 183–208.

4. Certain market imperfections have the same result. Firms may, for example, be too widely scattered to experience severe competition.

5. Any extra expenditure due to the extra wear and tear on equipment and so on *is* a sacrifice caused by the job, and should be included in

avoidable cost. This is a good example of the way in which the accountant's direct cost (based on the arbitrary classification of the ledger) can differ from true avoidable cost.

6. A job's full cost may include, besides the load for factory overhead, a second load for more remote overheads such as administration (usually found as a percentage of the job's direct cost plus the first load). The second is even harder to justify than the first, since a given job is not likely to add much to administrative expense or make much drain on administrative services.

7. For instance, the concept of profit target as a round percentage on past investment may strike many accountants as no more than a convenient simplification, which can be amended without inconsistency when circumstances demand something less crude. Again, the accountant (like other practical men) sometimes illustrates the master budget with a break-even chart whose lines are straight, in contrast to the economist's curves—thus seeming to imply that output and profit can expand indefinitely. If pressed on the point during discussion, the accountant will freely agree that the implication is absurd: he may explain away the absurdity by saying, for example, that nonmonetary factors, such as strain on management, will in fact check expansion.

8. I. F. Pearce showed in "A Study in Price Policy," *Economics,* XXIII (May, 1956), 114–27 that in one firm, whose managers firmly believed they worked on cost-plus, job prices found by cost-plus became actual prices in only a minority of cases.

9. For instance, a clerk can trace the historical cost of raw materials through his records from their purchase until they enter the final product, but the resulting "direct cost" may not show the sacrifice due to the decision to use materials in stock. This decision probably causes the purchase of new materials; if so, the sacrifice is not a figure already in the books, but the outlay on replacement.

Accounting Analysis for Short-Run Decisions— Production Policies

INTRODUCTION

The planning and control of manufacturing operations, which prompted and nurtured the development of many managerial accounting techniques, continues to present a major challenge to the accountant as a system designer and information analyst. This is hardly surprising in view of the multiplicity of decisions for which information is required and the variety of data which enter the information system. A major concern of management is the planning and control of each type of input cost, in each manufacturing center, both in absolute terms and in relation to the volume and mix of products manufactured. Since the manufacturing operations in even relatively small firms involve several types of inputs, several production centers, and several products, the need for a fairly complex scheme for classifying input and output costs becomes obvious.

217

Many input costs are "common" or "joint" with respect to two or more products, activities, or departments. This leads to a major problem in the analysis of the interactions between changes in cost inputs on the one hand and the changes in the volume and mix of output on the other. In the absence of a completely satisfactory theoretical solution to this problem, several practical techniques have evolved. These include the use of simple judgments which underlie traditional allocation processes, the use of statistical methods for cost behavior analysis, and the use of matrix techniques to develop comprehensive cost coefficients.

For any given business, a number of alternative cost systems, which differ as to input cost classifications and output cost allocation methods, might be appropriate. Hence the accountant is faced with the problem of choosing from among these after considering their respective marginal costs and benefits. Formidable though this task is, it is only one aspect of his total decision problem. The potential usefulness of a cost system is fully realized only if the information contained in it is presented effectively. Since a variety of reporting schemes are possible, the accountant faces another choice problem. Its complexity is especially large in the manufacturing area since several levels of responsibilities, several activity cycles, several input/output relations, and several individual and group behavioral patterns have to be encompassed.

The preceding description of the accountant's problem of choosing a cost system and a reporting system suggest that his system choice process is facilitated if he is familiar with the firm's decision process and with how individuals use and respond to information.

In making his choice decisions in practice the accountant may be characterized as adopting a heuristic process with two-way interactions between information made available and information requested or used by decision makers. Recent attempts to conceptualize the accountant's choice process are based on the premise that the firm's decision process can be approximated by formal decision models. Under this assumption, the parameters, variables, and structure of the decision models guide the accountant in designing the firm's accounting system and its subsequent output.

The readings in this section concentrate upon the problems of defining and measuring costs that are relevant to production decisions. The articles emphasize the interrelationship between cost determination and manufacturing output. This interaction is approached both conceptually and through examples of formalized decision processes and statistical methods of determining cost behaviors.

Bourke's paper, *What Does It Cost?*, explores several possible decision dimensions to be considered in classifying, summarizing, and reporting costs. His article serves to highlight the futility of debates over the two specific systems of absorption and direct costing. Bourke, by pointing out the wide spectrum of choices, implies that there are numerous systems that are not really mutually exclusive designs.

Hye's article, *Application of Linear Programming Analysis,* shows how a manufacturing process can be flowcharted and used to specify a related formal decision model using linear programming methods. Without burdening the reader with the computational techniques, the author conveys the power of formal models to improve the rationale of the decision process using essentially the same information that is available in most accounting systems. The reader should notice that the model allows one to specify the type of information required and to compare this against what can be expected of the accounting system. The article also shows that jointness of cost need not be a problem if the accounting system faithfully reflects such costs as joint. The alert reader should also notice that the measurement of cost is not necessarily in terms of past sacrifices, but it is often in terms of potential sacrifices given the alternative uses for the resources and their market prices.

Although costs which are "joint" need not be a problem, since decisions rely on marginal cost only; the task of separating joint costs from costs which vary with individual activities or products has not been resolved satisfactorily in extant systems. Despite widespread criticisms, the method of subjective allocation continues to be the major means of identifying marginal costs. Chiu and DeCoster's article, *Multiple Product Costing by Multiple Correlation Analysis,* is essentially a plea for exploring the scope of multiple regression analysis to estimate the marginal costs of multiple products or activities. The theoretical superiority of this approach compared to subjective allocation methods is obvious, although it must be recognized that choices in practice must weigh the relative costs as well as benefit from employing alternative methods of estimating marginal cost.

An area which is subject to much misunderstanding and confusion is that of estimating and reporting costs of facilities. Since facilities typically serve many time periods and several products within each period, the problem of determining capacity utilization costs included in product or activity costs has been an extremely baffling one. The traditional solution has been to amortize the historical cost using a depreciation formula and then assigning these costs to the product units via an overhead rate. Horngren persuasively discusses the irrelevancy of historical cost of facilities in guiding the allocation and utilization of fixed facilities or in evaluating actual utilizations of such resources, once the investment has already been made. Ideally the opportunity costs of fixed resources should be the guiding factor, but there are many practical problems in quantifying opportunity costs. Horngren, in *A Contribution Margin Approach to the Analysis of Capacity Utilization,* proposes a method for evaluating capacity utilization which uses the forgone or lost contribution margin as a surrogate for opportunity cost to assess the relevance of plans and the effects of variances from these plants.

What Does It Cost?

P. F. Bourke

It is generally accepted that the purpose of cost accounting is to provide data (incorporating costs and income) to enable product costing for inventory valuation and profit determination, and for planning and control. Cost accounting is a highly developed quantitative device for helping managers select and reach their objectives. It is a means to an end, the end being decision-making.

So the above points are really sub-objectives, as the justification for the management accountant's existence is the aid he gives management in making decisions. The decision maker requires from the management accountant relevant information in the right form at the right time. I stress the word *relevant*.

Cost Terminology

A multitude of terms has arisen to describe different types of costs. One wonders whether the variety of terms is not more confusing than illuminating. Particularly when a good proportion of them have no uniform and precise definition, and their meaning often varies from enterprise to enterprise, and accountant to accountant.

All these terms qualify the concept of cost in an endeavour to make the meaning of the particular cost known, or rather, to describe a particular concept of cost.

SOURCE: Reprinted with permission from *The Australian Accountant* (April, 1969), pp. 176–182.

THE CONCEPT OF COST

Two definitions of "cost" are given below:

a. "Cost means economic sacrifice measured in terms of the standard monetary unit incurred, or potentially to be incurred, as a consequence of business decision."[1]

b. "Cost is a general term for a measured amount of value purposefully released or to be released in the acquisition or creation of economic resources, either tangible or intangible."[2]

All costs are not measurable in monetary terms as these definitions imply. However, in a business situation as many factors as possible must be quantified, for quantitative factors are the bases on which the manager makes his decision.

The definitions quoted above are broad because of the complexity of the nature of cost. The term requires specific qualification to make its meaning clear as the items to be included in a particular concept of cost depend on the conditions under which the costs are required to be measured and the purpose for which the measurement is required. That is, there is no single concept of cost that is applicable in all situations.

THE CONCEPT OF RELEVANCY

Different costs for different purposes or different cost concepts for different situations, I would term "the concept of cost relevancy." If this concept is not observed by the management accountant, the data he provides is valueless for the question at hand. It would be interesting to analyse and trace decisions both good and bad, back to the cost data on which they were based.

It is likely that a good many decisions which have had undesirable results could be traced to cost data prepared without the understanding, or application, of the concept of cost relevancy.

Managerial Needs

Management requires different cost information to meet different needs in different situations. What are these situations and what are their needs? There are four distinct business needs, in the managerial sense, i.e.,:

1. Income measurement
2. Cost control
3. Profit planning
4. Special situations requiring special decisions.

It is important that the data provided for these needs be relevant, because there are different ways of handling the same cost data for the same purpose, but with different results. This is highlighted by the direct costing controversy.

Direct Costing and Absorption Costing

Probably the easiest way to define each of these approaches to cost accounting is to describe the difference between them.

The philosophy of direct costing holds that only variable production costs are "inventoriable," as they are the only costs that are created because of the manufacture of a product unit. These are often called product costs.

Fixed factory or production costs are related to capacity to produce and thus to time. They are not generated by the production of a specific product unit, and generally they are not varied by fluctuations in the level of production. These are sometimes called period costs.

The absorption costing view is that inventories should carry a fixed cost component, because both fixed and variable costs are necessary to produce. Therefore both of these costs should be attached to products and inventoried, regardless of the difference in their behavioural patterns.

It seems relevant to ask: Do either of these approaches provide the framework from which any of the multitude of cost concepts can be extracted to meet the concept of cost relevancy?

A modern cost system is surely based on standards, irrespective of whether it employs direct or absorption costing techniques, or whether the nature of its business requires the use of job or process costing methods. Such a cost system will equally as surely separate fixed from variable cost components and have established behavioural patterns for those costs.

Therefore, the real issue between the two approaches relates to periodic income determination through inventory valuation.

The Measurement of Income—Inventory Valuation

Both direct costing and absorption costing approaches seem illogical in one way or another. If we accept the point that fixed factory costs should be assigned to products and inventoried, is that as far as we should go?

Why should fixed costs other than factory costs not be included in inventory: for example, administrative costs? Substantial administrative costs are generated by the same factors as fixed factory costs: for example, certain senior executive salaries, the Accounts Section, the Supply Department, Stock Records and Costing. Surely a good proportion of these costs are applicable to products on the same basis as are factory costs. What logical reason is there for drawing an imaginary line, on one side of which fixed costs are added to products and find their way into inventories, while on the other side, fixed costs are written off against the period in which they were incurred, irrespective of the reason for their incurrence?

The only explanation appears to be one of practical expediency. It seems the accountant has enough problems in allocating fixed factory costs to products on the basis of some pre-determined notion of capacity, without having to do the same thing with other fixed costs.

The theory of direct costing is equally illogical. Are variable production costs the only true product costs? If this view is accepted, a rather ridiculous situation can arise. For example, a product manufactured on an operator-controlled machine is subsequently converted to an automated process involving high cost machinery, with no variation in material costs or variable manufacturing costs per unit, and the direct labour costs become part of the fixed cost associated with the machine. The result, therefore, is that the inventory cost would be reduced from direct materials, plus direct labour, plus variable manufacturing expenses to direct materials, plus variable manufacturing expenses only, simply because of a change in the method of manufacture.

The principal argument that the benefits of fixed costs expire with the passage of time and therefore must be absorbed by the revenues of the period to which they relate, ignores the point that the facilities represented by those costs are value creating.

The time period certainly receives the standby benefit of the facilities but actual production receives the usage benefit. The product cannot be manufactured without these facilities. They add value to the product, and the value is normally recovered in the selling price. It is therefore illogical that the unit of product does not carry the cost of facilities used.

So much for the lack of logic in these approaches. We now come to the question of relevance. To determine what costs are relevant in terms of inventory, we must first establish what inventory is. Inventory is universally accepted as an asset, and an asset could be defined as "an economic resource devoted to business purposes within a specific accounting entity. It is an aggregate of service potential available for or beneficial to future operations." Therefore, we could say that:

- Any cost is an asset if it will have a favourable economic effect on future costs or revenue.
- If a given cost will not influence either total future revenue or total future costs, it is not an asset.

Since this is so—

- Variable costs are relevant and inventoriable, because they have been incurred and the necessity to incur them again has been obviated.

- Fixed costs are inventoriable only when utilisation of these costs will have a favourable economic effect on the future. That is, when failure to produce now will lead to additional costs or loss of revenue in the future.

Inventories are designed *solely* for future economic benefit. Goods are retained in inventories for the purpose of being available for sale in the future, whether it be tomorrow, next week or next month. Therefore, fixed costs are relevant and inventoriable, and it is suggested that relevant fixed costs in this concept include fixed costs other than those classified as manufacturing expense.

Cost Concepts for Control

Cost data is required by management so that responsibility for cost incurrence can be identified. This requires a system of accounting which ensures that costs are accumulated by levels of responsibility within the organisation structure—and that each supervisor may be held accountable for the costs over which he has control, and the authority to incur.

For control purposes, other cost concepts, e.g., those used in product costing, are irrelevant. Only those costs directly controllable by a given level of managerial authority within a given time period are relevant. Controllable costs are not synonymous with variable costs nor are non-controllable costs synonymous with fixed costs.

Cost controllability is a matter of degree and is determined by (a) the managerial area of responsibility involved, and (b) the time period under review.

For example, a factory manager may have authority to purchase specified raw materials, in which case, the raw material price may be controllable by him because he can influence it. On the other hand, the foreman responsible to the factory manager, may have a strong influence on the usage of that raw material, but no influence on its price. So raw material usage is controllable by the foreman. If the factory manager entered into a set price contract, say for six months, then price is non-controllable by him for any period less than six months, but possibly controllable beyond that period.

It is important to remember that it is often the physical cost generator which is the relevant factor for control. The monetary unit is merely attached to the physical unit and simply follows the usage fluctuations of that physical unit.

An allocated (indirect) cost item, whether fixed or variable, is irrelevant, as is any direct fixed cost over which the respective supervisor has no control. Only direct variable costs (which should be measured in both quantity and price if possible) and direct fixed costs which the given manager can influence within the time period under review, are relevant.

The Income Statement

The conventional income statement, produced by either direct costing or absorption costing, often fails to distinguish between fixed and variable costs, controllable and non-controllable costs, direct and indirect costs and joint (common) and separable costs. These distinctions are vital for judging performance and for various marketing, manufacturing and financial decisions.

The direct costing controversy is an excellent illustration of the need for accountants to realise that no single version of inventory cost or income will be a valid guide to interpretation and action under all circumstances.

The income statement should be designed to facilitate its multi-purpose use. It should be designed to focus on the appropriate data for appraisals of performance. It should not aim to produce one income figure, because the singular concept of income is obsolete. It should be relevant to the multi-purpose requirements of modern management.

An income statement (see Exhibit 1) provides basic overall data which can be used for the following purposes:

- Performance appraisal
- Disclosing the effect of changes in cost, price and/or volume on profit
- Disclosing the effect of fluctuating inventory levels on profit
- Determining the impact on profits of two or more contemplated courses of action.

The income statement is only relevant if it reflects the effect on profit of all of the activities of the business. Fluctuations in the level of production can only be shown through sales and/or inventory variations. In Exhibit 1, the effect of inventory fluctuations on periodic profit is highlighted by separating the standard fixed cost content of that inventory variation.

In addition to highlighting the effects of inventory build-up (or reduction) on profit, Exhibit 1 has other features:

a. The contribution margin for the business and for segments is shown. This figure is important for decision making in particular. However, its use must always be considered in the light of the limiting factor, e.g. machine capacity, labour hours, etc.

b. The performance margin is particularly helpful in judging performance by segment managers, particularly when used in conjunction with the contribution margin. Direct controllable fixed costs are sometimes termed programmed costs, that is, they are relatively fixed costs arising from managerial policy decisions. Whilst they have no particular relation to any base of activity, they are controllable at least when they are planned. Such costs include advertising, sales promotion, engineering, research, management consulting and supervision costs.

EXHIBIT 1. A Relevant Periodic Income Statement

	COMPANY $000		SEGMENTS DIVISION A		DIVISION B		DIVISION C	
	B	A	B	A	B	A	B	A
Net Sales	$ 3,200	$ 3,000	$ 1,800	$ 1,500	$ 1,000	$ 1,000	$ 400	$ 500
Less standard variable manufacturing cost of sales	1,560	1,500	720	600	600	600	240	300
Standard Manufacturing Margin	$ 1,640	$ 1,500	1,080	900	400	400	160	200
Less standard cost variance	—	20	—	6	—	4	—	10
Actual Manufacturing Margin	$ 1,640	$ 1,480	1,080	894	400	396	160	190
Less variable selling and administrative costs	492	440	360	300	100	100	32	40
Contribution Margin	$ 1,148	$ 1,040	720	594	300	296	128	150
Less direct controllable fixed costs	385	380	210	200	100	100	75	80
Performance Margin	$ 763	$ 660	510	394	200	196	53	70
Less direct non-controllable fixed costs	140	140	80	80	20	20	40	40
Segment Margin	$ 623	$ 520	430	314	180	176	13	30
Less joint costs	270	270	—	—	Not Allocated		—	—
Net Unadjusted Profit	$ 353	$ 250						
Add (deduct) standard fixed cost content of inventory variation	(3)	5	—	10	—	—	(3)	(5)
Adjusted Net Profit	$ 350	$ 255	430	324	180	176	10	25
Standard fixed costs content of inventory variation								
Standard fixed costs in opening inventory	$ 56,000	$ 50,000	$ 26,000	$ 20,000	$ 20,000	$ 20,000	$10,000	$10,000
Standard fixed costs in closing inventory	53,000	55,000	26,000	30,000	20,000	20,000	7,000	5,000
Adjustment	$ (3,000)	$ 5,000	—	$ 10,000	—	—	$(3,000)	$(5,000)
Standard fixed cost absorption	$405,000	$400,000	$227,000	$220,000	$100,000	$100,000	$78,000	$80,000
Actual fixed cost Allocated as S.C. to production	390,000	380,000	210,000	200,000	100,000	100,000	80,000	80,000
Unabsorbed & included in above figures	$ 15,000	$ 20,000	$ 17,000	$ 20,000	—	—	$(2,000)	—

c. The segment margin is computed after deducting direct fixed costs which are generally non-controllable in the short run, for example, depreciation, insurances, certain executive salaries, rates and taxes, etc. This figure is helpful as an indicator to long run segment profitability but should not influence appraisals of current performance. A segment is any line of activity of the business for which cost and income data is required. In Exhibit 1, they have been called divisions, but they can be products, branches, departments, territories, customers, order sizes, distribution channels, etc.

d. The effect on profit of alternative courses of action can be easily seen; e.g. increase or decrease in volume, price variations, changes in product mix, etc. Through variations of the contribution margin, the effect of such alternatives is disclosed on the net unadjusted profit figure.

e. Joint costs are not allocated to segments as such allocation serves no useful purpose. These costs include those which have no clear relationship to segments and cannot be separated in any meaningful manner. However, attempts should be made to ensure that joint costs are really joint or common before giving up the attempt to identify them with particular segments.

Profit Planning

Profit planning is nothing more than a series of decisions between alternative courses of action. The sum total of such decisions is the optimum plan of operations, having regard to operating conditions, financial limitations and long term objectives.

Planning involves answering questions such as: "What would happen if the sales mix were changed this way or that? If we reduced the selling price of product X? If we increased advertising by X amount of dollars? If we changed our distribution methods to such and such? If we installed an automated machine process instead of the manual controlled machine process?, and so on.

Planning deals with the future and the alternatives considered are alternatives of the future. So, future costs are relevant costs in the planning function. However, all future costs are not necessarily relevant: only those future costs which will be different under each of the alternatives considered are relevant. For example, a company is considering re-arranging its finishing plant facilities with the aim of reducing direct labour costs per unit of product. This re-arrangement will generate additional fixed costs for the department concerned, will reduce direct labour costs per unit by 20% and is estimated to cost $500. (See Figure 1.)

	Unchanged	Re-arranged
Direct material per unit	$10	$10
Direct labour per unit	$5	$4
Variable overhead cost per unit	$3	$3
Total fixed costs per month	$1,000	$1,100
Production level per month	400 units	400 units
Cost of re-arrangement	–	$500

FIGURE 1.   Finishing plant.

All of the costs shown in Figure 1 (although based on historical costs, which are irrelevant), are expected future costs. But the relevant costs are direct labour per unit, total fixed costs and re-arrangement costs, for they are the only ones which are different.

Whatever costs are used within whatever framework, such as cost-volume-profit analysis, must be future costs to be relevant.

Pricing

Few businesses are in a position where costs are the only factor in determination of pricing policy. It is my experience that accountants and businessmen think costs influence pricing decisions, but their actions show that customer demand and competitor behaviour are the prime factors in determining pricing policy.

Price levels, in the main, are set in the market-place, and are subject to three main influences: customers, competitors and costs.

A businessman must examine his pricing problems through the eyes of his customer. The customer cannot be forced to buy a company's product. He can reject it and turn to competitors' or substitute products, for any of a variety of reasons.

Rivals' reactions, or lack of reactions, will also influence pricing decisions. Knowledge of the competitors' costs is important. Knowledge of his plant size, technologies and operating policies, help in estimating his costs, for it is often his costs that are relevant, not your own.

In the long run, all costs must be recovered through selling prices, otherwise the business will fail. In the short run, the minimum price should never be below the variable costs of accepting the order. Costs may determine the minimum price, but have no bearing on the maximum price, for the maximum price is the one which will not drive the customer away.

Where a company has discretion in price setting, customer demand at various price levels determines the sales volume. In this situation, cost-volume-profit analysis is useful in pricing decisions within the framework of market conditions, elasticity of demand, production capacity and competitors' reaction. When such is not the case, a company ordinarily accepts the price range that competition has set, and selects the level of production and sales which maximise profit.

An understanding of the interplay of price, cost and volume is a key factor in pricing. The cost-plus formula, often stated to be the most popular method, is in most situations the wrong approach, for several reasons:

- It ignores demand. What the market will pay bears no necessary relationship to the cost incurred by the manufacturer.
- It involves circular reasoning. Unit cost depends on volume which depends on price.
- It fails to adequately reflect competition. That is, what competitors' prices are and what alternative products are available and their price.
- Finally, and most important, the costs are often irrelevant. Not current costs or past costs but future costs are required. Relevant costs are future costs, whether they be unit variable, total variable or total fixed costs.

Often the relationship of cost to price is inverted. That is, costs are tailored to fit selling prices. An excellent example is in the case of timber components for metal windows. The market volume is known, as is the market price range, and estimates of volume can be determined for given price levels. Having determined the price, costs are determined as follows:

Pre-determined acceptable market price	$14
Less Desired contribution margin	$4
Unit variable cost	$10
Less Variable manufacturing, selling and distribution costs (including direct labour)	$2
Unit material costs	$8

Materials are sought which will produce an acceptable quality article at a cost not exceeding that determined by the above. If none can be found, then either the contribution margin and/or the price would have to be varied within the framework of the effect of such variations on volume and profit.

The study of pricing policy is complex because of the variety of influences all of which are inter-relating. No one concept of cost is relevant in all pricing situations. However, two are common to all: the concept of cost variability, and the concept that relevant costs are future costs.

Special Decisions

Special decisions which face management are many and varied and involve choosing between alternative courses of action. Such decisions take many forms, some of which are:

- The special order.
- Make or buy.
- Sell or process further.
- Drop a product line.
- Replacement of a machine.

Let us examine examples of three of the above; the special order, sell or process further, and replacement of machine. Relevant costs in every special decision are future costs that are different under each of the alternatives considered.

The Special Order.   The question is whether or not an order for 1,000 units of product at a price of $5 per unit should be accepted. The order could be fulfilled as capacity is available, and its acceptance is not likely to adversely affect the company's market. (See Figure 2.)

	Without special order		Difference			With special order
Sales (20,000 units)	$140,000		1,000 @ $5	= 5,000		$145,000
Factory costs						
Variable	92,000		1,000 @ 4.60	= 4,600	96,600	
Fixed	18,000	110,000		–	18,000	114,600
Gross Margin:		30,000		400		30,400
Selling & administrative costs						
Variable	1,400		1% $5,000	50	1,450	
Fixed	20,000	21,400		–	20,000	21,450
Net Profit:		$8,600		$350		$8,950

FIGURE 2.   Anticipated month's results.

Obviously, the order should be accepted because its acceptance will contribute an extra $350 to profit. Note that the relevant costs in this example are the variable costs. Fixed costs are the same under either alternative and could be completely disregarded. The relevant figures in the example are revenue and variable costs.

Sell or Process Further.   This is a fairly frequent question, whether to sell a given item at a given stage of completion or to process it further for sale at a higher price. The question in this example is whether Product B can be sold as such or processed further to make Product C. Figures involved are:

Costs of carrying on the joint process:	$36,000

Product A
Output 10,000 lb. at $3 per lb. Sales Value: = $30,000

Product B
Output 10,000 lb. at $1.50 per lb. Sales Value: = $15,000
    10,000 lb. of Product B plus $16,000 of additional
    processing will yield 8,000 lbs. of Product C
    which can be sold for a unit selling price of
    $4 per lb.

If the joint costs are allocated on any basis, different and irrelevant answers will be obtained, for cost allocation and past costs are irrelevant. The relevant costs are:

a)	Lost selling price of Product B:	$15,000
b)	Additional cost of producing Product C:	$16,000
c)	The revenue from the sale of Product C:	$32,000

The calculation is as follows:

The cost of not selling Product B:	$15,000
Add additional cost of processing to Product C:	$16,000
	$31,000
Revenue from Product C (8,000 × $4.00)	$32,000
Net Gain:	$ 1,000

The data that is relevant must include the revenue foregone by not selling the product. Costs to that point are irrelevant unless they are altered by the decision to process further. Incidentally, the same approach could be used even if Product A did not exist.

Replacement of Machine.   All historical costs are irrelevant in decision making, and this includes the book value of fixed assets. On the question whether an asset should be replaced or not, the only relevant factor in relation to the asset is its disposal value, if any, and then only if the value is different under available alternatives. For example:

- We have a machine, original cost $125,000, with a disposal value of $10,000 now or $5,000 in four years' time.
- The machine has a book value of $45,000 and a remaining useful life of four years.

- A new machine is available that will cost $60,000 with a zero disposal value at the end of its four year life.
- This new machine will reduce total variable operating costs from $80,000 per annum to $56,000 per annum.
- The annual revenue of $125,000 will not be changed irrespective of the decision.
- Annual other fixed costs of $100,000 will also be unchanged irrespective of the decision.

Many accountants and managers would not replace the old machine because it would entail recognising a $35,000 loss on disposal. The calculation in Figure 3 shows that this is faulty thinking because the $35,000 loss is not relevant.

	Retain	Difference	Replace
Net sales	$500,000	–	$500,000
Variable expenses	$320,000	– 96,000	$224,000
Depreciation/write-off			
old machine	45,000		45,000
Proceeds from disposal	– 5,000	– 5,000 –	10,000
New machine		+ 60,000 +	60,000
Other fixed cost	100,000		100,000
Total expenses	460,000	– 41,000	419,000
Net Profit	$ 40,000	+ $41,000	$ 81,000

Net added average annual income: $\dfrac{41,000}{4}$ = $10,250

Net added initial investment: $60,000 – 10,000 = $50,000

Rate of return on added initial investment: $\dfrac{10,250}{50,000}$ = 20.5%

FIGURE 3.   Replacement of machine (four years added together).

Note that the relevant figures in Figure 3 are variable expenses, disposal values of the old machine and the cost of the new machine. The book value of the old machine is the same under each alternative and thus irrelevant.

Here the accounting method of evaluation of return on investment is used, but the more intricate compound interest technique of discounted cash flow can be used. However, for this purpose, the emphasis is on the isolation and measurement of relevant revenue and cost items.

Conclusion

No single concept of cost is valid under all circumstances. We need different cost constructions and income concepts for different purposes. Costs take on a useful meaning only in relation to the specific objective for which they are accumulated. Whether for income determination, planning, control or special decisions, the cost data must be relevant.

It is the responsibility of the management accountant to learn the uses that are to be made of his data and to ensure that the data is relevant to the purposes for which it is to be used. Only then can an adequate answer be given to the question "what does it cost?"

The ability to discard the irrelevant and dwell on the relevant is a leading characteristic of outstanding executives and should be a prerequisite for management accountants.

Do we have this ability? Or more important, do we use it?

FOOTNOTES

1. *Handbook of Modern Accounting Theory,* Morton Backer.
2. Executive Committee of the American Accounting Association—*The Nature of Business Cost—General Concepts.*

REFERENCES

1. *Cost Accounting and Managerial Emphasis*—C. T. Horngren.
2. *Tailormaking Cost Data for Specific Uses*—W. J. Vatter.
3. *Cost Factors in Price Making*—H. C. Greer.
4. *N.A.A. Research Bulletin* on Direct Costing Nos. 23 and 31.
5. "Costs Included in Inventories"—*N.A.A. Research Bulletin* No. 10.

Application of Linear Programming Analysis to Determine the Profitability of Products Involving Joint Cost—The Plywood Manufacturing Case

Lee Meng Hye

The sales manager and the production manager of a plywood manufacturing company dropped into the office of the cost accountant one day and asked: "Can we ever find out what profit margins we are making on the various grades of plywood panels we sell?"

Pause . . . and then, the cost accountant looked up, unperturbed, "I am afraid we can't. It has been so for a long, long time. We just don't have any satisfactory way of assigning the joint-wood cost to the veneer used in constructing the plywood panels. You don't have to remind me again that wood cost makes up as much as 65% of the total variable cost of producing the plywood panels."

The conversation ended there . . . rather unsatisfactorily.

SOURCE: Reprinted with permission from *The Australian Accountant* (December, 1970), pp. 511–516.

THE PROBLEM

Most accountants use either a physical measure of the joint products or the net sale value of the products as a basis for assigning joint cost to the products. These methods are designed primarily for inventory valuation purposes in preparing financial statements. The product costs so computed are not suitable for use in management decision-making, and the accountant makes no pretence about it. It is stated that "no technique that is applicable to the problem of joint-product costing should be used for managerial decisions . . . [decisions] regarding whether a product should be sold or processed further."[1]

Two conclusions may be drawn from this. (1) The accountant has so far failed to find a way for allocating the joint cost to the product so as to make the product cost useful for decision-making concerning product pricing and so on. (2) The accountant feels that managerial decisions concerning joint products do not call for the allocation of the joint cost to the products.

Most accounting texts describe a joint cost situation as the one depicted in Figure 1 where the decision is whether to sell the products at the point of "split-off" or to process them further, *individually*. In such a situation, the decision is made by comparing the incremental revenue derived from the product and the cost of processing that product further. And the question whether the products should have been produced in the first place is settled by comparing the total cost of production with the total revenue derived from all the products combined (either sold at the point of split-off or processed further, whichever is more profitable). There is no question of producing one product without producing another because of the very nature of the joint-products. Thus, there is no need to know the profitability of the individual joint-products.

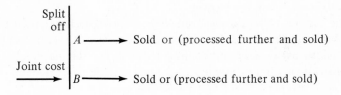

FIGURE 1.

However, plywood manufacturing faces a more complex joint-cost situation, one as depicted in Figure 2. Many grades of veneer are jointly produced from peeling a single log. The veneer might be saleable at the point of split-off from the individual manufacturer's point of view but for the plywood industry, the veneers are useful to the consumers only when they have been first turned into plywood panels. The major decision therefore is how to process the veneer further, and *jointly*.

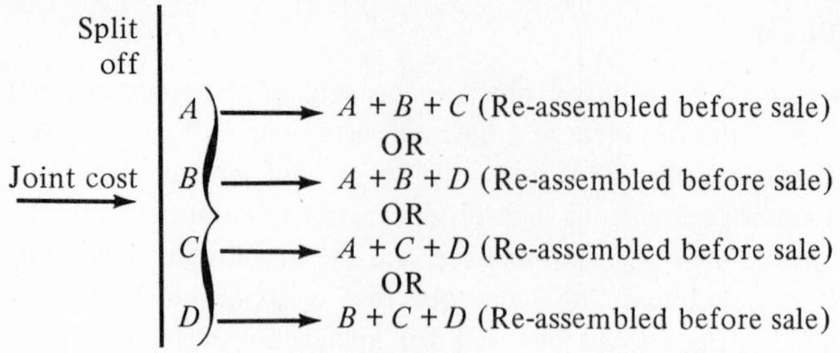

Split
off

Joint cost

A ⟶ $A + B + C$ (Re-assembled before sale)
OR
B ⟶ $A + B + D$ (Re-assembled before sale)
OR
C ⟶ $A + C + D$ (Re-assembled before sale)
OR
D ⟶ $B + C + D$ (Re-assembled before sale)

FIGURE 2.

The veneer may be combined in various ways to form panels of various grades and specifications. There is, therefore, the need to know the production cost of the various types of panels in order to intelligently set the sale price or in order to determine their profitability so as to produce the most profitable combination of panels, whichever is applicable.

The need to know the product cost for price setting purposes is often under-estimated because of the argument that in a perfectly competitive situation, the individual firms are "price-takers"—thus, there is no price setting problem! In perfect competition it is the industry (i.e. all the firms collectively) that helps to set the market price. The market price is determined by the inter-action of the industry's supply curve and the industry's demand curve. The writer wishes to emphasise that the supply curve of a product, be it that of an individual firm or that of the industry cannot be intelligently determined without the knowledge of the product cost. In a perfectly competitive situation the plywood industry, therefore, appears to have guessed the required product cost in arriving at the market price. The inputed product cost might not be at all realistic and yet no one may be wise to the fact.

In the case of a "price-leader" situation, knowledge of the product cost of the plywood panels will help the price-leader to know the profit margin he is placing on the panels when setting the prices. On the other hand, knowing the profit margins of the panels will help the price follower to determine the best product emphasis in his production and sale effort.

A SUGGESTED SOLUTION TO THE PROBLEM

It is not the objective of this paper to attempt to find a suitable way for allocating the wood cost to the plywood panels. It rather proposes to illustrate how, without allocating the joint-wood cost to the product, linear programming (L.P.) analysis may be used to give a good indication of the profit margins of the various types of plywood panels produced. However, it is not meant to imply that the usefulness of L.P. analysis is limited to analysing the profitability of the products. Other uses of L.P. analysis may also become evident in the course of this paper.

WHAT IS L.P. ANALYSIS?

A linear programming system defines a linear function to be maximised (minimised), subject to the constraint of a set of linear inequalities.[2]

At the beginning of a planning period the plywood manufacturer has a set of fixed factors of production, i.e. his production facilities. He also has access to the factor market where he can acquire certain amounts of logs of different grades and species and acquire the necessary human services to operate the production facilities, at some given or negotiated prices. A set of plywood panel sale opportunities are also available at a set of given or negotiated panel prices. A linear relationship between factor input and product output may be assumed.

Such a situation lends itself well to L.P. analysis. The analysis will indicate to the manufacturer the best programme of activities to adopt for the period in order to maximise his profit with the given opportunities.

Economic theory describes a firm as having reached its optimum programme of operation in the short run if its marginal revenue equals the marginal cost. However, there is no clear guide as to how a firm may arrive at this position, especially if the firm has many product lines and does not know its product cost, let alone the marginal product cost. As far as the writer knows, L.P. approach is the one practical way for the firm to arrive at the optimum position even without knowing the full product costs.

Most experienced L.P. users agree that the full benefit of the L.P. analysis is realised only by doing a sensitivity analysis after finding the optimum programme of operations. The sensitivity analysis shows how the optimum programme of operations will have to change and also how the total profit will change in response to any changes in the supplies factor and/or the market opportunities.

One product of the sensitivity analysis with which we are particularly interested here is what is sometimes called "shadow prices." The shadow price of a plywood panel tells us how much the total profit of the manufacturer will increase or decrease if one more or one less unit of that particular type of panel is produced and sold, where the rest of the operation of the business is best adapted to accommodate for this unit change.[3] The writer suggests that these shadow prices can be used to give a good indication of the relative profitability of the various types of plywood panel produced by a manufacturer.

SHADOW PRICES AND PANEL PROFITABILITY

The accountant measures the profit contribution of a unit of product by "sale revenue of product–variable unit cost of producing that product." This assumes that the sale of that marginal unit of product will not have any effect on the profitability of the rest of the operations of the business. In contrast, the shadow price of a unit of product is measured by "sale revenue of product – variable unit cost of producing that product plus or minus the consequent change in the profit of the rest of the operations of the business, after first being adapted to best accommodate for the marginal unit of product." The shadow price, therefore, measures the truly marginal profit contribution of a unit of a product under a given set of operating conditions. It is expected that the shadow price of the Nth unit of a product may be different from that of the $N + 1th$ unit.

The L.P. analysis gives the range of value for which a particular measure of the shadow price of a product is valid. It can also give the shadow prices for a whole range of units of a product. The shadow price curve may be visualised as a stepped function as shown in Figure 3 though the exact shape of the curve depends on the existing conditions governing the whole system of input-output of the business.

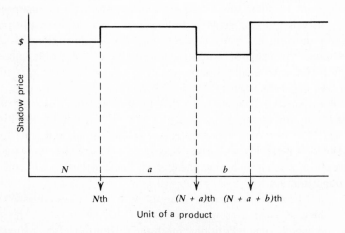

FIGURE 3.

Each shadow price curve of a particular type of plywood panel assumes a certain set of given log supply opportunities, and given sets of production facilities and of market opportunities for all other types of panels. Any change in one of the conditions may cause a shift of the shadow price curve or even a change of its shape. However, it may be expected that the shadow price curve of a product may be more sensitive to certain changes in operating conditions than to some other changes. The L.P. analysis can be used to produce a comprehensive set of shadow price curves so as to give a good indication of its sensitivity to changes in operating conditions.

The usefulness of shadow prices for helping to evaluate pricing policies or for selecting the best combinations of panels to produce is enhanced if the following conditions are fulfilled:

1. The L.P. analysis is used to produce a sufficiently comprehensive set of shadow price curves for each type of panel and under various operating conditions, especially those which have been found to have a significant effect on the shadow prices. With this it is possible to pick the shadow price that is most applicable then in gauging the profitability of the panel.
2. Where it is found more profitable to leave log supplies and production capacities unused than to produce a particular type of panel, then it is quite safe to assume that the panel is unprofitable unless either production cost or panel price, or both, are changed significantly.
3. Where the shadow price curves are converted into curves of marginal profit margin, i.e. shadow price/panel price, it will enhance the determination of the relative profitability of the various types of panels.

AN ILLUSTRATION

An actual L.P. analysis of a plywood manufacturing business is presented. . . for illustration purpose. The business studied (situated on the west coast of Canada) manufactures "soft-wood" plywood using mainly Douglas Fir. The study was carried out with a broader purpose in mind than just the analysis of the shadow price of the plywood panels. However, the usefulness of the shadow prices as an indication of panel profitability will be especially emphasised in this presentation.

CONSTRUCTION OF THE L.P. MODEL

Readers who so desire may refer to Appendix 1 for a brief description of the plywood manufacturing process. Figure 4. . .presents a configuration of the model constructed.[4]

The three major sets of questions the L.P. analysis was designed to answer were:

a. Which grades of logs to use and in what quantity combinations?
b. Which are the best construction structures to use for constructing the plywood panels?

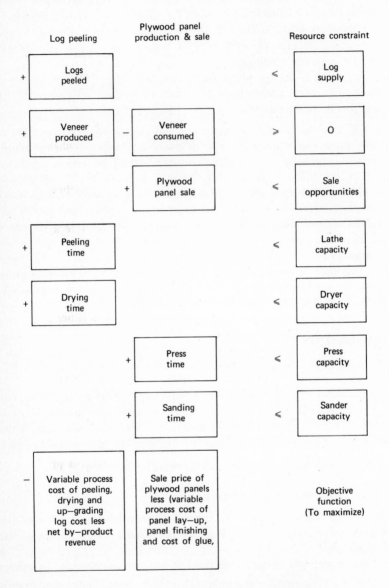

FIGURE 4.   L.P. model for plywood machines.

c. Which types of panels to produce and sell, given a set of log supply opportunities, sale opportunities, fixed production facilities and cost and prices anticipated for a planning period?

The firm had eight grades of logs to select from. It was thought that perhaps owing to the imperfect log price structure and/or the peculiarities of the veneer production facilities of the firm, certain grades of logs might yield a higher veneer value per dollar log cost as compared to some other log grades.

The logs were peeled for veneer in one of three thicknesses, namely 0.104", 0.130", and 0.171". There were several possible ways of laying up a plywood panel of some specified grade and dimensions. The model was designed to select the most economical panel construction. However, it was also encouraged to make use of all available veneer. This might mean having to use some less economical panel structure at times in order to use up some "odd" veneer being jointly produced with the rest. It is too difficult in practice to use veneer inventories for the purpose of co-ordinating veneer production and veneer consumption to the extent of seeing every piece of veneer used in the most economical constructions. That was why the L.P. model was designed without explicit provision for inventory change and veneer inventory accumulation was given a value of zero dollar.

The production and the sale of panels of all the grades and dimensions as commonly found in the market were programmed for in the model.

INPUT DATA FOR THE L.P. MODEL

Information on veneer yield from individual grades of logs had not been collected by the existing information collection system. A random sample of logs of various grades was processed under normal operating conditions to provide the necessary information on veneer yield and processing machine-time.[5]

Historical data on operating costs such as for labour and power were analysed to determine their variability with the level of operations. The variable cost of operating each process centre per unit time was computed. A time study was carried out to determine the process time needed for processing per unit of log or per unit of plywood panel of a particular type under normal operating conditions.

The log supply opportunities were determined from a projection of the past supplies from the company's own forest land and its experience with the open log market within its reach. The sale opportunities were projections based on past sales. Cost and prices anticipated for the period were used in the analysis.

The L.P. problem was solved and further analysed using the IBM LP-III 7040/7044 (a library computer programme) on an IBM 7040 computer.

SIGNIFICANT INFORMATION REVEALED BY THE L.P. ANALYSIS

On Panel Profitability.   The L.P. analysis suggested that it was better for the firm to leave production facilities idle and log supplies untapped than to continue producing the two thinnest types of panel for all panel grades. At that time about 20% of the firm's dollar sales were derived from these thin panels.

The shadow prices of the panels expressed as a per cent of panel prices appeared to be consistently higher with the increase of panel thickness and also higher for the 4′ X 10′ panels as compared to the 4′ X 8′ panels. Therefore, it was strongly suspected that the existing price structure was placing a high premium on panel thickness and on 4′ X 10′ panels. This might call for a re-examination of its pricing policy or a re-orientation of its sales policies.

On Log Prices.   The L.P. analysis also suggested that it was more economical to use logs of grades Peeler Nos. 2 and 3 and sawlog No. 2 than logs of grades Peeler Nos. 1 and 4 and S.F.P. (i.e. suitable-for-peeling). This suggested that the log price structure might be unduly favourable to log grades Peeler Nos. 1 and 4 and S.F.P., either unintentionally or due to some other competing uses for these particular grades of logs. However, to the company it provided a guideline for log purchasing or for determining the alternative uses for its own supply of logs. Though logs do not come in booms of a single grade or a specified combination of grades, there is a certain amount of room for choosing those booms with the more favourable combinations of grades.

CONCLUSION

So far no satisfactory method exists for allocating the joint-wood-cost to the plywood panel so as to make the panel cost useful for price setting purpose or for analysing panel profitability. Yet, panel prices have to be fixed somehow, or for an individual firm, guesses may have to be made as to which are the more profitable panels to concentrate on selling. Guesses may be unrealistic and yet no one may be wise to the fact!

One of the products of a linear programming analysis of a plywood manufacturing business is "shadow prices" of the various types of plywood panels. The shadow price measures the true marginal profit contribution of a particular plywood panel. Its measure is valid only for a certain range of the volume of sale of that particular panel and for a given set of log supply, production facilities and sale conditions. However, the L.P. analysis can produce a comprehensive list of shadow prices for various ranges of sale volume and various operating conditions. In this way, the shadow prices may serve as a good indicator of the profitability of the various types of plywood panels and are, therefore, useful for evaluating the panel price structure or helping a firm to best adapt its operations to a given price structure.

APPENDIX 1. Plywood manufacturing process.

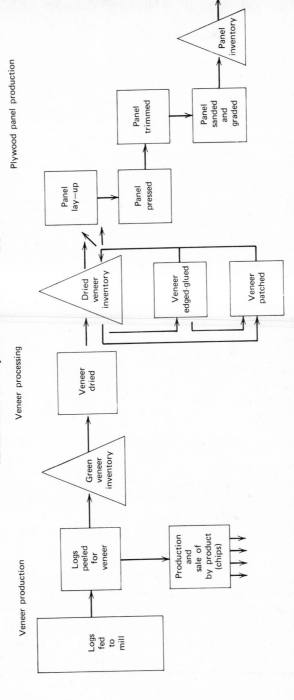

APPENDIX 2.   Representation of the Plywood Manufacturing L.P. Model

Description of columns Row description		Log peeling			Plywood panel production & sale			
		X_1	X_2	X_3	X_4	X_5	X_6	
Logs peeled—								
Grade $P \neq 1$		X_1	$+X_2$					$\leqslant 150$
Grade $P \neq 2$				X_3				$\leqslant 50$
Veneer input & veneer consumption								
4' X 8' X 0.104"	A	$8.4X_1$			$-5.0X_4$		$-5.0X_6$	$\geqslant 0$
	B	$4.2X_1$			$-7.5X_4$			$\geqslant 0$
	C	$3.5X_1$			$-10.0X_4$			$\geqslant 0$
4' X 8' X 0.130"	A			$7.2X_3$		$-5.0X_5$		$\geqslant 0$
	B		$3.8X_2$			$-5.0X_5$	$-5.0X_6$	$\geqslant 0$
	C			$3.0X_3$		$-7.5X_5$		$\geqslant 0$
4' X 8' X 0.171"	C			$11.0X_3$			$-7.5X_6$	$\geqslant 0$
Panel sale								
4' X 8' X 4/5"	$G1$				X_4	$+X_5$		$\leqslant 50$
4' X 8' X 3/4"	$G2$						X_6	$\leqslant 150$
Lathe capacity		$0.03X_1$	$+0.02X_2$	$+0.03X_3$				$\leqslant 100$
Dryer capacity		$0.12X_1$	$+0.11X_2$	$+0.12X_3$				$\leqslant 200$
Press capacity					$0.08X_4$	$+0.09X_5$	$+0.08X_6$	$\leqslant 150$
Sander capacity					$0.02X_4$	$+0.03X_5$		$\leqslant 50$
Objective function (to maximise)		$-240X_1$	$-230X_2$	$-160X_3$	$+670X_4$	$+660X_5$	$+520X_6$	

Legend to Appendix 2

Definition of the Units Used:
Logs are measured in units of 10,000 foot-board-measure each.
Veneers are measured in units of 100 sheets (or sheet-equivalent) each.
Plywood panels are measured in units of 250 panels each.
Machine capacities are measured in time units of 10 hours each.
The objective function is defined in dollars.

Definition of the Columns Used in the Matrix:
X_1: The value given to X_1 in the solution represents the number of units of log grade $P \neq 1$ being peeled for a veneer of 4' by 8' by 0.104". Each unit of log thus peeled yields 8.4 units of A veneer, 4.2 units of B veneer and 3.5 units of C veneer. Each unit of log thus peeled takes up 0.03 units of lathe time and 0.12 units of dryer time. The log cost plus the variable process cost of peeling and drying less the recovery of by-product is $240 per unit of log.

X_2: Similar to X_1, representing the peeling of grade $P \neq 1$ logs for veneer of 4' by 8' by 0.130''.

X_3: This represents the peeling of $P \neq 2$ logs for veneer of 4' by 8' by 0.171''. Each unit peeled yields 11.0 units of C veneer. Each unit of log takes up 0.03 units of lathe time and 0.12 units of dryer time. The cost of log plus the variable process cost of peeling and drying less by-product recovery is $160 per unit of log.

X_4: This represents the production (and sale) of plywood panels of 4' by 8' by 4/5'', grade $G1$. Each unit of panel is constructed with 5.0 units of A veneer, 7.5 units of B veneer and 10.0 units of C veneer, i.e., using a 9-ply construction. Each unit of panel takes up 0.08 units of press time and 0.02 units of sander time. The sale price of the panel, less the variable process cost of pressing and sanding the panel and the cost of glue is $670.

X_5: Similar to X_4, except that an alternative panel construction of seven plies, utilising veneer with a thickness of 0.130'' rather than veneer of 0.104'' is being used.

X_6: This represents the production (and sale) of panels of 4' by 8' by 3/4'', grade $G2$. Each unit of panel is constructed with 5.0 units of A veneer of .104'' thick, 5.0 units of B veneer of .130'' thick and 7.5 units of C veneer of 0.171'' thick. Since the surface of the panel is not sanded, no sanding time is required.

Definition of the Rows Used in the Matrix:

The purpose of the equations (or inequalities) is to define individually and/or jointly the limits of the values that each of the X variables may assume in the solution.

For example: Row No. 1:—$X_1 + X_2 \leqslant 150$. This means that the amount of $P \neq 1$ logs peeled (i.e. the value of X_1 and X_2) may at the most add up to 150, the amount of $P \neq 1$ logs available.

Row No. 3:—$8.4X_1 - 5.0X_4 - 5.0X_6 \geqslant 0$. This means that the amount of 4' by 8' by 0.104'' A veneer supplied (as determined by the value of X_1) is to at least meet the consumption requirements under X_4 and X_6.

Row No. 10:—$X_4 + X_5 \leqslant 50$. This means that the total amount of 4' by 8' by 4/5'' $G1$ panels produced and sold are not to exceed the expected demand of 50 units.

Row No. 12:—$0.03X_1 + 0.02X_2 + 0.03X_3 \leqslant 100$. This means that the total consumption of lathe time is not to exceed the 100 units available.

The Objective Function:

This measures the profit accruing to the plywood manufacturing business. The model is required to select the set of values for the X variables so as to give the maximum profit. The values of the X variables, of course, have to be within the limits set by the equations (or inequalities).

APPENDIX 3.   Veneer Recovery (per 10,000 FBM of Logs Peeled). Veneer Grades (after Upgrading via Patching and Edge-Gluing) in Units of 100 Sheets or Equivalent

Dimension 4' X 8'	Log Grade	A	B	B_1	C/F	U/C	Backs No. 1	Solid centres	Centres No. 1	XB	XC
.104"	Peeler No. 1	1.76	6.44	2.75	2.89	2.31	4.83	—	0.18	0.41	7.82
.130"	Peeler No. 1	1.47	4.07	3.59	2.59	0.35	4.52	—	—	0.37	7.04
.104"	Peeler No. 2	1.69	4.88	2.27	1.89	0.89	3.59	0.003	0.19	0.69	13.08
.130"	Peeler No. 2	0.71	2.55	2.50	0.67	5.00	5.32	0.004	0.22	0.33	6.31
.104"	Peeler No. 3	1.03	3.88	5.05	0.82	4.75	9.23	0.001	0.49	0.44	8.35
.130"	Peeler No. 3	0.80	3.02	0.64	1.63	3.01	8.50	—	—	0.46	8.70
.104"	Peeler No. 4	—	1.38	2.00	2.00	2.69	14.22	0.008	0.38	0.50	9.58
.130"	Peeler No. 4	—	0.72	2.30	0.88	1.97	12.28	—	—	0.43	8.17
.104"	S.F.P.	—	1.20	0.24	2.48	1.76	20.90	—	—	0.56	10.78
.130"	S.F.P.	—	0.90	0.65	1.69	3.72	12.98	—	—	0.48	9.13
.104"	S-Log No. 2	—	0.54	0.69	4.25	2.72	12.19	—	0.05	0.54	10.28
.130"	S-Log No. 2	—	0.34	0.41	2.61	1.87	8.54	—	—	0.48	9.22
.171"		—	—	—	—	—	—	1.09	11.93	0.77	5.04
.171"	S-Log No. 3	—	—	—	—	—	—	0.55	10.45	0.76	6.88
.130"	Interior	—	0.12	0.24	0.49	1.86	8.67	0.05	2.43	0.54	10.35
.171"	Interior	—	—	—	—	—	—	0.55	10.37	0.79	7.12

FOOTNOTES

1. C. T. Horngren, *Cost Accounting—A Managerial Approach,* Prentice-Hall, 1964.

2. Those readers who wish to know the history of the application of L.P. analysis in solving management problems may refer to the introductory chapter of R. Dorfman and others, *Linear Programming and Economic Analysis,* McGraw-Hill Co. Inc., New York, 1958.

3. A practical, but yet reasonably accurate approximation may be to use 250 plywood panels as per unit measure of plywood panels in the L.P. analysis.

4. See Appendix 2 for a representation of the L.P. model.

5. See Appendix 3 for details on veneer yield. There is hardly any published information on veneer yield of logs.

Multiple Product Costing by Multiple Correlation Analysis

John S. Chiu &
Don T. DeCoster

Many firms have production processes that result in a multiple product output from one primary input of materials or costs. Typical illustrations of this type of production are the petroleum, forestry, food processing, and chemical industries. Any attempt at product costing in these or similar industries highlights the apparent problem, that, when costs are incurred in a lump-sum aggregate to produce more than one end objective, the allocation of these costs is always based upon an individual value judgment—not upon an underlying self-evident truth. This was pointed out by Charles H. Griffin when he said that "logical and reasonable bases of association must be provided to identify cost measurements with the various classes of products manufactured."[1] It is impossible to discover *the* cost. Rather, attempts lead to finding *a* cost—a cost that is logical and reasonable.

ACCOUNTING AND MULTIPLE PRODUCTS

Accountants have defined joint products as those that are necessarily produced together. With this general definition as a point of departure, attempts to

---

SOURCE: Reprinted with permission of *The Accounting Review*, Vol. 41, No. 4 (October, 1966), pp. 673–679.

EDITORS' NOTE: A technical appendix has been omitted.

distinguish between joint products have relied upon their significance to the firm. For example, the National Association of Cost Accountants describes multiple products as follows:

> The products of greater importance are termed *major products* and the products of lesser importance are termed *by-products.* Major products are also called prime products or main products. . . .Where two or more major products appear in a jointly produced combination, these products are called *co-products* to indicate that they are products of like importance produced together.[2]

While there is no unanimity of opinion on these exact terms, there is definitely a consistency of approach as demonstrated in accounting literature.

The accounting motivation for developing product costs from joint costs has been primarily periodic financial reporting. The determination of inventory values and cost of goods sold requires that the joint costs be split between accounting periods and products. While the results from an approximate method of cost allocation are not ideal, they can be tolerated where it is believed that the actual results will have a minimum variance from the ideal situation. This will happen when the method is applied consistently over time periods and the inventories experience relatively small fluctuations. Where the beginning and ending inventories are zero, the allocation will have no effect upon periodic income. Warnings are given, however, in using these cost allocations for managerial decision purposes. "Where costs are wanted by internal management for evaluating alternative courses of action, it is often preferable to work with cost differentials and thereby to avoid allocating joint costs."[3] Two broad methods to allocate joint costs to co-products have been used by accountants. (Methods of by-product costing are not reviewed here since the principal topic is co-products.)

Allocation by Physical Attributes

The allocation of costs by physical attributes assumes that the products should receive costs relative to the benefits that the products received from the production process. Numerous physical factors are used including weight, volume, production run time, and qualitative weighted factors. Many industries can find unique physical measurements such as the petroleum industry has done with the barrel-gravity, gravity-heat, and BTU measurements. This method can achieve considerable sophistication when adapted by individual firms. All cost allocations by physical attributes, regardless of their degree of refinement, suffer from two potential weaknesses. First, there is the underlying assumption that the costs incurred vary in direct proportion to variations in the physical attributes. Second, all physical units are treated as homogeneous in nature, which may not be true.

Allocation by Ability to Carry Costs

Probably the most prevalent method used, and possibly the most acceptable by accountants, is the allocation of costs to the products on the basis of their ability to absorb costs. The allocation of costs by the relative sales value method results in costs for each product that are proportional to the sales value. This can be considered not primarily as a way of allocating the costs among the products, but, as a way of allocating the profit. As stated by one writer, "this is an arbitrary method of allocation and does not necessarily reflect the true cost of any particular type and grade of product. It simply spreads the cost in such a manner as to assign the same percentage of gross profit to each product produced. Thus, it does not provide a reliable yardstick for planning and directing manufacturing operations."[4] Changes in the market value of one or more of the products automatically cause a change in the cost-allocation basis. Yet, it is likely that any one product will cost no more or less because of the market change. The method can cause distorted income measurements as well as inaccurate managerial decisions when some of the products' market value remains stable while others fluctuate.

Accountants have utilized variations of these two methods for income determination with consistency, if not with deep satisfaction. This was stated well in the N.A.C.A. research study:

> While a chosen basis can be rationalized, it cannot be proved more correct than another by a process of objective measurement. . . .While satisfactory for over-all financial reporting, the study shows that management usually does not rely upon individual product cost or profit figures in making decisions with respect to joint products.[5]

ECONOMICS AND MULTIPLE PRODUCTS

A more fruitful method for managerial decision-making, as well as for income determination, in co-product cost allocation is a shift from consideration of their significance to the firm to the nature of their generation. Joel Dean distinguishes products by their generation when he states:

> For product-costing it is desirable to distinguish two broad categories of common products: joint products and alternative products. When an increase in the production of one product causes an increase in the output of another product, then the products and their costs are traditionally defined as joint. In contrast, when an increase in the output of a product is accompanied by a reduction in the output of other products, it is a case of what may be called alternative products.[6]

Distinguishing between types of multiple product outputs allows a more flexible approach to cost allocations. Instead of relying upon methods that do not provide reliable yardsticks for planning and control, a more discriminate method can be used where the products are controllable in output proportions. Discussing the appropriateness of cost allocations, Dean stated:

> Assigning common costs to individual products is more difficult and less useful when the products are joint than when the products are alternative. The cost of an alternative product can always be computed in terms of the foregone profits from the other product, whereas the cost of a joint product (as distinguished from the cost of the product package) is essentially indeterminate. When the proportion of joint products is fixed, cost allocation is impossible as well as footless, since there is no alternative but to produce the package. When proportions are variable, marginal costs with respect to changes in product-mix would be useful in deciding between alternative product-mixes.[7]

A study published by the National Bureau of Economic Research said essentially the same thing when it stated:

> A rational basis can be established for price and output decisions under conditions where joint products are made in variable proportions. In such circumstances it is theoretically possible, through a continuous variation of these proportions, to estimate the marginal costs of each separate product. Strictly, the marginal costs of a product thus determined would vary for different levels of total output. An enterprise will reach the correct economic combination of products for profit maximization when the marginal cost of each product equals the revenue increment from its sale.[8]

Accountants have not ignored the fact that products can be of either a fixed or variable proportion. For example:

> When two or more jointly produced products can be produced in varying proportions, or are not inevitably produced together, it is possible to determine the *differential cost* of each by varying the output of one or the other product. In essence this procedure is possible for all *substitute* or *alternative* products, although the cost of the determination may make it uneconomic to use it.[9]

There is tacit recognition that the proper way to develop cost-oriented decisions for products is to utilize the marginal cost of production. Yet, at the same time the methods of allocating costs do not yield marginal information. The use of multiple correlation analysis for product cost allocations generates an approximation of the marginal costs of the products. This knowledge can open the door to many valuable decision tools not otherwise available.

AN ILLUSTRATION APPLYING MULTIPLE CORRELATION

Table 1 shows the total cost, Y, of producing various levels of three alternative products X_1, X_2 and X_3 for ten consecutive periods.

TABLE 1.   Original Data

Periods	Y Total cost in thousands of dollars	X_1 Product 1	X_2 Product 2	X_3 Product 3
		(in same physical units)		
1	80.8	232	87	390
2	77.8	221	172	262
3	76.4	258	125	313
4	67.5	300	52	300
5	83.5	198	151	349
6	80.0	183	92	489
7	37.9	181	33	131
8	88.7	159	111	441
9	84.5	197	209	228
10	105.3	145	234	410
Total	782.4	2,074	1,266	3,313

By two different methods of computation to be described later, the application of multiple correlation to these data yields the following results:

A. The "standby cost" when zero output is produced is statistically determined at $10,193.15, designated as b_0.

B. The linear marginal costs for three alternative products are estimated as follows:

Product 1: $ 48.67 per unit, designated as b_1.
Product 2:   193.94 per unit, designated as b_2.
Product 3:   100.81 per unit, designated as b_3.

C. The probable statistical errors of these cost estimates (the b's), technically known as standard errors of regression coefficients, are estimated as follows:

Product 1: $31.69, designated as S_{b_1}.
Product 2:   22.20, designated as S_{b_2}.
Product 3:   12.75, designated as S_{b_3}.

These probable errors give a 95 per cent confidence that the "true" marginal cost of product 1 is in the range of -$28.99 to $126.33,[10] that of Product 2 between $139.55 and $248.33, and from $69.57 to $132.05 for Product 3. These confidence intervals can definitely be improved with more data, or less effectively, with wider ranges of fluctuation in the output levels of the products.[11] Unfortunately, the data extend only over ten periods.

One remarkable aspect of the computational results is the very high coefficient of multiple correlation $R = 0.9821$ out of the perfect correlation of 1.0000. This means that 96.44 per cent of the fluctuation in actual total cost (Y) is explained by the changes in the output levels of the products. This 0.9644 is technically known as the coefficient of multiple *determination* (mnemonically designated here as D) which is the square of the coefficient of multiple *correlation* (i.e., $D = R^2$). This R of 0.9821 can be viewed as a sample estimate of the true but unknown value of R. Checking this observed coefficient of multiple correlation, 0.9821, against a standard probability graph for R shows that the population value of R should be at least 0.92, with 95 per cent confidence.[12] This high value of R provides ample assurance that the linear multiple regression is a valid model. If this were not the case, nonlinear multiple regression might have to be considered. Although nonlinear models are not improbable to use, they can be messy, time-consuming, and difficult to interpret.

It is shown above that the three products taken together explain a high percentage, 0.9644, of the variation in total cost. How about each individual product? The three t-ratios listed below give the relative significance of each product:

Product 1:

$$t_1 = \frac{b_1 - \beta_1}{S_{b_1}} = \frac{\$48.67 - 0}{\$31.69} = 1.536.$$

Product 2:

$$t_1 = \frac{b_2 - \beta_2}{S_{b_2}} = \frac{\$193.94 - 0}{\$22.20} = 8.735.$$

Product 3:

$$t_3 = \frac{b_3 - \beta_3}{S_{b_3}} = \frac{\$100.81 - 0}{\$12.75} = 7.910.$$

To facilitate the interpretation of these t-ratios, the following hypothetical situation is used as an illustration. If the total cost (Y) were not affected by the changes in the output level of an individual product, say, Product 2, its true linear marginal cost, designated as β_2, would be zero. Even allowing random sampling and/or measurement error, the estimate b_2 of β_2 should approximate zero under the assumption of no relation between total cost and volume change in Product 2. b_2 can deviate from the assumed zero value of

β_2 dependent upon the size of the error which is estimated at S_{b_2} = \$22.20. Checking the deviation of observed b_2 from the assumed β_2 against the magnitude of the error S_{b_2} gives a ratio indicative of the size of the gap between the observation (b_2) and the assumption (β_2) relative to the probable error S_{b_2}. Thus, the ratio $(b_2 - \beta_2)/S_{b_2}$, which is conveniently called t, is formulated.

This t_2 should vary between the range from -2.45 to $+2.45$ with 95 per cent probability under the assumption of β_2 = 0.[13] Note that this range is centered around the assumed zero value for β_2. In other words, t can deviate as far from zero as -2.45 or $+2.45$ by random error even if the assumption of β_2 = 0 is true. If the t value falls outside of this range the assumption of β_2 = 0 cannot be made. The actual value of t_2 is $+8.735$ which is beyond the upper limit of $+2.3$. Therefore, it is positively concluded that the linear marginal cost of Product 2 is not zero. In other words, total cost definitely depends upon the output level of Product 2. This is scarcely surprising.

The next concern is the linear marginal cost of Product 2, assuming the conclusion is not zero. This goes back to the confidence limits described earlier for β_2 which is between \$139.55 and \$248.33. Conservatively speaking, the linear marginal cost of Product 2 is at least \$139.55. It could be as high as \$248.33. The "indeterminacy" within this range of \$139.55 and \$248.33 is due to the lack of perfect knowledge and the rather small amount of experience (merely ten periods). Applying exactly the same kind of analysis above to the other two products shows that t_1 = 1.536 is not within range to be absolutely conclusive even though it is usable. Ratio t_3 = 7.910 very definitely shows the linear marginal cost of Product 3 cannot be zero.

With due regard to its limitations, the main advantage in applying multiple regression to estimate the marginal costs of multiple products is its recognition of the *cost structure* of multiple products and hence its *simultaneous estimation* of *all* of the marginal costs. This statistical method corresponds to the *ceteris paribus* or "marginal" concept in economic theory, i.e., the estimated marginal cost is equal to the change in total cost, per unit change in the output level of any one of the multiple products, other things held constant. This method also corresponds to a very important concept in differential calculus, partial derivatives. Symbolically, the model postulated here is as follows:

$$Y_i = \beta_0 + \beta_1 X_{1i} + \beta_2 X_{2i} + \beta_3 X_{3i} + E_i,$$
$$\text{for } i = 1, 2, \ldots, n,$$

where $Y_1\ Y_2, \ldots, Y_n$ stands for the series of total costs over the n periods (in this case, n = 10); $X_{11}, X_{12}, \ldots, X_{1n}$ the series of varying output levels of Product 1; similarly, $X_{21}, X_{22}, \ldots, X_{2n}$ and $X_{31}, X_{32}, \ldots, X_{3n}$ for Products 2 and 3, respectively; and finally the $E_1, E_2, \ldots, E_n$ the series of random errors. These β's are the following partial derivatives:

$$\beta_1 = \frac{\partial Y}{\partial X_1}, \beta_2 = \frac{\partial Y}{\partial X_2}, \text{ and } \beta_3 = \frac{\partial Y}{\partial X_3}.$$

β_3, for example, measures the change in total cost Y per unit change in the output level X_3 of Product 3. The estimated marginal costs are given previously as $b_1 = \$48.67$, $b_2 = \$193.94$, and $b_3 = \$100.81$. Actually, these b's are the estimates of the partial derivatives. Thus the derivative of the regression function (a hyperplane) is equal to marginal cost.

Suppose that a simplified view were taken by ignoring the cost structure and accordingly estimating the marginal costs independently. The simple linear correlation of total cost with the output level of Product 1 yields a marginal cost of -\$117.96 which shows that the total cost will decline if the output volume of Product 1 is increased, an obviously absurd conclusion. Those of Product 2 and 3 are \$203.17 and \$112.10, respectively, which differ from the multiple correlation results above (\$193.94 and \$100.81). Although the differences are not large in this instance, there is no assurance that they are insignificant in other cases. The difference in marginal cost for Product 1 by simple versus multiple correlations is however large indeed; +\$48.67 versus -\$117.96.

MULTIPLE CORRELATION ASSUMPTIONS

The use of multiple correlation analysis for multiple product cost allocation can be of tremendous benefit. Like other methods of cost allocations it is not a cure-all to all problems. Nor can it be considered as a "perfect" answer to the problem. There are definite constraints in its use which must be recognized if it is to be used realistically.

Product Limitations.   The use of multiple correlation analysis is valuable with only one type of multiple products—those characterized by variable output proportions. Where the production output is fixed in terms of product proportions, the determination of marginal costs per product is impossible. In these cases accountants will have to continue the use of other methods such as the relative sales value or quantity methods.

Equation Limitations.   The reliability of the estimates from correlation analysis will depend to a large extent upon the ability to fit an appropriate curve to the information. In the previous example a linear relationship was used with good reliability. However, in other situations it may be necessary to develop non-linear curves. This poses few practical problems if the data are being analyzed electronically, but if the calculations must be done by hand it may limit the scope of analysis. Where linear equations are used, the marginal cost is a constant over the span of activity considered; in more complex situations this may be undesirable.

Period Limitations.   There are several problems which arise as a result of the use of discrete time periods to measure the observations. First, there is the unrealistic assumption that the "readings" of the data have been taken over a continuum. The measurements of the data are usually based upon different time periods. This requires an assumption that the relationships being measured have not changed over time. The statistical measure becomes an average for the time periods included. Hence, if production methods or raw material inputs have changed materially over time, an incorrect pattern of relationships may result. Second, the statistical relationship can be extrapolated, either forward or backward, over only the range of the observations. This relevant range may restrict the usefulness of the correlation in some circumstances. Third, and extremely important, is the number of observations required. Multiple correlation can be used with a very large number of multiple products only if a large number of period observations are available. To maintain the degrees of freedom necessary, there must be at least $K + 1$ observations in terms of the number of multiple products.

Causation Limitations.   The coefficient of correlation must be considered only as a measure of co-variation. Cause and effect relationships are not identified by the technique. It is possible that a variation of *either* variable may be caused by a variation in the other. Also, a co-variation in the two variables may be due to another variable not included in the analysis or it may be due entirely to chance.

In conclusion, multiple correlation analysis frees the accountant from making the assumption that marginal costs per product are always too difficult to unearth. For products that have an output proportion that is variable, multiple correlation allocates costs in a method valuable for decision-making. As with any statistical method, there are factors that lie in wait to trap the unwary. But in a practical setting these limitations will often fall by the wayside.

FOOTNOTES

1.   Charles H. Griffin, "Multiple Products Costing in Petroleum," *The Journal of Accountancy,* March 1958, p. 46.

2.   *Costing Joint Products,* National Association of Cost Accountants, Research Series, 31 (April 1, 1957), p. 7.

3.   *Ibid.,* p. 30.

4. Robert M. Simpson, "Accounting Problems of the Forest-Products Industry," *The Journal of Accountancy,* September 1957, p. 44.

5. N.A.C.A., *op. cit.,* p. 4.

6. Joel Dean, *Managerial Economics* (Prentice-Hall Inc., 1951), p. 317.

7. *Ibid.,* p. 319.

8. National Bureau of Economic Research, *Cost Behavior and Price Policy* 1943, pp. 177–178.

9. Robert I. Dickey, Ed., *Accountants' Cost Handbook* (Ronald Press Company, 1960), p. 135.

10. $b_1 \pm t_{n-k-1} S_{b_1}$ = \$48.67 ± 2.45 (\$31.69)
    = (−\$28.99, \$126.33)

    $b_2 \pm t_{n-k-1} S_{b_2}$ = \$193.94 ± 2.45 (\$22.20)
    = (\$139.55, \$248.33)

    $b_3 \pm t_{n-k-1} S_{b_3}$ = \$100.81 ± 2.45 (\$12.75)
    = (\$69.57, \$132.05)

11. The standard error is inversely related to the moment matrix (or the matrix of product sums). The magnitude of the moment matrix varies with the sample size n and/or the variances of the independent variables, $\sigma^2 x_1$, $\sigma^2 x_2$, and $\sigma^3 x_2$. See, for example, J. Johnston, *Econometric Methods* (McGraw-Hill, 1963), p. 110.

12. See, for example, M. Ezekiel and K. Fox: *Methods of Correlation and Regression Analysis,* 3rd ed. (John Wiley, 1959), p. 296, Figure 17.3.

13. The value of t ratio with $n-k-1 = 10-3-1 = 6$ degrees of freedom at $\alpha = .05$ is 2.45 which can be found in almost any statistics textbook or table.

A Contribution Margin Approach to the Analysis of Capacity Utilization

Charles T. Horngren

The analysis of variances is one of the major topics in our cost accounting courses. The volume (capacity) variance, which supposedly gauges the utilization of capacity, probably gets the prize as the most baffling measure[1] that is produced by variance analysis. What does it mean? Why should we compute it?

This article develops a conceptual framework that may prove better than traditional volume variance analysis because it (1) distinguishes long-range and short-range factors, (2) demonstrates the weaknesses of existing practices, (3) sharply pinpoints responsibility in relation to the purposes of short-range planning and control and separates the role of physical measures of capacity[2] from the role of valuation of that capacity, and (4) indicates how a contribution-margin or opportunity-cost approach to valuation is superior to a unitized historical-cost approach.

LONG-RANGE AND SHORT-RANGE FACTORS

Two Aspects of Capacity: Acquisition and Utilization

Organizations assemble human and physical resources that provide the capacity to produce and sell. These commitments often require heavy expenditures that affect performance over long spans of time. The implications for managers are two-fold. First, careful planning is obviously crucial to the wise acquisition

---

SOURCE: Reprinted with permission from *The Accounting Review*, Vol. 42, No. 3 (April, 1967), pp. 254–264.

of fixed resources. Second, the acquired capacity should be properly utilized if current net income[3] is to be maximized.

Many fixed costs result from capital budgeting decisions, reached after studying the expected impact of these expenditures on operations over a number of years. The choice of a capacity size may be influenced by a combination of two major factors, each involving trade-off decisions and each heavily dependent on long-range forecasts of demand, material costs, and labor costs:

1. Provision for seasonal and cyclical *fluctuations* in demand. The trade-off is between (a) additional costs of physical capacity versus (b) the costs of stock-outs and/or the carrying costs of safety stocks of such magnitude as to compensate for seasonal and cyclical variations, the costs of overtime premium, sub-contracting, and so on.
2. Provision for upward *trends* in demand. The trade-off is between (a) the costs of constructing too much capacity for initial needs versus (b) the later extra costs of satisfying demand by alternative means. For example, should a factory designed to make color television tubes be 100,000, 150,000, or 200,000-tube level?

Acquisition of Capacity and Follow-up

Suppose that management decided to build a factory that can produce 200,000 units yearly. Also suppose that the expected demand used to justify the size of the factory was a long-run average of 160,000 units for five to ten years. The larger factory was built because management decided that this was the most economical way to provide for seasonal, cyclical, and trend factors that may result in a demand at a peak rate of 200,000 units per year (practical capacity) during certain times.

A follow-up or audit of planning decisions is needed to see how well actual utilization harmonizes with the activity levels used in the plan that authorized the acquisition of the facilities. The follow-up helps evaluate the accuracy of management's past long-range planning decisions and should improve the quality of similar decisions in the future. The pertinent base for comparison is a particular year's activity level used in the capital budget that authorized the acquisition of facilities. Comparison should be done on a project-by-project basis to see whether the predictions in the capital budgeting schedules are being fulfilled. Such comparisons need not be integrated in the over-all information system on a routine basis.

Normal activity, 160,000 units in our example, is the rate of activity needed to meet average sales demand over a period long enough to encompass seasonal and cyclical fluctuations; it is the average volume level used as a basis for long-range plans. In our example, a comparison of currently budgeted sales or actual sales with the 160,000-unit normal activity might be suggested as the best basis for auditing and assessing the impact of long-range planning decisions. However, normal activity is an average that has little or no significance with respect to a follow-up for a particular year.

Moreover, normal activity should not be a reference point for judging current performance (i.e., the volume variance so often computed using historical costs). This is an example of misusing a long-range average measure for a short-range particular purpose. The acquisition of facilities and other fixed resources requires a planning and control horizon of many years—a horizon that fluctuates because various resources are often obtained piece-meal or on a project-by-project basis. In contrast, our concern here is with the planning and control of current operations; we shall see that the notion of normal activity has no bearing on this problem.

WEAKNESS OF EXISTING PRACTICES

Unitizing Historical Costs

How do accountants actually apply dollar measures to the utilization of capacity? They "unitize" historical fixed manufacturing costs and use the resultant unit rate to measure a volume variance (and to cost products). In our example, suppose that manufacturing costs are $131,200 per year. The accountant would relate this cost to the number of units to get a predetermined unit cost. He might select from several possible rates. Let us consider two:

Alternative A—Use practical capacity as a base:

$$\text{Unit cost} = \frac{\text{Total fixed manufacturing costs}}{\text{Practical capacity in units}} = \frac{\$131,200}{200,000 \text{ units}} = \$.656 \text{ per unit}$$

Alternative B—Use budgeted sales as a base:

$$\text{Unit cost} = \frac{\text{Total fixed manufacturing costs}}{\text{Budgeted sales in units}} = \frac{\$131,200}{164,000 \text{ units}} = \$.80 \text{ per unit}$$

He would use one or the other of these unit costs for costing product and for measuring volume variances.

There are numerous drawbacks to using a historical-cost approach for management planning and control. Historical costs have no particular bearing on the management problem of obtaining desired current utilization of existing capacity. For instance, let us compare the dollar results of using the above two historical unit costs:

Alternative A–Use a historical cost unitized at $.656 per unit:

Practical capacity 200,000 units; fixed costs to account for	$131,200
Actual production and sales, 140,000 units at $.656	91,840
Volume variance, 60,000 units X $.656	$ 39,360

Alternative B–Use a historical cost unitized at $.80 per unit:

Master budget* sales of 164,000 units; fixed costs to account for	$131,200
Actual production and sales, 140,000 units at $.80	112,000
Volume variance, 24,000 X $.80	$ 19,200

*"Master budget" is used here to designate the over-all, comprehensive financial and operating plans for the year.

Effect of Numerator and Denominator

Note that the fixed cost rate as traditionally computed depends on a numerator of historical manufacturing costs only. Fixed selling and administrative costs, which often can be huge, are not incorporated in the volume variance or in the cost of the product.

The unit cost is also affected by the denominator selected. Practical capacity as a denominator results in one unit cost, while master budgeted sales as a denominator results in another unit cost. The choice of the denominator thus affects the amount of the variances (and, incidentally, computed product costs). In our example, the volume variance is either $39,360 or $19,200, depending on whether practical capacity or master budgeted sales is selected as the denominator. Such variety in quantification is difficult to justify and explain.

Characteristics of the Volume Variance Based on Historical Costs

Most cost accounting systems simultaneously try to (1) accumulate costs for planning and control and (2) apply costs to product for inventory valuation and income determination. The approach to (1) and (2) for variable costs usually entails the use of unit costs for direct material, direct labor, and variable manufacturing overhead. No volume variances arise because the total variable costs incurred are equal to the total variable costs applied to product. However, analytical troubles begin when the same approach is attempted with fixed costs.

A volume variance arises because of the conflict between accounting for control (via budgets) and accounting for product costing (via unit costing rates for applying overhead to product). The development of a product-costing rate results in an artificial transformation. Traditionally, for product-costing purposes, all costs rank abreast; no distinctions between cost behavior patterns are appropriate. Thus, the fixed cost is accounted for in product costing *as if it were a variable cost.* A volume variance appears whenever the activity level actually encountered fails to coincide with the original activity level used as a denominator in the computation of a product-costing rate.

In a sense, the volume variance based on historical costs is little more than a bookkeeping bridge between the control and product costing purposes of the cost accounting system. It is difficult to see how such a variance could have been invented solely for purposes of current planning and control, our major concern here. Fixed costs and variable costs have different frames of reference, timing, and control features. Fixed costs simply are not divisible like variable costs. Fixed costs usually come in big masses, and they are related to providing big chunks of sales or production capacity rather than to the production of a single unit of product. To use parallel analytical devices (e.g., variances, unit costs) for costs with unlike patterns of behavior is illogical and is a reflection of the product-costing purpose's immense influence on cost accounting systems.

Efficiency Variances and Fixed Costs

Consider another example of the attempts to analyze variable costs and fixed costs in a parallel manner. Students of cost accounting are familiar with the usual way of computing efficiency variances for variable costs such as direct material, direct labor, and variable overhead:

$$
\begin{matrix} \text{Variable cost} \\ \text{efficiency} \\ \text{variance} \end{matrix} = \begin{pmatrix} \text{Actual hours of input} \\ \text{minus} \\ \text{Standard hours allowed} \\ \text{for units produced} \end{pmatrix} \times \text{Hourly rate}
$$

The same approach is commonly taken to the computation of an efficiency variance for fixed overhead:

$$
\begin{matrix} \text{Fixed} \\ \text{overhead} \\ \text{efficiency} \\ \text{variance} \end{matrix} = \begin{pmatrix} \text{Actual hours of input} \\ \text{minus} \\ \text{Standard hours allowed} \\ \text{for units produced} \end{pmatrix} \times \begin{matrix} \text{Hourly fixed} \\ \text{overhead} \\ \text{rate} \end{matrix}
$$

But the resulting variance should be distinguished sharply from the efficiency variances for material, labor, and variable overhead, because efficient usage of these three factors can affect total actual cost incurrence, whereas short-run fixed overhead cost incurrence is not affected by efficiency. Moreover, the managers responsible for inefficiency will be aware of its existence through reports on variable costs control; so there is little additional management information to be gained from expressing ineffective utilization of fixed factory overhead factors in historical dollar terms.

Lack of Economic Significance

The unit fixed historical cost measure has little direct economic significance for current planning and control. It is conceptually inferior to the lost contribution margin per unit notion, which will be examined in a later section. Unlike variable costs, total fixed costs do not change as volume fluctuates. Fixed cost incurrence often entails lump-sum outlays based on a pattern of expected recoupment. But ineffective utilization of existing facilities has no bearing on the amount of fixed costs currently incurred. The economic effects of the inability to reach target volume levels are directly measured by lost contribution margins, even though these often are approximations. The historical cost approach to current planning and control fails to emphasize the useful distinction between *fixed cost incurrence,* on the one hand, and the objective of *maximizing the total contribution margin,* on the other hand. These are separable management problems, and the utilization of existing capacity is more closely related to the latter. This historical cost approach may possibly be useful in looking backward for an evaluation of past capital budgeting decisions. But the contribution margin approach is more useful in looking forward for current planning and control.

SHORT-RANGE PLANNING AND CONTROL[4]

Measuring Activity

What information about capacity can help management in planning and controlling operations? The analytical framework in Exhibit 1, expressed in physical terms only, should be useful.

P = *Practical capacity or practical attainable capacity* is the maximum level at which the plant or department can realistically operate efficiently, 200,000 units in our example. When an organization has provided a given amount of practical capacity, little can be done in day-to-day operations to affect the total level of the associated fixed costs. The practical capacity acts as a constraint on subsequent performance. Practical capacity is ideal production capability less allowances for unavoidable operating interruptions such as repair time, waiting time (down time) because of machine set-ups,

EXHIBIT 1.   Summary Framework for Analyzing Utilization of Capacity

Time of computation and use			
When the master budget is prepared	P = Practical Capacity M = Master budgeted sales	200,000 164,000	36,000 units expected idle capacity variance (1)
At the end of the period, when results are being evaluated	M = Master budgeted sales	164,000	16,000 units, marketing variance (2a)
	S = Scheduled production (sales orders received)	148,000	
	A = Actual production (and sales)	140,000	8,000 units, production variance (2b)

24,000 units volume variance (2)

(1) $P - M$ = Expected idle capacity variance, a measure of the anticipated idle capacity.
(2) $M - A$ = Volume variance, the difference between master budgeted sales and actual sales. (Note that this is the same as the volume variance that is traditionally computed—provided that master budgeted sales, and not practical capacity or "normal or average" sales, is used as a basis for the computation.)
    (2a) $M - S$ = Marketing variance, a measure of the failure of the sales force to get orders equal to the current sales forecast in the master budget.
    (2b) $S - A$ = Production variance; a measure of the failure of the production departments to adhere to production schedules.

and operator personal time. N.A.A. *Research Report No. 39* describes one company's approach:

> . . . practical attainable *hourly* capacity is developed by one company. Daily, monthly, and annual capacity is determined by multiplying the number of working hours in these periods by the practical attainable hourly capacity. Additional allowances are made for events which occur during a day, month, or year, but not hourly. For example, an allowance may be required for cleaning up equipment at the end of each day and for model change-over time once a year. Industry practice and current management policy determines the number of shifts, number of hours worked per week, holidays, reserve capacity provided for contingencies, and other allowances entering into the number of working hours per period. It may be noted that this company measures annual practical attainable capacity both with and without use of premium wage time. Thus management knows how much additional production can be obtained by use of premium wage rate time.[5]

M = *Master budgeted sales* is that volume of activity employed in formulating the master budget for the period. In this example, it represents management's best single estimate[6] of expected sales for the period, 164,000 units.

S = *Scheduled production* is that volume of sales orders received and assigned for production in the immediate current period,[7] 148,000 units in this case. This may not agree with the master budgeted sales because the marketing department may eventually fail to sell the budgeted number of 164,000.

A = *Actual production* (and sales delivered to customers) is self-explanatory, 140,000 units in this case.

For clarity, the framework in Exhibit 1 simplifies matters by making the following assumptions:

a. There are no changes in inventory levels; that is, all units currently produced are currently sold.
b. The single product, single department case is examined here. The same fundamental analysis is applicable (but not without difficulty) in more complex cases on a product-by-product, department-by-department basis.[8]

Expected Idle Capacity Variance

The expected idle capacity variance $(P - M)$ should be computed when the original master budget is prepared. Management may then (a) obtain a specific measure of anticipated idle capacity early enough (b) to adjust plans in light of possible uses for the expected idle capacity. This may be a give-and-take process, in which the initial master budget is altered (for example, prices may be changed) in light of the initial expected idle capacity.

The responsibility for such a variance may be partially attributable to the sales department for inability to penetrate all possible market potential and partially attributable to the managers who may have wisely or foolishly over-built facilities to meet future demand. Other possible explanations may include general economic conditions or particular competitive circumstances.[9] The point is that the alternatives available under current planning and control are constrained by the past decisions which provided the present facilities. Current plans should concentrate on the optimum utilization of given facilities.

Note the difference in timing and in the frame of reference for evaluating different decisions. Practical capacity becomes important in the course of preparing the master budget. At the end of the period, however, the master budgeted sales is the key to the evaluation of results.

N.A.A. *Research Report No. 39* (p. 24) advocates evaluating performance by comparing practical capacity with scheduled production because it "measures the additional output that could be attained without incurring additional capacity costs." Advocates of practical capacity as a basis for the evaluation of performance rightly maintain that management should be regularly aware of all idle facilities. However, when do they need this information? The critical time is probably at the master budget planning stage, not the evaluation of performance stage. The master budgeted sales is the relevant base for analysis at the latter stage. The point is developed more fully below.

Total Volume Variance

The measurement system may be designed to follow up on various versions of capacity, each serving a different purpose. To continue our example, production for the current year was 140,000 units, although current production schedules called for 148,000 units. What measures would help management in the evaluation of current results? Variances should help pinpoint responsibility. Exhibit 1 shows a total volume variance (M - A), the over-all difference between budgeted sales and actual sales. In turn, this volume variance is subdivided into marketing variance (M - S) which, to the extent that it can be assigned, is usually the responsibility of the sales manager, and the production variance (S - A), which is usually the responsibility of the production manager.

Marketing Variance (M - S). The 16,000-unit deviation from the master budgeted sales (164,000 units less 148,000 units scheduled) is a measure that is primarily traceable, at least initially, to the sales arm of the organization. This *marketing variance* should be computed on a routine basis because it integrates the master budget with the results and helps explain the differences between original expectations and results. "Results," as far as the marketing department is concerned, consists of getting sales orders. That is why scheduled production (sales orders received) rather than actual production (sales delivered to customers) is used as the measure of results. Possible explanations of the variance include ineffective advertising or sales promotion, unexpected changes in economic or competitive conditions, poor estimates, and an understaffed or inefficient sales force.

The master budgeted sales, rather than practical capacity, is more germane to the evaluation of current results. Managers, particularly the sales executives, will feel much more obligated to reach the master budgeted sales, which should have been conscientiously set in relation to the optimum opportunities for sales in the current period. To have any meaning, marketing variance must at least crudely reflect the existence of a bona fide opportunity to sell. Consequently, on the operating firing line the marketing variance is much more meaningful than a variance related to practical capacity. For example, a practical capacity variance could be computed by subtracting scheduled production from practical capacity in Exhibit 1. But this would blend two unlike items: the marketing variance plus the expected idle capacity variance.

Production Variance (S - A). The production manager has two major responsibilities: to maximize efficiency and to meet production schedules.

The efficiency is monitored with the aid of standards and budgets for the variable cost factors, while the ability to meet production schedules is metered by some quantification of the difference between scheduled production and actual production.

The attainment of production schedules is a mutual effort by the producing departments and the production planning and control department. Common reasons for failure to meet schedules include poor direction of operations by factory supervisors; operating inefficiencies caused by untrained workmen, faulty machines, or inferior raw material; lack of material or parts; and careless scheduling by production planners. These reasons may be lumped together as possible explanations for a production variance.

Failure to meet a schedule would result in an unfavorable production variance. This is the most commonly encountered situation. However, it may happen that actual production exceeds scheduled production. In such a case, technically the variance would be favorable. But all unusual variances are supposed to be investigated, and the findings may or may not substantiate a favorable label in the layman's sense of the word. That is, sometimes unwanted excess production occurs because of misunderstandings of production schedules.

A common explanation for the bulk of the production variance is labor inefficiency, that is, inability to meet currently attainable standards. To pursue the example further, assume that the standard time allowance per unit is one direct labor hour, and that 148,000 actual direct labor hours were used but labor inefficiencies resulted in the production of only 140,000 good units. In such a case, the entire production variance may be attributable to inefficient labor rather than faulty scheduling or some other reason.

However, favorable or unfavorable variances in labor performance may not be necessarily related to the production variance. Departures from schedule could be caused by machine breakdowns, material shortages, poor production planning, or some other reason. Conversely, a manager can adhere to production schedules, but still produce the units inefficiently.

EXPRESSING VARIANCES IN DOLLARS RATHER THAN IN PHYSICAL MEASURES

Limitations and Uses of Monetary Measures

Supposedly, once a certain capacity is provided, the addition of one unit of product to sales will increase net income by the unit contribution margin. The fixed costs in the short run will be unaffected by changes in volume, so failure to utilize capacity fully represents a lost opportunity to increase net income by the contribution margin associated with the unsold capacity.

So far, we have deliberately avoided expressing variances in dollar terms for two reasons. First, it is often unnecessary and confusing to express control measures in dollars when the operation personnel being judged think in physical terms only. The general guide is to express a measure in terms best understood by the individuals affected. The object is to help managers operate effectively and efficiently. If this can be achieved without converting data into dollar terms, so much the better. Second, the approximation of opportunity costs, which are the pertinent dollar measures, is hampered by many practical difficulties. For instance, a uniform unit contribution margin is often assumed. In many cases, of course, the increases in unit volume may be attained only by reducing unit prices or by accepting orders that would entail extraordinary incremental costs. In these instances, the dollar measure of the variance would have to be adjusted accordingly. The main objective is to approximate the probable impact on current net income of the best alternative uses of available capacity.

Using Contribution Margins as Approximations of Opportunity Costs

What is the best way to measure the cost of unutilized capacity? The total fixed costs will be the same regardless of whether production is 140,000 or 164,000 units. Therefore, from a short-run total operating cost viewpoint, unutilized capacity will not affect costs as they are ordinarily recorded by accountants. However, from an economic viewpoint, there may be an opportunity cost as measured by the contribution margins foregone by failure to utilize capacity. This opportunity cost may be zero, particularly if the sales force has done everything possible to market the products and if there is no alternate use for the otherwise idle facilities. An example of alternate use would be doing sub-contracting work for some other manufacturer. However, to demonstrate the general idea, assume that uniform unit contribution margins per unit can be validly used.

In our example, assume a sales price of $10.00 less unit variable costs of $8.00, or $2.00 unit contribution margin. Exhibit 2 expresses the variances in dollar terms.

Contribution margins as an approximation of the opportunity cost notion may be especially pertinent when the master budget sales forecast is hovering near practical capacity. For example, production could be master budgeted *and* scheduled at the practical capacity level of 200,000 units, but, say, inefficiencies result in only 194,000 units being produced. The economic impact of this production variance is best measured by the lost contribution margin per unit times the difference between the 200,000 and the 194,000 good units produced ($2.00 X 6,000 units = $12,000 lost contribution margin).

Helping the Budgetary Process

The variances described above can also be useful in evaluating and revising the budget as the year unfolds. Even if the variances were not used to evaluate marketing and production management, they still could be useful to the budgetary process because they stress careful estimation in the first place—emphasizing consideration of alternative opportunities before the master budget

EXHIBIT 2.   Analysis of Volume Variance Using Contribution Margins.

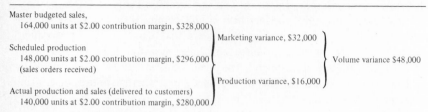

Master budgeted sales,
   164,000 units at $2.00 contribution margin, $328,000

Marketing variance, $32,000

Scheduled production
   148,000 units at $2.00 contribution margin, $296,000
   (sales orders received)

Volume variance $48,000

Production variance, $16,000

Actual production and sales (delivered to customers)
   140,000 units at $2.00 contribution margin, $280,000

Somewhere in the reporting scheme, management will probably want an explanation of why the target net income is not achieved. The above analysis dovetails well with the income statement. Assume that total fixed costs are $200,000. A summary analysis follows:

	Master budget 164,000 units	Actual results 140,000 units	Variance
Sales at $10.00	$1,610,000	$1,400,000	
Variable costs at $8.00	1,312,000	1,120,000	
Contribution margin at $2.00	$ 328,000	$ 280,000	$48,000U
Fixed costs	200,000	200,000	
Net Income	$ 128,000	$ 80,000	$48,000U*

*Explanation of variance: Failure to reach volume level originally budgeted resulted in inability to obtain the contribution margin originally budgeted:

Marketing variance:	
Sales department failed to obtain enough orders (164,000 units budgeted – 148,000 units scheduled for production) X $2.00	$32,000
Production variance:	
Production departments failed to meet production schedules (148,000 units scheduled – 140,000 units produced and sold) X $2.00	16,000
Total volume variance, which *in this case* wholly explains the difference in net income	$48,000

is adopted. Interim follow-up could prompt a revised master budget,[10] as is now done in practice. That is, although the illustration used a year as a time span for analysis, the same approach is applicable to monthly or quarterly periods.

The Opportunity Cost Approach

The illustrations in this paper highlight the essence of the problem of assessing how well capacity is being utilized. However, the use here of the lost contribution margin, a single product, and a single constraint oversimplifies the real world difficulties of trying to obtain variances which are the best available measures of opportunity costs. Most companies have many products and many constraints. Interactions are manifold:

> "Alfred Marshall asked the question, which blade of scissors does the cutting? If you analyze one blade at a time, you will never find out how a scissors cuts a piece of paper. There is interaction between two blades, which is the crucial element for cutting.

Many kinds of business and government phenomena that we observe can not be analyzed effectively one variable at a time. If you can analyze effectively one variable at a time, that is, by all odds, the means to use. But the crux of systems analysis is the application of the situation when you cannot explain the behavior of the system by looking at it one variable at a time—even if you exhaust all the variables, which may be many millions."[11]

How can an accounting system be designed that will tie in best with the decisions regarding the utilization of capacity? A logical first step is to try to formulate a reporting system that dovetails with a specific, well-defined decision model. Demski has developed what he calls an ex post model, based on the linear programming model, which envelopes shifts in the original master budget. It "compares what a firm actually accomplished during some planning period with what it deems on the basis of hindsight it should have accomplished—where accomplishments are measured in terms of the objective function in the firm's planning model. It is an opportunity cost approach in the sense that what a firm actually accomplished during some planning period is compared with what it should have accomplished by the ex post optimum program."[12] He ably demonstrated the feasibility of his model by applying it to the operations of an oil refinery. His approach was truly an opportunity cost approach because it considered the simultaneous changes in all relevant variables (mutatis mutandis) rather than one variable at a time (ceteris paribus). It produced variances that signaled the existence of opportunities and their exact sources and effects, as near as could be determined. The existence of well-defined decision models, such as linear programming, inventory, and queuing models, enhances the likelihood of implementing an ex post opportunity cost approach in practice.

SUMMARY

Distinctions between long-range and short-range factors and between hierarchies of responsibility in an organization help to develop a conceptual framework for analyzing the utilization of capacity.

For purposes of current planning and control, physical measures of capacity should suffice in many instances, at least at lower levels of the organization. If dollar measures are sought, opportunity costs, even if they have to be crudely approximated via unit contribution margins, are superior to historical costs for measuring the effect on net income of the utilization of existing facilities.

Lost contribution margins directly measure the effects of volume on profits. Therefore, they are a better basis for the computation of volume variances than historical fixed costs, which unitize total costs that are not affected by current fluctuations in volume. The volume variance based on historical fixed costs has little, if any, economic significance for current planning and control.

The development in many firms of more sophisticated management control systems, which often are linked with formal, well-defined decision models, will facilitate attempts to produce variances that better approximate opportunity costs.

FOOTNOTES

1. Don T. DeCoster, "Measurement of the Idle-Capacity Variance," *The Accounting Review* (April, 1966), pp. 297–302, discusses the "disparity that exists within accounting literature in quantifying the idle-capacity variance."

2. A thorough study of capacity would include a rigorous operational definition of the word "capacity." This is not attempted here because such a definition is sub-ordinate to the major purpose of this article. See Research Report 39, *Accounting for Costs of Capacity* (New York: National Association of Accountants, 1963), pp. 10–11. On page 10, Report 39 observes: "Capacity planning requires definition and measurement of capacity in a manner relevant to questions which arise in the planning process. This problem has two aspects. First, it is necessary to specify capacity in terms of how much the company should be prepared to make and to sell. Second, the capacity of specific facilities available or to be acquired must be determined. . . . A variety of alternative combinations of capacity and operating patterns is usually possible." There are many other difficulties of definition that are not being dealt with exhaustively in this article. *Variable cost, fixed cost,* and *contribution margin* are examples of concepts that raise difficult but not unsurmountable practical problems of definition and measurement. Contribution margin is defined here as the excess of revenue over all variable costs of manufacturing and non-manufacturing.

3. The focus here will be on the maximization of current net income, although long-run effects and other goals could be incorporated by extending the analysis. The expected inter-play of current net income and future net income obviously affects current decisions (e.g., pricing) even though these effects are seldom explicitly quantified.

4. Many of the notions in this and the next section originally appeared in Charles T. Horngren, *Accounting for Management Control: An Introduction,* (Englewood Cliffs, N.J.: Prentice-Hall, Inc., 1965), Chapter 10. However, a number of changes and embellishments have been incorporated in the present paper.

5. *Op. cit.*, p. 22.

6. The use of probabilities in estimating sales and in the analysis of variances is germane but is not discussed here. For examples, see Robert K. Jaedicke and Alexander A. Robichek, "Cost-Volume Profit Analysis Under Conditions of Uncertainty," *The Accounting Review,* October 1964, pp. 917–926; and Harold Bierman, Jr., Lawrence E. Fouraker, and Robert K. Jaedicke, "A Use of Probability and Statistics in Performance Evaluation," *The Accounting Review,* July 1962, pp. 409–417.

7. For simplicity we shall assume throughout the subsequent discussion that all orders received are immediately scheduled and that production should occur immediately upon being scheduled; in other words, there are no lags between orders, schedules, and expected production. In this way, we will not have to bother with some messy technical adjustments in the analysis of variances caused by, say, an order being booked in November, scheduled in February, and produced in April. These adjustments may be difficult to construct in a particular company, and they impede practical application of these ideas.

8. The linear programming model, using dual evaluators, will help management decide which combination of products will be most profitable when a given capacity must be utilized for their production or sale. When the primal solution shows the optimal production mix, the dual evaluators (shadow prices) of the constraining factors are the opportunity costs of their marginal products.

9. Conceivably, this variance could be sub-divided into two parts: (1) the difference between practical capacity and the activity level used for that particular year in a past capital budget; (2) the difference between the latter and the master budget. These subdivisions might help the evaluation of long range planning, particularly when excess facilities were deliberately acquired.

    In this context, where excess capacity is deliberately acquired, the opportunity costs of bearing this capacity could be regularly compared to the costs of its elimination (e.g., overtime premium, second shift premium, sub-contracting, etc.). Then management could choose whether to eliminate the capacity through disposition or lease.

10. This is akin to changing the optimal mix in linear programming in light of changes in constraints, prices, etc.

11. Comments by W. W. Cooper in Thomas J. Burns (Ed.), *The Use of Accounting Data in Decision-Making* (unpublished, The Ohio State University, 1966), p. 228.

12. Joel S. Demski, *Variance Analysis: An Opportunity Cost Approach with a Linear Programming Application,* unpublished Ph.D. dissertation, University of Chicago, 1966. Also, see J. M. Samuels, "Opportunity Costing: An Application of Mathematical Programming," *Journal of Accounting Research,* Autumn 1965, pp. 182–191.

Accounting Analysis for Long-Run Decisions

INTRODUCTION

Short-run decisions may be important for the immediate profitability of a firm, but long-run decisions are most critical to the very survival of a firm. Policies based on short-run factors can often be quickly changed if results are unfavorable, and the consequences of instituting such an undesirable policy may be slight. This is seldom the case with long-run decisions. These involve the irrevocable investment of relatively large sums of money in anticipation of future (though uncertain) returns. If future circumstances prove the investment to have been an unwise one, there is little chance of recouping the original investment.

Nearly every decision made by a firm concerns some sacrifice (cost) in anticipation of a related benefit. In most short-run decisions the costs and benefits are occurring simultaneously. Thus, if costs are exceeding benefits in the chosen alternative, a new alternative can be selected. For instance, if a firm increases the price of a product and finds that the volume of sales drops more than expected, the price can be reduced to its original level with the major

273

consequence being the loss of sales over a short period of time. On the other hand, when a decision is made to undertake a long-run capital investment project, there is a large immediate cost. This cost is expected to be more than offset by large net benefits over the future. However, if future benefits are less than expected they may never be large enough to offset the cost. Because the cost in this case is sunk, there is no way to select a different alternative and escape the consequences of the poor decision. Many firms have gone bankrupt because large outlays for investments were not followed by the anticipated level of benefits. This is especially true when an investment is financed through borrowing, and the future returns are not large enough to make the required payments on the loan.

There is general agreement that the long-run capital investment decision is extremely important; however, there is less agreement as to what type of decision system is best for making such decisions. The role of the accountant in this decision-making process is also a matter of controversy. Because this book is intended for accounting students, it is important to establish the accountant's function in the process, and then the decision system itself will be discussed from the accountant's viewpoint.

There are at least three roles the accountant could adopt. First, he could be merely the historian who records and reports the results of the firm's operations. As such he would produce only a small portion of the information needed for long-run decisions. Because capital investment decisions are based on predictions of benefits well into the future, there is no way that reports of past operations can be sufficient for making these decisions. In this role, there would be no need for accountants to understand or even be cognizant of the decision system. However, this role is based heavily on the stewardship function of the accountant and this narrow definition of accounting was rejected earlier.

A second possible role is that of information specialist. In this role the accountant would provide all information needed by those making capital investment decisions. The accountant's function would be to formulate an optimal information system. To effectively perform this function, the accountant must understand the decision system within the firm. He must know what information is desired by the decision maker, and he must also know the potential impact of that information on the decisions to be made. For instance, if capital investment decisions are made using a payback model, where all returns beyond year N are ignored, the accountant should not be spending time and money predicting the returns in year $N + 1$.

A third role for the accountant is that of being a member of the management team and consequently being a decision maker as well as an information supplier. The role arises often in large capital investment decisions which come up infrequently and involve many predictions and assumptions about the future.

In this role the accountant must not only understand the decision system used by the firm, but he must be able to judge this system vis-a-vis other possible systems. In other words, he must be able to create as well as understand decision systems. This takes considerably more ability and knowledge than does merely understanding the system.

The readings in this chapter were selected on the assumption that accountants must, as a minimum, understand existing capital investment decision systems. The literature in accounting, finance, economics, and operations research during the past decade has presented scores of alternative capital investment decision systems. The decision-maker who is intimately involved with capital investment decisions should be familiar with these alternatives. However, from an accountant's point of view, the critical aspect is understanding existing systems used by management, and that is what is emphasized in these readings.

In *Decision Criteria for Investment Strategies,* Meredith presents an excellent survey of the current state of theory and practice regarding models of project selection. When a capital investment project is proposed, a firm must have some criterion which specifies whether to accept or reject the project. This basically involves making a prediction as to whether the future benefits to be derived from the project warrant the investment that is required. Ideally a firm would accept any project that would increase the value of the firm. If only one of two projects could be accepted, the one that would increase the value the most would be accepted. However, because the method by which a firm is valued has not yet been conclusively determined, surrogates of the effect of a project on this value must be used. Meredith presents several surrogates and discusses the merits of each. The basic discounted cash flow approach is explained and various adaptations are presented. This approach is unquestioned if there are perfect capital markets and if the future can be predicted with certainty. However, capital rationing and uncertainty (or risk) cause complications which are considered by Meredith. Especially enlightening is his comparison of theoretical and practical attempts to deal with uncertainty.

While reading Meredith it is important not only to recognize the various decision criteria presented, but to consider the data requirements of the criteria. In no capital investment decision are historical data an adequate input to the decision model. Predictions are required, and these predictions must include not only future profitability estimates but also assessments of risk and alternative opportunities. The traditional historical accounting system does not supply the relevant data for these parameters.

The other reading in this section, *Empirical Evidence of the Adoption of Sophisticated Capital Budgeting Techniques* by Klammer, indicates what types of capital investment decision systems are in greatest use in a sample of large firms. Several findings should be especially noted. First, an extremely large percentage of the firms have a quite formal system. This percentage has been growing over the past decade. Second, the increasing use of an explicit recognition of risk in analyzing proposals is significant. Third, the payback criterion has been replaced by the discounted cash flow criterion as the most popular profitability standard for selecting projects. All of these results are consistent with the position that the sophistication of capital investment decision systems has been increasing over the past decade. The editors see no reason to expect this trend to change in the near future.

Despite the increasing sophistication of capital budgeting systems, there remain areas for improvement. The search for alternative investments and the predictions relating to these proposed investments are areas that hold tremendous potential for improvement in the capital investment decision system. Also, theoretical correctness in these systems must sometimes yield to practicality. Capital budgeting is an art as well as a science, and emphasis on the artistic (e.g., recognition of opportunities and prediction of the correct future parameters) rather than the scientific is often necessary.

The post-auditing of capital investment decisions is another area for improvement. This is an important aspect of a complete capital investment decision system. The traditional accounting model provides feedback regarding total costs and revenues from accepted projects, but there are at least two important weaknesses in this feedback. First, there is absolutely no feedback on rejected alternatives. This means that acceptance of unprofitable projects may become known, but the rejection of profitable alternatives is never indicated. This can bias decisions to be made more conservatively than is desirable. Second, the basis of reporting is inconsistent with the decision-making basis. While the timing and riskiness of future returns are important to the investment decision, the traditional accounting model deals only with actual dollar amounts. No adjustment is made for timing or risk. This means that a proposed investment could be expected to provide increased income in the future according to the accounting model, but it could be an undesirable investment because of a long delay before the returns are achieved or due to the uncertainty of the returns.

Decision Criteria for Investment Strategies

G. G. Meredith

INTRODUCTION

In the seventies the importance of the professional accountant's function as a classifier, recorder and reporter of financial data has assumed new proportions. However, without detracting from this important function, in many business entities, the accountant also "wears the hat" of the financial manager—a function that appears to be ever changing to include (among other things) determining the total amount of funds to employ in the business, allocating these funds as investment strategies and obtaining the optimum finance-mix to ensure that shareholders' (owners') wealth is maximized. The finance manager is concerned with three major decisions—the investment decision, the financing decision, and the dividend decision.[1] The three decisions are interrelated—an optimal combination of the three decisions maximizes the value of the firm to its owners (shareholders). The investment decision determines the allocation of funds to investment strategies. A decision to create, expand, or liquidate a company is an investment decision. Every item of expenditure within the firm should be seen as a component of an investment strategy—the result of a past investment decision. These decisions (or the results of the decisions) determine firm growth and prosperity, dividend payout, and the multitude of management's future decisions.

Management's financing decisions are concerned with determining the optimum capital structure for the firm. Assuming the aim of management is to maximize the value of the firm to its shareholders (as reflected by the market

SOURCE: Reprinted with permission from *The Australian Accountant* (November, 1971), pp. 439–447.

price of shares) this value will be influenced by the firm's capital structure. Capital structure reflects the asset structure of the firm, and both capital structure and assets affect business risk which in turn influences future financing policies.

Finally, the firm's dividend decisions determine retained earnings and these decisions can be made to maximize shareholders' wealth. The three decisions— investment, financing, and dividend—can be solved jointly; however this paper is concerned with the first—investment—and decision criteria for alternative investment strategies. The aim of the paper is to evaluate the position reached by academics and practitioners in trying to develop criteria which lead to optimum investment decisions. The paper will show that, while many unresolved problems remain, a set of investment decision rules for financial management can be established for practitioners in the market place.

Academic papers on capital budgeting have shown a spectacular growth over the past decade, reflecting both the increasing complexities of decision making in a world of large scale investment and the complexity of the capital budgeting problem. This interest by academics has had its influence on practice. The rigorous theoretical framework of economics is being applied by the financial manager. While the impact of theory on practice in Australia may be regarded as modest (see post), a graduate accounting profession will certainly influence the next decade of practice.

After summarizing the investment appraisal "problem," the paper evaluates the "present state of the game"—both theory and practice. A set of investment decision rules (1971 style) are then illustrated for practitioners and the paper concludes by reviewing some of the major unresolved problems that remain for academics.

THE INVESTMENT APPRAISAL PROBLEM

Capital budgeting involves business resource allocation over time. The *process* of capital budgeting includes the development of alternative investment strategies; projection of data flows for each strategy; evaluation of strategies; selection from alternatives based on some acceptance criteria and finally, the project reevaluation over time. In spite of contributions made by academics to the "science" of investment appraisal, the practitioner is faced with what may be regarded as a bewildering array of problems to face before the theoretical ideal of the "laboratory" can be applied in the market-place. Academics have had a great deal to say on:

- methods of investment appraisal,
- acceptance criteria,
- the influence of capital rationing,

- the problem of risk and uncertainty, and
- complications arising from mutually exclusive or contingent projects, and projects with varying life spans and initial outlays.

The key to the decisions by management is the method(s) of project appraisal and the acceptance criteria to be adopted. Before investment appraisal methods can be applied by practitioners, acceptable modifications to accommodate risk and uncertainty, capital rationing conditions, as well as complications arising from mutually exclusive and contingent projects, must be forthcoming from theorists. The practitioner must often feel that academics develop their theories in the "sterility" of the laboratory test room where the realities of risk, capital rationing, mutually exclusive alternatives and so on, are "assumed away." Unless the theorists can provide practitioners with decision criteria which can cope with the rough and tumble of the competitive world, the so-called "rule of thumb" methods of investment analysis and appropriate decision criteria can be expected to dominate company procedure manuals.

Given that management will be faced with an array of alternative investment strategies, proposals must be evaluated and ranked[2] and an acceptance criteria employed to provide an investment portfolio which maintains shareholders' wealth—by maintaining the present market price per share.[3] How proposals *should* be analyzed and acceptance criteria applied is not always clear-cut (see post).

Capital rationing is a capital budget constraint—a constraint of funds available for investment.[4] Capital rationing in one form or another exists for most businesses (small and large) quite frequently (see post). It is a condition that cannot be ignored in developing decision criteria for investment strategies.

Risk and uncertainty are also a reality for the business executive. Academics distinguish between a "risk alternative" and "uncertainty." Risk is a situation where a number of outcomes are possible for each strategy and from historical data, statistical probabilities associated with these outcomes can be determined.[5] For example, an oil company establishing service stations throughout Australia undoubtedly has sufficient experience to be able to determine the likely *range* of outlays required for a particular station, and the likely range of annual operating costs and the probabilities of each item in the range occurring. Uncertainty is a situation where a number of outcomes are possible from alternative strategies, but the probabilities attached to these outcomes are unknown. For example, a company may be assessing the impact of amalgamating interstate factories. A major factor in the analysis may be the effect (on demand/sales) of *withdrawing* manufacturing operations from a State or States. While subjective estimates of demand patterns are feasible, objective data would not be available.

Finally, the investment decision problem for practitioners is complicated by the existence of mutually exclusive projects, contingent projects and projects with varying cash flow patterns. A proposal is said to be mutually exclusive if its acceptance precludes the acceptance of one or more other proposals. For example, a business may be considering the purchase of a fleet of vehicles—on a fleet basis. A decision to favour one type precludes the purchase of alternatives. A contingent proposal is one whose acceptance depends upon the acceptance of one or more other proposals. For example, the purchase of plant and machinery for a new factory depends upon the commitment of funds to the construction of the factory building. Mutually exclusive, dependent and independent proposals may vary in lifespan, initial outlay and/or cash flow patterns. Decision rules must cope with these possibilities.

THEORY AND PRACTICE—THE CURRENT POSITION

Methods of Project Appraisal

Complete agreement exists amongst theorists on the validity of compound interest formulae in project appraisal. This position has been reached after some decades of debate and investigation.[6] In the fifties Professor Joel Dean made a major contribution to the introduction of compound interest methods to the business world in place of such methods as payback and "accounting" rate of return.[7] Academics claim that the compound interest techniques provide an essential link between business cash flows arising from projects and growth in shareholders' wealth.[8] Thus the techniques satisfy the accepted objectives of the firm whereas the so-called "rule of thumb" methods of analysis are generally regarded as not providing this necessary link although several attempts have been made to link payback and accounting rate of return and time-adjusted percentage rates.[9]

Although there exists a variety of compound interest models—internal rate of return,[10] present value,[11] profitability index,[12] uniform annual equivalent,[13] and terminal value[14]—the first two mentioned, internal rate of return and present value methods, are most frequently supported. The internal rate of return is defined as that rate of interest which equates the present value of project cash benefits and the cash sacrificed.

		Years hence		
0	1	2	3	4
−$3,170	$1,000	$1,000	$1,000	$1,000
		r% = 10		

The present value of a uniform cash flow of $1,000 for four years discounted at 10% is $3,170. Thus the company would just cover all costs (including interest) on the project if the funds were borrowed at 10% compound interest.

In the (net) present value method, annual cash flows are discounted at a predetermined rate. For example, in the above example, a predetermined rate of 7% results in a net present value of +$217. This means that if funds for the project are borrowed at 7% compound interest, the project's cash flows would cover all expenses (including interest) and provide a surplus equivalent to $217 in the initial year. Thus the net present value measures the rise in share prices which would result from the project's acceptance—assuming the results of the investment are communicated to the shareholders.

While it is sometimes argued that both methods provide management with the same accept/reject advice, complications found in the market place—capital rationing, mutually exclusive projects, risk and uncertainty, irregular cash flow patterns—require some modification to the techniques if they are to be applied in practice. Perhaps this fact partly (at least) explains why surveys in the United States of America, United Kingdom and Australia have shown that less than half of the executives of the *largest* companies employ the discount methods in project appraisal.[15]

Perhaps a major reason for the apparent reluctance of executives to employ discount methods, may be the difficulty in comprehending the implications from using the two main discount techniques. Consider the following character- istics of the I.R.R. and N.P.V. methods.

a. The internal rate of return remains unchanged by the scale of the investment, while the net present value increases in proportion to the investment scale.

Cash flows years				I.R.R.	N.P.V. (10%)
0	1	2	3		
$	$	$	$		
-1.95	1.0	1.0	1.0	25%	+0.54
-3.90	2.0	2.0	2.0	25%	+1.08

If an investment in one machine requires $1.95 and produces benefits of $1.00 in each of three future periods, these benefits indicate an internal rate of return of 25 per cent. The net present value when benefits are discounted at 10 per cent is +$0.54. If two machines are installed and benefits increase proportionately, the internal rate of return remains unchanged while the net present value increases in proportion to the scale of investment.

The fact that the internal rate of return is constant with increasing invest- ment outlays and benefits is logical since the interpretation of the index in terms of quantitative ($) return is that the profit accruing to the firm in each of the three years of the lifespan of the machine is 25 per cent of the initial outlay. Therefore, when two machines are installed (and outlays doubled) the absolute value of profit in each year also doubles.

b. Postponing an investment decision to future time periods has no effect on the internal rate of return, however for each year that the investment is delayed, the net present value is reduced by $1 \div (1 + i)$.

		Cash flows years				I.R.R.	N.P.V. (10%)
0	1	2	3	4	5		
$	$	$	$	$	$		
-1.95	1.0	1.0	1.0			25%	+0.54
	-1.95	1.0	1.0	1.0		25%	+0.49
		etc.					

c. A direct relationship exists between the rate of investment and net present value of the investment, however the internal rate of return is independent of the investment rate. The rate of investment may be defined as the number of units of investment approved by management in any time period. The rate of investment may be constant or may be at a decreasing or increasing rate.

		Cash flows years				I.R.R.	N.P.V. (10%)
0	1	2	3	4	5		
$	$	$	$	$	$		
-1.95	1.0	1.0	1.0			25%	+0.54
	-3.90	2.0	2.0	2.0		25%	+1.08
		-5.85	3.0	3.0	3.0	25%	+1.62
Total -1.95	-2.90	-2.85	6.0	5.0	3.0	25%	+2.85

While the internal rate of return remains independent of the investment rate, the net present value increases (.54 by X) times where X is equal to the number of investment units.

d. Both the internal rate of return and the net present value of an investment increase as project lifespan extends. However, the increase is not indefinite. For example, in the case quoted above, the internal rate of return for a two-year lifespan is 2 per cent. If the lifespan is extended to five years the internal rate of return increases to 42 per cent and continues to increase to 51 per cent for a lifespan of twelve years. Longer lifespans have no effect on this investment's rate of return.

In the same way, the net present value increases with extended lifespans but reaches a maximum when the present value factor of an annuity has a value of $\frac{1}{i}$.

e. A unique value for the internal rate of return may not be obtained when future investment benefits are both positive and negative. Multiple rates of return may be produced under these circumstances.

Cash flows years			I.R.R.	N.P.V.		
0	1	2		5%	15%	40%
$ -1.0	$ 2.4	$ -1.43	10% & 30%	-.011	+.066	-.016

The internal rate of return for the above project is both 10 per cent and 30 per cent, whereas the net present value is either positive or negative depending upon the discount rate. The net present value between 10 per cent and 30 per cent is positive, while the net present value for discount rates outside this range is negative.

f. Some cash flow patterns may result in an internal rate of return which is not a real number. For example, the equation for the rate of return of the investment below reduces to $i^2 = -1$. The net present value is negative for all feasible discount rates.

Cash flows years			I.R.R.	N.P.V. (10%)
0	1	2		
$ -1.0	$ 2.0	$ -2.0	--	-0.834

g. The internal rate of return assumes intermediate net cash benefits produced by a project are reinvested at a rate equal to the project's internal rate of return. The net present value method assumes intermediate net benefits are reinvested at the discount rate applied to calculate the net present value.[16] If the investment in (a) was financed by borrowing $1.95 at 25 per cent interest, the investment would break-even over the lifespan of the project. The loan cash flows—involving interest payments and principal repayments—are as follows:

Years			
0	1	2	3
$ +1.95	$ -0.49	$ -0.49	$ -2.44

The combined cash flow—the cash flow of the project and of the loan—takes the following pattern:

Years			
0	1	2	3
$ --	$ +0.51	$ +0.51	$ -1.44

If the net cash flows of $0.51 in the first two years of the investment are reinvested at 25 per cent per annum, the accumulated funds equal the $1.44 necessary to clear the debt at the end of the third year.

The present value of the project's benefits of $1 per annum for three years at 10 per cent is $2.49. This means that if it was possible to borrow $2.49 at 10 per cent interest per annum, $0.54 ($2.49-$1.95) could be distributed immediately as "profit" and the balance ($1.95) invested in the project. The project benefits of $1 per annum would be sufficient to repay the loan and interest as long as surplus funds were reinvested at 10 per cent per annum.

An important assumption made in the above illustrations is that the reinvestment rates are constant over the project lifespan. When theory is modified to accommodate risk and uncertainty, it may be necessary to abandon this assumption.

h. It is generally accepted that the internal rate of return and the present value method produce identical results in a two-period or point-input, point-output case where investment proposals are not mutually exclusive (for a detailed analysis of the relationship between the two rules, see Hirshleifer: 1958). Under these circumstances a project with an internal rate of return in excess of the cost of capital will also show a positive net present value discounted at the cost of capital.

Similarly, in the multi-period case, the internal rate of return method will produce the same decision-result as the net present value method if the problem is to accept or reject investment proposals which produce one or more net cash outflows followed by one or more net cash inflows.[17]

i. However, the present value method and the internal rate of return method will not always rank mutually exclusive proposals in the same order.[18]

This apparent contradiction is to be expected because:

a. the methods answer different questions concerning investment proposals analysed; and
b. the methods make different implicit assumptions.

While the internal rate of return method determines the rate of interest at which funds can be borrowed and repaid by the proceeds of the proposal without incurring any loss to the borrower, the present value methods show the minimum amount which at the current marginal cost of capital could be borrowed and repaid from each proposal's proceeds without causing any loss to the borrower. One method (the internal rate of return) determines an interest rate, the other an absolute amount of finance.

Furthermore, while the internal rate of return method explicitly assumes proceeds from proposals are reinvested at the return percentage, present value methods assume proceeds are reinvested at the discount rate. Thus whenever there is a wide divergence between the internal rate of return percentage and the net present value discount rates, these alternative methods may then rank projects in different orders.

Academics are not unanimous in the support for the alternative methods. It is probably fair to say that while some support the I.R.R. approach (e.g., J. Dean and Merrett & Sykes), a larger group support present value methods (e.g., Bierman & Smidt).

Acceptance Criteria

Quantifying cash flow patterns of alternative investment strategies do not reduce the significance of the decision-maker. Value judgements by management will remain (in the foreseeable future) as a vital segment of the capital budgeting process, however economic analysis of alternative projects is undertaken to provide the decision-maker with "all the facts," to the extent that they can be quantified. The decision-maker requires a "quantified" accept/reject criteria to select from possible alternatives.

The acceptance criteria generally applied with both the internal rate of return and present value methods is the "required rate of return" or "cut-off rate," representing an opportunity cost of funds available. This rate acts as the minimum required return when the internal rate method is employed, and also acts as the discount rate in the present value methods.[19] This approach would appear to provide a relatively simple selection method *as long* as the "required rate of return" can be determined with some confidence. In fact extreme difficulties are found in attempting to define and measure opportunity cost of funds in particular situations. Some funds (e.g., debt) clearly impose a clear obligation in terms of future cash flows which have to be met and therefore the cost of debt is generally expressed by the I.R.R. which equates the cash repayments and the amount borrowed.[20] While preference shares are not equivalent to debt in a legal sense, for cost of capital purposes, the effective cost is calculated in a similar manner. New share issues also carry a "cost." Investors subscribe on the expectation of dividends or capital gains. New capital projects should therefore only be accepted if the value of existing equity funds remains unchanged as the result of the investment. The "cost" of new share issues would therefore seem to be the discount rate which equates the expected future dividend stream to the market value of the firm's existing equity.[21]

An opportunity cost must be imputed for retained earnings since by reinvesting funds and paying lower dividends, management forces its share-holders to forego either funds for personal consumption or funds for alternative investment opportunities. This opportunity cost would be the investment rate of return at which the sacrificed dividends could be invested in the market place on an equivalent risk basis.[22] While there is *some* agreement on the above approach to the calculation of debt and equity as individual items of funds, there is less agreement on the practicability of calculating these costs, and the calculation of a combined debt equity cost. The traditional view of a weighted-average cost of funds assumes that extra debt funds added to the "mixture" reduces the average cost, although financial risk may be increased.[23] Most decision-makers probably agree with the "traditional" view—i.e., debt and equity capital can be mixed to produce an optimal (least) average cost of funds. However, this view has been challenged by Professors Modigliani and Miller and the debate continues.[24] If practitioners are to be given workable acceptance criteria for use in a business environment, the criteria must be developed recognising that capital rationing, risk and uncertainty are a reality.

Capital Rationing

Capital rationing may be defined as any situation in which a firm cannot or does not wish to raise funds for capital investment beyond a certain limit. This limitation of funds may be enforced by management either by making a fixed total available for the capital budget, or while allowing the total amount available to fluctuate to a certain extent, by applying very high cut-off rates as minimum desirable rates of return. In both cases the technique results in sponsored proposals competing for limited funds. In both cases some "profit-able" projects will be ignored; that is, some projects may promise a return greater than the cost of funds involved, and yet be rejected through a general restriction on investment.

A number of factors may force a firm to accept a policy of capital rationing. Low profitability may force a firm to curtail future capital investment because past profitability may have had the effect of increasing out of all proportion the cost of external funds available. A firm operating at a loss may be forced to rely on equity (high cost) funds for capital investments, whereas, if the firm had been operating at a profit, external debt funds might have been available—at a significantly lower cost. Thus it may pay management to delay desirable capital investment until a present profitability situation has corrected itself.

Extreme doubts as to the future certainty of operations may result in a capital rationing situation. All capital budgeting is carried out under conditions of some degree of uncertainty; however, management at any one time may consider the future to be so uncertain that capital projects readily acceptable under normal circumstances are perhaps better curtailed until future prospects improve. Funds from external sources may not be readily available if lenders believe the future is too uncertain to risk supplying unlimited quantities of funds for capital investments.

Government regulations could represent an external influence causing capital rationing within the firm. Nationalized industries of semi-governmental bodies may be restricted from time to time by government regulations or government policies, and the policies of the government-controlled banking system may also cause internal capital rationing among individual firms.

In spite of the influence of external factors in the capital rationing policies of individual firms, it is most likely that capital rationing in the majority of cases is self-imposed. Top management quite often is not prepared to borrow to the limit. Experienced management would probably consider that a certain reserve of borrowing power should be retained for emergencies in any one budget period. Possibly for this reason, many firms will restrict funds available for capital investment to a total represented by annual depreciation plus a fixed proportion of expected future profits. This will leave the company or firm in a position to approach the external market if any future emergencies arise. Management is generally not prepared to borrow to the limit of its capacity or the capacity of the firm, because such borrowing may lead to certain restrictions on operations imposed by lenders.

A recent Australian survey[25] has shown that between 80% and 90% of listed public companies experience capital rationing, and to a great extent, the rationing is imposed by internal management. The investment decision "rules" that what follows (see post) have been developed on the assumption that the influence of capital rationing cannot be ignored.

Risk and Uncertainty

Theories of decision-making under uncertainty have been developed by La Place (reported in Luce and Raiffa[26]), Wald,[27] Savage,[28] and Hurwicz.[29] The theories attempt to explain how decision-makers should act, and are rational to the extent of being mathematically well-defined and objective. In each case, given the end of profit maximization and the decision-maker's problem setting, the theories never lead to ambiguous selections under a given set of circumstances.

The La Place criterion states that given complete lack of knowledge about the relative probabilities of alternative outcomes, it can be assumed that equal probabilities should be assigned to each outcome. The strategy with the highest expected payoff or value is then accepted. This principle, "the principle of insufficient reason," and the assumption of equal probability involve a principle which is associated with Bayes. Since there is no apparent reason for one outcome to eventuate, it is assumed that one is as equally likely to occur as another. This criterion has been criticised rather strongly by Morris[30] on the ground that its application is complicated by difficulties in obtaining statements of possible futures which form collectively, exhaustive and mutually exclusive sets of futures. For example, for a decision to invest in a particular machine, it is generally not a simple matter to decide on all possible futures. Many alternatives exist, and the choice may well depend simply on which list of alternatives is used. In answer to this criticism, it could also be claimed that incorrect specification of states of nature is likely to affect all other criteria, so that this criticism should not be levelled at the La Place criterion alone.

The Wald criterion for selecting strategies under uncertainty is referred to as a criterion of pessimism, since it states the correct strategy is that which offers the minimum maximum loss. This minimax refers to selecting the strategy or act which will minimise losses if we suppose the worst might happen, or the strategy which will provide the maximum profit/cash recovery outcome when it is supposed that the future will cause losses to be minimal. The Wald theory is extremely conservative. The criterion selects a set of strategies which will give the decision-maker a given income with the smallest chance attached to it.

The Savage criterion is based on the assumption that the decision-maker will attempt to select the strategy which will minimize the maximum regret he will experience. This regret is measured in terms of the difference between the payoff the decision-maker actually receives and the payoff he would have received if he had known what was going to happen in the future. Like the Wald theory, the Savage criterion is conservative in assuming that the worst, the largest possible regret, will occur.

The Hurwicz or pessimism-optimism index considers both the best and worst payoffs for each alternative act. This criterion is based on the principle that most decision-makers find their outlook somewhere between the extreme pessimism of the Wald criterion and the extreme opposite of Wald's criterion.

The Hurwicz principle suggests that the degree of optimism of the decision-maker can be measured on the scale from zero to plus one. If the decision-maker is relatively optimistic his index will be close to one.

The most obvious operational criticism of this principle centres around the method for determining the proper value of the optimism-pessimism index. If values of the index for pessimism and optimism are to be determined, the values are equivalent to estimates of probabilities and these subjective probabilities (as they would be) should be used and the decision treated as one under conditions of risk. If the problem is to be treated as one under uncertainty, then by definition the probabilities are unknown and arguments based on them are irrelevant. Similar arguments can be made against the maximum principle and the regret principle.

In addition to the above criticisms of the theories, there are sound reasons for not incorporating these decision criteria within the programme.

a. There are no *a priori* theoretical grounds for selecting one of these theories over another. The preferred approach depends upon the decision-maker's psychological makeup and judgement. Hence there would appear to be no single best mathematical procedure for solving the decision problem under uncertainty if the alternative theories available are to be restricted to these four.

b. For the modern company, it is unlikely that pure uncertainty ever exists. Some knowledge of the state of nature and the limitations applying to alternatives will be available to management. On the other hand, it is most unlikely that management could be in a position to nominate possible *outcomes* for different states of nature. Within certain limits the possible future courses of action may involve a very wide range of alternatives and it may be completely unrealistic to apply the minimax principle or the regret principle, for example, to these situations.

Savage[31] has developed a second theory and in no way similar to his minimax regret criteria. This theory shows how subjective probabilities may be attached to various states of nature under uncertainty. The theory postulates that a complete preference ordering of all acts exists for the decision-maker, apart from any consideration of payoff relevant to each act. Under these conditions, an optimal set of the subjective probabilities can be attached to the states of nature, and in this way decision problems can be handled in subjective terms as a risk problem, provided only that the expected value of the pay-off distributions are considered by the decision-maker. Under the Savage subjective probability theory, subjective probabilities are assigned to each of the alternative states of nature and the expected values calculated for each alternative strategy.

Given that the uncertainty case can be "converted" to a risk situation (using subjective probabilities), the suggested treatment of risk is now examined. Academics have put forward a range of approaches—some simple (rule of thumb) and quite subjective, others requiring some knowledge of basic statistics.

a. Weighting investment outlays and costs through contingency allowances.[32]
b. Making not one but several estimates of outlays, costs and benefits representing optimistic, expected and pessimistic estimations.[33]
c. Calculating return on capital at risk as well as return on total funds involved in the project.[34]
d. Varying cut-off standards or discount rates to reflect risk.[35]
e. A certainty equivalent approach which requires the modification of expected annual (net) cash flows. Cash flows are modified with a "risk" coefficient, which reflects management's utility preferences with respect to risk. The greater the risk, the lower the coefficient. A risk-free discount rate (or standard) is then used in the decision-making process.[36]
f. Probability distribution approaches in which the probability distributions of cash flows are determined, under varying assumptions of dependence of cash flows from period to period. Management is given information about the expected value of the project return *and* the dispersion of the probability distribution of possible returns.[37] Using this method management can be given *additional* information to assist in decision-making, e.g., the expected return *and* standard deviation about the expected return *and* the probability of a return being equal to a standard or the probability of the net present value being zero or less, and so on. This information can be presented in chart form in the usual bell-shaped pattern or as a cumulative distribution.

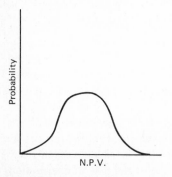
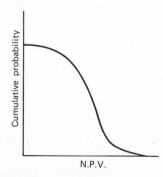

g. Simulating future expectations using computer or non-computer approaches.[38] Simulation is a technique whereby a model is constructed of a real situation, and by manipulating the model, conclusions about these real situations can be drawn by the decision-maker. All factors affecting the project are considered. Probability distributions are assigned to these factors, random numbers are generated and in one simulation trial, factors are selected to calculate the I.R.R. or N.P.V. The trials are repeated and a "picture" of the expected I.R.R. or N.P.V. developed and presented to management as graphs or as probability distributions.

h. The above techniques can be combined to provide solutions for investment opportunities which involve a sequence of decisions over time. The "decision tree" approach is one where various decision points are studied in relation to subsequent chance events. Management can then choose among alternatives in an objective and consistent manner.[39]

i. Direct incorporation of utility theory in capital investment analysis. Probability distribution approaches are based on the use of *monetary* values. They do not provide management with the "best" decision since this will depend on the utility preferences of management with respect to the risk borne by the firm. When using this approach, the investment alternative providing the greatest utility is the one accepted.[40]

In order to apply this approach the decision-maker's utility function must be derived. Expected utility values of investments are obtained by multiplying the utility value of particular outcomes by the probability of occurrence. Using this approach the decision-makers would attempt to maximize the expected utility value of all investments, subject to a budget constraint.

In the market place, practitioners are employing *some of* the less sophisticated techniques to allow for risk and uncertainty, but in general, the approach could be summarized as one of "risk avoidance" rather than risk analysis. A survey of Australian manufacturers in 1967 revealed the following approaches adopted by management:

a. A simple sensitivity analysis was used to highlight the significance of individual factors for project profitability. Rather than make use of one set of input factors for project evaluation, three estimates of each factor were made, one representing a pessimistic estimate, one an optimistic estimate, and a figure between these extremes which could be regarded as an assessment of expected values.

b. Contingency allowances—additional sums added to the expected initial outlay to cover unpredictable costs and thus reduce project profitability—have been used to ensure that project analysis has been based on a "conservative" figure. The size of the contingency allowance depends upon management's assessment of the risk and uncertainty associated with individual projects.

c. Where risk and uncertainty were recognised, projects were penalised by requiring a standard return on capital over a limited useful lifespan (for example, ten years) when it was specifically known that the lifespan of the investment would be considerably longer than this reduced figure (for example, twenty or twenty-five years).

d. Risk associated with a project is often highlighted through the construction of profit graphs and break-even charts to illustrate the return percentage necessary to break even, assuming that various initial outlays may be required to launch the particular project. The graphs also illustrate the minimum future benefits required to recover various possible outlays. Management's task is to assess whether the minimum future benefits would be realised and whether any excess benefits justify the risk that may be associated with the project.

e. Where project alternatives were present, these have been considered on technical grounds and only the most acceptable presented to top management with some financial analysis.

f. Executives of many mining companies suggested that additional funds were allocated to project investigation in an attempt to eliminate or reduce risk. For example, additional funds were often allocated to cover preliminary exploration in a mining venture, to reduce the possible risk of obtaining an unsatisfactory yield from the project.

g. Some firms reduce future trading risk and uncertainty through a policy of expansion by takeovers of firms already successful in related fields. The principle behind such a policy is to invest only in projects (that is, established firms) which have been proven financially successful in the past. Such a policy is often designed to reduce competition and increase market exposure of the firm's products.

h. Risk and uncertainty in product development is often reduced by introducing products which have already been tested by subsidiary companies, parent companies, or affiliated overseas firms. Most firms send technical staff regularly overseas to examine trends, methods of production, and successful new products.

i. New products introduced are often supplementary to those already proved successful on a consumer market. This may apply particularly to such products as items of furniture or building equipment, tools, etc., where a firm's success in one field may be followed by continuing success in related fields.

j. Production and supply risks are often eliminated through company organization whereby the firm is not dependent upon outside suppliers or manufacturers for key raw materials or parts. For example, a firm controlling raw material supplies, product manufacture and product distribution may eliminate risk and uncertainty associated with production and supply.

k. Market surveys before any product is launched, reduce risk and uncertainty associated with consumer product acceptance. Most firms rely, as well, on experience of affiliated overseas companies. Consumer goods may be imported initially from a parent company overseas, and tested on the

Australian consumer market before large initial outlays of capital expenditure are committed to the manufacture of the product in Australia.

l. Projects by some firms are classified as either single-purpose or multi-purpose. Greater risks exist for single-purpose projects. If they are unsuccessful an alternative use for assets established may not exist. Multi-purpose projects on the other hand, may have several alternative uses. Standards of acceptance set by the companies using this method are higher for single-purpose projects than for multi-purpose investments.

INVESTMENT PROGRAMME PROCEDURES

The following working procedures are based on the assumption that capital rationing is imposed by management; risk must be taken into consideration, and projects will vary in cash flow patterns.

a. Adopt a system of project classification to assist in the rational allocation of funds. Many alternative classification systems have been suggested, however a simple system could be: 1 essential, 2 replacement, 3 expansion.

b. Determine the upper limit of total funds for investment and allocate these funds to classification groups.

c. Prepare differential cash flows for all investment projects (other than "essential") and use subjective probability distributions for investments under risk. Convert cash flow distributions to "expected" cash flow patterns.

d. Select from mutually exclusive groups, those projects to include in final selection. Use differential cash flows and calculate I.R.R. in this selection.

e. Calculate the I.R.R. of all "expansion" projects and prepare a demand and supply schedule of funds for these projects. Compare the I.R.R. of the marginal project with the long-run cut-off rate for the firm. If the marginal I.R.R. is equal to or greater than this rate, rank all expansion projects according to a present value index or a terminal value index (to take into consideration varying outlays and lifespans).

f. Using the long-range cut-off rate, rank replacement projects in order of present value index.

CONCLUSIONS

This paper set out to evaluate the present state of investment theory and practice and to develop a set of investment selection procedures. It has been shown that while there remain considerable differences of opinion amongst academics on the complex areas of capital rationing and risk, practitioners can select and employ theoretically sound decision criteria for investment strategies.

FOOTNOTES

1. Van Horne, J. C., *Financial Management and Policy,* Prentice-Hall, 2nd ed., 1971, p. 9.
2. Bierman, H. and Smidt, S., *Capital Budgeting Decision,* Macmillan, 1971, pp. 3–4.
3. Van Horne, J. C., *op. cit.,* p. 57.
4. Elton, E. J., "Capital Rationing and External Discount Rates," *Journal of Finance,* XXV, June, 1970, p. 573.
5. Porterfield, T. S., *Investment Decisions and Capital Costs,* Prentice-Hall, 1965, Chapter 7.
6. Parker, R. N., *Management Accounting: An Historical Perspective,* Macmillan, 1969, Chapter 3.
7. Dean, J., *Capital Budgeting,* Columbia University Press, 1951.
8. Porterfield, J.T.S., *op. cit.*
9. Gordon, M. J., "The Payoff Period and the Rate of Profit," *Journal of Business,* XXVIII (October, 1955), p. 253.
10. Dean, J., *op. cit.*
11. Merrett, A. and Sykes, A., "Calculating the Rate of Return on Capital Budgets," *Journal of Industrial Economics,* IX, November, 1960, pp. 98–115.
12. Weingartner, H. M., "The Excess Present Value Index–A Theoretical Basis and Critique," *Journal of Accounting Research,* 3, 1966, pp. 213–224.
13. Meredith, G. G., *Capital Investment Decisions,* University of Queensland Press, 1966, pp. 6–10.
14. Meredith, G. G., "An Effective Rate of Return for Capital Projects," *Cost Accountant,* 42, August, 1961, pp. 295–299.
15. Parker, R. H., *op. cit.,* Chapter 1, and Meredith, G. G., *Administrative Control of Capital Expenditure: A Survey of Australian Public Companies,* University of Queensland Press, 1965.
16. Solomon, E., "The Arithmetic of Capital Budgeting Decisions," *Management of Corporate Capital,* edited by E. Solomon, Free Press of Glencoe, pp. 74–79.
17. Bennett, J. W., Grant, J. McB., and Parket, R. H., *Topics in Business Finance and Accounting,* Cheshire, p. 54.
18. Solomon, E., *op. cit.*
19. Solomon, E., *The Theory of Financial Management,* Columbia University Press, 1963, Chapter III.
20. Porterfield, T. S., *op. cit.,* pp. 44–51.
21. Bierman and Smidt, *op. cit.,* pp. 144–5.
22. Bierman and Smidt, *op. cit.,* pp. 152–5.

23. Solomon, E., *op. cit.*, Chapter VII.

24. Solomon, E., *op. cit.*, Chapters VIII and IX.

25. Morris, R. D., *An Examination of Cut-off Rate for Capital Expenditure Analysis under Capital Rationing*, University of Queensland Press, 1971.

26. Luce, R. D. and Raiffa, H., *Games and Decisions*, Wiley & Sons, 1957.

27. Wald, A., *Statistical Decision Functions*, Wiley & Sons, 1950.

28. Savage, L. J., *Foundations of Statistics*, Wiley & Sons, 1954.

29. Hurwicz, L., *Optimality Criteria for Decision Making under Ignorance*, Cowles Commission Paper No. 355, Chicago.

30. Morris, W. T., *The Analysis of Management Decisions*, Irwin, 1964.

31. Savage, L. T., "The Foundations of Statistics Reconsidered," *Studies in Subjective Probability*, Wiley and Sons, 1964.

32. Niland, P., "Investing in Automotive Equipment," *Harvard Business Review*, 35, 1957, pp. 73–82.

33. Wright, M. G., "Uncertainty and the Risk in Capital Investment," *Accountant*, CMV, 1966, pp. 628–631.

34. Merrett, A. and Sykes, A., *op. cit.*

35. N.A.A.: *Return on Capital as a Guide to Managerial Decisions*, Research Report No. 35, 1965.

36. Robichek, A. and Myers, S. C., *Optimal Financing Decisions*, Prentice-Hall, 1965, pp. 79–93.

37. Van Horne, J. C., *Financial Management and Policy*, Prentice-Hall, 1971, pp. 131–144.

38. Meredith, G. G., *Analysis of Capital Investments under Risk and Uncertainty*, A.S.A. Bulletin No. 9, August, 1969.

39. Magee, J. F., "How to Use Decision Trees in Capital Investment," *Harvard Business Review*, No. 42, 1964, pp. 79–96.

40. Swalm, R. O., "Utility Theory—Insights into Risk Taking," *Harvard Business Review*, No. 44, 1966, pp. 124–125.

Empirical Evidence of the Adoption of Sophisticated Capital Budgeting Techniques

Thomas Klammer

Previous research into capital budgeting procedures has usually shown the following picture. At any one time, at least some theorists and scholars are advocating relatively sophisticated capital budgeting methods. These methods are being used or seriously considered by a small number of firms, mostly large and in industries with high investment rates and rapid changes. Most remaining firms are relying on methods which are simpler and theoretically less satisfactory, although there may be considerable sophistication in the way in which individual practitioners apply formally simple capital budgeting methods.[1] For example, in the late 1950s theorists were advocating rate of return as a measure of an investment's worth, but this method tended to be in actual use only in some of the larger oil, chemical, and automotive products companies, while the majority of firms used relatively simple and formally unsatisfactory methods, such as payback.

In recent years, leading theorists have gone beyond rate of return, have attempted to deal more explicitly with the existence of risk, and have suggested a variety of applications of management science or operations research techniques to capital budgeting problems. Have there been similar changes in the practices of business firms? This paper reports on a survey aimed at answering this and related questions for large manufacturing firms in 1970.

SOURCE: Reprinted by permission of author and *The Journal of Business,* Vol. 45, No. 3 (October, 1972). Copyright 1972 by the University of Chicago.

EDITOR'S NOTE: The technical appendix has been omitted.

SURVEY PROCEDURE

Sample

The sample was drawn from the 1969 Compustat listing of manufacturing firms.[2] Firms in this list were omitted if they did not meet the following requirements: (a) The Compustat listing contained at least fifteen firms in the same major Standard Industrial Classification grouping (e.g., SIC no. 20, Food and Kindred Products). (b) The Compustat listing showed at least five firms in the same SIC subclassification (e.g., SIC no. 2082, Malt Liquors). (c) The firm made at least $1 million of capital expenditures in each of the five years 1963–67 as determined from the Compustat breakdown of capital expenditures.

These selection rules produced a sample of 369 rather large firms with sizable and continuing capital expenditure programs. Such firms would be expected to make relatively heavy use of the more sophisticated capital budgeting techniques covered in the survey questionnaire, as compared with all firms on the Compustat list.

Response Rates

The 369 firms were surveyed by mail in the first part of 1970. One hundred eighty-four firms, about half of those surveyed, returned questionnaires with some usable data. Table 1 shows the two-digit SIC classification of firms in the sample and of firms responding.

Measures of size and capital intensity were calculated for both responding and nonresponding firms. The response rate was higher for larger and more capital-intense firms.[3] Also, the response rate seemed to be higher for those industries that are subject to more rapid changes in technology and/or capital needs, such as chemicals, petroleum, and transportation equipment. Overall, it appears that firms that have found the greatest need for capital budgeting and therefore have the greatest interest in the practices of other firms were most likely to respond. The bias which this introduces in the results appears to be in the same direction as that already inherent in the sample: toward more use of sophisticated methods.

Questionnaire

All but one of the questions asked for yes-no or multiple-choice responses. Respondents were asked whether they used each of five specific administrative procedures, four specific methods of appraising risk (with an additional open-end question to cover any other method used), and eight management science techniques. Additional questions covered the proportion of projects for which

TABLE 1.   Sample Size and Response Rates by Industry

SIC No. and industry	Firms in sample	Responses received	Response rate (%)
20. Food and kindred products	45	21	46.7
22. Textile mill products	16	4	25.0
26. Paper and allied products	20	9	45.0
27. Printing, publishing, and allied products	8	2	25.0
28. Chemicals and allied products	72	40	55.6
29. Petroleum refining and related industries	31	21	67.7
32. Stone, clay, glass, and concrete products	17	6	35.3
33. Primary metal industries	20	10	50.0
34. Fabricated metal products, except ordinance, machinery, and transportation equipment	17	7	41.1
35. Machinery, except electrical	45	23	51.1
36. Electrical machinery, equipment, and supplies	43	20	46.5
37. Transportation equipment	35	21	60.0
Total	369	184	49.9

profitability estimates were made and the use and nature of minimum profitability standards, both primary and secondary.

Respondents were asked to answer each question for each of three time periods: the present, 1964, and 1959. There was a clear tendency for respondents to give less information for the earlier periods.

ANALYSIS OF RESULTS

In analyzing the results, I found that a major question is how to make use of the industry detail available. One might speculate that the sample design and the pattern of nonresponses would act to eliminate most of the potential interindustry differences, and this appears to be the case. In the absence of strong hypotheses about the nature of industry differences, χ^2 tests were performed on the responses to individual questions by industry. The mixed results, shown in table 2, do not provide strong justification for more elaborate analysis by industry. Accordingly, the analysis which follows will present and comment on the industry detail only where it seemed especially appropriate.

TABLE 2.   Significance of Differences in the Use of Capital
Budgeting Techniques by Industry

Industry and the use of:*	χ^2	Significance level†
Long-range capital budgeting	5.74	.45
Postauditing	5.46	.45
Full-time capital budgeting staff	9.38	.15
Formal method of considering risk	12.84	.05
Management science techniques	10.96	.10
Required profit rate—percentage of investments meeting	11.74	.08
Payback	4.76	.60
Accounting rate of return	7.51	.30
Discounting	5.27	.50

*The number of firms using and not using a technique was broken down for each industry with ten or more responses and a χ^2 calculated. The results of each of these χ^2s are reported in this table.

†Significance at this level or greater based on six degrees of freedom.

Administrative Techniques

Five questions covered techniques which the literature frequently emphasizes in discussions of desirable capital budgeting systems. The percentage responses are summarized in table 3.

TABLE 3.   Administrative Techniques Used

Technique	Percentage using in:* 1970	1964	1959
Search for alternative investments	94	87	82
Formal long-range capital budget	69	57	43
Postaudits of major projects	88	61	50
Standard forms for expenditure requests	97	90	84
Full-time capital budgeting staff	56	51	45

*Percentages shown are yes divided by yes + no multiplied by 100, disregarding non-responses. Nonresponse rates were higher for earlier years. For these five questions, yes + no answers ranged from 181 to 184 for 1970. For 1964 the corresponding range was 150–55 respondents, and for 1959 it was 137–48.

Usage of all of these techniques has been growing and is now high for most of them. Departures from 100 percent usage might be best explained as a result of careful reading of the question. It is hard to imagine a respondent making no effort to search for alternative investments at some point in the evaluation procedure, or having no long-range capital budgeting plan, but the questions may have put such emphasis on the formality with which these activities were conducted that some respondents answered negatively. The low reported usage of a full-time capital budgeting staff, reported as used by only a little more than half of the respondents, can only mean that some amount of financial, engineering, or other duties are often performed by even the most specialized individuals performing the capital budgeting function. This type of organization may well be consistent with a large and well-conducted capital budgeting activity. It does not, however, seem to give unqualified support to Terborgh's 1967 statement that most firms had specialized staffs.[4]

In general, the usage rates reported here for earlier periods are consistent with the findings of Istvan,[5] Pflomn,[6] and Terborgh[7] on the use of standard forms and postaudits.

A relationship appears to exist between the presence of a full-time staff and the use of a formal long-range capital budget. A χ^2 test showed less than a 5 percent chance of this relationship occurring by chance.[8] One might explain this association by pointing out that a full-time staff is more likely to have the time, opportunity, ability, and interest to maintain a long-range capital budget.

Risk Analysis

It is likely that nearly every firm has some method of dealing with risk, but only 39 percent of the respondents said they were using some specific formal method. Table 4 summarizes the percentage responses to the questions on risk analysis.

TABLE 4.   Risk Analysis Techniques

Technique	Percentage using in:*		
	1970	1964	1959
Raising required return	21	16	12
Shortening payback period	10	9	9
Determining probability distribution	13	7	7
Measuring covariance of projects	3	2	1
Other	7	2	1
At least one of above	39	24	19
Two or more of above	14	7	5
Three or more of above	5	3	1

*Percentages shown are yes divided by yes + no multiplied by 100.

Many firms which did report using a formal method tended to use more than one. In addition, some of the management science techniques covered in the next section undoubtedly included risk appraisal features, although the questions were not asked in such a way as to permit determination of a nonduplicating total of firms using at least one management science or other formal method of risk analysis. If we make the relatively conservative assumption that all firms reporting the use of probability theory are making formal risk analyses, ignoring the possibility that some of the other management science techniques are being used for the same purpose, the nonduplicating total of table 4 becomes 45 percent of respondents using some formal risk analysis method.[9]

Industry groups responded differently to the risk questions. Over 70 percent of firms in Petroleum Refining and over 50 percent of those in Chemicals reported using at least one method. In the remaining industry groups, less than 40 percent of the firms did so.

Management Science Techniques

Out of the many techniques associated with the approaches of management science and operations research, the questionnaire asked about eight. Percentage responses are summarized in table 5. Again, firms reporting any use often report the use of several of these techniques. And once again, firms in the Petroleum Refining industry reported the heaviest use: 85 percent of such firms say they used one or more of these methods. No other industry group reported usage greater than the all-industry average.

TABLE 5.   Management Science Techniques Used

Technique	Percentage using in:*		
	1970	1964	1959
Game theory	3	2	0
Linear programming	17	8	5
Nonlinear programming	4	3	1
Computer simulation	28	7	4
Probability theory	32	8	5
Decision theory	9	4	3
Pert/critical path	28	13	4
Utility theory	4	1	0
At least one of the above	51	22	13
Two or more of the above	32	11	7
Three or more of the above	21	4	3

*Percentages shown are yes divided by responding firms multiplied by 100, disregarding nonresponse. For this question, total responding firms are 184 in 1970, 157 in 1964, and 149 in 1959.

Project Evaluation Methods

Two questions covered the proportion of projects for which profit contribution estimates were made and on which minimum profitability standards were imposed. Recognizing that considerations of cost and the value of information would lead a sophisticated firm to avoid these procedures for some sorts of projects, it still seems likely that movement away from the lowest and toward the highest proportions indicates increased sophistication during the period covered by this survey. The results, as reported in table 6, show such movement. Even among the relatively sophisticated respondents of this survey, however, it remains true that about a quarter of the firms say they make profitability estimates for a quarter or less of their capital outlays and nearly a tenth say they impose minimum profitability standards on only a few of their proposals.

TABLE 6.   Project Evaluation Techniques

Technique	Percentage using in:*		
	1970	1964	1959
Profit contribution analysis required:			
For over 75% of projects	53	53	50
For 25%–75% of projects	41	40	34
For less than 25% of projects	6	7	16
Total	100	100	100
Minimum profitability standards required:			
For most projects	77	65	58
For some projects	13	23	20
For few projects	10	12	22
Total	100	100	100
Most sophisticated primary evaluation standard:			
Discounting (rate of return or present worth)	57	38	19
Accounting rate of return	26	30	34
Payback or payback reciprocal	12	24	34
Urgency	5	8	13
Total	100	100	100

*Percentages shown are yes divided by yes + no multiplied by 100.

Respondents cited a variety of projects as *not* subject to estimates of profit contribution. Most frequently, these were governmentally required projects such as those for safety or pollution control, replacement proposals, particularly in emergencies, and projects for employee morale, such as paving parking lots and the purchase of newer office furniture.

Lumping respondents who said that "most" and "some" projects had to meet minimum profitability requirements in 1964, we obtain results that are very similar to those obtained by Christy.[10]

When asked to designate their primary standard of project evaluation, a number of firms gave more than one answer. The percentages given in the lowest section of table 6 count only the most sophisticated method designated by each respondent, where "Urgency" is taken as the least sophisticated and any discounted net cash flow method is taken as the most sophisticated. The results show a clear majority using discounting methods in 1970.

The method of eliminating multiple answers entails an obvious bias in the direction of more sophisticated standards. For the current period, about one-third of the firms reporting the use of discounting as their most sophisticated primary method reported that they used more than one primary method. Furthermore, an additional 25 percent of the firms that used discounting as a primary method reported use of some nondiscounting method as a secondary standard. Thus, only about 25 percent of the respondents say they are using discounting standards exclusively, although 67 percent make some use of discounting methods. Beyond all this, one can make no further statement, from these data, about how and to what extent firms use any of these techniques.

Even with the bias just discussed, it is clear that use of one or the other of the discounted cash flow methods has been gaining over time and that payback methods have been declining in popularity. Previous surveys usually showed payback as the most widely used standard.[11] This is not strongly contradicted by the present survey responses for the two earlier periods, when we consider sample differences, normal errors of recall of earlier periods, and our method of eliminating multiple answers. The advanced theory of the 1950s has increasingly become the practice of the early 1970s.

FOOTNOTES

1. See, for example, George A. Christy, *Capital Budgeting–Current Practices and Their Efficiency* (Eugene: Bureau of Business and Economic Research, University of Oregon, 1966).

2. Compustat is a magnetic tape library containing financial information for over 1,000 companies including 678 manufacturing firms in 1969. These represent the major New York, American, over-the-counter, and regional stock exchange companies. Compustat is a service of Standard Statistics Company of New York.

3. Size is based on the average operating assets for an eight-year period, 1961–68. Capital intensity is the yearly depreciation divided by the yearly operating assets for each of the eight years 1961–68. The larger this ratio, the higher the capital intensity of the firm.

4. George Terborgh, *Business Investment Management* (Washington, D.C.: Machinery and Allied Products Institute and Council for Technological Advancement, 1967), p. xx.

5. Donald F. Istvan, *Capital Expenditure Decisions: How They Are Made in Large Corporations* (Bloomington: Bureau of Business Research, Indiana University, 1961), p. 29.

6. Norman P. Pflomn, *Managing Capital Expenditures,* Studies in Business Policy 107 (New York: National Industrial Conference Board, 1963), p. 30.

7. Terborgh, p. xx.

8. A series of χ^2 tests was made comparing the usage and nonusage of two capital budgeting techniques. These tests were designed to test the association of individual techniques.

9. A χ^2 test indicates that there is a strong relationship between risk analysis and management science techniques.

10. Christy, p. 12

11. *Ibid.*

Coordinating the Decision Process— Formal Planning Systems

INTRODUCTION

To understand the aggregate process of planning at the firm level, one has to transcend the logic at the level of individual decisions or even decision subsystems such as those presented in the preceding three chapters. This implies no denial of the logic underlying such decisions, but it suggests that the framework within which such logic is developed is subordinated to the rationale underlying the overall planning process. A firm's objective is not to make the most profit in any single transaction such as a sale or a purchase; rather it is to have an optimal pricing *policy* for a whole group of products for a relevant horizon, to have an optimal parts purchase *policy* for a class of products, and so on. Each design must support and be consistent with the management strategy which the firm pursues in exploiting specific product-market opportunities in their environment. Since an optimal production policy might conflict with an optimal purchase policy on the one hand and an optimal marketing policy on the other hand, it is clear that an optimal firm-wide plan is not an aggregation of the

305

optimal sequential plans. Similarly since the optimal firm-wide plan for one period might be in conflict with the optimal firm-wide plan for the ensuing period, it is clear that the firm's optimal long-range plan is not an aggregation of the firm's optimal short-range plans. In other words, a suboptimal plan in one or more subunits of the firm might be quite consistent with the firm's overall optimality. Similarly, a suboptimal plan in one or more short-run periods might be quite consistent with optimality over a longer range.

These considerations suggest the need for coordination, arbitration, and negotiations in order to achieve overall optimality. It is a difficult process because it involves potential sacrifices by the internal members of the firm for the common good of the investors of the firm who, interestingly enough, do not participate in the planning process. Explicit intervention is therefore necessary to transcend from segmental plans to a balanced, coordinated firm-wide plan. Such intervention is carried out by the top management who are as much concerned with the effectiveness of the overall plan as with the efficiency of the decision subsystems because they, more than other managers, perceive their rewards from the firm to be directly associated with investor satisfaction.

The total planning process is therefore an organized blending of several approaches which include:

1. the adoption of rational decision rules and standards governing specific, repetitive internal tasks;
2. employment of middle-level managers with demonstrated ability (1) in making "good" judgments in situations where the input/output relationships are not clear; and (2) in motivating the people they manage; and
3. imposing divisional performance targets adequate enough to provide a fair return to investors and to provide sufficient contribution towards the maintenance of management and their staff.

Thus, assuming optimal net benefit criteria at the core of the decision subsystem in the lower levels of management, top management views the planning criteria as providing sufficient slack in the system in addition to normal return on investment.

It is not surprising to find that the approach, both in theory and in practice, has been one of exploring one subsystem while holding all others constant. For example, output and marketing plans are usually analyzed holding plant size and investment level constant. Similarly, investment analysis usually subsumes outputs and pricing decisions within individual time periods. The previous sections of the book have set the prelude to the problem of overall balance and coordination which is the subject of this chapter. The title of formal planning systems is used to imply this balanced, integrated master plan.

Before we move on, we should point out that accounting plays an extensive and intimate role at all levels of planning. In the earlier chapters we saw the flow of accounting data in the decision subsystems. The articles in this section serve to highlight the crucial role that accounting measures, accounting models and accountants play in the formal planning area. Accounting methods serve not only to reflect the nature and expected results of an overall plan, but, more important, they also compel and marshall the planning processes, and they generally breathe life into what might otherwise remain as a collection of empirically sterile precepts of management process and organizational behavior.

In the opening article of this section, *Framework for Analysis,* Anthony introduces the problem of understanding the total planning and control system and suggests the need for recognizing several distinct processes. In his scheme of classification, these different processes are: strategic planning, management control, technical control, financial accounting, and information handling. In a related work[1] he discusses each of these subsystems at length. In the present article he confines himself largely to a discussion of management control and how it differs from strategic planning and technical control. The objective of management control is to encourage line managers throughout the firm to make the most effective and efficient acquisition and utilization of resources toward achieving goals of the firm.

One measure of success of a management control system in a firm is the extent to which it promotes congruence between individual managers' goals and the firm's goals, and the strength of motivation the system generates in the manager. One way of enhancing the effectiveness of the management control system is to separate tasks requiring considerable judgment from tasks where the input/output relations are readily determined or can be predicted with a high degree of accuracy. The latter then can be covered through technical controls exercised on a real-time basis at the operational level, since the decision rules for such tasks can be formalized through rational decision models and the related performance controlled by direct intervention. As a result, more of the manager's time is released for truly managing through the exercise of judgment, persuasion, and leadership in areas where optimal arrangements cannot be specified.

In his article, *Budgeting for Management Planning and Control,* Welsch advances the notion that a budgetary control system is the only practical link between sound management philosophy and the actual planning of operations. He does this by comparing the principles underlying budgetary control systems with those underlying a sound management philosophy. In the process he cautions the accountant to distinguish between the role of the specific accounting techniques and models used in coordinating the budget and the role of the principles of the budget control system. In order to be successful, the budgetary control system should be tailored to the unique needs of the firm and its objectives, the nature of operations, and the management structure.

One reason Welsch's cautionary remarks are often overlooked in practice and the planning process gets equated with the routine of fitting budget schedules is due to the sheer physical size of the paper work involved in planning. A lack of appreciation of the actual magnitude of the time required to plan, as well as the nature of the multiple interrelationships between the plans of the various segments of the organization, often leads to unrealistic budget completion dates. As a consequence, the budgets may not be timely for making decisions or for commencing operations. If this is the case the budgets become costly ornaments. When the managers are under pressure to complete their budgets in time, planning may be sacrificed for form filling, and the basic purpose of planning and the budget is foiled. Seen in this context, DeCoster's article, *The Budget Director and PERT,* is an eloquent plea for planning the planning process itself. Basically he calls for a realistic appraisal of the time required to develop plans in each segment and for the need for proper dovetailing of the plans of the various segments with the resources required to accomplish these tasks. Further, by choosing PERT as the specific technique used to illustrate the planning of the planning process, DeCoster manages to introduce the reader to the PERT technique, itself a useful planning and decision tool. There is another side benefit from this reading since it serves to show diagrammatically the flow of a budget program.

Accounting, by nature, is a repository of historical data. Planning and decision making, on the other hand, deal with the future. The measure of usefulness of the historical data depends upon how well it facilitates a prediction of the future and to what extent it supplements or complements nonaccounting data. Prediction, in addition to demanding available and relevant data, involves the choice of a forecasting model. Hall's article, *Forecasting Techniques for Use in the Corporate Planning Process,* provides a survey and appraisal of the forecasting techniques useful in planning. If the reader is bewildered by the variety of forecasting models and is at a loss as to how to make a choice, it is because the subject is truly vast and the process of selecting a forecast model seems to be more an art than a science at this stage.

The sheer magnitude and complexity of the overall planning process coupled with the problem of forecasting relevant data tend to force the management to terminate the planning process earlier than desired and to choose an overall plan without examining all the alternatives proposed. A partial solution to this problem is evolving with the development of computer technology and the increasing use of computers to simulate the real process which is being subjected to planning. Simulation models may range widely in sophistication, size, and applicability, but in the context of firm-wide planning, the financial planning simulation using traditional accounting models seems to have gained the most acceptance in firms. The reason for its success is due to the fact that managers can interface decision effects with it, much in the same way as they used to interface with traditional budget schedules. At the same time they can exploit the computer's facility and speed by asking several "what if" questions. The computerized simulation model thus actually aids the planning process by encouraging the manager to test his decisions before the fact while simultaneously facilitating the manager's learning process and by eliminating long feedback delays. Khoury and Nelson, in *Simulation in Financial Planning,* provide an excellent discussion of the general features of the financial simulation model of a large company, its uses and advantages, and the resources and type of organizational commitment necessary to develop the model.

Schiff and Lewin's article, *Where Traditional Budgeting Fails,* is an attempt to provide a down-to-earth description of the planning process of a large company. Although it is highly simplified, the reader will recognize the difficulty one company encountered in reconciling its practices and normative theories of planning. While formal decision models steer the mythical rational man to the optimal plan, the real-world managers who hold discretionary power use their volition to set respectable targets whose optimality or nonoptimality can hardly be verified. Once these plans are established, their attainment is made a condition for the continued participation of the lower-level employees with the firm. The authors point out that under such a set-up, an unintended consequence is the creation of slack at lower levels without the knowledge of top management. They further report that under such circumstances what passes for successful budgeting is no more than the "successful" manipulation of slack by the lower-echelon employees in such a way as to produce results consistent with the targets set by top management. These observations are very significant, but whether the existence of slack connotes a failure of formal planning process, as the title of their article implies, is open to question. Because the lower-level management is exposed to the risk of nonattainment of budget levels, the slack may be seen as a necessary premium paid to cover risk contingencies. Also, from the total firm point of view, the slack may be seen as a necessary cushion the firm needs to absorb unanticipated adversities without courting disaster.

FOOTNOTES

1. Robert N. Anthony, *Planning and Control Systems: A Framework for Analysis,* Boston: Harvard University Press, 1965.

Framework for Analysis *

Robert N. Anthony

Since dogs and humans are both mammals, some generalizations that apply to one species also apply to the other. It is for this reason that some new surgical techniques can be tested on dogs before being risked on humans. But dogs and humans differ, and, unless these differences are recognized, generalizations that are valid for one species may be erroneously applied to the other. For example, canine behavior can be largely explained in terms of conditioned reflexes, but human behavior is much more complicated. Similarly, some generalizations can be made about the whole planning and control process in a business; however, there actually are several quite different types of planning and control processes, and mistakes may be made if a generalization (principle, rule, technique) valid for one type is applied to the other.

The purpose of this article is to suggest a classification of the main topics or "species" that come within the broad term, Planning and Control Systems, and to suggest distinguishing characteristics of each. Hopefully, this will lead to a sorting out and sharpening of principles and techniques applicable to each species.

The particular classification chosen has been arrived at after careful analysis of how well various alternatives match statements made in the literature and, more important, what is found in practice. It is, however, tentative. Better schemes may well be developed, and we expose this one primarily in the hope that discussion of it will lead to agreement on *some* scheme, not necessarily this.

SOURCE: Reprinted by permission of *Management Services* (March/April, 1964), pp. 18-24. Copyright 1964 by the American Institute of CPAs.

*This article is based on research done for the Division of Research at the Harvard Business School and financed by The Associates of the Harvard Business School. Both the professional and financial aspects of this support are gratefully acknowledged. An expanded treatment of the subject is planned for publication by the Division of Research.

310

In this article, we shall focus on a process labeled *management control*. We shall describe its main characteristics, and distinguish it from processes labeled *strategic planning* and *technical control*. (Two other processes, *financial accounting* and *information handling*, are also relevant, but space does not permit a discussion of them here.)

Obviously, we do not assert that these processes can be separated by sharply defined boundaries; one shades into another. Strategic planning sets the guidelines for management control, and management control sets the guidelines for technical control. The complete management function involves an integration of all these processes, and the processes are complementary.

We do assert that the processes are sufficiently distinct so that those who design and use planning and control systems will make expensive errors if they fail to take into account both the common characteristics of a process and the differences between processes. This article will deal with these similarities and differences and point out some of the errors that are made when they are not recognized.

MANAGEMENT CONTROL

Management control is the process of assuring that resources are obtained and used effectively and efficiently in the accomplishment of the organization's objectives.

Management control is a process carried on within the framework established by strategic planning. Objectives, facilities, organization, and financial factors are more or less accepted as "givens." Decisions about next year's budget, for example, are limited by policies and guidelines prescribed by top management. The management control process is intended to make possible the achievement of planned objectives as effectively and efficiently as possible within these "givens."

The purpose of a management control system is to encourage managers to take actions which are in the best interests of the company. For example, if the system is structured so that a certain course of action increases the reported profits of a division, and at the same time *lessens* the profits of the company as a whole, there is something wrong. Technically, this purpose can be described as *goal congruence*.

"TOTAL" SYSTEM NECESSARY

Psychological considerations are dominant in management control. Activities such as communicating, persuading, exhorting, inspiring, and criticizing are an important part of the process.

Ordinarily, a management control system is a *total* system in the sense that it embraces all aspects of the company's operation. It needs to be a total system because an important management function is to assure that all parts of the operation are in balance with one another, and, in order to examine balance, management needs information about each of the parts.

With rare exceptions, the management control system is built around a *financial* structure; that is, resources and outputs are expressed in monetary units. Money is the only common denominator by means of which the heterogeneous elements of output and resources (e.g., hours of labor; type of labor; quantity and quality of material, amount and kind of products produced) can be combined and compared. (Although the financial structure is usually the central focus, nonmonetary measures such as time, number of persons, and reject and spoilage rates are also important parts of the system.)

The management control process tends to be *rhythmic;* it follows a definite pattern and timetable, month after month and year after year. In budgetary control, which is an important part of the management control process, certain steps are taken in a prescribed sequence and at certain dates each year: the dissemination of guidelines, the preparation of original estimates, the transmission of these estimates up through the several echelons in the organization, the review of these estimates, final approval by top management, dissemination back through the organization, operation, reporting, and the appraisal of performance. The procedure to be followed at each step in this process, the dates when the steps are to be completed, and even the forms that are to be used can be, and often are, set forth in a manual.

INTERLOCKING SUBSYSTEMS

A management control system is, or should be, a *coordinated, integrated* system: that is, although data collected for one purpose may differ from those collected for another purpose, these data should be reconcilable with one another. In a sense, the management control system is a *single* system, but it is perhaps more accurate to think of it as a set of interlocking subsystems. In many organizations, for example, three types of cost information are needed for management control: (1) *costs by responsibility centers,* which are used for planning and controlling the activities of responsible supervisors; (2) *full program costs,* used for pricing and other operating decisions under normal circumstances; and (3) *direct program costs,* used for pricing and other operating decisions under special circumstances, such as when management wishes to utilize idle capacity. ("Program" is here used for any activity in which the organization engages. In industrial companies, programs consist of products or product lines, and "product costs" can be substituted in the above statements.)

Line managers are the focal points in management control. They are the persons whose judgments are incorporated in the approved plans, and they are the persons who must influence others and whose performance is measured. Staff people collect, summarize, and present information that is useful in the process, and they make calculations which translate management judgments into the format of the system. Such a staff may be large in numbers; indeed the control department is often the largest department in a company. However, the significant decisions are made by the line manager, not by the staff.

STRATEGIC PLANNING

Strategic planning is the process of deciding on changes in the objectives of the organization, in the resources that are to be used in attaining these objectives, and in the policies that are to govern the acquisition and use of these resources.

The word *strategy* is used here in its usual sense of deciding on how to combine and employ resources. Thus, strategic planning is a process having to do with the formulation of long-range, strategic, policy-type plans that change the character or direction of the organization. In an industrial company this includes planning that affects the objectives of the company; policies of all types (including policies as to management control and other processes); the acquisition and disposition of major facilities, divisions, or subsidiaries; the markets to be served and distribution channels for serving them; the organization structure (as distinguished from individual personnel actions); research and development of new product lines (as distinguished from modifications in existing products and product changes within existing lines); sources of new permanent capital; dividend policy; and so on. Strategic planning decisions affect the physical, financial, and organizational framework within which operations are carried on.

IRREGULAR IN NATURE

Briefly, here are some ways in which the strategic planning process differs from the management control process.

A strategic plan usually relates to some part of the organization, rather than to the totality; the concept of a master planner who constantly keeps all parts of the organization at some co-ordinated optimum is a nice concept but an unrealistic one. Life is too complicated for any human, or computer, to do this.

Strategic planning is essentially *irregular*. Problems, opportunities, and "bright ideas" do not arise according to some set timetable, and they have to be dealt with whenever they happen to be perceived. The appropriate analytical techniques depend on the nature of the problem being analyzed, and no over-all approach (such as a mathematical model) has been developed that is of much help in analyzing all types of strategic problems. Indeed, an overemphasis on a systematic approach is quite likely to stifle the essential element of creativity. In strategic planning, management works now on one problem, now on another, according to the needs and opportunities of the moment.

The estimates used in strategic planning are intended to show the *expected* results of the plan. They are neutral and impersonal. By contrast, the management control process, and the data used in it, are intended to influence managers to take actions that will lead to *desired* results. Thus, in connection with management control, it is appropriate to discuss how "tight" an operating budget should be: Should the goals be set so high that only an outstanding manager can achieve them, or should they be set so that they are attainable by the average manager? At what level does frustration-inhibit a manager's best efforts? Does an attainable budget lead to complacency? And so on. In strategic planning, the question to be asked about the figures is simply: Is this the most reasonable estimate that can be made?

Strategic planning relies heavily on *external information,* that is, on data collected from outside the company, such as market analyses, estimates of costs and other factors involved in building a plant in a new locality, technological developments, and so on. When data from the normal information system are used, they usually must be recast to fit the needs of the problem being analyzed. For example, the current operating costs of a plant that are collected for measuring performance and for making pricing and other operating decisions usually must be restructured before they are useful in deciding whether to close down the plant.

COMMUNICATIONS ARE LIMITED

Another characteristic of the relevant information is that much of it is imprecise. The strategic planner estimates what *will* happen, often over a rather long time period. These estimates are likely to have a high degree of uncertainty, and they must be treated accordingly.

In the management control process, the communication of objectives, policies, guidelines, decisions, and results throughout the organization is extremely important. In the strategic planning process, communication is much simpler and involves relatively few persons; indeed, the need for secrecy often requires that steps be taken to inhibit communication. (Wide communication of the *decisions* that will result from strategic planning is obviously important, but this is part of the management control process.)

Strategic planning is essentially applied economics, whereas management control is essentially applied social psychology.

EXHIBIT 1.   Some Contrasts

	Strategic Planning	Management Control
Person primarily involved	Staff and top management	Line and top management
Number of persons	Small	Large
Mental activity	Creative; analytical	Administrative; persuasive
Variables	Complex; much judgment	Less complex
Time period	Tends to be long	Tends to be short
Periodicity	Irregular, no set schedule	Rhythmic; set timetable
Procedures	Unstructured; each problem different	Prescribed procedure, regularly followed
Focus	Tend to focus on one aspect at a time	All encompassing
Source of information	Relies more on external and future	Relies more on internal and historical
Product	Intangible; precedent setting	More tangible; action within precedent
Communication problem	Relatively simple	Crucial and difficult
Appraisal of soundness	Extremely difficult	Much less difficult

Both management control and strategic planning involve top management, but middle management (i.e., operating management) typically have a much more important role in management control than they have in strategic planning. Middle managers usually are not major participants in the strategic planning process and sometimes are not even aware of the fact that a plan is being considered. Many operating executives are by temperament not very good at strategic planning. Also, the pressures of current activities usually do not allow them to devote the necessary time to such work. Currently, there is a tendency in companies to set up separate staffs which gather the facts and make the analyses that provide the background material for strategic decisions.

These and other differences between management control and strategic planning are summarized in Exhibit 1, above.

Strategic planning and management control activities tend to conflict with one another in some respects. The time that management spends in thinking about the future is taken from time that could otherwise be used in controlling current operations, so in this indirect way strategic planning can hurt current performance. And, of course, the reverse also is true.

More directly, many actions that are taken for long-run, strategic reasons make current profits smaller than they otherwise would be. Research and some advertising expenditures are obvious examples. The problem of striking the right balance between strategic and operating considerations is one of the central problems in the whole management process.

CONSEQUENCES OF CONFUSION

Following are statements illustrating some of the consequences of failing to make a distinction between strategic planning and management control.

"We should set up a long-range planning procedure and work out a systemized way of considering *all* our plans similar to the way we construct next year's budget." (A long-range plan shows the estimated consequences over the next several years of strategic decisions already taken. It is part of the management control process. Although it provides a useful background for considering strategic proposals, it is not strategic planning. Strategic proposals should be made whenever the opportunity or the need is perceived in a form that best presents the arguments.)

"The only relevant costs are incremental costs; pay no attention to fixed or sunk costs." (This is so in strategic planning, but operating managers are often motivated in the wrong direction if their decisions are based on incremental costs; for example, in intracompany transactions.)

"We may be selling Plan X some day. We should therefore set up the operating reports so that management will have at its fingertips the information it will need when it is deciding this question. For example, we should show inventory and fixed assets at their current market value." (Operating reports should be designed to assist in the management of current operations. Special compilations of data are needed for such major, nonroutine actions as selling a plant. Collection of such data routinely is both too expensive and likely to impede sound operating decisions.)

"Our ultimate goal is an all-purpose control system—integrated data processing—so that management will have all the data it needs for whatever problem it decides to tackle. We should collect data in elemental building blocks that can be combined in various ways to answer all conceivable questions." (This is an impossible goal. Each strategic proposal requires that the data be assembled in the way that best fits the requirements of that proposal. No one can foresee all the possibilities. The "building block" idea is sound within limits, but the limits are not so broad that all problems are encompassed.)

"All levels of management should participate in planning." (All levels of management should participate in the planning part of the management control process, but operating managers typically do not have the time, the inclination, or the analytical bent that is required for formulating strategic plans. Furthermore, such plans often must be kept highly secret.)

TECHNICAL CONTROL

Technical control is the process of assuring the efficient acquisition and use of resources, with respect to activities for which the optimum relationship between outputs and resources can be approximately determined.

The definition of technical control refers to outputs and resources. *Outputs* are the accomplishments of the organization, what it does, and *resources* are the inputs which the organization consumes. For a whole business, the outputs are the goods and services sold, which are measured by revenues earned, and the inputs are costs and expenses incurred. In rough terms, "output" equals "results," and "resources" equals "cost."

One of the important tasks in an organization is to seek the *optimum* relationship between outputs and resources. For some activities, this optimum relationship is fairly easy to establish: To manufacture a given part should require such-and-such labor, a certain sequence of machine operations, and so on. For other activities, there exists no "scientific" (even in the loose sense of this term) way of establishing the optimum relationship; for these activities, decision as to what costs to incur depend on human judgment.

The term "managed costs" is a descriptive one for those types of resources for which an objective decision as to the optimum quantity to be employed cannot be made. An important management function is to make judgments as to the "right" amount of managed costs in a given set of circumstances. These are, by definition, subjective judgments.

Management control applies to the whole of an organization, and to any parts of the whole in which managed costs are significant. Technical control applies to those activities, and only to those activities, in which there are no significant elements of managed cost. Or more simply, in the management control process, management judgment is an important element; in the technical control process, the technique itself is dominant.

As an example of technical control, consider inventory control. If the demand for an item, the cost of storing it, its production cost and production time, and the loss involved in not filling an order are known or can be reasonably estimated, then the optimum inventory level and the optimum production schedule can both be calculated, and reasonable men will agree with the results of these calculations.

In other than exceptional circumstances, these calculations can determine the actions that should be taken. Management intervention is necessary only when these exceptional circumstances arise.

SOME AREAS CAN'T BE MEASURED

By contrast, consider the legal department of a company. No device can measure the quality, or even the quantity, of the legal service that constitutes the output of this department. No formula can show the amount of service that should be rendered nor the optimum amount of costs that should be incurred. Impressions as to the "right" amount of service, as to the "right" amount of cost, and as to whether the relationship between the service actually rendered and the cost actually incurred was "right" are strictly subjective. They are judgments made by management. If persons disagree on these judgments, there is no objective way of resolving the disagreement. Yet the legal department as a part of the whole organization must be controlled; the chief counsel must operate within the framework of policies prescribed by top management. The control exercised in this situation is management control.

Examples of activities that can be subjected to technical control are: auto-mated plants, such as cement plants, oil refineries, and power generating stations; the direct operations of most manufacturing plants (but often not the overhead expense items); production scheduling; inventory control; the "order-taking" type of selling activity; and order processing, premium billing, payroll accoun-ting, check handling, and similar paperwork activities.

Examples of activities for which management control is necessary are: the total activities of most manufacturing plants, which include such "judgment" inputs as indirect labor, employee benefit and welfare programs, safety activities, training, and supervision; most advertising, sales promotion, pricing, selling (as distinguished from order taking) and similar marketing activities; most aspects of finance; most aspects of research, development, and design; the work of staff units of all types; and management activity itself.

The control appropriate for the whole of any unit which carries on both the technical and the management types of activities is management control. The control of the whole accounting department is management control even though technical control is appropriate for certain aspects of the work, such as posting and check writing.

Some people believe that the distinction between the two classes of activities described above is merely one of degree rather than of kind; they say that all we are doing is distinguishing between situations where control is "easy" and "diffi-cult," respectively. We think the distinction is more fundamental than that, and hope this will be apparent from the following brief list of characteristics that distinguish management control from technical control.

Management control covers the whole of an organization. Each technical control procedure is restricted to a subunit, often a narrowly circumscribed activity.

Just as management control occurs within a set of policies derived from strategic planning, so technical control occurs within a set of well-defined procedures and rules that are derived from management control.

Control is more difficult in management control than in technical control because of the absence of a "scientific" standard with which actual performance can be compared. A good technical control system can provide a much higher degree of assurance that actions are proceeding as desired than can a management control system.

RULES CAN BE PROGRAMMED

A technical control system is a *rational* system; that is, the action to be taken is decided by a set of logical rules. These rules may or may not cover all aspects of a given problem. Situations not covered by the rules are designated as "exceptions" and are resolved by human judgment. Other than these exceptions, the application of the rules is automatic. The rules can in principle be programmed into a computer, and the choice between using a computer and using a human being depends primarily on the relative cost of each method.

In management control, psychological considerations are dominant. The management control system at most assists those who take action; it does not directly or by itself result in action without human intervention. By contrast, the end product of an inventory control system can be an order, or a decision to replenish a certain inventory item, and this order may be based entirely on calculations from formulas incorporated in the system. (The formulas were *devised* by human beings, but this is a management control process, not a technical control process.)

In a consideration of technical control, analogies with mechanical, electrical, and hydraulic systems are reasonable and useful, and such terms as feedback, network balancing, optimization, and so on, are relevant. It is perfectly appropriate, for example, to view a technical control system as analogous to a thermostat which turns the furnace on and off according to its perception of changes in temperature. These analogies do not work well as models for management control systems, however, because the success of management systems is highly dependent on their impact on people, and people are not like thermostats or furnaces; one can't light a fire under a human being simply by turning up a thermostat.

A management control system is ordinarily focused on a financial structure, whereas technical control data are often nonmonetary. They may be expressed in terms of man-hours, number of items, pounds of waste, and so on. Since each technical control procedure is designed for a limited area of application, it is feasible to use the basis of measurement that is most appropriate for that area.

APPROXIMATIONS MEET DATA NEEDS

Data in a technical control system are in real time and relate to individual events, whereas data in a management control system are often retrospective and summarize many separate events. Computer specialists who do not make such a distinction, dream about a system that will display to the management the current status of every individual activity in the organization. Although this *could* be done, it *should not* be done; management doesn't want such detail. Management does not need to know the time at which lot No. 1007 was transferred from station 27 to station 28; rather, it needs to know only that the process is, or is not, proceeding as planned, and, if not, where the trouble lies.

Similarly, technical control uses exact data, whereas management control needs only approximations. Material is ordered and scheduled in specific quantities, employees are paid the exact amount due them, but data on management control reports need contain only two or three significant digits and are therefore rounded to thousands of dollars, to millions of dollars, or even (in the U.S. Government) to billions of dollars.

A technical control system requires a mathematical model of the operation. Although it may not always be expressed explicitly in mathematical notation, there is a decision rule which states that given certain values for parameters *a, b, . . . n,* action *X* is to be taken. Models are not so important in management control. In a sense, a budget or a PERT network are models associated with the management control process, but they are not the essence of the process.

The formal management control *system* is only a part of the management control *process,* actually a relatively unimportant part. The system can help motivate the manager to make decisions that are in the best interests of the organization, and the system can provide information that aids the manager in making these decisions; but many other stimuli are involved in motivating the manager, and good information does not automatically produce good decisions. The success or failure of the management control process depends on the personal characteristics of the manager: his judgment, his knowledge, his ability to influence others.

TECHNIQUE IS ALL-IMPORTANT

In technical control, the system itself is a much more important part of the whole process. Except in fully automated operations, it is an exaggeration to say that the system *is* the process, but it is not much of an exaggeration. The technical control system ordinarily states what action should be taken; it makes the decisions. As with any operation, management vigilance is required to detect an unforeseen "foul-up" in the operation, or a change in the conditions on which the technique is predicated. And management will be seeking ways to improve the technique. In general, however, the degree of management involvement in technical control is small, whereas in management control it is large.

As new techniques are developed, there is a tendency for more and more activities to become susceptible to technical control. In the factory, the production schedule that was formerly set according to the foreman's intuition is now derived by linear programming. And, although not too long ago it was believed that technical control was appropriate only for factory operations, we now see models and formulas being used for certain marketing decisions, such as planning salesmen's calls and planning direct mail advertising. This shift probably will continue; it is a large part of what people have in mind when they say, "management is becoming increasingly scientific."

Following are statements illustrating the consequences of failing to make a distinction between management control and technical control:

"Computers will make middle management obsolete." (Although computers can replace human beings in technical control, they are not a substitute for the human judgment that is an essential part of the management control process.)

"Business should develop a management control system like the SAGE and SAC control systems that work so well for the military." (The military systems mentioned are technical control systems. They are not related to the management control problem in the military, let alone that in business.)

"The way to improve the management control process is to develop better management decision rules." (This implies that mathematics rather than human beings, is the essence of management control.)

"Transfer prices should be calculated centrally." (This gives no recognition to negotiation and the exercise of judgment by divisional managers.)

"If you follow the planning and control techniques described in this book, your profits are a near predictable certainty." (This implies that the technique, rather than the quality of management, is the principal determinant of success.)

SUMMARY

We have described several subsystems that come under the general heading, "planning and control systems." Although related to one another, they have different purposes and different characteristics; different ways of thinking about each of them are therefore required. Generalizations about the whole area are, if valid, so vague as not to be useful. By contrast, useful generalizations, principles, and techniques can be developed for each of the subsystems. Mistakes are made when those valid for one subsystem are applied to another.

Budgeting for Management Planning and Control

Glenn A. Welsch

In current literature, in speeches, in conferences, and in the classroom, we hear with increasing frequency that, to be effective:

- Management must plan
- Management must co-ordinate
- Management must control
- Management must practice management by exception
- Management must improve communication
- Management must make effective the principle of participation, etc.

All of these are basic dictates and we cannot seriously take exception to them. Yet we read and hear relatively little as to how a management—be it of a small, medium, or large firm—might make these dictates practical and effective.

Much of the current management literature deals in generalities that frequently leave the practical business executive, as well as the student of management, "wandering in the dark," knowing some broad principles but having little knowledge as to how such dictates may be made effective in practice.

In contrast, much of the accounting literature and discussions concerned with "managerial accounting" are devoted almost exclusively to the *mechanics and techniques* of such procedures as budgeting, standard costing, direct costing, break-even analysis, and cost analysis. No one can deny that such techniques have excellent potentialities in appropriate settings. More important, the critical test of their potentialities in a given situation is the extent to which management uses the results in the process of decision making and in planning and controlling operations.

SOURCE: Reprinted by permission of *The Journal of Accountancy* (October, 1961), pp. 37–41. Copyright 1961 by the American Institute of Certified Public Accountants, Inc.

In any given situation, a basic problem is to put the two together—*techniques* and *application*—so that the management has a system suited to the situation and fundamentally sound in principle and design, yet tangible and detailed enough for specific application as well as for broad use.

The central theme of this discussion is that budgetary planning and control as practiced today by the better managements provides the only systematic and tangible approach so far developed for bringing sufficient certainty to management planning and control and for applying the above-mentioned management dictates in a coordinated and practical manner.

Budgetary planning and control is a comprehensive system whereby all aspects of the management process may be brought into a coordinated whole, and where the loose ends of management action and operations may be carefully tied together. This all-inclusive concept of the budgetary process is frequently misunderstood by some managements, and by some accountants.

In order to comprehend the full importance of budgeting, we must make a careful distinction in budgetary planning and control between:

• Mechanics and techniques, and
• Fundamentals or principles (to use the latter word loosely)

Mechanics have to do with such matters as design of budget schedules, clerical methods in completing such schedules, and routine computations. The techniques of budgeting are many and varied. For example, we may note methods of developing the sales budget, breakeven analysis, capital budget procedures, cashflow analyses, and variable budgets.

For accountants the mechanical aspect of budgeting is a natural since there is much in common here with the accounting model. This fortunate situation not infrequently leads to serious pitfalls, such as an oversimplified view of the budgetary process and a possibly unjustified feeling of competence with respect to it. An unfortunate by-product is the possible failure to realize the full potential of budgetary planning and control in a given situation.

Frequently a budget program may be appropriately characterized as a mere mechanical or technical exercise with no deep-rooted management involvement. This situation occurs, for example, when the company accountant, the company budget director, or the independent CPA "draws up the budget."

Since this paper is not primarily concerned with techniques, let us say directly that they are important; that the characteristics and problems of the firm should determine the particular techniques to be employed as well as the way in which these should be adapted and applied.

To have an effective budgetary planning and control system, the mechanics and techniques of budgeting must be brought into complete harmony with management problems and needs. To accomplish this objective in any situation there must be a clear understanding of certain underlying fundamentals. These have much more in common with the process of management and enlightened human relations than with accounting. It is for this reason that CPAs and young people being trained for accounting careers need considerable depth of understanding of management methods, policy formulation, organization principles, and behavioral sciences.

FUNDAMENTAL PRINCIPLES

What are these fundamentals? They are concerned directly with the basic management functions of planning, coordination, and control. First and foremost, systematic planning for the individual firm for both the short run (one year or less) and the long run is essential. A recent survey of 424 better-managed companies revealed that over 96 per cent of them develop detailed and comprehensive short-range budgets on a formal basis. Approximately 65 per cent reported that they develop formal long-range budgets. A systematic and formal approach to planning is essential, particularly in view of the fact that indefinite plans seldom have meaning, are frequently forgotten or, at least, are inconsistently changed. Planning is essential to judicious employment of available resources; and a firm, no less than an individual, needs well-defined goals and objectives. Planning is the easiest function of management to put off. It seldom if ever forces our hand at the present—we can always temporize. The most effective planning in a firm generally comes from the combined efforts of the management team rather than from one individual or a single staff group.

The present-day concept of the planning budget (preferably *plan of operation*), coupled with the long-range budget, appears to be the only generally applicable, satisfactory approach so far developed to facilitate in a systematic manner the planning function of management. The planning budget expresses in financial terms management plans and policies for the period under consideration. It is the first step in effective profit engineering. From the mechanical point of view, the planning budget concept is simple for the accountant. From the point of view of technique, it becomes more involved, and from the point of view of "principles," simplicity ceases altogether. I would list the following as important fundamentals or principles relating directly to *managerial planning* through budgeting:

1. The principle of organization. Budgetary planning must rest upon sound organization structure coupled with clear-cut lines of authority and responsibility. Plans and budgets should be developed in terms of individual responsibilities. It is people who get things done. Planned performance must therefore be directly related to organizational responsibilities.

2. The principle of responsibility accounting. Budgeting requires an effective accounting system tailored to the organizational structure and to assigned responsibilities so that individual performance can be measured and evaluated. An accounting system tailored to external needs and to "generally accepted accounting principles" is essential but by itself is inadequate for management planning and control needs.

3. The principle of participation. This principle requires clearly defined responsibilities for input of planned data. It is basic that those having supervisory responsibilities should be responsible to the fullest possible extent for developing the plans for carrying out such responsibilities, in conformity with the plans and policies of higher levels of management. Achieving meaningful involvement in the planning process is not easy. Lower levels of management react favorably to participation, yet certain checks and restraints are necessary. Token participation is apt to create negative reactions. Participation by lower levels of management imposes a prior responsibility on higher levels of management to clearly define and circumscribe policies well in advance. Planning budget procedures provides a framework suitable for participating management. Accounting and budget experts may design and coordinate the planning system, but those who have to perform should build the budget and provide the input data. This procedure makes possible effective implementation of the participation principle in management.

4. The principle of timeliness. This principle holds that there must be a definite schedule for planning activities, preferably in the form of a written "planning schedule." Once a management firmly commits itself in this manner to budgetary planning, procrastination in planning largely ends. Successful managements today report this result to be one of the most important indirect benefits accruing from a budgetary program. Whereas before it was practically impossible to assemble certain management groups intact for planning sessions, following adoption of such a program this activity often takes precedence similar to that of a meeting of the board of directors. In many companies executives absolutely refuse to make outside commitments during the critical phases of budget planning. Many such companies which budget effectively report that for the first time both strategic and detailed planning are on a rational and timely basis. Nothing is more devastating to effectual planning than for the management to issue a budget some time after the beginning of the period involved.

5. The principle of confidence. The management must be confident that it can significantly influence the course of events for the company and that it is its duty to plan such influence. It must be convinced that realistic policies and goals can be developed in advance and that it is desirable to do so. It must operate under the belief that persons having management responsibilities

in the firm tend to tie their own success to that of the firm, and will therefore strive seriously and aggressively to attain *known* and *realistic* goals.

6. The principle of flexibility. This principle holds that there must be recognition from all levels of management that a budget will not manage the business, and that flexibility in applying the budget must be the rule so that no strait jackets are imposed and no opportunities passed up merely because "they are not covered by the budget."

7. The principle of realism. In budget planning the management must exercise neither undue conservatism nor irrational optimism. The objective should be to plan realistically attainable goals and objectives.

We have examined, rather briefly, systematic planning as a fundamental aspect of the budgetary program and some related principles. Now let us look, again briefly, at another concept, that of *control* as a fundamental aspect of budgeting.

In the process of control, problems of human relations stand out clearly as the most critical consideration. A management does not need a budget to practice poor human realtions; alternatively a budget program may be a vehicle for accentuating either enlightened or poor human relations. The weaknesses of a management in this respect are frequently attributed to budgeting.

PRINCIPLES OF BUDGETARY CONTROL

What are the essentials or "principles" related to effective budgetary control?

1. The principle of individual recognition. This is primarily a system whereby the individual is recognized, and both outstanding and substandard performance are revealed. The system of evaluation must be fair, understandable, and reasonably accurate. It should give recognition to the abilities of the individual, his aspirations, his reactions, and to the group pressures that affect him. The individual's dignity must be respected.

2. The principle of organization. This involves a principle mentioned earlier with respect to planning. Since control is exercised through people, there must be a clear-cut delineation of responsibilities from the organizational point of view as well as in terms of goals. What do we expect of the individual supervisor? Planning is fundamental in clarifying this situation; sound planning is thus basic in establishing effective control. The measurement and reporting of actual performance must be in terms of organizational responsibilities.

3. The principle of effective communication. Communication implies a common understanding between two or more individuals on a given point.

Communication for effective control should be such that both superior and subordinate have the same understanding of responsibilities and goals. The planning budget built in terms of responsibilities and developed to a large extent by the supervisor himself, assures a degree of understanding not otherwise possible.

4. The principle of a standard. A system of goals, objectives, or standards is vital to control. There must be bench marks to which performance may be related. Basically, standards are essential:
   a. to provide a target at which to shoot, and
   b. to provide a bench mark against which actual results may be compared in order to measure control; that is, to determine the degree of efficiency or inefficiency with respect to attainment of the goals.

5. The principle of management by exception. This principle holds that the busy executive should devote his time to the unusual or exceptional items, rather than worry about those matters that are not out of line. Dealing with out-of-line items is enough of an accomplishment, without having to pinpoint them. To make this principle effective, the control system must be designed so that the exceptions stand out. By emphasizing variations, budgetary planning and control provides a method whereby the attention of successively higher levels of management is called to the exception. This principle obviously requires comparison of an actual with a realistic standard. The usual comparison with last year's results is unsatisfactory since these frequently constitute an unreliable standard. Budgeting stands far out in front as the basic, practical approach to effective management by exception.

6. The principle of follow-up. This principle holds that both good and bad performance should be investigated, the purpose being threefold:
   a. in the case of poor performance, to lead to corrective action immediately and in a constructive manner;
   b. in the case of outstanding performance, to recognize it and perhaps provide for a transfer of knowledge to similar operations;
   c. to provide a basis for improved planning and control in the future.

7. The principle of flexibility. We see here another application of this basic principle. Expense and cost budgets must not be used and interpreted inflexibly. They must not prevent the making of rational decisions merely because the expenditure is not covered by the budget.

Variable or flexible expense budgets are frequently employed to meet the problems of expense control arising from the volume differential. To illustrate the point, assume that the budget for Department X carries an allowance of $2,000 for indirect labor; 10,000 units of production are planned. Now assume that unforeseen circumstances make it necessary to produce 12,000 units. Obviously, a comparison of actual costs incurred at 12,000 units with a budget allowance based on 10,000 units would show an unfavorable, and more significantly, a meaningless variation. The variable budget provides a means of adjusting the budget allowance to the actual volume prior to the comparison. This does not mean that because variable budget allowances are available they should be allowed to influence the effort to develop realistic volume forecasts initially.

8. The principle of cost consciousness. Both experience and investigation have demonstrated that attitudes of cost consciousness are fundamental to effective cost control. To illustrate, investigations have shown that if an executive is cost conscious, his subordinates likewise tend to be cost conscious by a margin of three to one, as compared to situations where the executive is not cost conscious. Here we are dealing with attitudes, with the psychology of the individual and of the work group. Our control system must be designed to take advantage of these psychological phenomena.

SUMMARY

There are three broad aspects of budgetary planning and control: the mechanics, the techniques, and the underlying fundamentals. Mechanics are relatively simple, yet undue concern with them may cloud our thinking with respect to the budgetary process. The techniques available must be known and understood. The underlying principles of the budget process are of primary significance; they have much more in common with the process of management and enlightened human relations than with accounting. Budgetary planning and control go directly to the heart of:

- Organization structure
- Delegation of authority and responsibility
- Accounting keyed to lines of authority and responsibility
- Effective communication
- Enlightened human relations

A budget program has great potential if designed and operated on a sound basis. The program must be sound mechanically and technically, but it must also rest on a firm foundation of basic principles. We must therefore conclude that a budgetary planning and control program is not simple, and that broad competence is essential on the part of those upon whose shoulders the task may rest.

What does all this add up to for the CPA in public practice? We are in a rapidly expanding profession. Recent evidence of this expansion is the tremendous interest shown in management services by practicing CPAs. The area of budgetary planning and control clearly stands out as a potential for the CPA interested in expanding his services. Management, particularly in medium and small firms, is in need of this kind of assistance. It has been estimated that practicing CPAs, with their present clients, could expand their practice by at least 15 to 25 per cent by focusing on this one area alone. This is possible because it would inevitably lead the CPA into organizational studies, accounting-system design and improvement, budgetary-system design and improvement, internal reporting problems, and direct advice to management concerning specific decisions. Budgetary planning and control provides the practicing CPA with an unequaled service for helping the client to stay in business and make more profits. Who can question the value of a realistic, well-designed road map for the immediate future, coupled with a simple control system, for the owner of a small business?

As members of a highly respected and highly competent profession we cannot afford to jump in without knowing how to swim. Budgetary planning and control is much more than a set of mechanics and techniques; it is intimately involved in the basic process of management. Too many accountants appear to dismiss budgeting because they appreciate only the mechanics. We must become acquainted with the fundamentals involved in order to appreciate the potentials, lest we commit serious errors. Self-study is required; the new course developed by the American Institute of CPAs is an important step in this direction.

The Budget Director and PERT

Don T. DeCoster

During the past few years, more particularly since 1958, PERT (Program Evaluation and Review Technique) has been attracting attention in the business and technical periodicals. This interest is not only academic but is based upon numerous successful applications of the technique to many highly complex scheduling problems faced by management. Among the military[1] and commercial[2] applications are:

1. Development and implementation of the Fleet Ballistic Missile Weapon System (Polaris).
2. Development and implementation of the Skybolt missile.
3. Development and implementation of the Nike-Zeus Anti-ICBM program.
4. Development of the B-70 Wing plans.
5. Current Development of the Dyna-Soar space glider.
6. Product development resulting in estimated time reduction of 28% (Deere and Company).
7. Plant Maintenance shutdown. Shutdown time reduced by 37% (Du Pont).
8. Equipment maintenance time reduced 27% with cost savings of $100,000 (International Minerals and Chemical).
9. 47 construction projects. Average time reduction 22%; expediting costs reduced 15% on the average (Catalytic Construction Co.).
10. Construction of plant property timed to growing season. Time reduction 25%; costs reduced about $1,000,000 (Sun Maid Raisin Growers).

Other areas suggested for potential applications of PERT include securities issues, long range planning, marketing problems, mergers and acquisition programs,

---

SOURCE: Reprinted with permission from *Business Budgeting* (March, 1964), pp. 13–17.

introduction of new products, installing management control systems, installing organizational plans and annual accounting closing procedures.[3]

PERT—TOWARD BASIC THEORY

There are two ingredients of the PERT technique which make it such a useful managerial tool. First, each activity or job which comprises any one of the parts of the project is located in a network according to its logical position related to all other activities. By use of the network, interdependencies between and among activities are easily ascertained and the questions "what must be done first" and "what must be done next" are readily answered. It has been stated by many users of PERT that it earns its keep through the benefits derived from the network alone.

The network is a diagramatic expression of the pattern of work. It consists of events (sometimes called milestones) and activities (sometimes called tasks). Activities represent "thing to be done" in going from one event to another event. Activities represent the passage of time in accomplishing the goals while events represent one point in time. Activities are shown on the network as solid lines which connect events shown as circles. Dummy lines (broken lines) are event constraints that do not require the passage of time.

Secondly, PERT embodies the ingredient of time—the time estimates which measure the probable time required to complete the activities within the network complex. Two time estimate techniques are commonly used. The three time estimate involves the use of an optimistic time (a) measuring the least time in which the activity can be completed; a most likely time (m) which measures the time in which the activity can probably be completed; and a pessimistic time (b) which is the estimated longest time than an activity should take. These three times are then combined by using the formula $\dfrac{(a + 4m + b)}{6}$ which produces the estimated activity time (t_e). Other firms use only one time, the most likely time, and use it for the estimated activity time. To distinguish between these two approaches, many experts call the three time estimate, PERT, and the one time estimate, CPM (Critical Path Method).

With time estimates super-imposed on the network the project manager has a method to determine: (a) the status of the project to date and the effects of this status on the project schedule at succeeding milestones; (b) the probability of accomplishing any milestone in the project within reasonable time limits; (c) the leeway or slack for every activity—the difference between the time it is expected to be finished and the time it must be completed; (d) the potential problem areas, thus allowing early remedial action in place of last minute "panic button" solutions; (e) the total elapsed time necessary to complete the project; (f) the effects of proposed changes in established plans; and (g) the longest time path necessary to accomplish the tasks, measured in terms of estimated activity times. This longest activity path is labeled the *critical path,* and any change of activity time along this path will change the project duration time.

IMPLEMENTATION OF BUDGETING WITH PERT

A dynamic budget is the result of coordinated line executives' budgeted allowances. To properly assimilate and coordinate these plans the budget director is faced with a scheduling problem. The components of the budget must be identified, matched with the responsible manager, and their interdependencies related to the completion schedule. After the budget estimates are set, they must be assembled and culminated into a master plan. Throughout this development, time is of the essence.

To demonstrate how PERT can assist the budget director fulfill his function, a simple network for sales budgeting is presented. The sales budgeting network assumes that the company under consideration computes three sales forecasts— a share of the market forecast, an opinion poll forecast, and a historical trend line forecast. These separate forecasts are combined into a composite forecast and then recast into forecasts by months, products, and salesmen.

The budget director, using Exhibit 1, can see the activities required to complete the sales forecast and their relationships with each other. For example, he can see that activity A-B must be complete before either activities B-E or B-F can begin. With estimated times added, the potential information grows.

1. The length in days of the project's *critical path.* Here it is 16 days identified by the heavy line which runs through the longest time path in the network.
2. The *earliest expected completion time* of any event (T_E) located in the circle by each event. The T_E for event G is 5. To get the T_E the longest time path to the event is traced from the start of the project. Two paths go to G: (A-B-G) and (A-B-F-G). A-B-F-G is 5 as opposed to 4 for A-B-G.
3. The *expected activity completion date* (T_X). Activity H-I is expected to be completed at the end of day 7. This is the sum of activities A-B, B-D, D-H, and H-I.
4. The *latest event time* (T_L) located in the square by each event. This is the latest time an event can be accomplished and not interfere with the completion date. The T_L for event G is day 6 determined by subtracting the t_c for activities succeeding activity G from the completion date (16).
5. *System slack* $(T_L - T_E)$. This is the surplus time available at an event. The system slack at event G is 1 day. This means that event G can be up to 1 day behind schedule and not endanger the project schedule.
6. *Activity slack* $(T_E - T_X)$. This is the surplus time available to perform an activity. The slack available to activity B-G is 1 day determined as follows: the

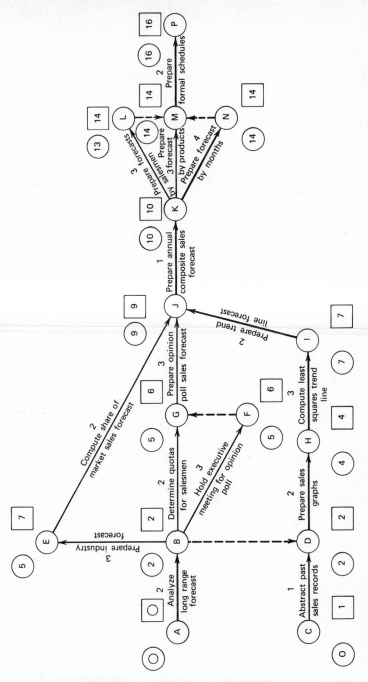

EXHIBIT 1. Sales forecast network

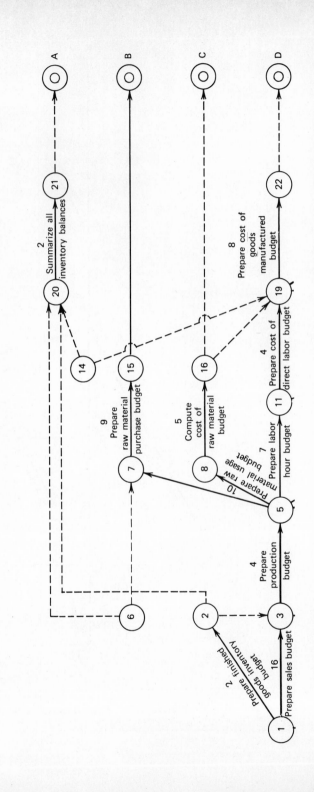

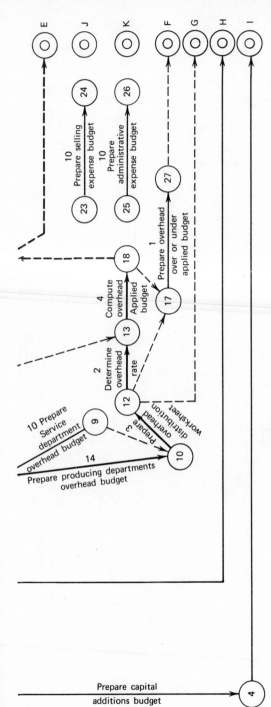

EXHIBIT 2. Master budget network

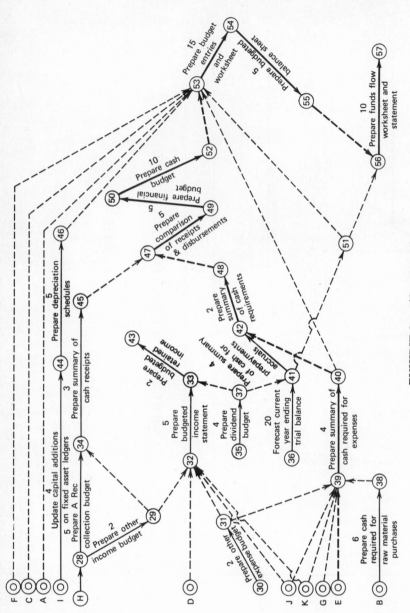

EXHIBIT 2. (Continued)

T_E for event G is 4 days and the T_X for activity B-G is 5 days. Their difference is 1. Thus activity B-G can be 1 day behind schedule and still not endanger the completion date.

By combining the series of subnetworks for budgetary planning, a master network, similar to Exhibit 2, can be developed. Exhibit 2 was developed from the integrated budget program shown in *Budgeting: Profit Planning and Control* by Glenn Welsch. Time estimates, in days, are shown on the network. Activity 1-3 represents the integration of Exhibit 1 into the overall budget plan.

GAINS FROM PERT

The biggest advantage of critical path scheduling is the identification of the sequence of jobs in which any delay will cause completion date setbacks. With the critical path activities highlighted, management knows upon which jobs to concentrate their attention. With only a small segment of the activities located on the critical path this is truly management by exception.

BRINGING PROBLEMS TO FOCUS EARLY

This initial network analysis is of future value if it is used as the basis of scheduling control, rescheduling, and revisions. The rapid processing of current status reports allows continuous, timely control. Reports, comparing actual results with network plans, show potential problem areas where action may be required. Reports should keep the manager's attention focused on future problems instead of allowing them to become crises demanding rapid, remedial action. To illustrate one type of report, Exhibit 1 has been redrawn in Exhibit 3. The network has been "squared up" with the horizontal dotted lines representing slack. If actual progress is plotted upon a transparent overlay, a continuous picture of status can be maintained.

PERT'S VALUE TO THE BUDGET DIRECTOR

The budget is the result of cooperation between the people responsible for its operation and fulfillment. PERT can be a boon to the budget director in achieving this cooperation. Developing a critical path generally allows the establishment of better relations between activity managers and general management since everyone contributes to the program development. These improved relations allow faster and more accurate communications while creating better morale. Through such an analysis the managers are cognizant of their role in the big picture. By knowing exactly which activities are important, the managers become more effective in their resource allocations.

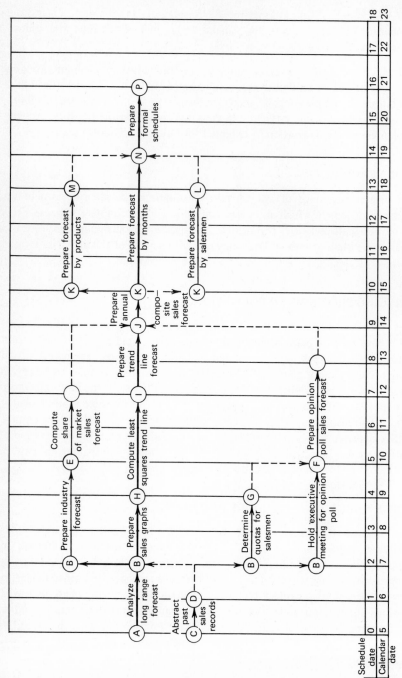

EXHIBIT 3. Project current status chart

FOOTNOTES

1.   Philip J. Klass, "PERT/PEP Management Tool Use Grows," *Aviation Week* (November 28, 1964), p. 85.

2.   J. W. Pocock, "PERT As An Analytical Aid for Program Planning—Its Payoff and Problems," *Operations Research* (November, 1962), p. 895.

3.   *Ibid.*, p. 896.

Forecasting Techniques for Use in the Corporate Planning Process

William K. Hall

INTRODUCTION

The development of good forecasting procedures is clearly essential in corporate planning, since the prediction and estimation of occurrences of future events provide a basic input into the planning process. Based upon these forecasts of future conditions, plans and policies can be developed to respond to future opportunities and react to future problems.

The significance of forecasting in the planning process has led researchers to develop an exceptionally wide variety of techniques to aid in the forecasting effort. Consequently the objectives of this paper are (1) to provide a systematic taxonomy for the most popular of these techniques, and (2) to provide further insights into the advantages and limitations of particular forecasting methodologies.

A basic taxonomy for existing forecasting techniques is provided in Figure 1. The primary classification is made to distinguish judgmental forecasting techniques from model-based techniques. A secondary classification exists within model-based techniques to distniguish explanatory (causal) models from statistical (data-based) models. These various taxonomies and the various techniques within each taxonomy will now be examined in more detail.

SOURCE: Reprinted with permission from *Managerial Planning* (November-December, 1972), pp. 5-10, 33.

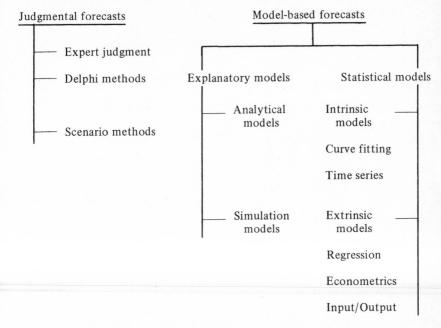

Figure 1.   A taxonomy for forecasting techniques.

JUDGMENTAL FORECASTS

The most fundamental (and perhaps most frequently used) prediction technique might be called judgmental forecasting. In judgmental forecasting, future values of a variable are predicted by directly specifying their levels. Although this technique is sometimes criticized as being unscientific, it is probably true that an experienced forecaster takes into account far more information and processes this information more consistently than many "model-based" techniques. The danger seems to come when inexperienced persons make forecasts and when individual forecasts are merged into "concensus" forecasts. In these situations, the lack of formality in both forecasting assumptions and analysis quite often result in inadequate projections at any point in time and in inconsistent projections through time.

The "Delphi" method is designed to remedy some of the problems which arise in concensus forecasts. The idea in this method is to maximize the advantages of group dynamics in forecasting while minimizing the problems caused by dominant personalities and silent experts. The procedure is characterized by three principles:

1. Anonymity of the forecasters (expert judges).
2. Use of iterative procedures in developing the forecasts.
3. Published statistical summaries of the forecasters' opinions at each iteration of the process.

The procedure is conducted as follows:

1. Each expert records (anonymously) his response to a well-defined forecasting question.
2. The responses are statistically summarized and returned to the experts.
3. Revised forecasts are prepared.
4. The procedure is repeated until concensus (or total lack of concensus) is achieved. (At later iterations additional information can be provided to the participants by having dissident forecasters record the reasons for their continuing differences of opinion.)

The primary use of the Delphi method has been in forecasting future technological events. Recently, attempts have been made to forecast future sociocultural events and to access social preferences through the use of the Delphi method. Still, as one corporate executive recently remarked: "The Delphi method can be used to predict when a well-defined event may occur, but it can't be used at all to predict or generate alternative futures which are not pre-conceived."

An alternative use of expert judgment structures this judgment into a "Scenario." Scenario forecasting techniques have been highly useful in long range forecasting, especially when predictions of future technologies and social conditions are highly imprecise. These procedures are initiated by postulating a formal set of assumptions (a scenario) about the future environment. Logical arguments are then utilized to develop various specific consequences of these assumptions, and these consequences form the basis for the forecast. The scenario forecasting technique is largely conceptual, but it has been found to be highly useful in structuring the analysis to determine projected consequences of a hypothetical future environment.[1]

MODEL-BASED FORECASTS

In many situations the objective of forecasting is to provide a formal, quantitative prediction of the future value or values of some variable. Here mathematical models are frequently of use and these forecasting models will be examined at this time.

Explanatory (Causal) Models

Perhaps the most difficult step in using models to forecast future values of a variable is to determine how these values are controlled by internal organizational decisions and policies. The extent of this control is highly dependent upon three factors: the variable being forecast, the functional level of decision-making within the organization, and the industrial situation being examined. For instance, consider the problem of forecasting future sales for a firm in a highly competitive manufacturing industry. In this case sales will be affected by the various product and marketing policies followed by the firm, and it is important to measure the extent of these effects in establishing good product and market plans.[2] However, if the industry is in fact highly competitive, other firms will quickly react to these plans, and in this way the effects of internal policies may be partially negated. Furthermore, general economic conditions may heavily influence future revenues, and various indices of economic activity may also diminish the effects of current market and product policies. Consequently, in developing revenue forecasting procedures, one must consider the effects of these uncontrollable factors in addition to the controllable factors as determined in the corporate planning process.

As a second example, consider the problem of demand forecasting faced by a public utility. Here future demands depend in part on the per capita usage of the utility's output, and this may be (partially) influenced by the marketing policies of the utility. But future demands will depend much more heavily on the real economic growth in the region served by the utility, and this growth process is largely independent of the internal policies and plans developed by the firm under consideration.

In other situations future values of a variable are much more controllable than in these two cases. Consider, for instance, the problem of forecasting future wage and salary expenses within a firm. In this situation, wage and salary expenses are directly dependent upon future wage rates and the number of employees, and these parameters can certainly be influenced by corporate policy.

The extent to which future values of a variable can be controlled by internal plans and decisions should heavily influence the forecasting model to be utilized. While statistical models are often used in forecasting the relationships between controllable and forecast variables, we shall see in the next section that these procedures are often misleading and are sometimes totally erroneous. Consequently explanatory models are frequently utilized to study the relationships between policy variables and the forecast variables of interest. For instance, these models can be used to predict future sales revenues as functions of marketing and product policies, wage expenses as a function of wage rates and employment levels, and other variables which are causally associated with controllable elements.

Explanatory models can be further subdivided into analytical and simulation models. In analytical models controllable inputs are related to various outputs through explicit mathematical relationships which have been developed by logical and/or empirical analyses. The classical "S" shaped function relating sales response to advertising expenditure[3] provides one simplified example of this class of explanatory model. In simulation models, on the other hand, input/output relationships are developed by making experimental inferences on a model of the situation. Hence, in this case, the causal relationships may be developed by implicit rather than explicit analysis. An example is provided by a decision process simulation model for sales forecasting developed by Schussel.[4]

The distinguishing characteristic of explanatory forecasting models is shared by both analytic and simulation models. This is the strong dependence on causal assumptions and subsequent logical analyses to derive the forecasts of interest. The causal assumptions are utilized to select the variables of interest and to develop the structure of the hypothesized causal relationship. Logical analyses can then be utilized to determine these relationships (which may be deterministic or stochastic) and to develop subsequent forecasts.

In situations where the structure or extent of the causal relationship is unclear, a useful modeling technique involves the decomposition of this relationship into its fundamental "causal" elements. For instance, consider the problem of predicting future industrial sales volumes as functions of advertising expenditure. Since the structure of this relationship is generally ambiguous, one approach might be to decompose the relationship into a set of sequential actions. Thus advertising expenditures can be directly related to message content and media mix. These two factors influence potential consumer exposure and recall, which in turn may sequentially influence consumer attitudes, purchase behavior and ultimately sales revenue. In many cases intermediate relationships in this "causal chain" of events can be developed by utilizing controlled experimentation. Alternatively, theoretical arguments and/or subjective managerial analysis can be used to quantify these intermediate relationships. The total forecasting relationship of interest can then be developed by systematically interfacing the intermediate relationships. The result should yield a causal model with significant explanatory power. More importantly, the procedure should improve the modeler's understanding of the causal phenomenon being considered, and this, of course, is the prime reason for model development in forecasting situations of this type.

Statistical Models

Statistical (data-based) forecasting models have experienced a tremendous growth in variety and popularity over the past ten years. The basic concept in statistical forecasting is the development of future projections of the variable of interest based upon historical values of the variable and/or historical values of various exogenous variables. When only historical values of the variable are used in deriving a forecast, the statistical model is called *intrinsic*. When exogenous information is utilized, the model is called *extrinsic;* a mixed or integrative statistical model arises when these techniques are simultaneously utilized in developing a forecast.

The simplest and very frequently utilized intrinsic technique consists of fitting some type of simple functional relation to the historical values of the series and extrapolating this relationship to forecast future values.[5] Straight lines, polynomials, and logarithmic functions are frequently used in this regard when certain "trends" or growth patterns seem to be present, and trigonometric functions (sines/cosines) are often used when cyclic tendencies seem to be present. Several problems are associated with these "curve-fitting" techniques:

1. It is difficult to accurately identify the appropriate functional relationships to fit to the data. For instance, fitting a "growth" curve to data may be erroneous if the series is actually following a cycle with a long period. In this case the curve will drastically "over-forecast" when the series turns downward. As a second example, consider a forecast derived by fitting an $(n - 1)^{st}$ degree polynomial to n data points. In this situation the curve will exactly "fit" the historical data, but it is likely to forecast future values with a very low precision.

2. Well-constructed forecasting curves may predict general tendencies in the series being considered but are unlikely to be very accurate in predicting specific future values of the series. This is especially true when there are highly-variable, random elements which may distort the series for short period of time.

3. The forecasts are not able to adapt to basic changes in the series (for instance, changes in the trend) without completely changing and/or refitting the assumed functional relationship.

A more advanced approach to intrinsic forecasting comes from utilizing weighted averages of historical values of the series to forecast future values. The simple "moving-average" forecast is perhaps the most elementary of these approaches. This technique "smooths" out highly variable components of the series, and "tracks" the less variable components. By employing weighted averages it is possible to adapt to changes in the series more rapidly than in the simple moving-average technique—exponential weighted average forecasting techniques are the most common of these. In exponential "smoothing," as the technique is frequently referred to, the weights decline through time according to an exponential function. The result is that the most recent historical values of the series are weighted most heavily. A peripheral benefit of exponential smoothing is that forecast values can be easily computed by taking a simple weighted average of the most recent value of the series and the forecast of the series for the most recent time period.[6] This facilitates computation and reduces data storage requirements, a significant advantage when many series are being routinely forecast.

Variants of simple exponential smoothing probably provide the most sophisticated intrinsic procedures statistical forecasting currently available.

Techniques have been developed to use exponential smoothing to forecast trend, cyclical, and highly variable components of a series separately, and then add these components together in order to obtain a forecast for the aggregate series.[7] An alternative technique can be developed by modifying the exponential weights through time so that these respond to changes in the structural characteristics of the series being forecast. "Adaptive" exponential-smoothing procedures are based upon this concept, and these procedures have recently been found to be highly useful in forecasting local area demand for public utility services.[8]

The primary advantages of intrinsic techniques arise from the ease of forecast computation and the minimal data acquisition and storage requirements. The major disadvantages arise from the inability of intrinsic forecasting procedures to predict major changes in the series. Since the forecasts are based entirely on historical data, they can only respond (or adapt) to such changes after they occur. In some situations, such as inventory planning, this forecasting "lag" may be acceptable. In others, the primary objective in forecasting is to predict such major changes. In these instances, forecasters have turned to extrinsic techniques.

The basic idea in extrinsic forecasting is to utilize exogenous information in deriving forecasts for a particular variable. This leads to two considerations: the choice as to the exogenous information to utilize and the choice as to the techniques to utilize in processing this information.

In general, the choice of the appropriate exogenous information to utilize involves a trade-off between information with high predictive power and the cost of obtaining and processing this information. In this regard, it is important to recognize that information with high predictive power may have no causal association with the variable being forecast. Thus, if a rise in women's skirt lengths is consistently followed by a rise in stock prices, skirt lengths may well be a good predictive variable for stock prices, independent of the true causal connections. It is also important to note that the common philosophy of throwing "everything" that may predict the variable of interest into a forecasting model is likely to have a very marginal value in forecasting accuracy. As Ackoff[9] has observed, "the less we understand a phenomenon, the more variables we require to explain it." Furthermore, high information processing and computation costs generally wipe out the incremental benefits associated with trying to use all available information. In the end, the choice of exogenous information to employ is largely a judgmental matter, and it will depend heavily on the potential use of the forecasting model being developed.

A wide variety of alternatives confront the planner in choosing an extrinsic forecasting technique. Perhaps the most frequently utilized extrinsic technique is to empirically develop associative relations between variables. This is generally done by using a multiple regression model to explain the variation in the forecast (dependent) variable as a linear combination of all extrinsic (independent) variables. Multiple regression forecasting models have been highly successful in certain applications. However, the user should be aware of the characteristics and limitations of these models:

1. The techniques assume a linear relationship among the variables or a relationship which can be transformed to obtain a linear function.

2. The techniques may be highly inaccurate when values of the independent variables are utilized which fall outside of the ranges of these variables which were utilized in empirically fitting the model to historical data.

3. The independent variables must lead the dependent variable,[10] or methods must be utilized to develop independent forecasts of these independent variables. This latter situation is in general very difficult.[11]

4. Although regression may be highly successful in explaining variations in the dependent variable,[12] if all variables (dependent and independent) are trend-dominated (as economic variables are likely to be), the multiple regression approach is likely to be very unsuccessful in forecasting the detrended series. This lack of success results from the percentage-wise increase, in variability in the de-trended series. Furthermore, it is very important, since it is likely that one will desire to predict deviations from the trend rather than the general average characteristic of the evolving series.

5. If any independent variables are controllable, the empirically-derived regression model can *never* be utilized to predict the consequences of changes in these. This fundamental, but often misunderstood point, is well-stated by Ackoff and Sasieni.[13] "If two variables are causally connected and if the statistical assumptions involved in correlation analysis are valid, they will usually (but not always) show a significant correlation. Hence, when the statistical assumptions are valid and two variables are not found to be statistically correlated, we can conclude (subject to measurable error) that they are not causally connected by a linear relationship. Therefore, at best, correlation analysis can only be used to tell us that a variable is not relevant. It is never sufficient to establish the relevance of a variable."

Attempts to resolve this latter problem have resulted in the development of econometric forecasting models. Econometric models attempt to take into account the cause-effect interaction between independent variables and the variable(s) being forecast. For example, certain marketing policies may influence future sales. These sales, in turn, may influence the firm to change future marketing policies. If the dynamics of these interactions can be logically specified, econometric methods may then be utilized to estimate parameters in the resulting models. This results in two questions which have dominated statistical thinking in this area: (1) Is it possible to estimate parameters in the model from a historical data base (the identification problem)?, and (2) How can these parameters best be determined (the estimation problem)? Although econometric textbooks are largely devoted to considering these two questions, a third question is perhaps much more fundamental in extrinsic forecasting: Should historical data be utilized at all in estimating the forecasting model parameters?

This latter question is often ignored in developing statistical forecasts when a large data base is available. For instance, consider the previously mentioned problem of forecasting wage and salary expenses as a function of wage rates and the number of employees. These can be related in a linear fashion, and a regression model can then be developed to forecast these expenses from historical wage and employee data. In this case, it is very likely that the resulting forecasting model will drastically under-forecast expenses, since it is essentially based upon the average wage rates over the time period considered rather than upon the forecasts of future wage rates. An alternative technique is to develop these forecasts directly by subjectively processing predictions of union settlements and employee benefit policies.[14] A second alternative is to forecast wage rates directly by using an intrinsic technique and then input these forecasts directly as coefficients in the wage expense model.

A variant of econometric analysis has resulted in what have been called input/output forecasting models. These models take into account intra-period dependencies between sectors of an economy as well as the inter-period dependencies between variables which are the focus of classical econometric approaches. For instance, in forecasting future demand for steel, a steel manufacturer might develop an input/output model showing the interaction between the producers and users of steel. This model can then show how changes in these interdependencies result in changes in the demand for steel. As such, input/output models can be used to study the sensitivity of forecasts to economic conditions and inter-industry dependencies.

Here again, multivariate statistical techniques may be developed to estimate the parameters of an input/output "table." As in the discussion of classical econometric models, however, non-statistical and "non-traditional" statistical estimation approaches may be more meaningful.

The idea of integrating intrinsic and extrinsic forecasting techniques is fairly new, and it is difficult to evaluate the resulting models at this time. Crane and Crotty[15] have utilized a two stage forecasting model, with exponential smoothing being utilized to forecast the independent variables in a regression model which subsequently forecasts the dependent variable of interest. Various econometric techniques are also being developed which combine lagged values of the variable being forecast with various exogenous information.[16] This area of forecasting methodology appears to offer substantial promise.

EVALUATION OF STATISTICAL FORECASTING MODELS

With an ever-increasing number of forecasting techniques and models being developed, the organization planner is faced with the complex task of selecting the technique or techniques to be utilized in his forecasting applications. While it is possible to evaluate alternative models on their theoretical characteristics, as a pragmatic matter the ultimate evaluation of a forecasting model must be based upon how well it performs.[17] In this regard statistical models are often evaluated by comparing forecast and actual values of the variable of interest over some sample time period, and then computing summary performance statistics such as the mean aboslute forecast error over the sample period or the mean square forecast error over the period.

The major problem with these evaluation approaches is that they fail to recognize that forecasts are being developed as inputs to the planning process. Hence, forecasts should be evaluated within the context of their role in this process, rather than in isolation. For example, the cost of underforecasting some variable may be far greater than the cost of overforecasting.[18] Alternatively, it may be exceptionally important to forecast the value of a variable at one future point in time; accurate forecasts in the neighborhood of this point may be far less significant in terms of their impact on the planning process. Finally, a large forecasting "error" may in fact be insignificant if this error does not lead management to an erroneous planning decision.

These problems point out the need for research directed at increasing our understanding of the role of forecasting in the planning process. This research is essential in obtaining new insights into the interactions between forecasting and decision making and in developing more effective ways of evaluating the role of forecasts in this interactive process.

FOOTNOTES

1. See, for instance, H. Kahn and A. J. Weiner, *The Year 2000,* Macmillan, 1967, for an extensive utilization of scenario techniques in forecasting long term social change.

2. In using sales forecasts to establish production schedules, however, the production scheduling department may view these as uncontrollable factors and consequently look at sales as a totally uncontrollable input to their functional activity.

3. See, for instance, K. L. Rich, *An Adaptive Optimization Model for Setting Advertising Budgets,* Marketing Science Institute, 1971.

4. G. Schussel, "Sales Forecasting with the Aid of a Human Behavior Simulator," *Management Science,* v. 13, 1967, pp. 593–611.

5. See, for instance, the recent article by R. E. Malcom, "Improving Forecast Effectiveness," *Managerial Planning,* July/August, 1970.

6. See, for instance, P. R. Winters, "Forecasting Sales by Exponentially Weighted Moving Averages," *Management Science,* v. 6, no. 3, 1960, pp. 324–342 for a discussion of this computational result.

7. See, for example, the discussion of Winter, *op. cit.*

8. See D. Dunn, W. A. Spivey, and W. Williams, *Analysis and Prediction of Telephone Demand in Local Geographic Areas,* Bell Telephone Laboratories, 1971, for a complete discussion for these applications.

9. R. L. Ackoff, "Management Misinformation Systems," *Management Science,* v. 14, no. 4, 1967, pp. 147–156.

10. That is, one must forecast the dependent variable in any future period as functions of exogenous variables observed in previous periods.

11. The reader is referred to an article by D. B. Crane and J. R. Crotty, "A Two-stage Forecasting Model," *Management Science,* v. 13, no. 8, for one approach to this problem.

12. As measured, for instance, by the coefficient of multiple correlation.

13. R. L. Ackoff and M. W. Sasieni, *Fundamentals of Operations Research,* Wiley, 1968, pp. 386–387.

14. In this case, the forecasting model is really not statistical, but instead is explanatory.

15. D. R. Crane and J. R. Crotty, *op. cit.*

16. See, for instance, J. Johnston, *Econometric Methods,* McGraw-Hill, 1960.

17. In this regard it is interesting to compare the simple national economic forecasting model developed by Laffer (*Time Magazine,* February 22, 1971) with the complex multi-sector national econometric models at certain research institutions (for instance, Wharton, Michigan, or the Brookings Institute). While these complex models may more adequately represent the "real world," the ultimate evaluation depends heavily upon how well they predict various economic indicators one year hence.

18. As, for instance, in the case of certain public utilities, who underforecast demand in the 1960's and consequently have insufficient plant capacity at the present time.

Simulation in Financial Planning

E. N. Khoury &
H. Wayne Nelson

Simulation, the mathematical representation of a system in order to see how a change in one of its elements will affect the others, is—at least potentially—one of the most powerful tools of operations research. It is finding increasing use in the solution of military and production problems.

In the financial area its application is less well known. Simulations of economic and financial processes have been employed mainly as research and teaching aids. Little has been done to develop simulation techniques to improve precision and response in the financial planning process within the corporate structure.

At Burroughs we have been experimenting with a simulation of the financial structure of the entire company. Our experience thus far has convinced us that this technique can provide management with an effective new planning tool.

This article, based on that experience, discusses the development of a financial simulation model structured around traditional accounting reporting practices. It emphasizes (1) the understanding of the business processes necessary to structure a useful model, (2) the model as a mirror of corporate policy, (3) the values and pitfalls in the use of a simulation model, and (4) certain methodological issues involved.

SIMULATION

Whenever the logical relations between the elements in the structure of a system can be quantified or expressed in measurable terms, a mathematical representation of these relationships can be formulated. The set of all these formal

SOURCE: Reprinted by permission of *Management Services* (March/April, 1965), pp. 13-21. Copyright 1965 by the American Institute of Certified Public Accountants.

statements is then a model of the system. When we manipulate this model, the technique is called simulation. (This definition lacks the precision that the professional operations researcher would require, but it is adequate for the needs of the financial executive.)

As a tool applied to management problems, simulation is comparatively new. Its development and application are closely tied to the development and application of computer technology. It has been used to study complex problems in military strategy, traffic control, machine loading, and process control that do not lend themselves to solution by mathematical programming and other optimization techniques.

Because simulation has generally been applied to the nonfinancial aspects of business, many financial executives are as yet unaware of it. Yet simulation has proved to be a powerful tool when applied to the planning process.

In almost everything we do the ultimate test of the adequacy of our decisions is the test of reality. But today business can seldom afford the luxury of testing the consequences of major decisions in the real world. Rather than determining the flight characteristics of a proposed missile by building and launching it, we now first simulate its performance on the basis of its design characteristics. In this way we can experiment without incurring the full cost of failure.

Similarly, in his role as planner, the executive is well aware of the magnitude of his investment decisions and the difficulty (sometimes the impossibility) of systematically evaluating all alternatives available to the company. He is also aware that he has at his disposal finite resources that have to be allocated among competing demands. Simulation techniques allow the businessman to examine the probable consequences of his decisions without the risk of real-life experimentation. They allow him to test the effects of his decisions on the whole corporation before these decisions are implemented.

Computers shorten the computational time period and thus permit repetitive use of the simulation model. This ability of the computer to compress the time needed to test the results of decisions makes experimentation much easier.

MANAGEMENT SCIENCE

Simulation is, of course, only one of a number of new mathematical techniques whose use has been facilitated by the availability of computers. During the past decade we have seen a growing recognition by management of its need for newer and more sophisticated planning tools. Operations research and other techniques now frequently referred to as management science have emerged to help satisfy that need. They are contributing new skills to aid management in meeting the complexities of the decision making process.

Not too long ago it was unusual to find a mathematician or statistician working in management. We had grown accustomed to his presence in the engineering department or the research laboratory, but we were surprised when we found him attacking such operational problems as production scheduling or inventory control. Now we even see him contributing to the financial planning function in such areas as capital budgeting, sales forecasting, and investment analysis. We see operations research and management science departments on the organization charts of many of our more progressive companies.

These professions, like all others, have developed their own characteristic approaches, methodology, tools, and techniques—decision theory, information theory, linear and dynamic programming, and network analysis, as well as simulation. These are now being applied to an increasing array of complex business problems.

Many of these techniques offer significant potential for use in financial planning. Simulation is particularly useful in this area because it can be applied to problems that are too complex and have too many variables to be reduced to optimization formulas. That is the reason we chose the simulation approach at Burroughs. It seemed to us the only means by which we could cope with the complexity of the financial planning process in the level of detail deemed essential while retaining the inherent flexibility needed to accommodate change.

SIMULATION MODEL

A financial simulation model can be defined as a formal statement of the relationships among the elements of a company's financial structure. The diagram (Figure 1) illustrates what we term the "accounting dependencies" within the corporate structure of Burroughs. It has some similarity to our ogranizational pattern in that the elements on the chart represent units of management responsibility and managerial control, but they are not necessarily described in their organizational hierarchy. The figure reflects one aspect of our accounting practice—the way we consolidate. As such, it defines the framework of our financial model.

Two key points in our concept of financial simulation are illustrated by this figure. The first is the concept of modular construction. The total Burroughs model is actually a set of sub-models, one for each of the management units shown. Specifically, we constructed individual models for each of these management units, expressing their output in accounting terms, and aggregated this output to produce the accounting consolidations indicated.

This design gives us the ability to identify and summarize the activities of each major corporate management unit. In addition, we can vary the form and

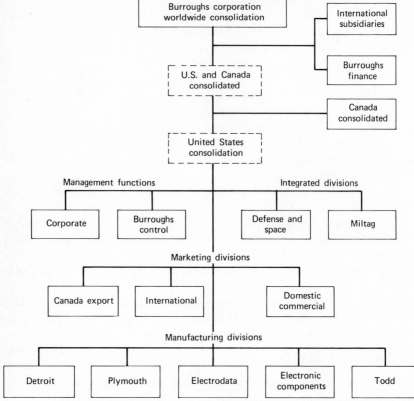

FIGURE 1. The "accounting dependencies" diagrammed above define the framework of the model

level of detail between organizational units as a function of their inherent characteristics and their contribution to the planning process. Finally, the modular construction provides us with great model flexibility; it facilitates the introduction of worthwhile change to the program.

The second point we mean to illustrate in the figure is that there is a logical sequence that must be followed. This sequence depends on the structure of the business. The output of certain models forms the input for others. The relationship thus created reflects the interplay between divisions. The ordering of the models is of prime importance.

If the model is to be an effective planning tool, it must explicitly reflect cause and effect both within the specific business process and between the business and the market in which it participates. In defining cause and effect in the model there are two considerations—the inter-model relationships and the intra-model detail. The former refers to the explicit identification of the cause and effect factors that determine the relationship and thus the ordering between the sub-models. The latter refers to the level of detail essential in structuring one of the sub-models per se. Let us discuss each of these factors.

CAUSE AND EFFECT RELATIONS

The importance of the inter-model relationship can be illustrated by discussing the relationship of demand to production in the total model complex. The marketing division models constitute the primary demand source within the total corporate model. The manufacturing divisions constitute the principal production source and capability since we make what we sell. Because the marketing divisions are organized on a geographic basis and within their respective marketing areas handle the full product line, there is no direct interdivisional relationship influencing the ordering of the marketing models. On the other hand, the stimulus for the manufacturing division models is the output of the marketing models. Here—given policy as to desired inventory and capacity constraints—production levels and manufacturing expenses are determined. The cost penalties of constraints (and of constraints masquerading as policies) can also, often, be determined. This creates opportunity to assess the value of making changes. The models must specifically describe the form in which marketing demands are translated into production requirements both as a direct functional relationship, acknowledging the explicit interplay of company policy, and in terms of the time transformation represented in this relationship. The output of both the marketing models and the manufacturing models provides input to the "management" model where we determine financial capacity, taxes, etc.

A complex interaction exists among our various manufacturing facilities. While they are each primarily identified with a specific product, each acts as a sub-contractor for assemblies, sub-assemblies, or parts to the other manufacturing facilities. Obviously, with this type of interaction any decisions made by the marketing organizations which affect demand rate will influence in varying degrees each of the manufacturing divisions, even though the decision might affect only one product in a wide product line. In order to create a useful planning tool, the development of the sub-models must explicitly include a formal statement of this inter-model cause-effect relationship.

In the Burroughs Financial Simulation Model the manufacturing interdivisional relation is accomplished by having the demand for all product lines carried to each manufacturing unit, even though they are primarily product organized, in order to acknowledge this inter-divisional relationship. The model itself does not allocate total capacity among products so as to maximize production efficiency. In other words, the production sites for the various products have been predetermined for any simulation run. If capacity of a given producing unit will not satisfy the generated demand, both primary and secondary, we do not automatically adjust the demand. Rather we determine the imbalance and generate a report which states the deficiency in terms of demand lost or added capacity required to satisfy the demand input.

During the development of our model we found it expedient to view the cause-effect relationship we have just illustrated in a serial fashion. A better understanding is obtained by viewing the process as continuous rather than as sequential. The marketing demand interacts in the manufacturing sectors with capacity constraints and inventory policy to generate a production requirement. When this production requirement is accepted and met, goods are provided to marketing to satisfy the demand. Pricing and other marketing policies then determine revenue potential. This, in turn, affects the capital position and debt level of the firm. The capital position in turn defines the limits for the marketing activity. The financial simulation model must reflect this feedback relationship explicitly or have some check and balance features incorporated to assure reasonable constraint.

EFFECTS OF INPUT CHANGE

To illustrate the level of detail which we felt necessary to reflect in the simulation structure, we will trace the impact of a hypothetical change in input to our simulation model. Assume that we desire to evaluate the aggregate impact of a change in sales manpower in one of our marketing divisions. We have structured our demand forecast to be a function of the amount of direct sales manpower and a productivity function. In addition to evaluating the impact of the proposed manpower change through the relationship just identified, we explicitly evaluate the impact of the demand change on equipment and services revenue, cost of sales, and finished goods inventory. The impact of the demand change together with an inventory policy allows us to determine the resultant production requirement. This production requirement is an input in determining the in-process inventory. The determination of the production in-process activity provides the necessary stimulus for the determination of the sub-assembly and part manufacturing requirements, which in our model interact throughout the whole manufacturing sector. We must further relate this activity to its effect on variable, semi-variable, and fixed costs of manufacturing, which collectively affect the burden absorption functions. Marketing expenses and commissions, freight and shipping costs, and interest expense will be affected. The change will affect the tax provision, after-tax profits, accounts receivable, and liabilities. It will affect the equity section since dividends and retained earnings are both functions of net income. Indeed, it will be essential to evaluate the magnitude of funds required to carry out the suggested program which in itself has a feedback to marketing, where we began the illustration.

PROCESS VS. POLICY

Two categories of causative action are involved—one a function of the physical process, the other a matter of corporate policy. The establishment of an appropriate training pipeline to support a desired sales force represents a cause-effect relationship that is related to the "physical process" of the operation of the corporation; it also illustrates the introduction of a balancing and control mechanism on the marketing assumption. On the other hand, the inventory policy, which affects production requirements, is a reflection of corporate policy.

There is no pat answer to the choice of level of detail which must or should be represented within the simulation model. Nevertheless it is important that those specific considerations to which system performance is sensitive be separately identified and treated within the models. Certainly, all aspects of policy should be separately identified. The aggregation of details not only masks their individual impact but makes it difficult to use the results of the simulation; through lack of detail, precise responsibility for a change is unknown. Either condition makes it difficult to interpret an output of a simulation run for planning purposes. In creating a useful planning model, prudence cautions against presenting too much detail, but an excess of detail is preferable to over-aggregation.

We have discussed the kinds of effects on the corporate plan caused by introducing a single change of input to the marketing division sub-model. We have mentioned the complex functional relationships that are affected throughout the system. It is important to re-emphasize that the complexity of this relationship is not only a functional interaction but is also compounded by a time dimension; the nature of the relationship explicitly changes as time passes. For example, expenditures for research and development are not expected to produce revenue in the same period. These expenditures are investments in future revenue. We could term R&D a "lead" factor. It is important that we know, or make assumptions about and test the sentivity to, the exact form of this time translation. On the other hand, administrative expenses may follow changes in revenue and thus, in certain instances, could be classed as a "lag" function. In many situations the semi-variable costs in the manufacturing sector show "asymmetric" properties relative to changes in production volume. That is, changes in semi-variable costs may lead changes in production volume when they are increasing but lag changes in production volume in a down trend. These relationships must be derived. Their specific form is in most instances unique to a particular firm. It is essential that the relationships used in the model be adequately representative of the corporation's own processes.

A financial simulation model must not only reflect cause and effect within the firm and between the firm and its market. It must also be logically consistent with the financial practices of the firm and be a true representation of management policies and plans. These relationships are not simple—they are not God-given. To establish an adequate representation that will assure an effective planning tool requires a rigorous and continuous study program within the firm.

So far in our discussion we have used some language that may be peculiar to Burroughs' operations. It is not our intent, however, to emphasize our unique operating characteristics. The most important point is this: Since we have unique characteristics in our operations, our model must be structured to acknowledge and represent them. Furthermore, we are not unlike any other dynamic organization. The interactions within our corporate structure are complex. The relationships are varied. The importance of the planning process to our operations forced us to seek new tools. In order to use simulation techniques effectively, we had to establish a program which would result in a better understanding of our business in order that we could identify and quantify the essential cause-effect relationships and assure a realistic representation of management policies and their effect on the firm.

USES OF THE MODEL

Because of the complexity of the interactions that take place within the firm, it is difficult if not impossible for a human to think through all of the ramifications in the systematic form demanded for proper planning. Without the assistance of the simulation technique, we would have an overwhelming computational task and a very nasty communications problem in trying to respond to today's demands for planning information. The simulation model lessens the communications problem through the definition and quantification of the relationships within the system. We cannot emphasize too strongly that you must be honest with yourself; you must learn about yourself and the way you do business; you must explicitly define and quantify the relationships applicable to your operation and your business. Otherwise a simulation model will produce uninteresting irrelevant or erroneous information.

Our experience has verified that financial simulation can add a new dimension to the planning process. Simulation provides flexibility by making it possible to generate a number of different plans quickly, easily, and cheaply. By forcing management to define and to quantify the relationships existing within the system and the interactions among its elements, it brings into clearer focus the hidden determinants of policy and practice. By making automatic the process of tracing the effects of decisions throughout the system, it solves the problems of communication that exist within any dynamic and diversified organization. By integration with management information systems, it provides the potential for the development of feedback control systems. The following are some examples of the uses we have made of our financial simulation model:

At the division level

1. To learn the combined influence of independent decisions
2. To improve decision making ability:
    a. To enforce discipline through formal relationships
    b. To allow the testing of independent decisions
    c. To point out problem areas
    d. To point out some inconsistent areas in decision making
3. To allow division to make several test runs before preparing their detailed forecasts.

At the corporate level

1. To learn the effect on the corporation of a proposed divisional plan
2. To evaluate divisional "profit plans" and study alternative plans with respect to:
    a. Growth objectives
    b. Asset management
    c. Profit maximization
    d. Cash flow
3. To evaluate corporate decision alternatives
4. To prepare long-range financial and debt management plans

Clearly, financial simulation increases the effectiveness of the financial analyst. The responsible analyst has, of course, always been aware of the interactions among elements in the system and has considered these in the development of his projections. At the same time, however, he has been hampered by the restrictions placed on him by computational limitations. He has had to ignore variables and relationships that he knew were important, simply because they could not be considered with the time and manpower resources he had available. He has been curious about the effects of altering certain basic assumptions but has never been able to test more than a few alternatives.

Today, burdened by increasing demands from top management, faced with more complex systems to analyze, and operating within the complex organizational and communications structure of a diversified corporation, the financial analyst needs the assistance that the technique of simulation can give him.

Through the use of simulation, he acquires the potential for doing his job the way he has always wanted to do it.

DO'S AND DON'TS

Now that we have examined the concepts of a financial model and seen how financial simulation contributes to the planning process, it may be helpful to summarize what we have learned about setting up a simulation program and the steps that must be taken in its implementation.

Construction of a model is an expensive, time-consuming process and requires the cooperation of middle and some lower management across the organization. Without the active interest and participation of top management, the project is doomed to failure from the start. This fact is of primary importance.

A second ingredient essential to the success of the project is the joint participation of the operations research or management science staff and the corporate financial analysis group in the development of the model. This inter-disciplinary approach is necessary to provide a balance between simulation technique on the one hand and financial logic and knowledgeability on the other. In our case the operations research man acted as the hub of the simulation team. At the same time, participation by financial analysis guaranteed that the operations research techniques were not applied in a vacuum but were kept within the bounds of logical and meaningful financial relationships.

A fine measure of success of a financial simulation program is its actual use by management in the planning process. If executives' participation has been enlisted in the development of the model, they will become knowledgeable concerning the nature and use of the approach. They will understand how the model works, how to use the model to simulate various policies and plans, and how to interpret its output. This understanding on the part of managers and their willingness to participate adds realism to the model and facilitates its acceptance as an official corporate planning tool.

In developing a model, it is necessary to examine a multitude of data. Sound research and financial logic are required in order to extract from the total information stream those data that reflect cause and effect. Initial efforts should be directed toward examining past research and making use of relationships previously developed and tested. Where previous research has not provided an adequate base for model design a research program must be initiated. If historical data are inadequate or judged not to be indicative of the future, one is forced to depend upon estimated relationships. Here the judgment of the informed manager is of great value in developing the necessary estimates.

After this approach has created an initial model, the model should be tested with actual data to measure the reasonability of its results. It is then modified and re-tested in a process continued until a simulation close enough to reality is obtained. No generalized criteria can be provided. What we are in fact doing is engaging in a formal validation procedure, to ensure that the model actually mirrors the corporate financial structure and that it truly reflects the effects of policies, plans, and actions.

A financial model must be dynamic in nature. It must be periodically reworked in order to improve the precision with which functional relationships are stated, to incorporate the organizational changes that occur in any dynamic organization, and to reflect changes in accounting practice which could lead either to changes in established relationships or changes in the accounting structure of the model.

A simulation model, like anything else in life, can always be improved. We can simulate, test, modify, and simulate again, until we get as close to reality as we wish. However, in expending this effort, we should try to strike a happy and acceptable balance between realism on the one hand and cost, time, and complexity of the model on the other.

In guarding against over-simulation, however, we should not go to the other extreme of oversimplification. For then the accuracy and the realism of the model are destroyed, and the effort expended becomes a costly exercise in futility.

THE PLANNING PROBLEM

The effort is worthwhile, for corporate planning—in particular, long-range planning—is a complex and difficult task. It requires sophistication and know-how on the part of the corporate executive who must formulate the corporate policies and plans that determine the future course of his organization.

The planning function is, first of all, a complex process. The executive is seeking to identify the alternatives available and assess their relative worth. The identification of reasonable alternatives is in itself a time consuming task, requiring the executive to sift through and analyze volumes of information. The determination of the relative desirability of these alternatives is made more difficult because of the element of uncertainty about the future within which each has been cast.

Uncertainty and change must be acknowledged as paramount forces to be coped with in the planning process. The balance between the need to make decisions and take action and the need for flexibility to permit adaptation to change remains a matter of judgment.

Changes are not only external. The organization, through expansion and diversification, may become more complicated as well. The economic environment, the acceptance of the company's product in the market place, and the company's cost of doing business are all affected in subtle but powerful ways by the complex interactions taking place between the enterprise on the one hand and government, labor, competition, and consumer demand on the other.

In addition to being complex, the planning process is a difficult one, increasingly so because of the shrinkage of time allowed the executive for response. As he attempts to cope with the complexities of his environment, the executive finds that his traditional patterns of decision making are breaking down in the face of ever increasing demands for faster reaction times. He recognizes the need for new planning tools to assist him in his planning role.

Traditionally, management has relied upon the financial segment of the organization for counsel in formulating plans. All activities have cost consequences. Hence, regardless of who else takes part in planning, the financial staff is an essential participant.

Top executives recognize the importance of the financial ramifications of planning. They are aware that decisions on budgets, appropriations, new product development, plant acquisition, and resource allocations made anywhere within the corporate structure have a far-reaching effect on the total fabric of the organization. They realize that policies and plans to achieve desired corporate objectives are embodied in these decisions.

Today we find the role of the financial manager in a corporation to be of primary importance. The financial manager is being asked to share the increased planning burden, to produce more planning exercises, to explore more alternatives, to provide information in greater detail, and, most significantly, to respond more rapidly.

The financial manager enjoys the confidence of top management because of his contribution to the planning process. The financial people have dedicated themselves to the development of technical competence and the accumulation of the experience necessary to act as consultants and advisors to top management. They have evolved accounting systems and analytic tools to aid them in performing this function.

The pressures under which the financial manager must now operate are obviously not due to any decrease in his capability. Instead, they stem from the increased demands now being put upon him by top management. The problem facing the financial manager, then, is only in relatively small part that of developing new theory, for the existing body of theory has proved generally adequate. Instead, he must acquire new tools, tools that are appropriate to his changing planning environment, tools that permit him to respond more quickly, more flexibly, and with greater accuracy and precision to requests from top management.

An attempt to use the traditional management structure of the corporation for financial planning creates significant communications problems that do not satisfy the executive response requirements. If management finds it necessary to communicate with all echelons and activities in order to determine the ramifications of a single "I wonder what would happen if" condition, the planning potential of the organization is limited. Yet relying solely on the experience of executives around the board room table does not satisfy today's need for explicit and systematic testing of the impact of change.

In financial simulation we have the potential for an effective solution to this problem. If a sound program—based upon top management participation, an interdisciplinary approach, and a thorough preliminary study phase—is established, this potential can be realized.

The structuring of a financial model is a difficult and sensitive task. We must learn and understand a great deal about the behavior of our organizations before we can produce workable and meaningful models. There is no cheap way to buy the tool. There is no such thing as a general financial simulation model that will act as an effective planning tool for a specific organization. There are no general equations applicable to every organization. While some equations in functional form can be expressed so as to be universal, their real value is in providing a guide for study and development. Even if our study provides a validation of their applicability we have, in fact, developed our own.

Thus, Burroughs' experience and Burroughs' model are hardly to be taken as universal. Indeed, our experience may not even provide an adequate sample from which to state a set of hard and fast rules. However, our experience has been sufficient to identify some important do's and don'ts. And this description of the relationships and circumstances that have produced an effective planning model may be useful as a general guide to those interested in applying the technique.

Where Traditional Budgeting Fails

Michael Schiff &
Arie Y. Lewin

A number of investigators have lately been concerned with the relationship of reported corporate income to true income. One hypothesis is that top management behaves as if it were "smoothing" reported income. This thought was first explicitly stated by Gordon,[1] who showed that reported income of the U. S. Steel Corporation appeared to be smoothed through judicious application of accounting methods. Schiff,[2] in his study of the Chock Full O'Nuts Corporation, has noted that management appears to have deliberately evened out reported income by decisions to expense or defer advertising costs of new products. This was apparently motivated by the management's desire to project an image of company growth. Lewin and Seidler[3] conclude that "income management"—the discretionary use of accounting methods—is seemingly painless to apply and is, therefore, preferred by top management to the difficult alternative of correcting internal problems that can be rationalized as temporary.

The question of reporting results exists not only in the relationship between the corporation and its external environment but, on a greater and more sophisticated scale, between divisions within the corporation itself. This article reports the results of a pilot study exploring the internal practices of managing reported results, vis-a-vis the budget and control system, from a behavioral decision-making viewpoint.

The most prevalent management accounting model is founded on the classical economic theory of the corporation and traditional organizational theory. Caplan[4] has compared and contrasted the assumptions which underlie the management accounting model based on the traditional attitudes of behavior with the modern organization theory, which represents the behavioral decision-making view. The fundamental difference in the two approaches is in their treatment of

SOURCE: Reprinted by permission of *Financial Executive* (May, 1968), pp. 51–52, 55–58. Copyright 1968 by *Financial Executive*.

the role of humans in the organization. In the traditional approach, humans are viewed as passive members of the system,[5] whereas in the decision-making problem-solving process the human and his ever-changing value system and limited information processing capability are emphasized.

It appears that most current budget and control systems are based on the traditional accounting model. Some of the unintended behavioral results of such a model have been reported by Argyris[6] and Dalton.[7] The latter, for example, reports on how lower level managements circumvent the budget and allocate resources to what they perceive as justifiable purposes.

It seems to us, however, that use of a budget and control system based on the traditional accounting model has unintended results which are especially serious with respect to the internal accounting for revenues, costs, and expenses.

Our views of the budget and its role within the firm are similar to those of Cyert and March in their treaties, "The Behavioral Theory of the Firm."[8] The budget in any company has the dual role of being a forecast of the year and a yardstick for managerial performance. The budget in its final form, however, is an explicit elaboration of organizational commitments for the year and reflects the resolution of demands for resources made by the various subunits of the firm.

Contrary to what Becker and Green[9] believe, the budget preparation process is a highly participative effort on the part of all managerial levels. This is because managers bargain about the performance criteria by which they will be judged throughout the year and for resource allocations. The outcome is a bargained budget incorporating varying degrees of slack.

Cyert and March see organizational slack in terms of the firm's cost function as the difference between minimum necessary costs and the actual costs of the firm. Organizational slack, in the Cyert and March view, arises unintentionally in the bargaining process, and its primary role is to stabilize performance despite fluctuations in the firm's environment. Basically, then, organizational slack would rise in relatively good times, providing a pool of emergency resources to be drawn upon in poor times, thus permitting the maintenance of organizational aspirations.

We believe as does Williamson[10]—contrary to Cyert and March—that managers consciously and intentionally create and bargain for organizational slack. Managers are motivated to achieve two sets of goals—the firm's goals and their personal goals. Personal goals are directly related to income (salary plus bonuses), size of staff, and control over allocation of resources. To maximize personal goals while achieving the goals of the firm requires a slack environment. This suggests that managers intentionally create slack.

Furthermore, the traditional budget and control system operates on the principle of management by exception. Since budgets are the criteria for measuring performance and management participates in their formulation, it clearly serves management's interests to have slack in the budget. Lower level management, therefore, usually attempts to have a budget which it feels is attainable and, at the same time, meets top management's requirements for a desirable net income.

All the above is not meant to indicate that top management is not aware of "padding" and "sandbagging." Numerous cases can be cited in which top management simply imposes increased profit requirements at the end of the long process of preparing the budget. These higher demands, often achieved, affirm the existence of slack. Frequently, however, top management accepts proposed budgets without change (normally in favorable years), thus implicitly legitimizing the creation of organizational slack and increasing the long-run cost function of the firm.

The purpose of our study was to determine whether the creation of slack occurs in the course of budget preparation; if so, what mechanisms are used, how extensive is the slack and its creation, and in what depth does top management recognize the existence of slack and counteract its growth?

MODE OF INVESTIGATION

The three independent divisions (segments of large companies chosen from *Fortune's* 100 largest corporations) which participated in the exploratory phase of the study are referred to as divisions A, B, and C. The consent for the study was obtained from the corporate headquarters of these companies with the understanding that this was not to be viewed as a consulting assignment, that the interviews were to be held confidential, and that the principal investigators would have access to all necessary documents and reports. The investigation, which was made with strict adherence to this agreement, relied mainly on personal interviews and detailed study of the relevant materials. This procedure occasioned frequent visits to each location and frequent re-interviewing. Our observations were made as the budgets developed and are based on cumulative insights.

In each of the three company divisions, the work centered on the division president, the controller, the vice presidents of planning, marketing and production, and their staffs. The interviews in every case ranged over the roles of all persons involved in the planning and budgetary process. In one instance, interviews were held with a random sample of men from the field sales force. The interviews gave a picture of each individual's job, his role in the division, and, moreover, his estimate of how other key people influenced the system as well as his specific activities.

The three divisions differed according to the business of their company. Division A, a producer of heavy industrial equipment, also produces and markets the consumables for its equipment and consumables for equipment produced by competitors. Division B, in a competitive and technologically sophisticated market, sells its products mainly to original equipment manufacturers. Division C, the second largest U. S. producer of its product, sells to both the consumer and industrial markets.

Fortunately for us, the three divisions also differed in their economic climate. Division A has a history of successful operations evidenced by a steady sales growth, high gross margins, and decreasing manufacturing costs. Sales at A in 1967 approximated $70 million and the immediate future of the division seems secure. Division B has been since its inception a loss operation in spite of a 140-fold increase in sales during the last five years (sales in 1967 were about $32 million). Division C has been historically profitable and has grown steadily in sales (1967 volume $100 million) and in earnings, and is reputed to be the low-cost producer in its industry. However, in 1967, due to an unexpected sales slump in one of the company's major products, C did not expect to achieve, for the first time in years, its budgeted profit.

PLANNING PROCESS

In each of the three divisions, planning for the ensuing year was synonymous with the budget preparation for that year. Although each division has a so-called five-year plan, little effort is devoted to the preparation of plans for the other four years. The so-called long-range plans are created by lower level staff after the following year's budget has been completed. These long-range plans are usually based on simple extrapolation of trends, reflecting division management aspirations for future resources commitments.

In all divisions, budget preparation began toward the end of May with a letter from the group controller containing information on timing schedules and accompanied by outlines of company policies and objectives, observations on expected economic climate, and occasional guidelines as to corporate expectations regarding the division's performance for the coming year. The objectives or company goals are stated either in relation to past attainments or in non-operational terms. None of the companies expect budgets that *maximize* profits; the objective is to obtain *satisfactory* returns.

Corporate memoranda are translated into internal guidelines for budgetary purposes by division management. The following are excerpts from letters accompanying internal budget messages reflecting division managements' general solutions to their budget problem:

"The base line for our 1968 Financial Budgets will be the attainment of 1968 sales volume within the framework of 1967 operating allowances. In brief, your 1968 budget will be the amounts allotted to you for 1967."

"Preliminary estimates indicate the 1968 sales quota will rise approximately 10 per cent above the 1967 quota."

"To assure that budgets reflect the best thinking of the product line teams and not of any one particular person. To assure to the best of our ability that the budgets submitted are not only accurate but are also *reasonably attainable.*"

The first step in the planning process of the three divisions was estimating next year's sales. There was a staff member in each division whose task was to perform industry analysis, compute product market shares, and prepare a qualified statistical forecast of the coming year's sales by product, region, and, sometimes, customer. The statistical forecasts were in all cases generalized extrapolations of past history based on these rules: (1) Total market share is computed from industry sales. (2) Next year's market share is derived from market share trends. Next year's market share is taken as a linear extrapolation of the market share trend when it is rising. When it descends, next year's market share equals last year's. (3) With a given estimate of next year's market share, that year's sales are directly obtained from the forecasted total industry sales for the coming year. The figure is derived from various trade reports.

We next examined the detailed steps in the budget process for each of the divisions according to differences in organization, roles of the executives, and what might be called "styles" in development of slack.

DIVISION A

A group controller is responsible for the mechanical aspects of the budget for this and other divisions in the group. The controller, who plays a passive role in the budget process, is satisfied to act as a collector of information. The key participant in division A is the vice president of marketing, despite the fact that there are two sales forces concerned with marketing his product: his own force and a force calling on distributors selling the products of the entire group, including division A.

Starting with a statistical sales estimate, the marketing vice president of division A formulates a sales estimate based on his projection of profits acceptable to corporate headquarters. His estimate at the time of our study assumed a "normal" sales and profit growth. In preparing the rough first estimate, the vice president of marketing in division A used average prices at the lower end of the expected range of prices contemplated for the following year. Product managers reporting to him assisted in the task.

With only minor modifications, the vice president's estimates served as a basis for developing detailed expense and capital budgets for 1968. It should be noted that the field sales force was also asked to submit estimates of 1968 sales. *The differences between these and the ones prepared by the vice president were negligible since the crude extrapolation done in totals at the home office was being repeated by each district field sales office as well.*

The aggregate budget and projected income statement, employing standard factory costs reflecting current year-to-date experiences, was then completed. Significant in the development of projections of operating expenses was frequent use of the expense-sales ratio to test the acceptability of expense budgets, especially those relating to marketing functions.

The budget as presented was reviewed with some concern at a division meeting because the final profit figures did not quite approximate the amount they thought corporate headquarters would accept. A modest increase in volume and price was therefore included as well as a decrease in standard unit factory cost produced by the factory cost accountant. These changes yielded a suitable increase in the over-all net income.

Corporate headquarters nevertheless rejected the budget with a request for additional profits. These were finally achieved by another increase in the expected average unit selling price for the products of division A, at which point the budget for the division became the formal approved plan for 1968.

A significant number of field salesmen in division A were interviewed. These men set sales goals which were generally achievable without much alteration in their approach to the market or in their time allocations. It appeared that, if pressed to increase sales, there was reasonable expectation that they could do so by "reallocating their time." Indeed, one of the salesmen, through what appeared to be self-motivation, doubled his sales volume in three years in a hitherto "stable territory."

Finally, the group controller at division A estimated that there was about 20 to 25 per cent slack in the number of division employees, exclusive of manufacturing, but he was "in no position to do anything about it."

DIVISION B

There are two organizational characteristics which affect the budget process and the "style" in this division. The controller is so much a part of the process that he makes modifications in key estimates. He reports directly to the division president and is strongly relied upon as chief financial officer of the division.

The products of division B are marketed by a group field sales force which sells products of other divisions as well. This sales body is assisted by a small group of field application engineers who are members of the marketing department of division B. The group field sales force is salaried but operates under an incentive bonus based on performance above dollar sales quota.

The initial sales projection, developed by the marketing research manager early in May 1967, indicated 1968 sales of 14 million units at $2.20. Working independently, the product marketing managers submitted an estimate of 18 million units at $2.20. (The five-year plan, used as a basis for capital budgeting, had indicated an expected sale of 20 million at $2.00.) A third input was the field sales force estimate of sales of 10 million units at $2.00, which was immediately modified to 13 million at $2.00 by the group marketing manager. It was observed by division B's management that the field force estimate was always kept low because of their desire to assure the earning of a bonus by setting a base which is readily achievable.

After a lengthy negotiation which involved the group vice president, a sales goal of 16 million at $2.00 was accepted. It should be noted that the unit price selected was at the low end of the estimated 1968 prices. (At the close of 1967, average prices were $3.68.) The various functional departments were then asked to submit expense budgets and the factory management was requested to develop standard costs. A profit and loss statement was subsequently developed which revealed a multi-million-dollar loss despite a prior directive from corporate headquarters requiring this division to at least break even in 1968.

The controller of division B began his budget adjustment process by raising the estimate for average prices. The revenue gained from this move, however, was somewhat offset when sales volume estimates had to be adjusted downward, based on more recent reports of actual results of the current year. He "recognized" then that some plant personnel would be employed only part of the year, although the initial budget showed them as full year. This difference amounted to a saving of $200,000. The controller next reviewed advertising expense with the product managers and trimmed another $120,000, *which was half the original advertising budget.* He also questioned the group marketing allocations to division B and obtained a $40,000 reduction—only a token, since the allocation was more than $1 million. Review of other costs yielded $140,000 more. The end result was a budget that still projected a loss but reflected total cost reductions of $500,000. All this was done with the support of the division president. The revised budget was then presented to corporate management, where it was again rejected with the clear directive to achieve a breakeven operation.

The divisional controller produced a new series of increased revenues and decreased costs. Average estimated price per unit was raised almost to the expected average high for the year with a resulting $720,000 in additional revenue. Postponement of more hiring of sales personnel added another $300,000. An accounting adjustment calling for deferral of the capitalization of new equipment until mid-year yielded a further saving of $100,000 by avoiding a depreciation charge for one-half of the year. With some other cost postponements and elimination of marginal product lines, the final budget projected a very minor loss for 1968.

It is clear from the above example that, contrary to theoretical expectations of Cyert and March, slack is also incorporated in the budgets of loss-producing divisions. We have specifically observed how slack appears in a budget through bargained sales goals, low average prices, manipulation of personnel requirements, marketing expenses, and accounting adjustments.

DIVISION C

As noted earlier, division C experienced a significant decline in sales in 1967 which was accompanied by an unanticipated labor rate increase of 6 per cent. Theoretically, slack previously incorporated into the budget would now be drawn upon to ameliorate expected profit decline. Therefore, we elected to examine *ex post facto* budget decisions for 1967 as well as the budgetary process for 1968.

Sales, at the end of January 1967, were below estimate in one product line and slightly up in the second. (The two lines account for the total sales of the division.) This trend became more pronounced by the end of March, when it was clear that one group of products had suffered by a 10 per cent sales slump while the second line exhibited a modest increase. Corporate headquarters may have been advised of this, but the division's forecast committee's monthly work sheets showed no attempt to modify the budget recognizing the sales slump, which continued through April. A small downward revision was made, however, at the end of that month. It was not until September that the forecast committee explicitly recognized the 10 per cent decline.

The division controller, an important member of the committee, activated a program officially referred to as "profit recovery." This was a device used by the controller fundamentally to plan slack in the budget. It should be stressed that corporate management accepts the profit recovery program as a means for improving performances by spending less than budget or selling more goods at better prices, which reflects a tight and efficient management. The extent of such built-in budgetary cushions is evident from a comparison of the projected profits prior to slack recovery with the actual profit in 1967. The sales slump, according to the controller, would have resulted in a 40 per cent drop in the division's profit. The final profit for 1967 was expected to be only 10 per cent off forecast! Profit recovery achieved this impressive result in spite of the unexpected 6 per cent labor cost increase granted production workers.

The profit recovery program in general led to cost savings over budget by postponing built-in overhead expenses, thus creating favorable efficiency variances, increasing prices, and cutting marketing expenses.

The 1967 budget called for hiring additional staff in various departments, yet none were hired. This counteracted the projected profit decline by 8 per cent. By re-evaluating marketing expenses, including advertising, the contribution gap was reduced another 15 per cent. This was accomplished by cutting travel expenses, cancelling technical and sales meetings, and reducing special promotional efforts.

Favorable efficiency variances were created by introducing process improvements which had been previously developed but not incorporated in standard costs. This reduced the contribution gap another 6 per cent. The eventuating figure, however, was partly cancelled by the wage rise to production workers. A selective 3 per cent price increase further lowered the contribution gap by 16 per cent.

This summary does not cover the total cost savings and accounting adjustments allowed within the 1967 budget, yet it is obvious that, through incorporating into the budget a formal profit recovery program, division C management created and controlled budgetary slack.

This was the actual climate or setting for the preparation of the 1968 budget. An operations controller, reporting directly to the division controller and responsible for sales forecasts, presented in June 1967 his projection for 1968. Prior to presenting it to the executives of the division, however, the projection was reviewed by the division controller and an upward modification was made to yield a more desirable profit. This projection was derived by using history, industry statistics, and general economic data. Division C has its own field sales force, but this force was not asked to submit sales estimates.

Sales estimates were used, nevertheless, as a basis for expense budget and standard costs. Current standard costs ignoring any improved process modifications were also employed, and budgets were prepared utilizing current expense-sales ratios. A final budget, yielding the expected profit and varying only in minor details from the original estimate of the controller, was submitted and approved by corporate headquarters.

That the profit recovery program was built into the 1968 budget is evident from the fact that the twenty-four men for the marketing organization, budgeted in 1967 and not hired, were incorporated in the 1968 budget! Similarly, standard costs for 1968 did not incorporate process improvements operationally available in December 1967. These improvements would have reduced standard unit manufacturing cost by 15 per cent.

STUDY RESULTS

It became cumulatively certain in our study that budgetary slack can be incorporated into both revenue and cost projections, and that internal slack may arise through accounting adjustments. We saw that sales objectives were arrived at on the basis of simple decision rules, resulting in the establishment of sales goals which are the most likely to be attained. Sales estimates often fell below a division's attainable estimates primarily due to interorganizational conflict.

Average price estimates seem to be initially budgeted at the low of their expected range and are generally finalized into the budget below their expected average. The greater the discrepancy between budgeted average prices and actual prices, the greater the slack and the ease of achieving or exceeding budgeted contribution.

On the cost side, we have seen that opportunities for incorporating slack are numerous and appear to require intimate knowledge of the budget and control system. Two main cost categories permit major slack manipulation: manufacturing cost standards and operating expenses. The inclusion of standard costs was at first surprising to us, but in retrospect appears simple and logical. Slack in standard cost arises from the discrepancy between the costs budgeted and what they actually would be if various known cost improvements were introduced. We have seen in at least one case that such improvements, producing efficiency variances, were included when needed and not when developed.

Marketing expenses result from many programs (for example, training meetings, special promotions, and the like) which are viewed by management as niceties. These programs appear on budgets, but the commitment of resources to them is contingent on progress made during the year in attaining the budget. Advertising budgets, which are treated in a similar way, strongly suggest that management formulates them on a basis of "how much can we afford," rather than on a basis related to an objective.

In the matter of operating expenses, which include budgetary allocations for new as well as replacement of personnel, it appears that budgeting for personnel and delay in hiring is extensively practiced and is a simple method for creating slack.

Accounting adjustments are also occasionally made to effect slack, but within divisional units over-all use of adjustments for this purpose is marginal. It seems that internal slack in organizations originates mainly through the mechanisms described above.

In our exploration, we concluded that slack may account for as much as 20 to 25 per cent of divisional budgeted operating expenses. The response of key people supports our conclusion. The group controller of division A estimated that slack in the administrative personnel category of the division was between 20 and 30 per cent. His estimate was based on a reorganization of the administrative unit in another division which had resulted in 25 per cent fewer people.

One division president, who was relatively new on the job, felt that the main office staff could be trimmed 20 per cent. He noted that in the past the main office force had been increased on a 1:1 ratio with sales, and questioned the need for it. In this same division, a number of people in the controller's group asserted that the controller could easily maintain the reported division contribution within 25 per cent.

Our results amply support the behavioral implications of the occurrence of slack as an unintended result of the budget and control system, especially where the system is based on the traditional accounting model of the firm. The management accounting control model assumes a plan—or budget—as the means to achieving profit goals based on maximal uses of resources. The system is based on such principles as responsibility accounting, variance analysis, management by exception, and so forth. It focuses on results after the budget by comparing the actual results to the budget.

Contending that the traditional system, contrary to expectations, does not result in maximal use of resources, we have shown on the basis of our pilot study how management can and does create slack to achieve attainable budgets and to secure resources for furthering their personal goals and desires. This behavior seems universal among managers; it occurs in profitable and unprofitable companies, whether stable or growing. Our study also suggests that the practice is widespread among controllers who are closely aligned with top management and assume the dominant role in the budget and control process of a decentralized control system.

REFERENCES

1.   M. J. Gordon, B. N. Horowitz and P. T. Meyers, "Accounting Measurements and Normal Growth of the Firm," *Research in Accounting Measurement* (Jaedicke, Ijiri, and Neilsen, Ed.) American Accounting Association, 1966.

2.   M. Schiff, "Accounting Tactics and the Theory of the Firm," *Journal of Accounting Research*, Vol. 4, No. 1 (Aug. 1966) pp. 62–67.

3.   A. Y. Lewin and L. J. Seidler, "Income Management: The Alternative to Cutting Organizational Slack," working paper, Graduate School of Business Administration, New York University.

4.   E. H. Caplan, "Behavioral Assumptions of Management Accounting," *Accounting Review*, Vol. XLI (July 1966) pp. 496–509.

5.   J. G. March and H. A. Simon, *Organizations*, Wiley, 1958, p. 6.

6.   C. Argyris, *The Impact of Budgets on People*, The controllership Foundation, 1952.

7.   M. Dalton, *Men Who Manage*, Wiley, 1959, pp. 31–52.

8.   R. M. Cyert and J. G. March, *A Behavioral Theory of the Firm* (Prentice Hall, 1963) pp. 36–38.

9.   S. Becker and D. Green, "Budgeting and Employee Behavior," *Journal of Business*, Vol. 35 (October 1962) pp. 392–402.

10. O. E. Williamson, *The Economics of Discretionary Behavior: Managerial Objectives in a Theory of the Firm* (Prentice-Hall, Inc., 1964).

Excerpt from Barron's

We finally got around to reading that famous brokerage report, issued about three weeks ago, recommending Bausch & Lomb. All in all, we thought the thing was a reasonable job, although, we hasten to add, it didn't shake our skepticism toward the wild enthusiasm for the soft contact lens. We did get a chuckle, though, out of the appendix. (This is a pretty fancy report.) Specifically, that part dealing with the third of "three broad assumptions" used in making estimates.

"Direct and indirect costs are totally variable. Thus, we have assumed that these costs are a constant percentage of sales. We realize that this will not be accurate, but we think that this margin of error is relatively unimportant given the uncertainty of our assumptions."

SOURCE: Reprinted by courtesy of *Barron's National Business and Financial "Weekly,"* May 31, 1971.

Coordinating the Decision Process— Formal Control Systems

INTRODUCTION

The term "planning and control" has been used extensively in accounting literature. Springing primarily from the management literature, the activities of planning and control are often considered the fundamental functions which management performs.

The managerial function of control is the measurement, reporting, and subsequent correction of the performance of the worker to insure that the firm's objectives and plans are achieved. The control function is the activity which makes sure that the actual work is done so as to fulfill the original intentions. As Goetz says; "Managerial planning seeks consistent, integrated and articulated programs," and "managerial control seeks to compel events to conform to plans."[1] If the forgoing view of control is accepted, there can be no control without the existence of goals and plans. Without plans there would be no vehicle to insure that subordinates are operating in the desired manner since the desirable behavior would not be specified. The plan may be as vague as a fantasy in the manager's mind or as definitive as an integrated budget; it may cover only a single day or it may cover a 20-year time span. Naturally the more complete and integrated the plans are and the greater the time span encompassed, the more complete managerial control can be.

A manager cannot control the past. This should be self-evident. A study of the past may provide clues about what happened and why, but it will not rectify the past events. It is only if history is assumed to repeat itself that past results allow the manager to take steps to avoid unwanted expereinces in the future. Control of necessity must look forward, not backward. Ideal control is one that corrects deviations *before* they occur. The next best control method is to determine deviations from the planned actions simultaneously with their occurrence. The longer the time span between the action and the report of deviations, the more ineffective becomes the control function.

It is reasonable to expect the control function to vary according to the sensitivity of the decisions. Robert Anthony in his article *Framework for Analysis* in the previous section suggested a classification system of managerial plans and controls. Strategic planning is concerned with long-run policies and objectives of the firm, while managerial control is the general "process of assuring that resources are obtained and used effectively and efficiently in the accomplishment of the organization's objectives." According to Anthony, management control is a process carried on within the framework established by strategic planning. Technical control, on the other hand, deals with assuring the optimum relationship between outputs and inputs. On the surface it is a reasonable hypothesis to postulate that technical control is the most sensitive to current data and hence, requires the most timely data. Strategic planning, however, is broader in scope and would be expected to require less timely data than either management control or technical control.

Accounting is a major source of control data, although it is by no means the only source of relevant data. The annual balance sheet and income statement as presented in the annual report fail to provide timely data for managerial and technical control. This control data must come in more timely and less condensed form. Standard costs are one example of the accounting profession's attempts to provide timely, relevant, and meaningful data for managerial and technical control. The setting of standards provides a predetermined plan, which if implemented would result in efficient costs of production. A standard cost system provides a detailed guide to resource consumption and a comparison of plans and actual activities through the generation of variances at the time the transaction is recorded. If the standard cost system is implemented correctly, the actual cost of production should be incurred so that it is congruent with the standard cost, and the variances should be zero. If the actual costs differ from the standard costs, the process may be out of control and managerial action should be considered.

An adequate control system must do more than report deviations expeditiously. Since events must be controlled through people it is mandatory that controls reflect the organization pattern. It is through the organization that the activities are coordinated, and it is through the organization that control is manifest. This recognition of the fact that the accounting flow systems and data reports must be synchronized with organizational structure has led to the development of cost centers and responsibility accounting. Responsibility accounting is a system tailored to match inputs and outputs of operations with the person responsible for them. Without some form of responsibility accounting the control data will not be properly matched with the person who can affect the operating activities.

The type of managerial control just discussed is a decision-oriented, dynamic control. The object of this view of control is to insure that the decisions and choices made by management are operationally activated. There is another type of control sometimes assigned to the accounting function. This could perhaps be labeled "compliance control." Where there are legal requirements, such as legal restraints in registering before the SEC, legal requirements that managers safeguard company assets or regulatory account structuring as required by the ICC for railroads, the accountant, through the historical records and subsequent audit, provide post hoc control records that the requirements have been met.

There are other implications of a control device. First, a control system must withstand a stringent cost/benefit analysis. Stated simply, a control system must provide data that justify their cost of collection. This is often difficult to assess in practice since the incremental benefits of being "in control" and the incremental costs of being "out of control" are difficult to assess. Second, the controls used must be understandable. One of the continuing problems of control devices, particularly those based upon the more complex mathematical models, is that they are not understood by the managers who use them. This opens up the entire field of communication theory. Data are not useful in and of themselves. It is only when those data convey to the manager information that he can convert into effective action that communication exists. Too often the data specialist becomes overly enamored with the data and forgets to ask himself the necessary question, "Does anyone understand or use the data?"

Finally, it is generally assumed that one of the major purposes of control systems is to "motivate" management to make optimizing choices. If motivation is conceived of as an activating force upon the manager, the control system, with its ability to report favorable or unfavorable deviations from normative behavior, should motivate (activate) the manager. It is generally assumed in the accounting literature that if management participates in the development of the firm's goals and plans, it will be positively motivated to fulfill or meet these plans. In addition, the presence of a control system provides a negative motivation. If the manager fails to meet the plan, the control system will generate unfavorable deviations and the manager will be subject to censure or dismissal.

The first article, *Budgetary Control Is Obsolete* by Morris, seriously questions the validity of business budgets as a control tool. His questioning is based upon the premise that budgets have conflicting functions—planning and control. He postulates that the planning and control functions are substantially different and therefore have different data requirements. It is generally held in the accounting literature that it is possible to integrate the planning models and the control tools along parallel lines. Mr. Morris believes there are too many differences to make this integration possible.

Mr. Pick, in his article, *Is Responsibility Accounting Irresponsible,* attacks another of accounting's sacred cows. Since Mr. Higgins first article on responsibility accounting in *The Arthur Andersen Chronicle,*[2] the advocacy of responsibility accounting has continually increased. Mr. Pick believes that it has built-in weaknesses that may prejudice the apparent accounting conclusions. He feels that motivation begins with the organization structure and is influenced by the techniques for collecting, measuring, and valuing data and the decision-making process. For one thing, responsibility accounting assumes an individual as a focal point while in many instances decisions are a group responsibility.

The final article in this section, *The Relevance of Probability Statistics to Accounting Variance Control* by Koehler, stresses the belief that management control designers should focus on broadening the base of variance controls. The author wants to expand the definition of variance controls by applying the concepts of statistical control charts. By moving from a single-point control measurement to an acceptable band of control he believes that managers can avoid the situation where performance is either at or above standard and therefore acceptable or else below standard and therefore unacceptable. Rarely do accountants discuss the concept of an acceptable "range" of behavior. Too often it is either/or.

Is it possible that a series of single-point estimates is too sensitive and that reporting these estimates to each responsibility center is too insensitive to be functional for effective management controls?

FOOTNOTES

1.   Billy E. Goetz, *Managerial Planning and Control* (New York: McGraw-Hill Book Company, Inc., 1949) p. 229.

2.   John A. Higgins, *The Arthur Andersen Chronicle* (April, 1952).

Budgetary Control Is Obsolete

R. D. F. Morris

The theme of this paper is that today the concept of budgetary control is no longer a viable proposition. This statement is based on the fact that the majority of budgetary control systems are attempting to perform two different functions: the functions of forward planning and of control.

If one looks back into the history of accounting one sees that companies once used to have only one set of accounts. This set of accounts was used both for informing the owners about their investment in the company, and for aiding the managers in the day-to-day operation of the company.

In the course of time it was recognized that accounting information assembled to inform the owners ('stewardship accounting' it is sometimes called) was not always adequate to serve internal management purposes. This led to the separate development of management accounting, using concepts and conventions that often varied from more traditional practice.

A similar situation now exists in relation to management accounting, the cornerstone of which is the budgetary control system. The information contained in a budgetary control system for planning purposes is not necessarily compatible with the information required for control purposes.

In 1939 Scott said:[1]

> The term budgetary control is applied to the system of management control and accounting in which all operations are forecast and so far as possible planned ahead, and the actual results compared with forecast and planned ones.

SOURCE: Reprinted with permission from *The Accountant* (May 18, 1968), pp. 654–656.

EDITORS' NOTE: This essay was the winner of the 1968 Reed Executive Selection Limited Essay Award Competition. The award is made only for the best essay submitted on a named topic of special interest to accountants. Reed Executive Selection Limited are the leading authority in the United Kingdom on the recruitment of accountants. Copyright by Reed Executive Selection Limited.

In the light of the state of knowledge at that time, this was a logical view. That this view is still widely accepted today, or if not accepted at least reflected in practice in the majority of companies (even the advanced ones), indicates a failure to keep up with the developments in theory which have taken place in the last twenty years.

This is not so say that cost or management accountants have not made significant progress in this period. The more widespread use of standard costing and marginal costing techniques, and the growing use of computers in processing information, are quite clear evidence to the contrary. There does, however, appear to be a need to make further advances in an area where the accountant's contribution is rapidly becoming inadequate.

WHAT IS A BUDGET?

The word budget has been defined in the *Terminology of Cost Accounting* of The Institute of Cost and Works Accountants as:

> A financial and/or quantitative statement, prepared prior to a defined period of time, of the policy to be pursued during that period for the purpose of attaining a given objective.

In other words, a budget is a statement or plan consisting of a number of targets which are to be achieved by the managers and departments in a company. If all these targets are achieved then performance will be in line with the budget.

WHAT IS CONTROL?

Control is less easily defined. Concepts of control range from the systems, engineering and cybernetics approach framed essentially in terms of feedback to the human relations approach as typified by management objectives.

To some extent Henrici[2] has defined what is not control. He says:

> The difference in a given time period between actual costs and standard cost, known as the "variance," tells management to what extent costs can be controlled. The variance itself is not a control, for costs are not controlled by compiling statistics about them. The control consists of the steps that management take to regulate or limit costs. And the effectiveness of these steps is gauged by the degree to which actual costs approach standards; in other words, the size of the variance.

The many definitions of control have much in common. The essential differences between them lie in the extent to which they regard the original target-setting process and the taking of corrective action as elements of control.

It seems somewhat difficult to envisage a situation as being under control when targets are being achieved, but the targets set are inappropriate. It seems equally difficult to regard a situation as being under control when planned levels of performance are not attained and yet no corrective action is taken. For these reasons it is maintained that both the target-setting and the corrective action are elements of control.

Here the term 'control' is assumed to include at least the following three elements:

1. Setting targets at the appropriate level to achieve the required performance.
2. Measuring actual performance and comparing this with target.
3. Taking corrective action in the event of actual results deviating from target results.

DIFFERENCES BETWEEN BUDGETS AND CONTROL

It may be argued that control as outlined above is exactly what budgets provide. They set targets, performance is measured and compared with these targets and finally, information is provided that leads to corrective action. That this is *not* so will become more apparent if these elements of control are considered in more detail.

1. Setting Appropriate Targets

Whether a target is appropriate or not depends on the purpose for which it is set. One purpose of budgets in many companies is to enable the company to plan the financial resources which will be consumed and generated during the course of the budget period: that is, amongst other things giving an indication of the extent to which the company will need to raise additional finance, the time period for which it will be required, or the extent to which the company is able to repay loans, pay dividends or invest surplus funds, etc.

The budget which is most appropriate for this financial planning is a statement of the most likely outcome of events. In some circumstances it may be that the most appropriate budget for this purpose is a conservative one; i.e., a budget that assumes that expected improvements in efficiency will not all be attained, and perhaps that there will be a falling off in achievement in some areas. For control purposes it is far from certain that this will provide the most appropriate target.

Target-setting for control must be based on some theory of human motivation; three alternative theories spring immediately to mind:

a. That people do the best they can, irrespective of the level of target set. Hence the target-setting process is not very important.
b. That people are highly motivated by achievement. Therefore the target must be one that the individual is highly likely to attain.
c. That individuals will try hardest if the target which they are to attain is

very difficult. In this case very tight targets (i.e., targets which are difficult to attain) are appropriate.

If the budget is used for planning purposes and the targets included are the ones which are highly likely to be achieved, then theory (a) or (b) is being used as the basis for control. If, on the other hand, theory (c) is believed to be true, the targets set for control purposes may well need to be different from those set for planning purposes.

Stedry[3] draws attention to the not uncommon practice of setting targets or quotas for salesmen. These quotas are designed to motivate salesmen to achieve higher volumes of sales. They are often accompanied by some form of reward or penalty structure which is designed to reinforce the motivation of the salesman. In many instances where this sort of system is operated, there is little direct relationship between the sum of the quotas set for salesmen and the budgeted volume of sales.

This form of target-setting is based on theory (c) of human motivation. What is true of the motivation of salesmen may well be true of the motivation of many or perhaps all managers. That is to say tighter targets may lead to higher levels of performance; though this is not to say they will result in achievement of these targets.

Stedry goes on to suggest that up to the point known as the 'discouragement point,' a manager's efforts to reduce the discrepancy between actual costs and budgeted costs will vary with the size of this discrepancy. On this basis the optimal target for a manager will be one that is set to give the maximum variance which does not exceed the discouragement point. In this case, however, actual achievement is very likely to be lower than the target. Clearly, therefore, this target cannot be used as a budget for financial planning purposes.

Care needs to be taken that the discouragement point is not exceeded and at a more extreme level the 'failure point' is not exceeded. It is postulated that if the discrepancy exceeds the failure point, it is likely that the manager will resign.

There is no suggestion here that setting tight targets is the only way in which managers can be motivated to high performance. Clearly, motivation can be achieved by a system of rewards related to performance. These two approaches are not incompatible.

One danger of a system of rewards based on improvements over a target performance is that there may be a reluctance to accept tight targets as interfering with the opportunity provided for attaining this reward. At least one company has divided its reward system in two parts.

One part of the reward—in the form of bonus payments—is made for producing results at an efficiency greater than the target or standard. This reinforces the pressure to achieve targets which arises from personal disinclination to be criticized. The other part of the reward is given as a bonus for improving the target or standard. This provides compensation for reduced opportunity to beat the target.

2. Measuring Performance and Comparing with Standards

Budgets contain a system of numerical targets, very often expressed in financial terms. Control also requires a system of targets, but it is arguable whether these are best expressed in financial terms for this purpose.

For a manager to be able to use control information it is necessary for him to understand it. Much accounting is based on the use of conventions and it is far from certain that all managers understand the implications of these. In particular in a period when the value of money is changing, measurement in money terms is rather like using an elastic ruler.

Apart from this, the purpose of measuring performance and comparing it with budget is presumably to enable corrective action to be taken. Argyris[4] has undertaken some studies which suggests that operating managers do not find budget variances very useful for this purpose.

Firstly, these operating managers complain that what the budget system throws up as the cause of variances are seen by shop floor managers as results from other deeper and perhaps more complex causes. Argyris quotes the comments of factory supervisors on this point:

> Let's say the budget tells me where I was off. I didn't make it. That's of interest. But it doesn't tell me the important thing of why I didn't make it or how I am going to make it next time. Oh sure, they might say all I need to do is increase production and cut out waste. Well, I know that. The question is how to do it.

Or:

> Budgets show a nice average for the month, quarter, or whatever it is. If I had 1,000 jobs in a month and I made my budget, that's fine. But, the fact that I made it doesn't describe how, and what I had to do to make it. The budget never shows how I had to work, the headaches I had to surmount, especially with bad jobs.

This latter comment raises another issue, that of frequency of reporting variances. Most budget systems report variances with a frequency which is related to the availability of financial information. For control purposes the requisite frequency of reports may be entirely different and may depend on the batch size, production time cycle or some other fact unrelated to normal accounting procedures.

3.   Taking Corrective Action

Corrective action is a futuristic concept. Action cannot be taken to alter what has happened in the past, it can only be concerned with what is to happen in the future. This action can be considered in two parts.

If it is accepted that the original setting of targets is a significant feature of control, then the review and possibly resetting of targets must be a significant feature of corrective action. The factors which influence the original target-setting need the same consideration when resetting targets.

That is to say, the same considerations of appropriateness need to be taken into account. There is no reason to believe that targets set originally and considered at that time to be most appropriate will continue to be the best after the passage of even a short period of time. The situation needs re-examination in the light of what has happened in this period. This re-examination may, of course, confirm the appropriateness of previously set targets, but it may not.

The other part of corrective action is not so relevant to this paper and is only mentioned to avoid a serious omission. Corrective action may involve processes which are separate from target-setting. These processes include changing people's behaviour. Cyert and March[5] have drawn attention to the operation of behavioural rules which underline much organizational behaviour.

Corrective action with budgets is also a matter of revising targets. On the other hand, frequent revisions of detail in a budget add little or nothing to its value for planning. The revisions which are important for budget purposes are those which have significance in relation to the overall company plans, or to major segments of the company. This would include such revisions as those which result in a significant difference in product profitability or the viability of an investment decision.

CONCLUSIONS

A non-accountant may well conclude that if budgets and control are so different, the accounting profession must be very incompetent to have talked of budgetary control for so long. This is not true for two reasons. Firstly, the concept of using targets as a specific form of motivation to achievement is not so well-established that it is easy to apply. Secondly, and perhaps more importantly, this paper so far has ignored all the difficulties of running a planning system and a control system in parallel.

The management accountant has always been concerned with both planning and control. That the same sets of figures should be used for both purposes has been inevitable in the past, because of the formidable volume of information processing needed to run two sets of figures. Discussions with accountants in a wide range of companies show that many companies are in the position in which their ideas for improving the value of their accounting system run far ahead of their capacity to handle the work involved.

The discussion so far has not been very constructive. It has essentially been concerned with what is wrong with current practice, rather than what should be done in future. The seeds of an alternative approach have been indicated, but it is necessary now to consider this more purposefully.

If it is impossible to perform the two functions of control and planning using the same set of figures, it is necessary to have two sets. For discussion here, they will be named the control records and the planning records. To be effective these records will need to be closely related. It is probable that the only practical way to maintain these records and handle the increased volume of information processing is by the use of a computer.

The basic record would be the targets set for the purposes of control. These targets will differ from those set for planning purposes in several ways.

Firstly, they will differ in time scale. The time scale for which they are set, the frequency with which performance is monitored and compared with target, and finally, the frequency with which they are reviewed and revised, will be a function of the factors surrounding each individual process. This frequency may be very different for different targets within any one department.

Secondly, these targets will be more numerous and detailed in some areas than is conventional when using budgets. The purpose of control targets is to enable the individual to examine his own progress. The result will be to involve the lowest levels of management in the control process; a result which would bring great benefit in view of the research evidence which exists showing that this level of management can significantly affect a company's costs.

Thirdly, the targets set would be of a different nature. Targets would be set which demanded the highest possible levels of achievement. In addition, they would be set in terms which are significant for the individual for whom they are set. They would still be quantitative but they would be much less likely to be in financial terms. This would overcome the problems inherent in using tools for which individuals are inadequately trained.

This would result in a control record which was continually being updated, which used measures designed to be intelligible to the individual whose performance was being monitored, and which set targets representing not what can be attained on average but the best that can be achieved.

From this control record a separate budget record would be produced which was more conservative. The basic information in the control record would be converted into financial terms. Factors would be applied to the targets set for control to adjust them to an average level of performance which could be expected to be maintained.

The rate of change of the planning record would be more modest. It could be updated in line with the frequency at which financial information was available.

It would take account of allocated costs—a factor which is largely irrelevant in the control record. Targets would only need to be adjusted when some significant change occurred in the level of performance, and this change could be maintained.

This planning record would be the source of marginal costs or standard costs, or such other management accounting information as is used for the company's normal planning, forecasting and decision-taking exercises.

As a final comment it is worth reiterating what this paper is about. It is concerned with a change of emphasis in control from results that can on average be achieved, to emphasis on the highest possible levels of achievement. The determination of what is possible is always open to dispute but at the least, what is possible is the best that anyone has achieved. The control records would need monitoring to ensure that the targets set were not only the best which had been achieved in a particular department, but the best that had been known to be achieved anywhere comparable.

If this approach was used for setting control targets in every area then most targets would need to be tightened and some targets would need to be altered dramatically. Without empirical evidence to support the ideas put forward here it is impossible to predict the extent of the improvements which would result from this change of approach, but it seems inconceivable that they would result in anything but an immense release of energy.

FOOTNOTES

1. *Budgetary Control and Standard Costs.* J. A. Scott (Pitman, 1962).
2. *Standard Costs for Manufacturing.* S. B. Henrici (McGraw-Hill).
3. *Budgetary Control and Cost Behavior.* Andrew C. Stedry (Prentice-Hall, 1960).
4. *The Impact of Budgets on People.* Chris Argyris (Controllership Foundation, 1952).
5. *A Behavioural Theory of the Firm.* Richard M. Cyert and James G. March (Prentice-Hall, 1963).

Is Responsibility Accounting Irresponsible?

John Pick

FUNDAMENTALS

Nature, Objectives and Fields

Perhaps the most significant developments in accounting during the recent years were 1) accountancy's shift of emphasis from external reporting to management services and 2) the use of the computer to process basic data and to combine them in numerous ways. Jointly, both factors promoted responsibility accounting. That accounting system—sometimes also called profitability accounting, profit center accounting, and activity accounting—intends ". . . to tag each official [in a company] as a center of authority, responsibility, and accountability . . ."[1] Its reports cover the activities of every manager—from foreman to president—and, starting with the lowest level, build up one upon the other.

Its main objectives are to furnish data for the evaluation of a manager's performance and to supply that manager with feedback information for remedial action, if needed. The system principally seeks to accomplish these ends by defining as responsibilities of a manager only those activities which he controls and the improvement of which can be expected from him. However, at times, certain transactions not entirely controllable by an official are included in his charge. In that case, either significant influence on, instead of full control of, transactions, is deemed sufficient for responsibility, or the responsible manager is expected to "pressure" those that share in the control.[2]

Meant for all managerial levels, responsibility accounting is applied to expense centers, profit centers, and investment centers. In expense centers, the input is measured in monetary terms. In profit centers that measurement includes the output. In investment centers, management's efficiency in the use of capital is evaluated too; investment centers usually are large units and may be parts of a conglomerate. In all cases, the aim is the promotion of efficiency and profitability through the control of operations.

SOURCE: Reprinted by permission of *The New York Certified Public Accountant* (July, 1971), pp. 487–494.

Control Systems

Industrial control systems, in general, involve communications from and to an official, the furtherance of his motivation, and the detection of unfavorable performance variances that should be corrected by him. A system is called "operational control" if the efficiency and effectiveness of the fulfillment of specific tasks is at stake, and it is labeled "management control" if the efficiency and effectiveness of the use of resources with regard to the company's goals is watched.[3] The two systems use different means.

Operational control uses standards for engineered (predictable) costs on one hand and budget allowances for managed (discretionary) costs on the other hand: through comparison of intended and actual costs it leads to "management by exception."

Management control, on the other hand, emphasizes the construction of those cost and evaluation concepts that motivate an individual to make decisions in line with company policy and aims; (for example, different concepts of investment bases for return-on-investment computations may direct an executive toward different decisions). The desired effect of management control is called "goal congruence"[4] or "harmony of objectives."[5] Its value is obvious. Less obvious is its compatibility with responsibility accounting. Conceptually at least, the managerial control over and the full responsibility of an official tend to interdict each other. Anyhow, a brief look at industrial responsibility is in order, even though philosophical discords are not the topic here.

Industrial Responsibility

Responsibility can be defined as an individual's (or group's) identification with a role to be played or a task to be fulfilled. It usually contributes to industrial productivity. Feeling responsible is itself ordinarily a motivation. The average American longs for responsibility, because it conveys challenge and esteem together with the feeling of competence. Thus responsibility is a job-satisfier, and together with other job-satisfiers (e.g., remuneration, the work itself, and advancement) causes efforts toward desirable results. Even the burden of reasonably tough responsibilities boosts performance. Such burden may cause tension. Yet, up to a degree, tension evokes action and thought.

Need for Reappraisal

Nevertheless, the question must be asked whether an accounting system based on a behavioral science concept like responsibility can do justice to such base or whether it has inherent weaknesses in that respect and, accordingly, has practical difficulties. The question implies the need for reappraisal. That need cannot be ignored under any circumstances by a CPA engaged in management services who desires to serve his client and the public well. Accounting procedures incompatible with findings of sociology and psychology may cause, in the long-term, the loss of profitability for the client and serious damage to his sociopolitical environment, even though those procedures may assist him in short-term profits.

The reappraisal requires first of all a scrutiny of organization theory. A firm's organizational make-up affects the motivation of employees and especially of those at lower levels.[6] Performance measurement at those levels constitutes the basic phase of present responsibility accounting. Besides, responsibility accounting historically is tied to the traditional organization theory with its hierarchical patterns and should not be judged without regard to it.

The following, therefore, deals first with both the traditional and the modern organization theories, and their support of responsibility accounting systems. Thereafter, the systems' techniques and results as to data collection, measurements, evaluations, and decision making will be explored.

THEORY

Hierarchical Structures

The traditional organization theory conceives business organizations as hierarchies. Ideally, such structures assign the responsibility for one specific function to one specific person and through a chain of commands to his superiors. They allegedly avoid overlapping responsibilities and provide for adequate authority. Those structures (and responsibility accounting) emphasize the control of the decisions of the heads of the lowest units.

To stress decision making and responsibility at the lowest levels is supported by behavioral research.[7] Questionable, however, is whether the conventional view of the business organization, with its chain of command and clearly delineated responsibility assignments, is not mostly a fiction, unaware of modern industry and disagreeing with behavioral sciences. Some of the rebukes of the conventional view are:

1. Not being links in the chain of command, staff advisors do not fit into the hierarchical structure and thus would have to be considered irresponsible.[8]
2. Individuals, each of whom officially has a different responsibility assignment, often are in fact not independent from each other. Overlapping fields of responsibility are quite common.
3. The responsibility for an act may not rest fully with the person officially charged with it but may be shared by his superiors. As mentioned, though, several researchers believe that—instead of sole control—significant influence is sufficient for an official's responsibility.

4. The behavior of subordinates is not only affected by their supervisors' directives but also by such factors as individual needs, informal groups, and company policies. Yet, in the hierarchical structure, supervisors are held fully responsible for the performance of subordinate supervisors and work groups.

5. The hierarchical structure is apt to restrict a department supervisor's thoughts to his own department and cause him to promote it at the expense of the overall success of the firm.

6. Usually authority cannot be delegated effectively but depends on its acceptance by subordinates. Such acceptance may depend less on the supervisor's official status than on his personality and the subordinate group's disposition.

7. The conventional organization theory neglects group responsibility.

Democratic Structures

The flaws in the hierarchical organization concept seriously weaken the function of industrial responsibility as an accounting base. However, there still remains the possibility that other forms of business organization may furnish firmer support.

Searching for new ways, McGregor named the hierarchical organization Theory X and contrasted it with Theory Y.[9] The latter represents a structure in which employees are *counseled* rather than *commanded*. The supervisor is assigned the roles of discussion leader and expert, and management is made participative by giving employees a voice in the decision making.[10] That structure is called "organic organization"[11] or, more often, "participative management." In such organization the human assets—e.g., employees' sentiments—are to be included in accounting reports, and information is to be shared freely.[12]

Although participative management is not generally extant in the American economy, it has to be taken into consideration. Future developments are difficult to predict. One writer, for example, believes that both structures may have each its own field in future: the hierarchical structure might prevail in mass (process) production and the organic structure in individual (job order) production.[13] Recent reports show a growth of the democratic industrial organization form and illustrate the increase in efficiency and profitability resulting in major firms from the conversion to it.[14] Its merits, indeed, are substantial in comparison with its shortcomings.

Participative management may fail in situations where time is of the essence, maximum short-run productivity is desired, repetitive work is involved, and the orderliness of operations is of paramount importance. It also fails where no goal congruence exists between the company and its employees. Happy workers are not necessarily productive workers, unless they identify their goals with those of the company; they should have a personal involvement in and a responsible concern for their activity or product.

On the other hand, participative management allows employees a fair chance at self-actualization by letting them solve problems and determine their work rules. The drive for self-actualization in industry is more relevant today than formerly because of the widespread satisfaction of such lower-level drives as physical, safety, and social needs. Participative management also recognizes the group and its responsibility. The last point is decisive for the overall choice between the two organization forms.

Group Responsibility

The recognition of groups and their responsibilities is important for the following reasons among others:

1. The Hawthorne studies have shown that the average employee is not an "economic man" and that the wage amount, unless it denotes social status or falls below a minimum, is not the primary source of employee morale but that intrinsic job values are more important and that the feeling of belonging to a cohesive employee group vastly enhances those values.[15]

2. The importance of the informal group is also demonstrated by the fact that without informal groups in the factory the turnover of employees and their absenteeism are high.[16] Scientists believe that employees' tensions become unbearable in the absence of such groups.[17]

3. Through social facilitation the levels of morale spread—positively or negatively—within the group. A group's decision is more easily accepted than a supervisors' directive because of the accompanying social pressure; and groups are more effectively addressed as to a correction of behavior than are single individuals.[18]

4. Shared responsibility usually is more easily accepted and carried out than individual responsibility because of the diminished anxiety and increased mutual help.

5. Shared responsibility does not only represent sharing within the group but also sharing between the group and its supervisor. The permissive, democratic supervisor still has responsibility for the assigned tasks. His responsibility is rather augmented than curtailed. Besides being charged with leadership, counseling, and maintaining a supportive (positive) climate in the group, he still may be coresponsible for the timeliness, quality and/or quantity of the group's production. Such sharing of responsibility between a supervisor and his group has advantages:

a. If the group's behavior needs to change, responsibility for the change is shared between changer and changee. Correcting one's own behavior pattern is learning, and learning is improved if the learner feels responsible for it.[19]
b. In case of failure, the sharing of responsibility lessens the supervisor's frustration and risk of becoming rigid, aggressive or disinterested.
c. Not only the reaction to failure is lessened but also the fear of failure. Decrease of that fear increases the probability of the setting of realistic aspiration levels (goals); fear may produce aspiration levels that are either too high or too low.

Obviously, the opportunity for shared responsibility boosts the democratic organization and its utility for responsibility accounting. The question is whether such accounting is technically feasible there. The techniques in question refer to data collection, measurements, data evaluations, and decision making. To discuss them solely in the frame of the conventional business structure would be wasteful, because that organizational concept does not present sufficient support for responsibility accounting. The inclusion of modern organization views in the discussion permits its further pursuit.

TECHNIQUES

Data Collection

Responsibility accounting assumes control by a specific individual or work group over the activity to be reported on. However, specifying the point of control and of the corresponding data collection often is difficult. For example, the foreman usually has little power over costs. Ordinarily, he has no say at all about material and labor prices; on the assembly line, material quantity and labor volume too are put out of his grasp; and the responsibilities for quality control and equipment maintenance quite often are shared with other officials. Such diffusion of control impedes the fair administration of data collection. When sufficiency instead of exclusivity of influence on an activity is the criterion for accountability, the questions arise how such influence is measured and what degree is relevant. No general indications are available. Organization networks are too peculiar and complex.

Another difficulty is encountered in expansion projects. There the follow-up on project realization can be quite frustrating. The collection of progress data that can be compared with original plans and computations is often technically impossible.

Measurements

The difficulties with data collection are outdone by those arising with measurements. Any doubt about it is dispelled by another look at the lowest responsibility level, i.e., the first-line-supervisor in the hierarchical organization and the work group in the democratic structure.

Measuring a First-Line-Supervisor's Performance

The foreman's position has undergone a radical change in this century. Around 1900, his importance in the factory was undisputed. Since then, the introduction of scientific management and of the assembly line have restricted his functions to the assignment of men and machines in the factory, to the breaking-in of new employees, and to maintaining discipline and morale in his group. In fact, the foreman could be dispensed with commonly, if emergency decisions would not have to be made at times and if the human factor were not significant in the production process.

The task of caring for the human element in the factory is both important and difficult. It is important because primarily management is the management of people. The group leader is a key factor here; he is the official who is in immediate contact with the work force; his success may determine the long-run prosperity of the company.[20] The foreman's task is difficult because his leadership should be permissive instead of authoritarian and employee-oriented instead of production-oriented in order to advance workers' productivity by maintaining a democratic climate. The behavioral skills needed for such leadership are difficult to learn.

The first-line-supervisor must understand the dangers of frustration and of other emotional disturbances of his subordinates. He must be able to gain their confidence and liking, and make them feel free to unburden themselves in talks with him. Such confidence he may gain by taking care of the employees' interests, by informing them about developments in the plant, and by heeding their self-respect through involving them in decision making and leadership functions. He will maintain discipline mainly not by coercive power or by rewards, but by the demonstration of expertise and by the referent power flowing from the attractiveness of his personality.

The display of such social skills is not measurable in dollars and cents; in fact, what measures ideally apply to interpersonal skills is presently unknown. On the other hand, where the foreman still has functions measurable in money such as cost reduction, a single criterion may produce a false overall judgment. Besides, with cost control in particular there is the danger that the supervisor by stressing it exclusively may lose rapport with his workers; the latter then will turn on their union shop steward for support and leadership, and the proper spirit in the factory will be difficult to attain. There exists then the unfortunate burden of two conflicting goals; the short-run profitability obtainable through strict cost control, and the long-run profitability depending on the maintenance of wholesome attitudes in the work force.

Foremen sometimes avoid the dilemma by reporting half-truths; that certainly defeats the purpose of accounting. However, the alternative to dishonest measurements may be a situation where (1) an individual has to incriminate himself or his workers, although (2) he was not given the necessary control to prevent whatever he or his men are held responsible for now and although (3) he still has to maintain the confidence and morale of his work group. An accounting system creating such situations cannot be upheld.

Measuring Group Performance

Group performance measurements, too, have undesirable features or are difficult to accomplish. To expect a group to render adverse reports about itself is unrealistic. To measure shared-responsibility achievements in dollars and cents is questionable. Generally, ratings—based on several criteria like production quantity and quality, employees' dependability and loyalty—will be more adequate than cost and output figures alone, even when the latter are accompanied by explanations of variations. In an organization both material and non-material values are important, and a group's present achievement is not indicative of the future, if it was obtained by pressure under disregard of such non-material values as willingness and cooperation.[21] Any changes in those values make themselves felt sooner or later and affect productivity in the end. Present responsibility accounting, restricted as it is mainly to measurements of costs (or profits), thus has a good chance to be dysfunctional.

Data Evaluation

The dismal picture of measurements naturally is reflected in data evaluations. For example, standards applied to lower management's achievements should be accepted as fair by the employees; otherwise, the measures may be felt as threats and do more harm than good. Such standards sometimes are difficult to set. Standards for transportation expense are one case. Another is the cost of absenteeism and of the break-in of substitute help. That cost might not appear at all in a separate account and standard, although absenteeism may be due to top-management's actions and should not be charged then to foremen and their groups.

Furthermore, individual variances from standards at the lower levels may offset each other in cumulative reporting, when achievement reports are prepared for scrutiny by higher executives. The grading of the lower ranks' performance by top management then loses most of its value.

The valuation of higher level performance, in turn, generally cannot be properly based on a single criterion either. The real characteristics of managerial excellence—i.e., not only a manager's actual achievements but also the quality of his objectives and of his attempts to overcome obstacles—are best judged by rating them in such various aspects as realism, flexibility and farsightedness, if these can be measured. Yet, such multiple criteria may make decentralization hard to maintain.

If the evaluation of higher level performance is restricted indeed to one single aspect, periodic net profits or returns-on-investment are used. That too can cause problems. Profit centers may lack clear delineation, and revenues and their matching costs may partly originate in different departments. It would be illogical then not to assign profits to all departments involved. Transfer pricing has to be used, and a choice becomes necessary between the various transfers such as actual full cost, standard absorption or direct cost, standard cost plus normal profit, actual marginal cost, and market price. Whatever the choice is, the departmental or divisional managers concerned should share in it. However, disputes often end up in company headquarters, which may decide contrary to the wishes of some of the executives facing achievement evaluation. The resulting antagonisms and accompanying feuds can make the whole procedure self-defeating.

Decision Making—Influence of Evaluation Procedures

The shortcomings of responsibility accounting in the measurement and evaluation of management performance have a counterpart in the decision making especially of divisional executives. Return-on-investment (ROI) instead of net profit often is employed to judge their efficiency. However, the usefulness of the ROI largely depends on the type, size, and mix of operating assets and on the executive's power to determine these factors. Great care must be exercised in the admission of assets to the investment base, because the divisional manager —if he is able to influence the capital investment—may strive for a high ROI by manipulating the investment base and may make harmful decisions by doing so. For example, he may decide to operate with fully depreciated equipment instead of replacements in order to keep a small investment base or he may delay a necessary replacement in order to avoid showing a loss on disposal of under-depreciated assets, when such assets are included in the base at net book value computed by unit depreciation. On the other hand, if equipment is included in the investment base at gross book value and depreciated at a composite rate, the divisional executive might replace some assets prematurely with more efficient ones in the opinion that this action will be judged by the ratio of cost savings over the total plant's gross-book-value increase (and not by the much lesser ratio of savings to the new acquisition's cost). The divisional manager may also abstain from keeping an adequate inventory or from procuring it in economic lot sizes—incurring thereby avoidable high set-up and stock-out costs—in order to obtain a certain ROI, whenever current assets fully enter the investment base. How to preserve in such situations goal congruence between the evaluating company and its executives is by and large an unsettled question.

Decision Making—Influence of Feedback Procedures

Another problem results from the effect of the feedback of evaluations on the decision making especially of middle and lower management and of work groups.

Some authors believe that informing employees of their deficiencies may create insecurity in them and make matters worse.[22] Other researchers, on the contrary, state that the learning process of employees can be speeded up by the knowledge of performance results and that such information is especially effective if it is imparted in dollars and cents. A similar opinion argues that the feedback of a group's success is very important and that achievers regard information about their accomplishments highly. Apparently, the value of the feedback function in responsibility accounting can be argued. The usefulness of the knowledge of one's own performance has not been proven. In some cases, a high sense of responsibility may be accompanied by intolerable feelings of frustration if failure is disclosed.

The statement, therefore, that "nothing will be accomplished unless subordinates are told of their shortcomings"[23] does little to settle the question. Providing subordinates with that knowledge does not insure that they are going to use it for the right decisions.[24] Stedry believes that the reaction of a department head to a discrepancy between aspired and actual achievements varies and depends on the value where discouragement starts (discouragement point) and on another value where failure is admitted (failure point).[25] Any firm is bound to have personnel with different discouragement and failure points and, therefore, with different reactions to similar disclosures. Thus, the effects of the feedback are difficult to predict. It may stimulate morale or destroy it. Above all, it may cause decisions incompatible with company goals. For example, the feedback of unfavorable cost figures to a foreman in possession of some cost control may result in a lowering of quality, or in cost savings at the expense of some other department, or in undue pressure on subordinate employees.

Decision Making—Influence of Accounting Procedures

A further setback for proper decision making arises from the practice of some companies to include non-controllable costs in a manager's responsibility report.

Divisional executives, for example, are sometimes charged with a share of corporate headquarter's research and development costs in order to evoke their interest in those undertakings; and lower level managers at times are charged with a share of common costs in order to broaden their outlook beyond the affairs of their own department.

Absorption costing in responsibility accounting has been defended with the reasoning that all segments contribute to the overall profits of the company, should share in the overall costs, and should be made conscious of that aspect. Ferrara, for example, believes that lower-level responsibility reports should use standard absorption costs.[26] However, absorption costs are apt to cause confusion as well as bitterness, although the underlying attempt to extend a supervisor's horizon is worthy. Cost allocations are seldom understood by foremen;[27] large allocations may make controllable costs appear negligible; and the fairness of allocations may be hard to prove. Sales managers, for example, often protest cost assignments that allegedly prevent them from meeting competition.[28]

Similar difficulties can result from the tie-in of responsibility accounting with budgeting. The responsibility budget frequently is not only considered a whip by employees, and its preparation is not only felt as a burden by the supervisors participating in the formulation; the budget also may cause wrong decisions. A manager may be tempted to slow down production or to neglect the cutting of expenses in order not to have his load increased in future.

CONCLUSION

The picture presented here of the theory and practice of responsibility accounting perhaps appears too grim. Admittedly, this accounting system has attractive features that explain its being favored in the accounting world. Though Freudians do not esteem it, the concept of responsibility has rational appeal; it is part of the accounting profession's own ethics. Moreover, the assignment of responsibility is a management tool thoroughly familiar to accountants and is, indeed, one of their touchstones of internal control. Finally, responsibility accounting in the overall is as systematic as can be expected in present accountancy. However, all that does not obliterate responsibility accounting's defects:

1. Its theory is presently tied to the conventional view of business organizations, and erroneously takes the existence of perfectly structured hierarchies for granted. The same theory imputes responsibilities to managers as isolated individuals, whereas few employees can function apart from their peers and environment, and nobody should be held responsible for what he cannot do. The importance and responsibilities of the groups representing the informal organization within the firm are ignored.

2. On the other hand, the techniques needed for responsibility accounting within a democratic business organization are not yet complete. In fact, present responsibility accounting fails oftentimes because of its short-comings in the techniques of data collection, measurements and evaluations, and because of its propensity to induce wrong decisions.
3. Accordingly, both logic and fairness often are wanting. First-line super-visors are a striking example; they usually have responsibility without com-mensurate authority.

Not surprisingly, top management frequently dislikes responsibility account-ing and finds distasteful the (disciplinary) decisions called for by it.[29] The CPA, too, should approach it with a critical mind in each case; it likely can cause behaviorally disastrous and economically destructive results. Applying it in absolute unawareness of such dangers is surely unprofessional. Using it without probing the hazards or despite admitting their unpredictability is not taking a risk but is sheer irresponsibility. Yet, to be acceptable, accounting must not only be rational and systematic but also by all means be responsible and sound.

REFERENCES

1. Heckert, Brooks J. and Kerrigan, Harry D., *Accounting Systems—Design and Installation* (New York: The Ronald Press Company, 3rd ed., 1967), p. 406; cf. Beyer, Robert, *Profitability Accounting* (New York: The Ronald Press Company, 1963), p. 73.

2. American Accounting Association (AAA), Committee on Cost Concepts and Standards, "Tentative Statement of Cost Concepts Underlying Reports for Management Purposes," *The Accounting Review*, Vol. XXXI (July, 1956), p. 189.

3. Anthony, Robert N., Characteristics of Management Control Systems, in *Management Control Systems*, Anthony, Robert N., Dearden, John, and Vancil, Richard F. Ed. (Homewood, Ill.: Richard D. Irwin Inc., 1965), pp. 2 ff.

4. Anthony, Robert N., *Management Accounting*, 3rd ed. (Homewood, Ill.: Richard D. Irwin, Inc., 1964), p. 362.

5. Horngren, Charles T., "Choosing Accounting Practices for Reporting to Management," *National Association of Accountants (NAA) Bulletin* (September, 1962), p. 7.

6. Benston, George J., "The Role of the Firm's Accounting System for Motivation," *The Accounting Review*, Vol. XXXVIII (April, 1963), p. 348.

7. Argyris, Chris., *Interpersonal Competence and Organizational Effectiveness* (Homewood, Ill.: The Dorsey Press and Richard D. Irwin, Inc., 1962), p. 3.

8.   Bass, Bernard M., *Organizational Psychology* (Boston: Allyn and Bacon, Inc., 1965), p. 237.

9.   McGregor, Douglas, *The Human Side of Enterprise* (New York: McGraw Hill, 1960).

10. Maier, Norman R. F., *Psychology in Industry* (Boston: Houghton Mifflin Company, 3rd ed., 1965), p. 175.

11. Argyris, Chris., *Integrating the Individual and the Organization* (New York: John Wiley and Sons, 1964), p. 185.

12. Likert, Rensis, *New Patterns of Management* (New York: McGraw Hill, 1961), p. 71.

13. Patten, Thomas H., Jr., *The Foreman: Forgotten Man of Management* (American Management Association, 1968), pp. 132 ff.

14. Gooding, Judson, "It Pays to Wake Up the Blue-Collar Worker," *Fortune,* Vol. LXXXII (September 1970), pp. 158 ff.

15. Viteles, Morris S., *Motivation and Morale in Industry* (New York: W. W. Norton and Co., Inc., 1953), p. 205; Roethlisberger, F. J. and Dickson, William J., *Management and the Worker, An Account of a Research Program Conducted by Western Electric Company,* Hawthorne Works, Chicago (Cambridge, Mass.: Harvard University Press, 1964), p. 588.

16. Mayo, Elton, *The Social Problems of an Industrial Civilization* (Andover, Mass.: Andover Press, 1945), p. 111.

17. Argyris, Chris., *Personality and Organization, the Conflict between System and the Individual* (New York: Harper and Bros., 1957), p. 230.

18. Leavitt, Harold J., Applied Organizational Change in Industry: Structural, Technological and Humanistic Approaches, in *Handbook of Organizations,* March, James G. Ed., (Chicago: Rand McNally Company, 1965) ch. 27, p. 1164; Maier, *op. cit.,* p. 160.

19. Leavitt, Harold J., *Managerial Psychology: An Introduction to Individuals, Pairs, and Groups in Organizations* (Chicago: University of Chicago Press, 2nd ed., 1964), p. 162.

20. Rowland, Kendrith M. and Scott, William E., "Psychological Attributes of Effective Leadership in a Formal Organization," *Personnel Psychology* (1968), p. 375; Walker, C. R., Guest, R. H., and Turner, A. N., *The Foreman on the Assembly Line* (Cambridge: Harvard University Press, 1956), p. 11.

21. Stogdill, Ralph M., *Individual Behavior and Group Achievement* (New York: Oxford University Press, 1959), p. 203.

22. Maier, *op. cit.,* p. 254; Chapanis, Alphonse, "Knowledge of Performance as an Incentive in Repetitive, Monotonous Tasks," *Journal of Applied Psychology,* Vol. 48, No. 4 (1964), pp. 263–267.

23. Huttner, Ludwig and O'Malley, Thomas R., "Let Them Know," *Personnel Psychology* (1962), p. 186.

24. Locke, Edwin A., "Motivational Effects of Knowledge of Results: Knowledge or Goal Setting," *Journal of Applied Psychology,* Vol. 51, No. 4 (1967), pp. 324–29.

25. Stedry, Andrew, *Budget Control and Cost Behavior* (Englewood Cliffs, N. J.: Prentice-Hall, Inc., 1960), pp. 24 ff.

26. Ferrara, William L., "Responsibility Accounting vs. Direct Costing—Is There a Conflict?" *Management Accounting,* Vol. XLVIII, No. 10 (June, 1967), p. 48.

27. Kellog, Martin N., "Fundamentals of Responsibility Accounting," *NAA Bulletin* (April, 1962), p. 15.

28. NAA, Research Report No. 37, *Current Applications of Direct Costing* (January, 1961), p. 52.

29. Holmes, Robert W., "Executive Views Responsibility Reporting," *Financial Executive,* Vol. 36 (August, 1968), p. 40.

The Relevance of
Probability Statistics
to Accounting
Variance Control

Robert W. Koehler

It is generally agreed that the primary objective of the widely used standard cost accounting systems is to indicate areas where some follow-up is desirable. To accomplish this objective great effort is typically expended in developing realistic standards. Periodically, detailed procedures are employed to report actual performance so that the variances can be determined. Often these variances are then classified by source into one of the following components: materials price, materials usage, labor rate, labor efficiency, fixed overhead budget, volume, and variable overhead efficiency.[1]

After all this precision, it seems ironic that decisions relative to which variances to investigate are made without an organized framework for evaluating the relevant factors pertaining to the decision. The variances are termed significant if they exceed some subjectively determined dollar amount or percentage of the standard. Such a procedure does not give enough attention to the concepts of chance and probability which are inherent in performance standards.

Over the last 15 years utilization of statistical tools to analyze the significance of variances has been recommended in several books[2] and numerous articles. These recommendations have gone unheeded. In some general inquiry from some prominent corporations I was unable to find a single use of statistical procedures for variance control.

From this almost total lack of response, it would appear that these writings either contained some fundamental fallacies or that accountants are so uninformed about statistical procedures that they have been unable to implement

SOURCE: Reprinted by permission of *Management Accounting* (October, 1968), pp. 35–41. Copyright 1968 by the National Association of Accountants, New York, N.Y.

them. While some have questioned the applicability of statistical procedures for accounting problems, no basic fallacies of statistical methods of variance control have been noted. In general, accountants are not as statistically sophisticated as they should be. This situation is, however, improving as more rigorous mathematics and statistics requirements are being introduced into college accounting curricula. Currently there are many accountants equipped to instigate such procedures. The fact that this is not being done implies that the reasons for applying statistical procedures to variance control are not sufficiently compelling. As a result, the statistical talents of the accountants are being utilized in other areas.

One difficulty in developing a concept for variance control hinges on the fact that accountants have not recognized a conceptual distinction between a significant and an insignificant variance.

THE NOTION OF CHANCE

The literature in the field of quality control[3] recognizes that performance varies due to a host of unexplainable reasons which are identified as chance. In other words, there is an omnipresent non-uniformity which cannot be eliminated. This non-uniformity is a natural phenomenon—even plants or animals experimentally developed under the same conditions are not identical. Likewise, tasks performed by the same worker under the same conditions are not identical. The reasons for such variation are unknown to man and have been identified by quality control engineers and statisticians as chance. Formally, chance is defined as "the absence of any known reason why an event should turn out one way rather than another."[4]

This concept of chance can be visualized by assuming that you record the number of seconds it takes you to shave for some period of time—say three months. You will soon discover that your performance varies. On some days you may explain that the blade in the razor was dull. Hence, you required more time than normal. On other days, cold water may cause your performance to vary. Occasionally, you may cut yourself and require extra time to scar the cut. The dull blade, cold water, and cut are known as assignable causes. If these are eliminated from your record, you would still find some variability in the number of seconds it takes you to shave. This is referred to as chance variability; its causes cannot be identified.

CHANCE IN ACCOUNTING VARIANCE

At this point, the reader may argue "Chance does not affect all variance classifications." Such an argument is quite convincing in that chance would not usually affect the materials price of labor rate variances and neither would it normally affect many components of the fixed overhead budget variance. There are, however, some exceptions to these generalizations. Chance may affect the materials price variance in situations where materials prices adjust rapidly to reflect the changing conditions of supply and demand. The labor rate variance may be affected in cases where workers with only slightly different wage rates perform a number of different functions depending upon a current need. The worker performing a given task at a given time depends upon the aggregate of other current needs. These needs at a given time may be influenced by chance. The wage rate for the task will depend upon the worker performing it. Therefore, the wage rate and corresponding rate variance is influenced by chance.

Chance may also affect the labor rate variance in firms which normally use some overtime. Since workers get a premium for overtime, the average wage rate depends upon the actual amount of overtime used and also upon the tasks (with their corresponding worker classifications) which are to be performed during overtime.

These are just a few examples; other situations may also introduce the chance concept. Whether chance is relevant must be decided on an individual basis. However, chance will not affect the materials price variance for materials which involve administered prices. Likewise for companies which have rigid job classifications with a specific wage rate for each classification and which do not normally use overtime, chance would not appear to affect the actual results for labor rates. In the short run, it may occasionally be wise to use a worker with a different job classification than that established for a job or to use overtime; but if these situations are not usual, they should be explained as the reason for the rate variance.

In general, chance is expected to cause variation in labor and overhead efficiency, material usage and overhead volume variances. It also causes variation in certain non-manufacturing costs such as clerical efficiency. There is a fundamental difference between these variance classifications and the ones discussed in the preceding paragraphs. Efficiency cannot be predetermined like a wage rate, the price of material, the amount of depreciation, or the property taxes. The human element with its inherent non-uniformity enters the picture for all variance classifications which involve efficiency of one kind or another. After all known causes are eliminated, the above items would vary for reasons which cannot be explained. To reiterate, chance variation is attributed to an inherent non-uniformity which also accounts for differences in the sizes of plants and animals developed under the same conditions.

At this point, it is important for the reader to understand the difference that the recognition of chance makes to variance control. We expect actual results to equal standard only for variance classifications which are not influenced by chance. The materials price and labor rate variances, along with many components of the overhead budget variance, will frequently be included in this group. For these we would often want to know the reason for any deviation. Only for these is the typical accounting definition of control ("The method and manner by which a person, or an organization, operation, or other activity is conformed to a desired plan of action"[5]) a realistic explanation of the control process.

For variance classifications which are influenced by chance, we do not expect the actual results to equal standard. Some variances are expected to occur even when no assignable causes are present. These chance variances should fall within predictable patterns so that variances not falling within the pattern could be identified as pertaining to an assignable cause giving rise to further inquiry.

It is suggested here that accountants give formal recognition to the chance concept in their definition of control. As a noun, control or variance control could then be defined as Koehler defined statistical quality control: "the state of equilibrium reached when deviations from a given norm (such as the process average) are only random in character and without assignable cause."[6] It is informative to note that Koehler does not recognize the relevance of chance or random concepts in his definition of control[7] but he does include them in his definition of statistical quality control.

The verb control would then be defined as consisting of those procedures designed to maintain the results within limits due to chance. Only those variances outside the limits due to chance would have to be subjected to analysis and investigation. Analysis and investigation of variances due to chance would obviously be wasteful.

LOGIC BEHIND STATISTICAL APPLICATIONS

With the establishment of this conceptual base, it would now seem like a fairly simple procedure to observe actual performance under established conditions for the purpose of determining the limits within which chance is operative. The difficulty is that the distribution of values due to chance overlaps the distribution of values due to assignable causes. That is, chance is also operative when assignable causes are present.

Overlapping distributions can be visualized by referring again to the shaving analogy. Assume that it takes you an average of five minutes to shave when only chance causes are present. Suppose, however, that it takes you an average of six minutes to shave with cold water. When you look at the distributions upon which these averages are based, you find that 95 percent of the time it takes you four to six minutes to shave when no assignable causes are present (i.e., only chance is present) and five to seven minutes to shave with cold water (an assignable cause plus chance). Thus you cannot tell whether chance alone or chance and cold water are present simply by looking at a performance value between five and six minutes. The dilemma remains: where should the control limits be placed?

Recognition of chance factors provides the clue for confronting this problem and for utilizing more objective criteria for significance determination. Since probability statistics is an area concerned with procedures for evaluating the patterns of chance influences, its use is a logical extension from the recognition that chance factors distinguish between significant and insignificant variances.

Thus, statistical applications to variance control are not just some tools that are pulled out of the air and applied to satisfy someone's academic fancy. There is a logical and compelling reason for their use. Stated succinctly, chance affects some variance classifications; probability statistics evaluates patterns of chance occurrences; therefore, probability statistics is useful to analyze those variances affected by chance.

Some may think that the relationships between chance and variances on one hand and between chance and statistics on the other are so obvious as to be unworthy of mention. Yet it is my belief that failure to recognize these relationships has caused accountants to overlook or ignore statistical applications to variance control. Once the importance of these applications is established, experimentation with various statistical models will almost certainly enhance their usefulness.

PROBLEM OF OVERLAPPING DISTRIBUTIONS

The shaving analogy was used above to illustrate how the distribution of values due to chance overlaps the distribution of values due to assignable causes. This phenomenon results in the dilemma of where to place the control limits and establishes the need for statistical techniques.

To elaborate further upon this, I will return again to the shaving analogy. This example is independent of the last one. To facilitate the use of greater detail, the unit of measurement will be seconds rather than minutes.

TABLE 1.   Probability Distribution of Chance Performances

Seconds			Probability
At least 270	but less than	280	.05
280		290	.10
290		300	.15
300		310	.40
310		320	.15
320		330	.10
330		340	.05
			1.00

Suppose that Table 1 represents the probability distribution of the number of seconds it takes you to shave when only chance is operating.

The mean of this frequency distribution is 305 seconds, as calculated by the formula ΣXoP, where Xo = each respective class mark and P = the corresponding probability for each class. The calculation is illustrated below:

Xo	P	XoP
275	.05	13.75
285	.10	28.50
295	.15	44.25
305	.40	122.00
315	.15	47.25
325	.10	32.50
335	.05	16.75
		305.00

Notice that you have been able to complete the task in as few as 270 seconds without a permanent increase in your speed. On the other hand, it has taken you as long as 340 seconds without discerning an unfavorable assignable cause. This variation is attributed to chance.

TABLE 2.   Probability Distribution of Cold Water Performances

Seconds		Probability
At least 290 but less than 300		.02
300 300		.10
310 310		.20
320 320		.35
330 330		.20
340 340		.10
350 350		.03
		1.00

Now suppose that Table 2 represents the number of seconds it takes you to shave with cold water. The mean time is now 325 seconds. This table shows that chance factors also prevail when an assignable cause (cold water) is operative. That is, performance also varies for cold water performances. The task has been completed in as few as 290 seconds; but it has, on occasion, taken as long as 360 seconds. The difference between the two distributions is that performance varies about a mean of 305 when only chance is operative, whereas it varies about a mean of 325 when cold water in addition to chance affects performance.

A comparison of Tables 1 and 2 shows an overlap between values 290 and 340. Only for results between 270 and 290 is there assurance that only chance has affected the variation. Similarly, it is clear that factors other than chance alone are attributed only to results higher than 340 seconds.

It is not possible, however, to identify the cause from mere knowledge of the number of seconds in the range from 290 to 340. Exhibit 1 illustrates these overlapping populations diagrammatically. The solid curve shows the distribution of chance performances alone and the dotted one shows the cold water and chance distribution.

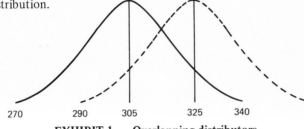

270   290   305   325   340

EXHIBIT 1.   Overlapping distributors

In the range from 290 to 340, the cause can be determined only by an investigation. In industrial situations investigations for each occurrence in this interval would be too costly. Hence, decisions to investigate are made under uncertainty. These decisions introduce the possibility of two different kinds of error.

First, for any upper control limit less than 340 there is the risk of investigating a chance performance. These unwarranted investigations are known as Type I errors. Assume that the upper control limit is set at 330. Now all performances over 330 will be investigated. Since 5 percent of the chance performances are over 330 (shown on Table 1), the probability of committing a Type I error is .05.

The other kind of statistical error involves failure to investigate when an assignable cause is present. This is identified as a Type II error. With an upper control limit of 330, the probability of committing a Type II error is .67.[8] (Table 2 shows that 67 percent of the cold water performances have values less than 330.)

After a cursory glance, an accountant might observe that the probability of committing a Type I error could be reduced to zero by increasing the upper control limit to 340. The difficulty is that this would raise the probability of committing a Type II error to .87. It is always true that the probability of committing a Type II error is increased if the probability of committing a Type I error is reduced by altering the control limits. Likewise, the converse is true. The problem to be resolved involves striking the best balance between commiting these two types of error.

COMPARISON OF CONVENTIONAL AND STATISTICAL APPLICATIONS

An example will serve to contrast a statistical approach with the approach to variance control conventionally used by accountants. Bower Company manufactures classroom tables for colleges and universities. One of the standard sizes requires a standard time of 40 minutes for one man to assemble. When a worker acquires the skill to perform the task in an average time of 35 minutes, he is given a raise and moved to a more complex assembly job. If a worker takes significantly longer than 40 minutes, an investigation is undertaken to determine the difficulty.

Initially, then, we can think in terms of three distinct populations. The values of individual performances can come from a population of values attributed to standard times, improved times, or unfavorable significant times. As the foreman receives the results of individual performances, he has the task of deciding which population each performance comes from and taking or recommending action accordingly. The worker may also be charged to make a decision relative to these populations and report to his foreman performance which does not fall into the standard population.

The accountant is in a position to be helpful in this aspect of control by providing guidelines in the form of control limits for the worker and his foreman.

Now let us see what kinds of guidelines might result from applying conventional and statistical control methods. As previously indicated, accountants commonly define control as "The method and manner by which a person, or an organization, operation, or other activity is *conformed* to a desired plan of action."[9] Strict adherence to this definition would require that all performances less than 40 minutes be classified as coming from the improvement population and that all performances over 40 minutes be identified as unfavorably significant. In practice, however, some variation from standard is allowed before a performance is classified as out of line and an investigation is undertaken. For this reason, this definition of control is not operationally meaningful. It does not explain the application of the control process.

The amount of variation allowed in practice is subjectively determined. What factors the analyst considers have not been set forth in the literature. In talking with cost accountants, I have been unable to identify any criteria they apply when they determine significance. From a methodological standpoint, they most frequently seem to identify a variance in excess of 10 percent of standard as significant although 5 or 7 percent may also be used as cut-off points.

For our example, let us assume that the 10 percent cut-off point is used. Therefore, performance is followed up if a worker completes his task in less than 36 minutes or if he takes longer than 44 minutes (40 ± 10% of 40).

Statistical procedures with various degrees of sophistication may also be used with various control limits resulting. The simplest of these procedures just makes use of the chance concept. Two ingredients are necessary. A probability distribution of chance performances must be constructed and the analyst must specify the probability that he is willing to run of incurring a Type I error. The probability distribution would be prepared from performance observation with intuition used to cast out performances resulting from non-chance causes. At the margin some investigations may be undertaken to substantiate intuition. Assume that the distribution shown in Table 3 . . . results.

TABLE 3.   Chance Probability Distribution of Times Taken to Assemble a Certain Line of Tables

Minutes		Probability
At least 32 but less than 33		.01
33	34	.04
34	35	.05
35	36	.06
36	38	.14
38	40	.20
40	42	.20
42	44	.14
44	45	.06
45	46	.05
46	47	.04
47	48	.01
		1.00

Now the analyst chooses a control limit which corresponds to the probability that he is willing to risk committing a Type I error. Probabilities between .01 and .05 are most commonly designated. A .05 probability would result in control limits of 34 and 46, whereas 33 and 47 would be the control limits with a .01 probability. The reasoning behind this is that 5 percent of the chance performances are completed in less than 34 minutes and 5 percent take longer than 46 minutes (See Table 3).

Given that a performance is completed in 34 minutes, 5 percent of the time an investigation would fail to reveal an assignable cause because only chance would be affecting performance. Thus, the probability of committing a Type I error (making an unwarranted investigation) is .05.[10] The same logic can be used to substantiate 46 as an upper control limit associated with a .05 probability of committing a Type I error and also to verify 33 and 47 as control limits for the .01 probability of committing a Type I error.

This procedure of selecting control limits is called statistical because it involves explicit consideration of chance factors. It is very elementary, however, because the probability of committing a Type I error is arbitrarily chosen. Some accountants have associated this with the control chart because quality control engineers frequently portray on such a chart performance results along with control limits determined in this simple manner.

The control chart is simply a visual representation of results. An example is shown in Exhibit 2. Performances which fall outside of the control limits would signal the need for a follow-up.

Let us assume that the analyst designates a .05 probability of committing a Type I error so that the control limits are 34 and 46. These contrast with the control limits of 36 and 44 that would result from the application of the accountant's conventional 10 percent cutoff point. One may now ask, "Is this difference between 34 and 36 and between 44 and 46 really enough to affect control?" Well, reference to Table 3 indicates that 16 percent of the chance performances are completed in less than 36 minutes and another 16 percent have taken longer than 44 minutes. This means that 32 percent of all chance performances would be investigated under the conventional 10 percent rule in contrast with 10 percent investigated under the statistical method (with the .05 level of significance considering both tails). Which method is superior depends upon:

1. How often an assignable cause would be detected under the accountant's conventional approach (with tighter control limits in this case) that would not be detected until later under the statistical approach.[11]
2. How costly the delay in detection of an assignable cause is.
3. How much more costly the additional investigations under the accountant's conventional approach would be.[12]

These factors were considered in a simulated model designed to test variations of several statistical approaches against the accountant's conventional approach.[13] The approaches were tested under several different conditions. In seven out of eight situations, each statistical approach was more economical than the conventional approach.[14] In the other situation, only one of the six

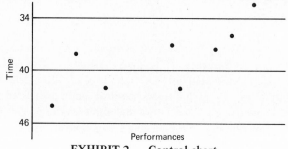

EXHIBIT 2.   Control chart

statistical approaches yielded poorer control than the accountant's conventional approach. By far the most significant conclusion of this study is that the accountant's conventional method produced the poorest control results.

DEFICIENCIES OF FOREGOING STATISTICAL APPLICATION

The foregoing statistical procedure is the one most frequently used by those considering the use of statistics for variance control. The reader will recall that the procedure is statistical because it considers the probability distribution of chance performances. This distribution enables the analyst to select the probability of committing a Type I error that he is willing to risk. This particular procedure appears to be incomplete because it does not consider the probability of committing a Type II error. Moreover, it does not consider relevant economic factors such as the cost of making an investigation or losses that would result from delays in detection of an assignable cause.

The reasons for these omissions seem clear even though they are not generally identified. General acceptance of statistical procedures for variance control can be gained more quickly by recommending simple procedures that can be easily applied. This simple procedure has been used for quality control for at least 20 years. From all indications it has provided satisfactory results and has certainly been more effective than arbitrary intuition. There is little evidence to suggest that more advanced techniques have been widely adopted for quality control.[15]

A further deterrent to the use of more sophisticated procedures is that there is no clear-cut way of applying them. For example, a Type II error is unique to some *particular* alternative non-chance population[16] with a specified distribution and mean. Certainly there are difficulties inherent in estimating such distributions.

In addition to this problem, there are always *several* alternatives to a chance population. That is, assignable causes may result from improvement, faulty equipment, faulty materials, illness, laziness, poor attitude, etc. Each of these populations has a separate distribution and each has a separate probability of committing a Type II error in conjunction with the specified probability of committing a Type I error. The amount of work is now substantially increased because estimates of the distributions associated with *each* assignable cause must now be made. But what distribution do we use in determining the probability of committing a Type II error? It would be possible to use the one associated with the assignable cause considered most likely to occur or to use the one most feared. One might also use an average. Should it be a simple average or a weighted average? Progress on these problems will require additional research.[17]

Difficulties also arise in estimating the cost of an investigation and the losses that would result from delays in detection of an assignable cause. For example, the cost of an investigation will vary depending upon the cause of the variance. Some assignable causes will be detected before others, depending upon the ordering of the steps in the investigative procedure. If only chance is present, the cost is higher than it would be for an assignable cause because the investigation must eliminate all other causes before it can be known that a Type I error has been made. Considering this, which estimate of costs should be used to incorporate the cost of an investigation into the model? Here again, additional study is needed.

In summary, more advanced statistical procedures can accommodate estimates of the:

1. Probability of committing a Type I error.
2. Probability of committing a Type II error.
3. Cost of an investigation.
4. Cost of delay in detection of an assignable cause.

It is even possible to conceive of using such additional factors as:

1. The prior probability that a given assignable cause is present.
2. The probability that a given variance is associated with a given assignable cause.

After the estimated value for these factors are obtained, there is the additional problem of developing a model capable of organizing the factors to give the desired control limits. Of the several possible models one may yield more effective control limits in one case while another model may be better for another situation.

THE WAY TOWARD PROGRESS

The fact that the above factors all require estimation and that they are not conclusive should not mitigate against their use in the statistical techniques. Most information[18] obtained for decision-making is estimated. We concentrate on determining what information is relevant and on how to best estimate this information. We certainly do not eliminate techniques just because they involve the use of estimates. If we did, we would be left with very few tools or perhaps with no field of accounting.

Considerable thought, much research, some experimentation, and reports of experiences will be needed to select the best combination of factors to improve on the estimates, and to develop the best model. Better control limits are bound to result by increasing the number of factors to be incorporated into the model, but one must always determine whether the utility of this increased information is worth its cost of acquirement. Now is the time to begin researching, experimenting and reporting on the use of more advanced statistical procedures. Those firms which do not have the necessary expertise to develop and experiment with the more advanced techniques can use the simple statistical application that was outlined above.

AVAILABILITY OF QUALIFIED ACCOUNTANTS

In a telephone conversation on July 21, 1967, Mr. Justin Davidson[19] estimated that 25 percent of the companies that employ standard cost accounting have internal talent capable of working with statistical models. The remainder would need outside help. Mr. Davidson thinks that all of the big eight Certified Public Accounting firms have staff skilled in statistical applications. Some of the smaller national firms also have personnel proficient in this field.

There is a growing awareness in the business community of the advantages of statistical and mathematical applications. Accordingly, at the college level, business curricula are requiring heavier emphasis in these areas. At the postgraduate level, there have been an increasing number of mathematics and statistics seminars to better acquaint professional people with the advantages of applications in these areas. There are, then, at least a sufficient number of personnel available to begin establishing systems for statistical variance control and others are being educated for such work.

RECOMMENDATIONS

It is, therefore, recommended that statistical control limits be established at the performance level. Perhaps it would be wise to begin with a few of the more important operations. If the savings from more effective control readily compensate for the set-up costs as Mr. Davidson and this writer feel they will, these procedures would logically be extended to include more operations.

CONCLUSIONS

The purpose of this paper has been to set forth the compelling reason for using statistical applications for accounting variance control. This reason emanates from the fact that chance factors cause variation in labor and overhead efficiency, material usage, volume, and in some non-manufacturing expenses. Since probability statistics evaluates patterns of chance occurrences, its use in variance control is logical. A simulation model referred to in this paper indicated that statistical techniques also yield more economical and effective control.

One simple statistical application was outlined. The use of more advanced applications poses a host of problems which should be resolved through additional research and experimentation.

BIBLIOGRAPHY OF BOOKS INCLUDING STATISTICAL APPLICATIONS TO ACCOUNTING VARIANCE CONTROL

1. Harold Bierman, Jr., Lawrence E. Fouraker, Robert K. Jaedicke, *Quantitative Analysis for Business Decision,* Richard D. Irwin, Inc., Homewood, Ill., 1961, pp. 108-152.
2. Harold Bierman, Jr., *Topics in Cost Accounting and Decisions,* McGraw-Hill Book Company, Inc., New York, 1963, pp. 15-23.
3. Stanley B. Henrici, *Standard Costs for Manufacturing,* McGraw-Hill Book Company, Inc., New York, 1960, pp. 262-623.
4. Charles T. Horngren, *Cost Accounting A Managerial Emphasis.* Prentice-Hall, Inc., Englewood Cliffs, N. J., 1962, pp. 748-749.
5. Robert M. Trueblood, and R. M. Cyert, *Sampling Techniques in Accounting,* Prentice-Hall, Inc., Englewood Cliffs, N. J., 1957, pp. 138-147.
6. Lawrence L. Vance, John Neter, *Statistical Sampling for Auditors and Accountants,* John Wiley and Sons, Inc., New York, 1956. The statistical approach in this book was covered in connection with analysis of deviations from clerical work standards in Chapter viii.

FOOTNOTES

1. Different breakdowns or further refinements may be used.
2. See the Bibliography at the end of this article.
3. See for example, Frank M. Gryna, Jr., Chapter 13, *Quality Control Handbook,* Ed., J. M. Juran, McGraw-Hill Book Company, Inc., New York, 1962. Also, W. A. Shewhart, Chapter 1, *Economic Control of Manufactured Product,* D. Van Nostrand and Company, Inc., New York, 1931.
4. C. L. Barnhart, Ed., *The American College Dictionary,* Random House, New York, 1960, p. 200.
5. E. L. Kohler, *A Dictionary for Accountants,* third edition, Prentice-Hall, Inc., Englewood Cliffs, New Jersey, 1963, p. 127. [Emphasis Mine.]
6. *Ibid.,* p. 127.
7. *Ibid.,* p. 127.
8. This probability assumes, of course, that cold water is the only other alternative to chance. The probability of committing a Type II error is conventionally calculated for a specified mean (325 in this case) other than the standard. Complications would arise in calculating this probability if we wanted to consider the probability distributions of more than one assignable cause. In such an example I have used an averaging procedure for the computation. This procedure is not difficult; but since it is not central to the intent of this paper, it is not illustrated here.

9. Kohler, p. 127. [Emphasis Mine.]

10. This discussion involves separate consideration of each half of the distribution. That is, if a certain performance takes 34 minutes, concern is whether or not improvement has occurred—not whether an unfavorable assignable cause has occurred. Similarly, when a value of 46 occurs, concern involves whether an unfavorable assignable cause is present and not whether inprovement occurs. Despite the fact that 10 percent of the chance values fall outside of the control limits of 34 and 46, (5 percent less than 34 plus 5 percent over 46), the probability of committing a Type I error may be stated at .05 if for a given variance concern rests with either unfavorable significance or favorable significance but not both. In statistical terminology, this is called a one-tailed test. If the overlap between favorable and unfavorable populations is so great that, with the occurrence of a given variance, concern is over both favorable and unfavorable significance a two-tailed test should be used. If a two-tailed test were used in conjunction with Table 3 the probability of a Type I error would be .10, corresponding to control limits 34 and 46.

11. In some cases the statistical approach could yield tighter control limits than the conventional approach. For these cases, the statistical approach would detect assignable causes earlier than the conventional approach.

12. For those circumstances in which the statistical approach yields tighter control limits, the statistical approach, not the accountant's approach, would produce greater investigation cost.

13. Robert W. Koehler, "An Evaluation of Conventional and Statistical Methods of Accounting Variance Control," (Unpublished Doctoral Thesis, Department of Accounting and Financial Administration, Michigan State University, 1967), Chapter Six.

14. *Ibid.*, p. 256.

15. This is the author's belief based upon reading articles in *Industrial Quality Control.*

16. The non-chance populations used in this manuscript were cold water in the shaving example and improvement in the assembly example.

17. One possibility was used in my Ph.D. dissertation, Robert W. Koehler, "An Evaluation of Conventional and Statistical Methods of Accounting Variance Control," (Unpublished Doctoral Thesis, Department of Accounting and Financial Administration, Michigan State University, 1967), Chapter Six.

18. Even reported periodic income is an inconclusive figure. Financial accounting theory is concerned with how to best measure or estimate periodic income. It is even concerned with criteria for income recognition. We are all familiar with the many acceptable alternatives.

19. Mr. Davidson is a partner with Touche, Ross, Bailey, and Smart. He has been active in applying statistical techniques to auditing and accounting problems.

Planning and Control Systems for Profit and Investment Centers

INTRODUCTION

It is clear from the discussion in the preceding chapters that a main objective of the planning and control process is to ensure that decisions and performance throughout the firm lead to maximal attainment of the firm's goals. The planning and control process at the lower levels is relatively simple. Labor and material standards for each task and each worker can be established with reasonable precision. If the worker's performance stays within these standards, it will be considered congruent with the firm's goals. However, as we move up the organizational hierarchy, the planning and control process ceases to be simple because the criteria for goal-congruent performance at the higher levels are difficult to define. In addition to hours and physical resources consumed, other dimensions of performance become relevant. Standards and budgets, if formulated, lack certitude because input/output relations are complex, incompletely specified, and span several time periods. The accomplishment of the firm's goals depends as much upon cooperation among departments as upon the internal efficiency of each department, and these two aspects might be mutually conflicting. Problems of this type are particularly predominant in the planning and control of decentralized divisions where the divisional management has considerable autonomy regarding investment and operations within the divisions.

The pronounced trend toward decentralized divisionalization in large companies in the last two decades has forged considerable interest in the criteria used for planning and control of divisional performance. Several alternatives are observed in practice and each has been the subject of much criticism.[1] Much work remains to be done at the theoretical level also. A complete discussion of the choice of criteria is beyond the scope of this book. The articles included in this section are therefore selected for the purpose of highlighting three major problem areas.

Ma, in *Project Appraisal in a Divisionalized Company,* seeks to answer the question, "How can firm-level financial objectives be translated into divisional-level planning criteria for the purpose of investment analysis and funds allocation?" In developing his proposed criterion of risk-differentiated divisional cost of capital, he borrows concepts from the financial theory of cost of capital and portfolio investment. Despite many useful insights developed in Ma's discussions, he notes that his proposals are at best tentative.

In *A New Way to Measure and Control Divisional Performance,* Clayden discusses the potential for adverse motivational consequences that could arise from improper criteria for divisional performance evaluation. The criterion he favors is the residual income concept, originally developed in the General Electric Company. Clayden notes certain deficiencies of even this criterion and suggests ways to eliminate some of them.

Both Ma's and Clayden's attempts represent a search for goal-congruent divisional-level criteria, in the former case for investment analysis and planning, and in the latter case for performance evaluation and control. It is interesting to make a combined analysis of these two articles since the criteria for planning and those for control must be also congruent with each other if each is to be congruent with the firm's goals.

In developing their arguments Ma and Clayden have ignored the problems caused by the interdependence among divisions, but practical situations are often characterized by an interdivisional flow of resources which compounds the problem of measuring and evaluating divisional performance. Dearden's article, *Interdivisional Pricing,* is noteworthy for its specific concern with the problems due to an interdivisional flow of resources. Adhering to the basic principle of goal congruence, Dearden discusses the approaches a firm might adopt to organize and value the interdivisional transfer of resources under varying market and internal considerations.

Admittedly, the articles in this section are to be seen as introductions to the problems and suggested solutions in the area of divisional planning and control. Hopefully, they provoke the serious student to pursue these issues further.

FOOTNOTE

1.   John J. Mauriel and Robert N. Anthony, "Misevaluation of Investment Center Performance," *Harvard Business Review*, XLIV (March-April, 1966) 98–105.

Project Appraisal in a Divisionalized Company
Ronald Ma*

There is a large, growing, and relatively sophisticated, body of writing on the capital budgeting problems of single companies which carry on one business.[1] Considerable work has also been done on the problems of companies whose operations are decentralized; in particular, analysis has centred on the thorny problems of transfer pricing and internal profit measurement. It is somewhat surprising, therefore, that so little attention appears to have been given to the special problems of capital budgeting in companies with two or more operating divisons.[2] It is proposed in this article to look at some of these problems, in particular those relating to project appraisal, and to suggest an approach towards their solution.

Many of the problems in project appraisal are the same for a divisionalized company as for the single company, but there are some distinguishing features. This article will be concerned with the relevant criteria to employ in appraising divisional projects; whether there should be a common return standard for all divisions based on the company's cost of capital or whether different divisional rates should be employed. The problems relating to a relatively small but distinctive group of projects, common service projects, are next examined. Some recommendations are then made on the construction of the master budget in a divisionalized company. It is seen that the resolution of the company's capital budgeting problems, namely the volume and source of funds to be raised in the current budget and their allocation between the divisions, is significantly influenced by the criteria adopted for accepting divisional projects.

SOURCE: Copyright 1969 by Sydney University Press. This paper is reprinted from *Abacus, A Journal of Accounting and Business Studies (*December, 1969), published by Sydney University Press, Australia and is reproduced by permission.

*I am indebted to Dr. G. D. Quirin for many of the ideas presented in this article. I am also grateful to Professors A. S. Carrington and R. L. Matthews, the late Mr. R. P. Brooker and my colleagues for their constructive criticism. The usual disclaimer applies.

THE OBJECTIVES OF DIVISIONALIZATION

The existence of several operating divisions within a company may be traced to a number of motivating factors, of which the two most fundamental are decentralization, as a means of attaining greater efficiency, and diversification, as a means of spreading risks.

The economic philosophy that lies behind the decentralization motive relates basically to the belief that a significant improvement in efficiency results from employing market-based prices in the internal transactions of the large company.[3] The most efficient economic system is one in which the marginal cost of the company's output is equal to its marginal revenue, which in a perfectly competitive market is given by the product's price. The process by which this desirable state is brought about is that of the market mechanism, that is, the free interplay of market demand and supply factors. These market forces may be visualized as an open sea and individual companies as islands. We know that all transactions that take place at the boundaries of an island and the sea are economically efficient transactions, but there is doubt concerning transactions in the interior. It is therefore proposed that to promote efficiency in the internal trade, inlets should be developed into the island, dividing it into sectors, to permit the same market forces that determine the volume and direction of intercompany trading to flow in and govern the interdivisional transactions as well.[4]

The primary object of decentralization is the improvement of efficiency and profitability and the evaluation of sectoral performance. A decentralized company may have production, marketing, and research and development divisions, all operating within the one industry. An entirely different situation is created where diversification is the major objective, and the company consequently has two or more divisions operating in different industries. The object in this case is the reduction of the overall riskiness of the company, and the issues raised are central to the capital budgeting function.

It may be desirable, at the outset, to distinguish between risk in its technical sense and uncertainty. Risk refers to the variability of outcomes of a certain event, where the probabilities can be statistically determined; the typical capital investment proposal contains uncertainty, which refers to varying degrees of confidence in the variability estimates.[5] Both future cash flows and their associated probabilities represent expectations held by management, and are therefore subjective estimates. For analytical purposes, the business uncertainty situation is treated as one of quasi-risk, and we shall employ the term risk in this paper to denote business uncertainty.[6]

The riskiness of an individual project can be defined as the variability of its earning stream. But there is a complex relationship between project risks and overall corporate risk.[7] Because of this relationship a company can seek to reduce its overall riskiness by adopting a diversification strategy. The case is succinctly put by Quirin.

When we combine any two operations, each of which generates income as a random variable, we get a single probability distribution of income in which the two separate probability distributions of the individual projects are merged. The expected value of the income for the resulting distribution will be the sum of the expected values of the original distributions. The coefficient of variation of the new distribution is unlikely to be any greater than that of the most variable of the original distributions (barring the case where the expected income of one is negative) and may well be substantially less, because fluctuations in the income from one project may be offset by fluctuations in the income of the other.[8]

Thus it is evident that the benefits to the company's risk structure from adopting a new project will depend not only on the quality of that project's income stream but also on whether it is independent of, or correlated in some way with, the income stream generated by existing projects. A sophisticated capital budgeting model, based on the principles enunciated by Markowitz,[9] that takes into account the interrelationships of project risks and their impact on corporate riskiness has been attempted.[10]

Divisionalization offers an alternative approach by which the beneficial effects of diversification on overall corporate riskiness are not pursued on a project by project analysis, but through a judicious combination of divisions, each of which has its own distinctive risk attributes.[11] Thus divisionalization provides the company with an operational model by means of which it can seek to achieve an optimal risk structure through the development of separate divisions in conformity with a central plan which embodies the company's growth and profit objectives.

It has often been stated that the company's sole objective is the maximization of profits or, in a more sophisticated version, of net worth.[12] When the assumption of certainty implicit in the above proposition is relaxed, it is discernable that a tradeoff relationship between wealth maximization and risk may exist. It is not proposed to argue here whether the risk consideration constitutes merely a constraint on the pursuit of maximum wealth; rather, it will be assumed that to achieve an optimal risk structure, given other corporate goals, can be a valid objective for a company operating under conditions of uncertainty.

This approach is amply supported by the results of a recent empirical study in New Zealand, in which 90 percent of the sample nominated 'survival' as a critical sub-goal.[13] Carrington concludes that this attitude 'reflects itself in various forms of risk avoidance which may be carried so far as to make implausible any assumption of even constrained profit maximization as the dominant goal.'[14] An assumption that this attitude also reflects investors' preferences at the margin can be maintained, and if this assumption were justified, the conservative management policy noted above would lead to a maximination of corporate values on the stock exchanges, at least in the long run.

INTERRELATIONSHIP OF DIVISIONAL RISKS

It is useful, before discussing the capital budgeting problem, to consider briefly the risk structure of a company with several divisions operating in different industries. The riskiness of the individual divisions and their interrelationships determine the overall risk structure of the company.

The most favourable situation is where the expected income streams of two or more divisions are compensating or negatively correlated, as for example, in the case of a company with two divisions, one producing a luxury good the income elasticity of demand for which is positive, and the other an inferior good for which the income elasticity of demand is negative. Where such a favourable relationship holds it may be possible to eliminate risk altogether, at least in a theoretical model.

Negatively correlated investment projects are relatively rare and the relationship is not likely to be stable. Consider, for example, the case of a company whose divisions produce competing products (such as gas and electricity), or a company in which the output of one division constitutes the factor input of another division (such as a rubber estate and a rubber-tyre manufacturing plant). In both cases it is essential to distinguish the varying risk relationships which obtain under different economic conditions. The divisional income flows in the two companies are negatively correlated under normal business conditions, and they are positively correlated under certain adverse conditions. Such a change in divisional risk relationships may occur for a variety of reasons; for example, the arrival on the scene of a more efficient competitor, such as nuclear energy may constitute for the first company, or synthetic rubber for the second.[15]

A further instance of diversification is given by the company the income streams of whose divisions move independently of one another, so that the overall riskiness of the company is less than the average of the divisional risks. This too is a favourable case but the benefits of diversification would be less pronounced than in the case of negatively correlated incomes.

Most investment projects, however, are positively correlated because of mutual dependence on the general economic environment. The acquisition and operation of two or more divisions whose expected incomes are positively correlated may be deemed favourable if the incremental contribution of each division to profitability more than offsets the incremental increase in risk to the company.

Thus the combination of divisions is governed by a tradeoff between profitability and risk that reflects the preferences of management. If these are coincident with the preferences of investors at the margin, then the policy will achieve the maximization of the long-term share price.[16]

If the combination of divisional incomes and risks is judged to be favourable, the market value of the company would be greater than the sum of the values of the separate divisions.[17] But where the divisions have high positive to perfect correlation, then it is likely that on account of the risk aversion of rational investors the value of the company will be less than the totality of divisional values. A comparison of these two values would confirm whether integration has been wise (although it is more difficult to say whether the divisional balance is optimal), or whether there has been an injudicious combination of businesses which should have operated as separate autonomous entities.

The market value of the company is given by the sum of the values of the different classes of capital, that is, equity, preferred and bond capital on the stock exchanges.[18] Divisional values are more difficult to obtain, but they may be computed in some such manner as follows, to give acceptable approximations.

The net operating income of the company may be allocated to the divisions and capitalized at divisional discount rates to obtain divisional values.[19] It is proposed that the divisional discount rate should be an average rate based on the company's costs of the different classes of capital currently employed, and weighted in accordance with a notional framework based on the capitalization patterns of competing single companies operating exclusively or substantially in the same industry as, and on a similar scale to, the particular division.[20]

There are complications connected with the allocation of the company's net operating income, but these need not be insuperable, since a condition of efficient divisionalization in the first place is the existence of separable costs and revenues.[21] Generally, all direct costs should be allocated, but co-ordinating costs, such as, say, the cost of the capital budgeting work, should not be apportioned. It might be argued that, since total costs are not exhausted in the allocation process, the divisional capitalization rates should be raised to reflect this. This objection may not be substantial. First, most operating costs would be separable and would have been allocated. But if significant joint operating costs exist some arbitrary apportionment of these costs would be necessary. Second, the divisional cost of capital based on the capitalization patterns of the single companies mentioned above has a built-in bias which will tend to offset any cost omissions.

THE CASE FOR A SINGLE RETURN STANDARD

The case for a single return standard for projects in all divisions has been put by Solomons.

Should a single rate of interest be used to represent the cost of capital in all divisions? Should we not recognize that, if the divisions were separate businesses, by reason of the variations in the riskiness of their undertakings they would not all have to pay the same price for the capital raised? The answer to these questions is to be found in the fact that the divisions are not separate businesses and their effect on the riskiness of an investment in the parent corporation cannot be assessed by looking at them one at a time. Just as an insurance company reduces the uncertainty of its loss experience by increasing the spread of the risks it insures, just as an investor reduces the uncertainty of his investment income by increasing the size and variety of his portfolio, so diversification in a divisionalized business aims to reduce the risks borne by the corporation. It does this by offsetting the risks associated with the separate divisions. Thus the addition of a divisional activity which is in itself quite risky might actually *reduce* the riskiness of the whole corporate enterprise. For this reason, the riskiness of a division is not to be assessed by looking at it in isolation from the rest of the business. For this reason, also, a single corporate cost of capital can quite appropriately be used throughout the company, without regard to the supposed riskiness of any division considered as a separate entity.[22]

We find this argument unconvincing. It is undoubtedly true that one of the main objectives of divisionalization is the reduction of risks borne by the corporation, but the adoption of a single return standard would seem to work against this objective, as it would stifle the expansion of the low-risk, low-return divisions, while it favours the expansion of high-risk, high-return divisions.[23] *Thus an unbalanced development may lead to a deterioration in the company's overall risk structure.*

THE USE OF MULTIPLE RETURN STANDARDS

Divisionalization offers the company a practical approach to the search for an optimal risk structure. But in taking a decision to divisionalize concurrently with diversification, the company has recognized the existence of operating sectors with different risk characteristics.[24] Because of these different risk characteristics, the rates of return in the individual divisions will not be the same, since broadly speaking, their rates of return reflect the different risks. Thus different evaluation criteria are necessary for the appraisal of projects in the respective divisions. Generally, divisional discount rates are the proper criteria to employ in appraising divisional projects.

The discovery of the divisional discount rates presents considerable conceptual problems, but it seems reasonable to extend the principles underlying the corporate cost of capital to the computation of divisional return standards. These principles can be briefly stated. Management, by and large, represents the interests of the ordinary shareholders; thus it should accept any project which would increase the market value of the ordinary share capital and reject any project which would lower this value. Acceptance is indicated where the return opportunities exceed the cost of the investment; the relevant discount rate is the company's cost of capital.

The cost of capital is a controversial concept which awaits definitive clarification. But the issues are adequately discussed in the literature,[25] and it is not proposed to take up the arguments here, since these are not problems arising on account of divisionalization. The measure that has won the largest degree of acceptance among economists is a borrowing rate computed as a weighted average cost figure. The costs of the different classes of equity and of loan capital are forward looking magnitudes that represent the opportunity costs to the company of raising funds. A system of weights based on the company's existing capital structure at market values is employed to combine the costs of the various classes of capital into a weighted average corporate cost of capital. This is a measure of the long-run average cost which, given certain assumptions, is coincident with the long-run marginal cost of capital, the relevant criterion for appraising investment worth.[26]

Thus, one possible approach to discovering the divisional rate is to base it on the experience of comparable competing independent companies in the same line of industry and with similar growth potential. The capitalization patterns of these competing single companies can be employed to determine a nominal capital framework that adequately reflects the business uncertainty in that particular industrial sector in which the division operates. The use of this framework to provide weights for the company's respective costs for each class of capital funds gives a weighted average cost which can serve as the cut-off point for divisional projects. It is appropriate to use the company's own capital costs in this exercise, and not those of competing single companies mentioned previously. This is justified not on grounds of convenience, but because the company's own capital costs may be expected to be relatively low, *vis-a-vis* those of the single companies, if diversification has brought about the consequences expected; and because their use facilitates divisional expansion, and thus the proper allocation of investors' fund.

The question may be raised as to whether divisional discount rates should be adjusted to take account of exceptionally favourable interrelationships between divisional risks, as where there are compensating or negatively correlated divisional income series. A strong case can be made for reducing return standards employed in these divisions to permit their joint expansion.

But it does not follow that return standards in competing divisions with high positively-correlated income streams should be adjusted upwards, since the adjustment would render their expansion prospects and competive ability with respect to single companies less favourable. It must be assumed that the co-existence of competing divisions in the same organization is justified by benefits in other directions, as, for example, in the sharing of technical know-how, and that their coexistence has not led to a reduction in the overall market value of the company to a figure below the sum of the divisional values.[27] Thus it may be argued that an upward revision of return standards in competing divisions is not desirable.

THE NEED FOR A UNIFORM INVESTMENT POLICY FOR COMMON SERVICE PROJECTS

Common service projects have two characteristic features. The assets necessary to provide the service are identical in nature in all divisions in which they are used; and they are employed for identical purposes in some or all divisions. Further, investment in these projects does not expose the company to the distinctive and specific risks associated with divisional projects.

It is envisaged that the investment in common service projects would be a relatively minor proportion of total investment in any one division, and its contribution to divisional earnings relatively unimportant. Thus the existence of common service projects and earnings associated with their use has been disregarded in our computation of divisional values in an earlier section. Nevertheless the investment policy for this relatively small group of projects deserves special treatment.

A typical example is the replacement policy for identical assets employed in two or more divisions. Replacement analysis shows that the point of replacement occurs when the present value of incremental cost savings (or incremental net receipts) in future years resulting from replacing the old equipment equals the net outlay on the challenger asset. Because of the wide variation in profit potential between divisions, it has been known that one division will replace a piece of equipment at an earlier point of time than another division which earns a higher rate of return on its investments. But for one division to replace an asset, say, trucks, every four years while another division replaces the identical asset every five years is illogical. This is evident if we assume that a special service department is set up to supply transport to all divisions. In this case, irrespective of how the transfer price is determined, or assuming even that a differential transfer price system is used (based on some criterion of incremental costs or of competitive charges for the facilities), the replacement policy would be uniform for all trucks in service.

The apparent inconsistency between the uniform investment policy proposed for common service projects and the dissimilar replacement policies that would have been followed had the divisions been independent entities can be explained. Given that the costs of capital of single companies in different industries are likely to differ significantly on account of dissimilar business uncertainties in the respective industries, and that each company will expand until incremental returns on projects equal the incremental costs of raising funds, widely divergent replacement policies are likely to emerge. The situation in a divisionalized company is not the same. While rates of return may differ as between divisions there is only one cost of capital, that of the company itself.[28]

A uniform investment policy for all common service projects can be implemented in one of several ways. For example, a service department can be set up as a separate operating department; or, where decisions are taken at divisional level, the announcement of a common company policy on certain types of investment formulated with the needs of the various divisions in mind may ensure uniformity. The relevant standard for evaluating common service projects should be a common rate given by the company's cost of capital.

Even where a uniform rate is employed, a further problem can arise. Investment in common service projects often generates a low rate of return, but might be desirable from a company-wide long-term view. In order to encourage a division with a high rate of return to invest in such projects, its profit objective must be revised. For, suppose, a division having a rate of return of 20 per cent has submitted a project which is expected to earn 5 per cent; if the project is approved, then the division's profit potential must be adjusted downwards in subsequent years. Though this is a problem of management evaluation, this and other similar factors cannot be ignored in the company's budgeting strategy.[29]

THE MASTER BUDGET

Capital expenditures often represent irreversible commitments that fundamentally determine the long-term future of the company. They are also intimately and inseparably interwoven with the capital financing function. The capital budgeting process, in short, must generate an overall plan that translates the company's multiple goals into action. Ideally, therefore, it should be centralized at a high level in the management hierarchy. Top management can use its budgets as means of coordinating and regulating operations of the entire company, thus facilitating the delegation of authority and responsibility, including responsibility for profit, to divisional managers.

Supporting arguments can be found for removing much of this kind of decision making from the divisional level. The possibility of conflicts between divisional interests and company interests is commented on below. Further capital investment decisions impinge directly on divisional profitability, by which divisional management is evaluated. Divisional decisions therefore tend to be coloured by the divisional manager's personal utility function, his attitudes towards prestige, job safety and the annual bonus, which are not likely to reflect shareholders' preferences.[30]

There are alternative methods of constructing the master budget. One procedure is as follows. Divisional managers first rank divisional projects by income and risk characteristics and arrange those projects in order of priority. Second, from the divisional priority lists is derived a master priority schedule, and this is then reviewed by the central budget committee. It would appear necessary to adjust the project evaluations originating from divisions by weights which reflect divisional risks. Thus proposals emanating from a low-risk, low-return division would be 'upgraded' and similarly proposals emanating from a high-risk, high-return division 'down-graded.'

This proposal does not have a strong appeal, as it is likely to lead to a higgledy-piggledy expansion of the various divisions.

An alternative approach would be to formulate at board level a comprehensive policy on the expansion of the company and of each division based on investment opportunities in the divisions and funds available for their financing. Given the budget constraints, the allocation of capital funds to divisions is dictated by the compromises, between profitability and risk, between long-term goals and short-run expediency, reached as integral parts of the comprehensive plan. The advantage of this procedure is that the desired rate of growth of the individual divisions is reviewed in the process. The final selection of the optimal parcel of projects in each division can then proceed as for a single company which faces a constraint on available capital funds.

It may be appropriate to note that an overall review of divisional budgets is essential even where the company has a surfeit of investible funds. Conflicts between divisional interests and company interests often arise. Many examples of such conflicts are seen in the field of transfer pricing, but they may exist in the budgeting sphere as well.

> The idea of external economies and diseconomies has taught us to beware of policies which yield optimal results for each of the various divisions of a firm taken by themselves, because by not taking into account the effects of its decisions on the rest of the company, policy-making, division by division, may yield results which are far from optimal for the company as a whole.[31]

CONCLUSION

Most companies do not employ sophisticated analytical techniques in their capital planning. Many decisions result in satisfactory consequences even though they are based on cruder methods or on intuition.[32] The purpose of our theoretical exercise is to attempt to gain some insight into the nature of the capital budgeting problem in the divisionalized company. If a conceptually valid approach to this complex problem can eventually be developed, we shall have a valuable benchmark by which to evaluate the more pragmatic procedures adopted in the name of expediency.

FOOTNOTES

1. The phrase 'single company' is used of a company which is not part of a group of companies in the sense in which 'group' is used in the literature of company law and accounting, and which is not a party to a price fixing or other restrictive trade practice which would cause it to be collusive in its operations. Clearly, a sole trader or a firm or partnership having several operating divisions would be faced with similar problems to those discussed in this article.

2. These special problems are well illustrated in a case study, 'Consolidated Electrical Products, Inc.,' in R.F. Vandell and R.F. Vancil, *Cases in Capital Budgeting,* Homewood, Ill. 1962, pp. 3–16; 17–26; 75–82; 183–93 and 373–5.

3. There is a voluminous literature on the transfer price problem. *See,* for example, P.W. Cook, 'Decentralization and the Transfer-Price Problem,' *Journal of Business,* April 1955, pp. 87–94; J. Dean, 'Decentralization and Intracompany Pricing,' *Harvard Business Review,* Vol. XXXIII, No. 4, 1955, pp. 65–74; J. Hirshleifer, 'On the Economics of Transfer Pricing,' *Journal of Business,* January 1956, pp. 172–84.

4. Decentralization has created so many intractable problems of measurement and control that the efficiency argument may be no more than an economic rationale for an inevitable development, the delegation of authority and decision making dictated by the sheer size of modern businesses. The economic rationale itself depends on the large assumption that significant external economies and diseconomies are not present.

5. S.H. Archer and C.A. D'Ambrosio, *Business Finance: Theory and Management,* New York 1966, p. 235.

6. Business uncertainty refers to the variability in operating earnings of an enterprise from technological or market factors or both.

7. G.D. Quirin, *The Capital Expenditure Decision,* Homewood, Ill. 1961.

8. Quirin, p. 223. It is implicitly assumed that 'a measure of dispersion is a sufficient indicator of risk for decision-making purposes . . ' fn. 15, p. 206.

9. H. Markowitz, *Portfolio Selection,* New York 1959.

10. Quirin, Ch. 11.

11. This argument rests on the assumption that the risk characteristics of projects tend to be similar within divisions and dissimilar between divisions.

12. E. Solomon, *The Theory of Financial Management,* New York, 1963, pp. 19–25.

13. M. C. Wells, 'Professor Machlup and Theories of the Firm,' *Economic Record,* Vol. 44, No. 107, September 1968, pp. 357–68.

14. A.S. Carrington, *Profitability Estimates for Investment Projects,* New Zealand Institute of Economic Research, 1967, p. 11.

15. Assuming adaptation is not possible.

16. See the discussion in J.C. Van Horne, *Financial Management and Policy*, Englewood Cliffs, N.J. 1968, Ch. 5.

17. The computation of divisional values is explained below.

18. This assumes that the company is a quoted public company, whose issues are widely traded on efficiently functioning stock exchanges.

19. 'The (net operating income) method (employs) the capitalization principle to determine . . . the investment value of the entire capital structure of the business—bonds and stocks.' Comment by C.J. Anderson in D. Durand, 'Cost of Debt and Equity Funds for Business: Trends and Problems of Measurement' in E. Solomon (Ed.), *The Management of Corporate Capital*, New York 1959, p. 120. This approach conforms with the Miller-Modigliani theorem and gives a lower total capitalization value than the net income capitalization method.

20. This procedure is further discussed and its justification attempted in a later section.

21. Divisional financial measures for this purpose would depart from the conventional measures, for example, in the recognition of price level changes, gains on inventories, and unrealized profits on internal transfers. As an extreme case, research and development and long-range advertising expenditures may be given special treatment. See J. Dean, 'An Approach to Internal Profit Measurement,' in H.R. Anton and P.A. Firmin (Ed.), *Contemporary Issues in Cost Accounting*, Boston 1966, p. 282.

22. D. Solomons, *Divisional Performance: Measurement and Control*, Homewood, Ill. 1965, pp. 158–9.

23. The association of risk and return is explained by the return differential constituting a premium for bearing the risk, Quirin, p. 213.

24. There is a basic assumption that the continued existence of all divisions is justified. The discontinuance of an existing division or the setting up of a new division necessitates special analysis that is beyond the scope of this article. It is also assumed that individual projects do not exert a disproportionate effect on divisional or company risk structures. Where a project is exceptionally large, its impact on the overall corporate profit-risk structure must be separately considered. See, for example, Quirin, Ch. 11.

25. See, for example, the discussion in E. Solomon, *The Theory of Financial Management*, and, *The Management of Corporate Capital*.

26. Quirin, pp. 137–40. It is assumed that the company achieves an optimal capital structure in the long run and that it does not face a rising supply curve of funds.

27. The case of General Motors of Detroit is an outstanding example.

28. The same argument does not apply to divisional projects. The distinction between divisional projects and common service projects is explained in terms of the different riskiness associated with the degree of specificity of assets in relation to their uses.

29.   Some of these problems are raised in J. Dearden, 'Limits on Decentralized Profit Responsibility,' *Harvard Business Review,* July–August 1962, pp. 81-9.

30.   This ideal must be qualified on account of the high implicit cost of decision making at the highest level. Decisions on projects which are obviously urgent or projects which conform to arbitrarily set limits are often undertaken at divisional level, but such expenditures should subsequently be reported and justified to the central budget committee. There is a further consideration of a different nature. Considerable project generation potential as well as screening power exist at the divisional level.

31.   W.J. Baumol, *Economic Theory and Operations Analysis,* Englewood Cliffs, N.J. 1961, pp. 274-5.

32.   *See* Vandell and Vancil, *Cases in Capital Budgeting,* pp. ix–xi.

A New Way to Measure and Control Divisional Performance

Roger Clayden

The decentralized corporation, in which the corporate entity is divided into portions that are considered small enough for traditional general management, is now well established as an organizational format. In many cases these divisions are involved in different markets, have different performance histories, and undoubtedly have different planning strategies.

An increasingly popular but nonetheless hazardous method of measuring and controlling decentralized investment centers is the so-called return on investment technique. The purpose of this article is to review the problems of using the return on investment technique for control of decentralized investment centers and to suggest another technique, the residual income method, which better aligns divisional goals with those of the corporation.

There has been some argument over the distinction between decentralization and divisionalization. In this article the terms are treated as synonymous and as referring to delegation of responsibility for the planning, the execution, and the profitability of operations.

The reasons for decentralization can be classified into two main categories:
Operational—Sometimes technological or geographical specialties make each division essentially independent. In the case of conglomerate acquisition there may also be the desire to retain an old system—at least for the time being.
Motivational—In a very large company long chains of command result in an impersonal organization structure. Decentralization of decision making provides local motivation and encourages internal competition, taking advantage of developed traits common in the make-up of the industrial manager.

SOURCE: Reprinted by permission of *Management Services* (September/October, 1970), pp. 22–29. Copyright 1970 by the American Institute of CPAs.

To achieve the benefits expected from decentralization it is, of course, essential that top management have the means both to measure and to control the actions of its division managers. In fact, the desire of top management for better control is always a major factor in any decision to decentralize. It has always been obvious that profits alone are an inappropriate measure of performance because some divisions are several times as large as others. A technique is necessary for comparing and contrasting the performance and prospects of the separate divisions, and the one that has gained the broadest acceptance is the "return on investment ration" (ROI), sometimes called "return on assets employed."

In a 1966 survey of major United States industrial corporations Mauriel and Anthony[1] found that of 2,658 respondents 60 per cent were using the investment center concept, 21 per cent were using profit centers but not investment centers, and 74 per cent of decentralized companies were using ROI or a similar technique. In some industrial groups the percentage using ROI was considerably higher—86 percent for scientific instrument manufacturers, for example. The authors concluded that divisional ROI had not only become an established performance measurement but had also displaced profit as the most widely used basis for measuring the performance of divisional managers.

The predominance of ROI is not difficult to understand. The economic prospects of a corporation are broadly defined by the price investors are willing to pay for a share in the company's future. Since the overall return on investment for the company is an essential ingredient of any decision the prospective investor makes, it is natural that the top managements of decentralized companies should want to delegate responsibility along the same lines. In this way the division manager should be motivated to make the same decisions that would have been made by top management. However, while theory and practice support the thesis that the division manager will react to the stimulus of the ROI control, an analysis of the economics of his decisions will show that in many cases they may not be in accord with the objectives of top management.

THE CONTROL PROBLEM

Unfortunately, the application of a simple ROI indicator to decentralized investment centers is fraught with hidden dangers. As early as 1956 Ralph J. Cordiner, an advocate of decentralization, stated,

> The traditional measures of profits such as return on investment, turnover, and percentage of net earnings to sales provide useful information. But they are hopelessly inadequate as measures to guide the manager's effectiveness in planning for the future of business—the area where his decisions have the most important effects.[2]

Nevertheless, as was reported earlier in this article, ROI is now firmly established in the hierarchy of measurement techniques and furthermore is probably used as a basis for long-range business decisions more often than any other factor.

Professor John Dearden of Harvard, a leading critic of existing ROI methods, has written several articles on this and related subjects for the *Harvard Business Review*. He classifies the inherent limitations of ROI into two types: "technical" and "implementation."

> "The first type," he says, "are those conditions which cause incongruities between divisional objectives and company goals, and which result in motivating division managers to take uneconomic actions. The second type includes those conditions that result from the inability, under many circumstances, to evaluate accurately the profit performance of division managers."[3]

This paper is concerned solely with the first type of limitation. Its objective is to formulate criteria that will align divisional goals with those of the company.

GOAL INCONGRUITY

To explain how simple ROI can lead to divisional decisions that are not in the best interests of the company, let us look at a few examples.

Division A is mature and produces an ROI of 30 per cent. Division B is young and has a target ROI rate of 5 per cent. Both divisions are considering increasing inventory for seasonal demand. Division A will not add an inventory of $100,000 unless it can yield at least $30,000 that year since a lower yield will reduce divisional ROI; Division B, however, will add inventory of $100,000 even though it yields only $5,000. Let us assume that the additional capital for this inventory can be directly attributed to a short-term bank loan at 8 per cent. We can see vividly that Division A may be foregoing up to $22,000 of additional profit to the company. Division B, however, could equally well reduce total profits by as much as $3,000.

Let us consider now the same two divisions contemplating the purchase of a piece of cost-saving equipment. Assume that it would be operating the same number of hours in each case, saving the same number of dollars. Clearly there is a range of returns which would be attractive to one division but unattractive to the other. From the corporate viewpoint, however, the capital acquisition uses the same source of funds and produces the same profits.

As time goes on, Division A's performance drops at a rate of 5 per cent per year because of a diminishing market, until it eventually falls below the company average. However, at the lower ROI, Division A is motivated to increase its inventory and purchase additional warehouse space, thus artificially enhancing its twilight years to the detriment of the corporation.

These are some examples of obvious anomalies that may result from ROI controls. In general, the limitations of simple ROI can be grouped into the following categories:

1. *Current investment*—The use of a different target rate for each division will not maximize profits realized from the company's management of liquid assets.
2. *Fixed asset investment*—Certain methods employed for including fixed assets in the investment base can lead to unfortunate management. If any technique is used that does not charge to the division the capital loss from scrapping an asset, then a division manager may be tempted to dispose of any asset that is not yielding his target ROI. The problem is even greater if fixed assets are constantly valued at cost (as in the gross book value method).
3. *Allocations*—To make divisional and corporate ROI comparable, centralized assets are apportioned according to some measure. While these allocations may appear neat and tidy from a bookkeeping standpoint, they can be just as misleading as allocated expenses are in costing. Consider the division that found it could get its data processing done by a service bureau for $20,000 a year more than it was paying the company's unit. However, the asset value of the facility was apportioned according to usage, and in this case $100,000 was allocated. If the divisional ROI objective were 30 per cent, then the additional cost of $20,000 would be more than offset by the reduction of $100,000 in its asset base. It is more than likely, however, that such an action would not be in the best interests of the company as a whole.
4. *Transfer pricing*—The problem of intracompany pricing is a result of decentralization, not of the use of ROI per se. However, since ROI control is often the only common quantitative measure among divisions, it is frequently expected to supply the solution. There is no doubt that transfer pricing can be a serious administrative problem, especially in companies whose divisions perform sequential tasks (such as the oil industry). Where divisions are heavily dependent on each other, price manipulation can play havoc with ROI controls.

COST OF CAPITAL

Capital funds come from three major sources: stockholder's equity, long-term debts, and short-term debts.

The cost of new equity capital can be measured approximately by the following formula:

$$C_0 = \frac{E_0}{P_0} + g \text{ (After Bierman and Smidt[4])}$$

Where C_0 = Cost of equity capital

E_0 = Current earnings per share

P_0 = Current net value per share (cost of issue deducted)

g = Expected annual percentage rate of increase in future earnings expressed as a decimal fraction.

Another source of new equity capital is retained earnings. The cost of retained earnings has been a point of argument,[5] but for the purpose of this analysis we shall assume that some cost C_r can be established that can be related to the cost of capital from common stock issue. A popular estimator is:

$$C_r = \frac{E_0}{P_0} \, (.80) + g$$

The .80 factor makes a rule-of-thumb allowance for the tax benefits of retained earnings to the investor.

The cost of long-term debt capital is the current effective interest rate for long-term securities held by the company's creditors. Because the market price for bonds may change from time to time, the nominal interest rate for the bonds cannot be used, and an effective interest rate must be calculated by selecting the rate that makes the present worth of all future payments equal to the market price.

Short-term debt capital comes from several sources; bank or institutional loans, trade credits, customer prepayments, accrued expenses, and accrued taxes are the most important. There is no one interest rate that can be applied to such debt, and in certain cases an average rate could be misleading, particularly since it is sometimes possible to assign the cost to some capital asset that has been used as the collateral for the borrowed funds.

The cost of debt capital (short- or long-term) can, however, be calculated with reasonable accuracy. If we excluded any fluctuation in the national economy that will seriously affect the value of bonds, then, since the future interest payments are certain costs, it is possible to establish a cost for the capital. If equity capital were also able to yield such a certain benefit, the same argument would apply, but under such conditions, of course, the investor would be unable to differentiate between the two, and there would be no need for alternative sources of capital.

In reality, finding the cost of equity capital is not a simple analytical task. The name itself is misleading because it suggests a definite price paid for new capital whereas the "cost" is the return expected from the use of the capital in a future that is far from certain. Furthermore, any changes in the capitalization of a company may result in a change in the market price for its stock. Uncertainties like these make the measurement of capital cost more difficult; they must be considered in any analysis. As Ezra Solomon points out,

If the purpose of a target or minimum rate is simply to prevent unwise investment decisions, it is easy to set a rate high enough to avoid such sins of commission. But its purpose is also to ensure that investment proposals which can be expected to increase net present worth are not rejected. This requires a more exact basis for setting screening standards, and for altering them in the light of changes in the capital markets and variations in the quaiity of returns expected from the investment or reinvestment of funds. The problem is a complex one . . .[6]

Some companies allow for these uncertainties by increasing the target rate of return as a hedge against risk. If all the proposals considered for investment bore the same degree of uncertainty, then the technique might have some validity. But the chances are that risk will not be apportioned consistently and that relatively risk-free investments will be foregone because their expected yield is below the target rate, even though it is above the expected average rate of return.

It is essential, then, to set a real target rate through analysis of past performance, through a forecast of desired future performance, or through a combination of both. When capital comes from several sources, the target rate must be calculated by taking a weighted average of the component costs. In the method for performance evaluation that is proposed in this article the measurement of capital costs from its various sources is an indispensable prerequisite.

RESIDUAL INCOME

We have considered the anomalous decisions that might result from the use of ROI. There are two basic problems. The first is the fact that a single criterion is being used for both measurement and control. This criterion is supposed to guide the manager in his decision making, which looks to the future, and to afford an evaluation of his performance, which looks to the past. Unless an extremely long evaluation period is used (at least three years), the two are likely to be out of phase. Divisions with poor performance, for example, will be set achievable target rates, which will be used to make investment decisions that will extend their poor performance for years to come. The second problem arises because, in order to arrive at a single divisional ROI, a single target rate of return has to be used for all classes of investment—and this technique is unable to accommodate the short-term changes in a company's financial positions.

These disadvantages are the trade-off for simplicity. ROI is easy to understand and is appealing to the ratio cult of business and finance. However, while it is not possible to devise a technique as compact as ROI that doesn't also have its pitfalls, it is possible to develop a technique that is equally simple to understand and avoids most of those pitfalls. This technique is a development of the concept of residual income.

To equal the company's target ROI, a division must make a certain profit using the assets it has. If it exceeds the target ROI, then its profits also exceed its share of the target profit level. The excess profit is called residual income. In principle, it is as if the division were borrowing its capital at an interest rate equal to the company's target rate. If the capital charge were made at a single rate for all assets, the control method would encounter some of the problems of ROI. However, it is possible to expand the residual income method so that different classes of assets can collect different capital charges, a capability not available with ROI.

The fixed assets of the division will collect a capital charge equal to the long-term cost of capital for the corporation (or an assignable charge such as mortgage interest). Part of the company's current assets will also be using capital from equity or long-term debt, but the remainder will probably be financed by short-term debt capital from bank loans, trade credits, etc. A case is sometimes put for the indistinguishability of capital employed; in other words, no asset class can be said to use capital from any specific source. But, while there is some interdependency of capital, within certain limits we can see that that argument is invalid. It may be possible, for example, to borrow from a banker in order to increase receivables. It would be a frivolous banker who would loan money to finance specialized equipment for a research venture (without some other collateral).

MULTIPLE CAPITAL CHARGING

A simplified capital charge schedule for a division might appear as in Figure 1 . . . The cost of long-term capital is at a rate of 20 per cent, so that assets employing this capital are so charged. The portion of the division's current assets to be charged at the long-term rate is a decision for top management. The charge may be allocated simply as a percentage of sales or by comparison with other companies in the same business as the division. Whichever method is used, the total of all the capital in the company charged at this rate must be equal to the company's long-term liabilities. In Figure 1 several assets have been charged at rates other than 20 per cent. There are $1,000,000 of accounts receivable charged at 8 per cent, for example. This means that loan capital at 8 per cent has been allocated against excess receivables held by the division. The division has a warehouse (Building No. 5) financed by a mortgage at an interest rate of 6 per cent on the debt outstanding ($1,000,000).

The capital charge for each asset is then calculated as shown in the next column. The current capital charges for the division's $65 million of assets total $12,740,000. If the division were an average performer for the company, its ROI would be $12,740,000 ÷ $65,000,000 or 19.6 per cent. If it were expected to yield this rate of return on all capital, it might mistakenly get rid of receivables costing the company only 8 per cent or a building costing 6 per cent.

Asset class	Asset value (000's)	Capital ratio	Capital charge (000's)	Additional capital approved (000's)
Current assets:				
Cash	$ 5,000	20%	$ 1,000	$ 100
Acc. rec.	10,000	20	2,000	200
	1,000	8	80	0
Inventories	15,000	20	3,000	0
	0	5	0	2,000
Others	3,000	20	600	0
Fixed assets:				
Land & buildings	20,000	20	4,000	100
Building No. 5	1,000	6	60	0
Equipment	10,000	20	2,000	200
	$65,000		$12,740	

FIGURE 1.   A Divisional Capital Charge Schecule.

The possibility of an uneconomic decision if its ROI were higher or lower than average has been discussed. Let us see now how the capital charge method can direct the division manager to make correct decisions.

In the last column of Figure 1 are listed capital amounts that are available for the division's use for the next fiscal period. Long-term capital has been allocated according to the capital budget; the division in the example has planned an expansion, and capital has been set aside for this expansion. This does not mean that absolutely no other funds can be made available. As with any capital budget, a review period must be established at a frequency sufficient to avoid financial traffic jams caused by changes in divisional plans. An annual review may be sufficient, but in a young company without financial stability it may be necessary to review divisional budgets as often as quarterly.

In our case, when the finance budget for the year was prepared, a capital excess was forecast, and a decision was made to buy short-term securities at 5 per cent with the capital unless it could be better employed within the company. It was further decided that this capital should be offered to the divisions for increasing inventory levels. Although the division in the example is paying 20 per cent on its current inventory, it can add up to $2,000,000 more inventory at only 5 per cent. However, because this cheap capital may be available for only a short period (two years, say) an advisory note would be included to prevent the division from increasing its inventory excessively.

If we look now at receivables, we can see that a $200,000 budgeted increase is available at 20 per cent. No additional capital is available at 8 per cent. It might seem peculiar that, with an expected capital excess, increasing receivables should be made unattractive. But this is a hypothetical example designed to demonstrate the method, so let us assume that top management believes that the company's receivables are getting out of hand and have been a reason for the fall in the price of its stock.

DIVISIONAL GOALS

The example has shown how, in principle, the division manager will be motivated to make decisions in the best interests of the company. So far, however, we have not set a target, except perhaps that profits should exceed the capital cost. The actual target is set in much the same way as a divisional ROI target, but, instead of dividing the target profit by the asset base, we subtract the capital charge for the assets from the target profit level. The final goal for the division is the residual income, which can be improved by either reducing assets or increasing profits in much the same way as an ROI target.

With this method it is possible that divisions with performances below average for the company will be set a negative goal. Technically this is no problem, but motivationally it may be distasteful. Fortunately, for reasons that will be explained in the next section, the problem will arise less frequently than we might at first expect.

ASSET MEASUREMENT

With the ROI technique it is common to allocate centralized assets. The reason for this, as was explained previously, is to produce a ratio that can be related to the world outside. The knowledge of this ratio is certainly useful; firstly, for measurement, because the comparison of a division's performance with outside competitors provides an important perspective for both top management and the division manager; secondly, to facilitate long-range planning where a division's growth and potential are conveniently quantified. However, from the standpoint of control, the inclusion of centralized assets is completely erroneous. In order to allocate assets, it is necessary to devise a convenient rule, e.g., so many dollars for each sales dollar or so many dollars for each fixed asset dollar used by the division. Whatever the rule, the division is able to reduce its allocated assets more directly by lowering its allocation base than it can by reducing its use of the centralized assets.

The same argument applies to the residual income method, and therefore we can make a general rule that only assets controlled by the division should be included in its capital charge schedule. The only exception to the rule occurs where an allocated asset is truly dependent upon the size of the allocation base. An example of this is cash. More often than not the company has one central banking function and divisions do not control their own cash. However, an increase in a division's activity will immediately increase the cash required for payroll, for example. Proper allocation of cash to the capital charge schedule is important to prevent a division from overrating the benefits of increased activity.

What about the increase in headquarters facilities necessary to accommodate continually expanding divisions? Perhaps the simplest answer is another question: What happens to the excess facilities that result from divisional reductions? Apart from the problem of finding a suitable allocation base, the headquarters changes would not be proportional to divisional changes—especially in the case of marginal variations. If it is important to allocate an asset, then the basis must be carefully chosen to avoid the pitfalls mentioned.

When assets are not allocated, the algebraic sum of the residual incomes from all divisions is equal to the capital charge for the unallocated assets. The existence of this divisional excess has a beneficial by-product; it means that fewer divisions will be set negative targets for residual income—a problem discussed earlier.

At the beginning of this section, the possibility was discussed that top management may want to make comparisons among divisions and between its own divisions and outside competitors. The residual income method does not always offer as convenient a comparison as ROI. However, all the information required for the ROI calculation has been collected in order to measure residual income, and it is therefore a simple matter to calculate an ROI. If an ROI is calculated, of course, it must not be involved in the formal procedure for measuring divisional performance.

REMAINING PROBLEMS

The residual income method resolves some, but not all, of the problems associated with ROI. The most significant problem remaining is that of setting a value for depreciable assets.

A piece of equipment may be purchased that is expected to yield a rate of return equal to the long-term capital charge rate. As the asset gets older, its book value decreases, and, consequently, so does the capital charge. If the operating benefits produced by the piece of equipment are uniform, then the residual income from it increases with time (see Figure 2 . . .). This not only makes the residual income measurement inconsistent, but it may also deter a division manager from making an investment because of the short-range reduction in residual income that would follow. Straight line depreciation was used in the example. If an accelerated depreciation method were used, the variation would be even greater.

	Net Book Value				Residual Income	
Yr.	At start of year	Average for year	Cash flow after tax	Capital charge at 15%	Before deprec.	After deprec.
1	100,000	90,000	30,000	13,500	16,500	–3,500
2	80,000	70,000	30,000	10,500	19,500	– 500
3	60,000	50,000	30,000	7,500	22,500	2,500
4	40,000	30,000	30,000	4,500	25,500	5,500
5	20,000	10,000	30,000	1,500	28,500	8,500

FIGURE 2.   Effect of Decreasing Book Value on Residual Income.

To overcome this problem, the annual capital charge plus the depreciation must be constant and should be equal to the capital recovery amount for the asset over its useful life. However, to prevent the improper disposition of assets, they must always appear on the asset list at their salvage value—or at as good an approximation as possible. The existence of these two constraints makes the problem theoretically insoluble.

Anthony has suggested a solution which he calls the annuity method.[7] He achieves the constant capital recovery amount by having an increasing rate of depreciation which compensates for the decreasing capital charge. The asset, therefore, decreases in book value slowly at first and then more rapidly as time goes on. While no depreciation method consistently values assets at their salvage value, the annuity method rarely comes even close. The tax laws being what they are, the annuity method would also be unattractive for cost accounting, so that in order to use the method two sets of records would have to be maintained.

There is a far simpler, albeit artificial, means of fixing the capital charge for depreciable assets. Property ledgers are usually kept in a form that shows the depreciation period for the asset and either the number of years' reserves that have accrued or the number of years' depreciation remaining. It is possible—and, if the files are on EDP equipment, easy—to subtotal these assets according to their remaining life. When this has been done, the capital charge can be calculated by multiplying each subtotal by the appropriate future benefit charge rate (see Figure 3 . . .). This way the capital charge will be equal to the expected benefits from investments uniformly yielding the company's target rate of return. Therefore, at all times assets will be valued at net book value, while the capital charge will be commensurate with the annual benefit expected from a wise investment decision.

As is shown in Figure 4 . . . the method has one drawback: An investment that produces the uniform benefits originally expected of it actually shows a residual income increasing with time. The reason for this is that a uniform benefit does not recover the principal uniformly; the interest component is higher in

Let r = target rate of return for equipment investment.
        n = number of years of depreciation (useful life) remaining.

An item of equipment should be retained if the present value of the future benefits resulting from its use is greater than current salvage value. For this to be true, the annual future benefit must be equal to the capital recovery amount at r% for n years (assuming a uniform series).

Define the future benefit capital charge for n years remaining:
$$f_n = \text{(Salvage value)} \times (crf - r\% - n)$$
where $(crf - r\% - n) = \dfrac{r(1+r)^n}{(1+r)^n - 1}$ is the capital charge rate.

This charge includes recovery of principal. If depreciation is recovered separately, then the capital charge
$$f_n = \text{(Salvage value)} \times (crf - r\% - n) - \text{(Depreciation)}.$$

Note: In practice it will often be necessary to assume that the salvage value is equal to the net book value of the asset.

FIGURE 3.   Future Benefit Method of Capital Charging.

*Yrs. of life remaining, N	Average net book value	After tax cash flow	$(crf-15\%-n)$	Capital charge f_n	Residual income
5	$100,000	$30,000	.30	$30,000	$ 0
4	80,000	30,000	.35	28,000	2,000
3	60,000	30,000	.44	26,400	3,600
2	40,000	30,000	.62	24,800	5,200
1	20,000	30,000	1.15	23,000	7,000

*Beginning of year used to facilitate calculations.

FIGURE 4.   Use of the Future Benefit Method for Capital Charging.

the early years. The only way to make the residual income uniform is to have an increasing rate of depreciation as in the annuity method. The disadvantages of this method have been explained.

Let us review again the purpose and technique of the residual income method. The division manager needs to be motivated to make economic decisions. At any point in time the division manager will be faced with two alternatives: either to scrap or to retain an asset. The basis of his decision should be to compare the present value of future benefits with the salvage value for the asset. If we accept the idea of a uniform benefit (which does not apply in every case but is the best generalization available), then, in the marginal case the forecast uniform annual benefit will be equal to the forthcoming capital charge, and, therefore, the manager will be properly motivated by the capital charge to make an economic decision.

What of the excess residual income from older assets? Will the manager's performance look better than it actually is? The answer is no because the residual income target is simply set as the difference between projected profit and capital charge. There is no absolute measure of residual income. The important consideration is that the future benefit method of capital charging for depreciable assets directs the division manager to make decisions that will increase his residual income and at the same time improve the performance of the company.

Finally the problem of transfer pricing deserves comment. Many pages have been written on methods for equitable transfer pricing, and it is generally agreed that where an outside market price is available this should be charged internally. In the more complex case of no outside market there is little agreement. In this situation, the residual income method should be used with the selling division's residual target set at zero. The buying division thus indirectly pays for the use of the selling division's assets. If the buying division contemplates an increase in sales, then its cost analysis allows for the increase in assets necessary to operate the selling division. Thus, the system is self-compensating.

SUMMARY

This article has demonstrated that, while ROI is an appealing method for division measurement and control because of its simplicity and its independence of divisional size, its use will often lead to divisional decisions that are not in the best interests of the company. Supplementary controls may be used to minimize these unfortunate decisions, but the very presence of these additional restrictions will remove the motivational benefits that make decentralization attractive.

The residual income method overcomes the deficiencies of ROI if it is applied in the following manner:

1. Capital charges should be made at various rates, according to the cost of capital employed by each type of asset.
2. Assets should be valued at their worth to the company. If assessments of value are not possible annually, then the net book value of an asset should be used as an alternative.
3. The future benefit method should be used for charging capital costs against depreciable assets.
4. Intracompany prices should be fixed at the open market price if prices are known. When there is no market price, the selling division should set its prices so as to earn zero residual income. A division that falls partly into the latter category must apportion its assets so as to yield zero residual income on the assets used for intracompany business.

By using these techniques, top management will align the goals of its division managers with those of the company and prevent a manager from making decisions that will improve the performance of his division but at the same time lower the overall performance of the company.

FOOTNOTES

1.   John J. Mauriel and Robert N. Anthony, "Misevaluation of Investment Center Performance," *Harvard Business Review*, March–April, 1966, p. 98.

2.   Ralph J. Cordiner, *New Frontiers for Professional Managers*, McGraw-Hill Book Company, New York, 1956, p. 95.

3.   John Dearden, "The Case Against ROI Control," *Harvard Business Review*, May–June, 1969, p. 124.

4.   Harold Bierman, Jr., and Seymour Smidt, *The Capital Budgeting Decision*, The Macmillan Company, New York, 1964, p. 135.

5.   Benson Hunt, Charles M. Williams, and Gordon Donaldson, *Basic Business Finance*, Richard D. Irwin, Inc., Homewood, Illinois, 1966, pp. 427–430.

6.   Ezra Solomon, *Theory of Financial Management*, Columbia University Press, New York, 1963, p. 35.

7.   Robert N. Anthony, John Dearden, and Richard F. Vancil, *Management Control Systems; Cases and Readings*, Richard D. Irwin, Inc., Homewood, Illinois, 1965, p. 343.

Interdivisional Pricing

John Dearden

An interdivisional pricing system is required whenever a company having internal financial transactions decentralizes profit responsibility. Under a system of decentralized profit responsibility, the interests of the company must coincide with the interests of the division; that is, the action a divisional manager takes to maximize divisional profits should also maximize company profits. In developing an internal pricing system, the most important consideration is that it support the financial control system by maintaining consistency between company and divisional interests.

In this article I shall (1) consider some aspects of interdivisional pricing that are particularly important in the proper functioning of a financial control system; and (2) describe methods which have been used to establish and administer successful systems of interdivisional prices. I shall be concerned only with companies that have a significant amount of internal financial transactions; the discussion, generally, does not apply to companies with little or no internal sales and purchases.

FINANCIAL CONTROL

The problems of establishing and administering an interdivisional pricing system so that it is consistent with the financial control system are neither theoretical nor academic. Profits have been lost (and, for that matter, are probably still being lost) because this consistency was not observed, and the effectiveness of financial control systems has been impaired because internal pricing systems were inadequate. To demonstrate the importance of this point, let us look at four actual cases:

SOURCE: Copyright 1960 by the President and Fellows of Harvard College; all rights reserved. Reprinted by permission from *Harvard Business Review* (January/February, 1960), pp. 117–125.

- The first two illustrate how profits were lost because pricing rules created a conflict between divisional and company interests.
- The third demonstrates how profits were lost when prices were not maintained in accordance with the rules, even though the rules were correct.
- The fourth case describes the effect that arbitrary pricing methods have on the acceptance of the financial control system by divisional personnel.

Case 1:   Design Changes

So that the manufacturing divisions of one large company would have an incentive to initiate design changes that would result in reduced manufacturing costs, the following rule was established:

> Once it has been established that a supplying division's price for a part or component is at competitive levels, any savings made by a supplying division by means of an officially approved design change, initiated by the supplying division, is to accrue to that division until the end of the model year.

Instead of creating the desired results, this rule encouraged the supplying divisions to hold off initiating design changes until the beginning of a model year. For example:

If the model year started in October, a change initiated in August would benefit the division for only two months. There would be every incentive to hold off the change until October, at which point the savings would accrue for a full twelve months (assuming, of course, that the part did not go out of production).

The situation was corrected by allowing the manufacturing division to keep the savings for exactly twelve months.

Case 2:   Negotiation

A division was purchasing an identical part from both an outside source and a company division. The rules provided that, in cases of this type, the internal price would be exactly the same as the outside price. The buying division would be able to negotiate prices with the outside source more effectively if it knew the manufacturing cost of the part. But the selling division was reluctant to give any information to the buying division that would reduce the outside price because the inside price would also be reduced. Although a lower price was clearly to the benefit of the company, it was to the disadvantage of the division.

The conflict of interests was resolved by making a price reduction by an outside vendor effective internally one year later, *if* the selling division assisted the buying division by providing the necessary cost information.

Case 3:   Cost Reduction

For three years a manufacturing division had been supplying a part to another division of the company for a price of $10.00. The rules provided that this part should be priced at competitive levels. When the buying division discovered that it could have been buying the part from an outside company for $8.50, a price reduction was immediately requested. The manager of the manufacturing division stated that the outside price figure could not be correct because his costs were $9.25.

The dispute was submitted to a central staff group for arbitration. After reviewing all the circumstances, the central staff group concluded that the $8.50 price was valid. The divisional manager then promptly took steps to reduce the cost of the part by making some design changes, effecting savings in direct labor costs, and improving material utilization. His costs were reduced to $8.00 a unit and the division was again in a profit position. It was evident that the failure of the buying division to maintain prices at lower levels had resulted in a loss of profits to it of as much as $1.25 a unit for three years.

Of course, it may be argued here that the poor cost situation should have been corrected by the manufacturing division without the pressure of a price reduction. This may be true, but the fact is that, rightly or wrongly, there is a tendency to assume that costs are satisfactory when profits are satisfactory. Without pressures of some kind, manufacturing processes tend to stabilize because the easiest, least risky course of action is to maintain the status quo.

If possible, divisions should be subjected to the same competitive pressures on costs that are experienced by independent companies. If prices are allowed to remain at levels higher than competition, this benefit is lost. Worse, management may be led by the artificially high profits of the selling division to believe that all is satisfactory in it, while improvements that may not be feasible are looked for in the division that is paying these prices. This kind of trouble can be avoided, as I shall show later, by a decentralized profit control system.

Case 4: Arbitrary Arbitration

An interdivisional price dispute was submitted to the central staff for arbitration. The difference between the buying division's proposal and the current price was $0.40 a unit; the volume was about 100,000 units a month. The staff decided to "split the difference" and the price was reduced by $0.20 a unit.

The plant manager of the selling organization was very disturbed when he heard of this decision. It reduced his profits $20,000 a month, and he had worked all year to reduce his costs $10,000 a month. A "split-the-difference" reason was not too convincing in such circumstances. As he might have pointed out, arbitrary pricing methods tend to defeat one of the most important purposes of decentralizing profit responsibility—to make divisional personnel profit-conscious.

OVER-ALL APPROACH

How can management develop an internal pricing system that is consistent with the objectives of sound financial control? I should like now to outline the main features of a complete internal pricing system. Although, to my knowledge, no single company has a pricing system exactly like the one I propose, all the methods and techniques which I recommend are being successfully used in some company at the present time.

Parts & Service Groups

One of the most important day-to-day activities that is affected by the internal price level is the analysis of make-or-buy problems. Because it is important for interdivisional prices to be at the level that will provide a proper basis for these decisions, there is a definite advantage to classifying all parts and services sold within a company according to the possibility of buying them from an outside source. As I shall explain later, this will also simplify the administration of the pricing system.

Parts and services may be classified in three categories:

A. *Items that will probably never be produced by an outside supplier*—Parts in this category include: (a) those for which no outside source is available; (b) those made within the company because of the necessity for maintaining secrecy; and (c) those which it is company policy to manufacture because control over the production process is essential (to maintain quality standards or meet some other goal). To illustrate, in the case of one of the large automobile manufacturers this category of parts would include engines (for which there is no outside supplier) and body stampings (which may be manufactured inside for reasons of secrecy).

B. *Items for which a change from manufacturing to buying or vice versa must be made on a more or less long-term basis*—Items in this category include parts requiring a substantial investment in specialized equipment or trained personnel. If a company is to start producing a part of this kind, it must generally be committed for a considerable future period because of the investment required. Conversely, if the company stops producing the part, it could involve idling (and possibly disposing of) equipment and also separating trained personnel. This would imply a more or less permanent withdrawal. To use the example of the automobile industry again, automatic transmissions would fall into this classification.

C. *Items for which the source may be changed on a short-term basis*—This category includes parts produced on general-purpose equipment or equipment involving a relatively small investment.

Pricing Rules

The first step in the recommended pricing system is to classify all parts into one of the three categories just described. The general pricing rules applicable to each of these categories follow:

Class A. I propose that, whenever possible, parts that require no make-or-buy decision be priced at long-run competitive levels. Since no direct competitive information is available for many of these items, it is generally not practicable to compare productive efficiency. For this reason, as well as the fact that decisions on choice of supplier do not depend on the prices of the items, it is not quite so compelling that exact competitive levels be maintained. However, it is desirable, although not imperative, to maintain prices at competitive levels so that the profits of a division making Class A products will be comparable to the profits of the other divisions.

Class B. I recommend that items requiring a long-term make-or-buy decision be priced at the long-term competitive price level. If the prices are allowed to reflect temporary fluctuations resulting from short-run supply and demand conditions, management might acquire a mistaken idea about their profit contribution to the company. To illustrate:

Assume that a company has its own forging plant manufacturing gear blanks exclusively for other divisions of the firm, and that these particular parts necessitate a substantial investment in specialized equipment. Assume further that during the past year several large companies have integrated into the manufacture of forgings by building their own forge plants. Excess capacity has thus been created in this segment of the industry. As a result, gear blank forging prices have fallen to the point where this business is not yielding a satisfactory profit to the efficient producers. At what level should interdivisional prices be set?

They should not be based on the low prices *if* these prices are temporarily depressed and *if* it is expected that they will rise as soon as some of the companies either go out of business or enter some other field of endeavor. Short-term low prices such as these are not valid as a basis for establishing interdivisional prices because management might be misled into deciding the company should stop producing these forgings (which might be just what competitors are hoping for, for it would relieve some of the industry's excess capacity and help prices return to the previous level).

Regardless of other considerations, a price that is expected to increase if a company stops manufacturing the item would be incorrect for internal pricing under the proposed system. It is not the lowness of prices that makes them invalid. Temporarily high prices are an equally poor base for pricing Class A items. What matters is the fact that the levels are temporary while the choice of source must be relatively permanent.

The answer to the question, "How long is temporary?" will differ in each case. Generally, it should be related to the effective life of the equipment involved. If, for instance, equipment is subject to obsolescence and has to be replaced every three years, a price that is likely to hold for three years would be considered long term and valid for interdivisional pricing. In the absence of any specific termination period, I have found that three to five years is a good general measure of what is "long term."

Class C. Items that require relatively little capital investment or that are manufactured on general-purpose equipment, and that therefore require only a short-term make-or-buy decision, may be priced on the basis of current competitive price levels (whether temporary or not). A temporary price is a perfectly good basis for a temporary make-or-buy decision. If, for example, the price of a part is temporarily depressed, it may be purchased until such time as the price increases to the point where it becomes profitable to manufacture it again.

SOURCE DETERMINATION

Many discussions of interdivisional pricing include the generalization that the buying and selling divisions should deal with each other as though they were independent companies. The procedure usually requires the manufacturing division to submit a bid (along with a number of outside firms) to the buying division; to the buying division, on the basis of these bids, decides which source will supply the part.

This procedure has the advantage of simplifying the administration of the internal pricing system because the divisions treat each other as if they were independent companies. It is my opinion, however, that giving the buying division the right to decide whether or not to buy a part from within the company can prove to be a very costly method of administration. In effect, make-or-buy decisions are being delegated to a divisional purchasing agent (or even a buyer). The buying division, whose profits may be relatively unaffected, is responsible for deciding whether a part is to be made within the company or purchased from an outside source. But the selling division, whose interests coincide closely with those of the company, must compete on the same terms as any outside company.

In general, would it not be more logical to let the *selling* division decide whether it will produce a part or not? Any change in company profits from the decision either to make or buy will be reflected in the financial statements of the selling division. It is, therefore, in a position to evaluate the desirability from a company-wide point of view of manufacturing a part. (This may not be strictly true if the selling division buys component parts from some other division. But, secondary company sources are usually minor. If there are significant purchases from a second company location, the two manufacturing divisions should prepare a joint study.)

On the other hand, the buying division is not in a position to evaluate a make-or-buy decision from a company viewpoint. On the contrary, its interests are frequently to buy from outside sources, even at the same price. I have known of instances where a division has placed business outside the company because it was able to put more pressure on the outside supplier for service. The value of this extra service was small but the cost of idle facilities was considerable.

Recommended Policy

I believe that it is neither practicable nor desirable for divisions to deal completely with each other as though they were independent companies. I suggest the following alternative:

1. The original source of Class B parts should be determined by a central staff group (either purchasing, finance, or manufacturing—or a committee of all three), and subsequent changes in source of supply should be made by mutual agreement between the divisions or, in case of dispute, arbitrated by the central group.
2. In the case of Class C parts, the selling division should have the right to appeal to the central group in any case where it believes that what the buying division wants to do is contrary to company interests. In most transactions, however, no quarrel is likely to occur. From an administrative viewpoint, therefore, it is more practical to let the buyer make the preliminary decision whether to purchase outside or inside. If the seller does not object, the decision stands; on the other hand, if the seller does object, an appeal can be made on behalf of the selling division's and the company's interest.

The proposed method of source determination retains much of the administrative advantage of allowing the divisions to deal with each other as independent companies because Class C parts normally constitute a large portion of the total number of parts, although a small portion of the total dollar sales. Most transactions, therefore, will be negotiated at the local level, and the central staff will not be bothered. At the same time, the company is protected against uneconomic actions in choosing suppliers.

ESTABLISHING PRICES

What specific techniques are helpful in establishing and maintaining interdivisional prices? Let us turn to this question now, keeping in mind that pricing a part depends partially on its classification. I shall assume, therefore, that parts classification as well as decisions involving sources of supply have been made in accordance with my previous recommendations.

Class C Parts

In general, the pricing of Class C parts will be the easiest of the three groups. These parts may be priced with a minimum of administrative effort because the negotiating divisions can deal with each other at arm's length (or close to it). If satisfactory prices cannot be agreed on, the buying division may be given the right to have the part made by an outside supplier, subject to appeal by the selling division.

As I have indicated, the prices of Class C parts should be established and maintained on the basis of current competitive levels. The division should meet competitive prices no matter how low, or give up the business.

Prices may be changed any time that competitive price levels change, subject only to agreement between divisions. For example, the buying division may request a price reduction from the selling division whenever the part can be purchased more cheaply from another vendor, provided there is no time limit on the agreement. If a time limit exists, the manufacturing division must meet the lower price on expiration of the agreement or give up the business.

Class B Parts

As earlier suggested, Class B parts should be priced at current competitive levels, adjusted for any short-term abnormalities. But may it not be difficult to determine the level of competitive prices exactly? Fortunately, where the competitive price level is difficult to estimate, there is frequently little opportunity for changing the sourcing pattern of a part and, therefore, little danger of choosing the wrong source of supply if the internal price varies somewhat from the competitive level. Conversely, where there is the real and continuing alternative of buying a part from an outside source, competitive price levels are usually available.

Here are some of the methods that have been used successfully in obtaining or approximating competitive prices:

1. *Published price lists*—Wherever possible, it is desirable to use a published price list for establishing interdivisional prices because this is usually the cheapest and most exact source of competitive price data. Price lists exist for many raw materials such as steel or glass and for standard parts such as nuts, bolts, tubes, and so forth. In certain specialized areas (e.g., meat packing), market prices are available at several points of production.

2. *Price quotations*—Published price lists and market quotations are often unavailable. To obtain data on differentiated products, management must turn to other means. Quotations from outside suppliers are one of the best sources of competitive price data for these products. The quotations must, of course, be obtained in good faith and not merely to help set internal prices. Not only is it unfair to request a quotation from a company when there is no intent to award it the business, but the supplier soon discovers what is happening and prepares his quotations accordingly.

3. *Current prices*—If a buying division purchases identical parts from both inside and outside sources, the price paid to the outside source—adjusted, of course, for differences in the conditions of the sale—may be used for internal pricing. Similarly, if a manufacturing division is selling an identical part to an outside source as well as to the inside source, the outside price provides a simple and accurate basis for setting the internal price.

4. *Prices formerly paid to an outside supplier*—When the source of a part is changed from an outside vendor to an inside division, the last valid price paid for this part will generally be a satisfactory basis for the internal price. (This price will, of course, have to be adjusted periodically for the effect of design changes as well as for changes in the general cost levels of raw material and labor.)

But caution should be exercised in deciding what the last valid price is. For instance, a vendor may adjust his price either upwards or downwards when he knows that he is to lose the business. Such price changes, frequently the direct result of the change in source, should be reviewed carefully to be sure that the new price is at a reasonable, long-term competitive level.

5. *Prices paid for similar parts*—Some internal prices may be based on the price of a similar part that is either purchased from an outside supplier or sold to an outside purchaser. The price of the outside part can be adjusted to reflect differences from the item produced inside the firm. Note that in the case of design differences which require different processing systems and therefore different costs, management wants to know what the cost differential would be if the part under consideration were produced as efficiently inside the firm as the outside item with its different design is produced.

6. *Historical price data*—Most companies have a wealth of historical data that may be used as a basis for establishing competitive price levels for internal parts. The extent that this information may be used and the methods for using it depend, of course, on the problem to be solved.

For example, one company needed to establish prices on a group of castings sold entirely within the organization. No outside quotations existed for these parts. The purchasing department obtained the price that was currently being paid for all castings purchased from outside vendors. It also took the data on parts purchased within the past three years and brought these prices up to date by making adjustments for changes that had occurred in the general level of casting prices.

Each of the castings was then brought into a conference room, weighed, and classified into one of several groups, depending on its size and complexity. A price per pound was established for each group based on the outside purchase prices. The prices per pound were, of course, established on a judgmental basis, rather than according to the arithmetic average of all the castings in a particular group. Some prices had to be discarded completely because the part was produced in very low volume or had design peculiarities.

The final step was to classify all of the internal parts into groups corresponding to the classifications of the outside parts. Prices were calculated by multiplying the appropriate price per pound by the weight of the part.

This method proved to be an effective and reasonably simple means for setting the prices of a number of complex castings. Incidentally, the study more than paid for itself since it pointed out several inconsistencies among the prices of outside parts, and the company was able through negotiation and changing sources to effect an over-all reduction in the cost of purchased castings.

Adjusting for Changes

Periodically, prices should also be adjusted for changes in competitive conditions. Once a year, perhaps, the buying division should request reductions if prices have gone down for any of the outside-purchased Class B parts that formed the basis for establishing the interdivisional prices. In the case of increases, the supplying division should initiate the necessary price action. More frequent adjustment tends to create an unnecessary work load, and less frequent adjustment leads to the danger that interdivisional price levels may get too far out of date and create a distortion in the divisional profit statements.

Price adjustments should not, of course, be made for changes in the efficiency of the manufacturing division. Such changes rarely, if ever, affect the competitive price level. Furthermore, if prices move up and down as efficiency is reduced or improved, the supplier would have little incentive to work on his costs.

Class A Parts

There are two pricing categories into which Class A parts may be divided: (1) those parts for which competitive prices may be approximated, and (2) those parts for which competitive prices cannot be reliably estimated. The first group may be priced in the same manner as Class B parts; the second group requires some other techniques.

The main need is for prices that will provide an incentive to maximize the rate of return on the investment under the control of the divisional manager. Rules for calculating these prices must be established with sufficient precision to allow the divisions to negotiate and establish their own rates. Although each case should be treated individually, the following methods have proved useful in establishing prices on manufactured parts for which no competitive standards exist:

1. *Calculate the cost of producing the part to be priced*—This should be the expected cost of a modern, efficient producer using the best methods and equipment.
2. *Calculate a profit allowance*—This profit, expressed as a percentage of the necessary investment, should be equal to the return that an efficient producer would expect to earn. The investment should include an allowance for working capital and be based on the current replacement value of the equipment used in making the cost estimate. When costs are based on equipment

actually in use, the book value of that equipment may be used instead of the replacement value.

3. *Calculate the price by adding the cost and the profit*—This is the final step.

It will be necessary, of course, to provide the divisions with specific, detailed instructions so that they will have a basis for negotiations. And if the part is very complicated, it may be necessary for the central staff to establish the initial price for it.

Once a price is established, it should be adjusted periodically for changes in design and changes in costs that are not controllable by the manufacturing division. It should *not* be adjusted for changes in efficiency or for facilities added to gain efficiency.

In the case of complicated assemblies does this approach result in an excessive amount of work? Such might appear to be the case, particularly when current facilities and methods are out of date and the price must be calculated on hypothetical costs and facilities.

However, the analysis necessary to establish a price is precisely the same type of analysis that should be undertaken to plan the action needed to correct the out-of-date condition. Further, when the interdivisional price is based on an efficient level of cost and the difference between the actual and the efficient cost level is reflected as a variance from profit objective, management is constantly made aware of the profit effect of the outdated facilities and inadequate methods.

A simpler version of this technique is to use actual costs as a basis for the price in combination with a profit markup that is less than the divisional profit objective; the purpose is to give the divisional management an incentive to improve efficiency. For instance:

It was decided in one case that the current manufacturing costs of a part were not at an efficient level. The price could be calculated by adding a 10% return on the investment to the actual costs of production. If the profit objective was then set at 20%, the division would be under pressure to correct the inefficiencies.

Although this method has the advantage of ease of calculation (because it does not require the costs of some hypothetical producer), it has disadvantages: (1) a plan to improve efficiency should be made whether or not interdivisional pricing is involved, and (2) it is an arbitrary method and may tend to undermine the acceptance of the financial control system.

SPECIAL PROBLEMS

In almost every decentralized financial control system, special pricing problems arise that are not covered by any of the preceding methods. Four problems in particular deserve attention here.

Separate Marketing Division

In some instances it may be desirable to have a separate division whose principal function is to market a line of products. Assume that Division A is responsible for marketing a line of electrical appliances that are manufactured by Divisions B, C, and D of the same company. How should the prices that Division A is to pay be calculated?

Some companies establish the purchase price to Division A on the basis of a percentage of the outside selling price. For example, the percentage might be 80%, leaving a margin of 20% to cover the division's sales promotion and administrative costs as well as profits. But this method is undesirable because it gives the merchandising division only a small part of the benefits of judicious pricing— usually one of its principal responsibilities. And, worse, it could create an incentive to keep prices low at the expense of profits because the merchandising division would be relatively unaffected by price reductions. To illustrate:

If an appliance sells for $100, Division A pays 80% of the selling price ($80), leaving $20 to cover profits and costs. A reduction in price of 10% means a new selling price of $90, a new purchase price of $72, and a new cost and profit allowance of $18. Although company profits have been reduced $10, Division A has absorbed only $2 of the loss. It can make up this loss with a relatively slight increase in volume.

A more realistic price to the merchandising division would be one based on the cost of manufacture, preferably, the efficient-producer cost of the Class A parts. In this way, the full impact of price changes falls on the merchandising division, where it belongs in such a case.

What about having the division pay a price per unit? This may tend to keep the selling price too high because the benefits of higher volume resulting from greater utilization of fixed plant and equipment do not accrue to the merchandising division. To correct this situation, the price paid by Division A could be divided into two parts: (1) a unit price based on the variable costs plus a profit on the variable assets; and (2) a fixed amount, charged each month, based on the fixed costs associated with producing the assemblies plus a profit on the fixed assets used.

If this approach is used, the merchandising division's efforts to maximize divisional profit will also maximize company profit.

Interdivisional Disputes

An interdivisional pricing system must provide in some way for the possibility that two divisions may not be able to settle a price. There are several methods in common use for settling such disputes:

1. Both of the divisional managers involved in the dispute meet with a top executive (e.g., the president, executive vice president, or vice president of finance). The meeting is generally conducted informally with no written presentation; the price is usually settled during the course of this meeting without a detailed review of each of the division's proposals. The decision is quick but arbitrary.
2. The dispute is submitted formally to a committee established for the purpose of arbitrating price disputes. Each party generally submits its position to the committee in writing. The committee, with the help of a staff, analyzes the proposals of both parties and publishes a decision.
3. Disputes are submitted to a central staff (probably finance or purchasing). The staff analyzes the proposals of each party and publishes a decision.

Probably no single one of these methods is completely satisfactory. In any case, however, the individual or group with final authority must be high enough in management to assure acceptance of the decisions, and to make it extremely difficult for divisional managers to apply undue pressure.

It helps to assign to a staff office (usually finance or purchasing), the task of recommending a settlement, but giving divisional management the right to appeal. If the staff recommends an appropriate settlement and either party disagrees with its recommendation, the matter is then referred to management for final arbitration—to a top executive or committee if the problem is a major one, to lower-level managers if it is not.

Always, however, it is important to keep alive the possibility that *any* recommendation may be appealed to top management. This assures the divisions that a careful and unbiased study will be made by the staff group responsible for reviewing price disputes.

Chronic Quarreling

One of the most annoying problems associated with many interdivisional pricing systems is the acrimonious debate and the resulting ill feelings which so frequently accompany price negotiations.

Inasmuch as the selling division is not concerned about selling its product and the buying division is not concerned about its source of supply, divisional personnel can be much more cavalier in the treatment of each other than if they represented independent companies. Sometimes this animosity between divisions can reach ridiculous extremes. I know of one instance in which the engineers of a buying division were refused admittance to a company plant that was freely accessible to engineers from a competing concern.

I know of no completely satisfactory answer to this problem. One of the most important considerations is the choice of people to conduct the negotiations. Many difficulties can be attributed to those who are doing the negotiating, rather than to the technical problems associated with establishing the price, as the following example clearly illustrates:

For a period of three years, in one instance, a division had to have nearly every price settled by arbitration. After the person responsible for settling price disputes was replaced, the division successfully settled all such problems thereafter without arbitration.

Although disputes are the result of many causes, it may be well to review the personnel involved in areas where the number of price disputes is inordinately large.

Accepting the Costs

In making a decision to decentralize, the cost of establishing interdivisional prices should be included as an added expense of the move. If the decision for decentralization is made because the change seems profitable, the cost of regulating interdivisional prices should *not* be considered a waste any more than the cost of preparing divisional financial statements. The direct savings from price negotiations—frequently significant—should not be expected to equal the direct cost of administering the internal pricing system.

Of course, I do not imply that every effort should not be made to keep the system as simple and inexpensive as possible, consistent with the objectives of the financial control system. My point is simply that there is no royal road to interdivisional pricing, that a naive internal pricing system will not support a sophisticated and complex financial control system. Short-cutting the pricing process will often weaken financial control in the same way that reducing the analysis of a proposed budget can weaken budgetary control.

CONCLUSION

Interdivisional pricing is a means to an end, not an end in itself. It is an essential part of a decentralized profit control system in any company where divisions buy from and sell to each other. The financial control system is only as good as the interdivisional prices on which the financial statements are based.

The most important requirement of interdivisional pricing is that it be consistent with the financial control system. The division and the company as a whole have vital mutual interests. The interdivisional pricing system can lend valuable support to these interests—or work against them. It is all up to top management.

9805